CRITICAL RACIAL AND DECOLONIAL LITERACIES

Decolonization and Social Worlds

Series Editors: **Alana Lentin**, Western Sydney University, **Ali Meghji**, University of Cambridge, **Syed Farid Alatas**, National University of Singapore and **Jairo I. Fúnez-Flores**, Texas Tech University

---

This series provides a radical new platform for high quality monographs which respond to the call for a decolonial revolution in sociology and the social sciences. Taking us beyond the boundaries of Eurocentrism, the series aims to expand the scope and imagination of the field.

Scan the code below to discover new and forthcoming titles in the series, or visit:

bristoluniversitypress.co.uk/
decolonization-and-social-worlds

CRITICAL RACIAL AND DECOLONIAL LITERACIES

Breaking the Silence

Edited by
Debbie Bargallie and Nilmini Fernando

With a Foreword by
Parlo Singh

First published in Great Britain in 2024 by

Bristol University Press
University of Bristol
1–9 Old Park Hill
Bristol
BS2 8BB
UK
t: +44 (0)117 374 6645
e: bup-info@bristol.ac.uk

Details of international sales and distribution partners are available at bristoluniversitypress.co.uk

© Bristol University Press 2024, excluding Chapter 22 © Ambelin Kwaymullina 2024

British Library Cataloguing in Publication Data
A catalogue record for this book is available from the British Library

ISBN 978-1-5292-3439-8 hardcover
ISBN 978-1-5292-3441-1 ePub
ISBN 978-1-5292-3444-2 ePdf

The right of Debbie Bargallie and Nilmini Fernando to be identified as editors of this work has been asserted by them in accordance with the Copyright, Designs and Patents Act 1988.

All rights reserved: no part of this publication may be reproduced, stored in a retrieval system, or transmitted in any form or by any means, electronic, mechanical, photocopying, recording, or otherwise without the prior permission of Bristol University Press.

Every reasonable effort has been made to obtain permission to reproduce copyrighted material. If, however, anyone knows of an oversight, please contact the publisher.

The statements and opinions contained within this publication are solely those of the editors and contributors and not of the University of Bristol or Bristol University Press. The University of Bristol and Bristol University Press disclaim responsibility for any injury to persons or property resulting from any material published in this publication.

Bristol University Press works to counter discrimination on grounds of gender, race, disability, age and sexuality.

Cover design: blu inc
Front cover image: *Annihilation of the Blacks* (1986) by Fiona Foley
Bristol University Press uses environmentally responsible print partners.
Printed in Great Britain by CPI Group (UK) Ltd, Croydon, CR0 4YY

Contents

Series Editors' Preface vii
List of Figures and Tables ix
Notes on Contributors x
Foreword by Parlo Singh xvii
Acknowledgements xxi

1 Introduction: Articulating a Critical Racial and Decolonial 1
Liberatory Imperative for Our Times
Debbie Bargallie and Nilmini Fernando

PART I Going beyond 'Decolonize the Curriculum'

2 Being Woke to Anti-Intellectualism: Indigenous 13
Resistance and Futures
Bronwyn Carlson and Madi Day

3 Decolonizing Australian Universities: Why Embedding 32
Indigenous Content in the Curriculum Fails That Task
David Hollinsworth

4 Let's Get Critical: Thinking with and beyond the 49
'Dead White Men' of Social Theory
Na'ama Carlin

5 (De)constituting Settler Subjects: A Retrospective 62
Critical Race-Decolonizing Account
Joseph Pugliese

PART II Being in the Classroom

6 Shedding the Colonial Skin and Digging Deep as Decolonial Praxis 79
Faye Rosas Blanch

7 Racially Literate Teacher Education: (Im)possibilities 93
for Disrupting the Racial Silence
Susan Whatman and Juliana Mohok McLaughlin

8 In Conversation with Helena Liu: Redeeming Leadership – a 111
Project of Critical Hope
Debbie Bargallie, Nilmini Fernando and Helena Liu

| 9 | The Provocateur as Decolonial Praxis
Fiona Foley | 123 |

PART III Doing Race in the Disciplines

10	Decolonizing the Curriculum in the Colonial Debtscape *Maria Giannacopoulos*	137
11	Race-ing the Law *Jennifer M. Nielsen*	152
12	Assembling Decolonial Anti-Racist Praxis from the Margins: Reflections from Critical Community Psychology *Christopher C. Sonn*	164
13	Unravelling the Model Minority Myth and Breaking the Racial Silence: A Collaborative Critical Auto-Ethnography *Mandy Truong and Jessica Walton*	178
14	Counter-Storytelling as Critical Praxis *Nicole Watson*	190

PART IV Building Critical Racial and Decolonial Literacies beyond the Academy

15	*Incantation*: Insurgent Texts as Decolonial Feminist Praxis *Nilmini Fernando*	205
16	Race at Work within Social Policy *Zuleyka Zevallos*	227
17	'The Sole Source of Truth': Harnessing the Power of the Spoken Word through Indigenous Community Radio *Sinead Singh, Susan Forde and Jyi Lawton*	246

PART V Resistance, Solidarity, Survival

18	Death Can Be Clarifying: Considering the Forces That Move Us *Samantha Schulz*	261
19	In Conversation with Yassir Morsi: Slow Ontology as Resistance *Debbie Bargallie and Yassir Morsi*	276
20	Teaching Race, Conceptualizing Solidarity *Andrew Brooks*	290
21	In Conversation with Alana Lentin: Racial Literacy – an Act of Solidarity *Debbie Bargallie and Alana Lentin*	305
22	Teacher/Decolonizer *Ambelin Kwaymullina*	317

Index 322

Series Editors' Preface

*Syed Farid Alatas, Jairo Funez-Flores,
Alana Lentin and Ali Meghji*

The *Decolonization and Social Worlds* series began at Bristol University Press as a response to the ongoing coloniality of knowledge. The series is co-edited by Syed Farid Alatas, Jairo Funez-Flores, Alana Lentin and Ali Meghji, along with an international advisory board featuring some of the leading figures in the field.

A central aim of the series is to excavate how coloniality works – both historically, and in its contemporary expressions. It is undeniable that the social sciences emerged in the high era of colonial imperialism. Classical social scientists – from Durkheim to Weber, and Giddings to Geddes – were prominent exponents of the politics *and epistemologies* of European empires. From Weber's Orientalist reduction of the 'Hindu', 'Muslim' and 'Confucian' worlds, to Durkheim's assertion of Indigenous people as being pre-modern, Geddes' colonial town planning in India and Palestine, and Giddings' endorsement of 'democratic imperialism', social scientists have had significant relationships to colonial imperialism. We are now at a stage in social science where we know quite well the histories of these relationships between social science and empire – both from the perspective of how social scientists worked in the service of empires (such as Britain's training cadets in sociology to better administer colonial populations), and from the perspective of how social scientists reproduced the epistemologies deployed by empires to legitimize colonialism (such as the idea of the colonized being in need of development and progress). While the *Decolonization and Social Worlds* series seeks to continue these discussions about social science and colonial imperialism, we also seek to further push the boundaries of social science knowledge by considering alternative histories, theories, movements, and social relations from the borders of the colonial world system.

Within the series, we therefore seek to address multiple areas of social scientific inquiry. To name just some of these areas, we are interested in unearthing the work of forgotten (or denied) scholars, in decolonial and anticolonial social movements and struggles, in new ways of thinking about the historical and contemporary relationships between the metropoles and colonies (or core, semi-peripheries and peripheries of the world system), in social scientific histories of colonial imperialism, in the evolution of empires, in Indigeneity and Indigenous critiques of coloniality, and in the historical and contemporary incarnations of the coloniality of being, knowledge and power.

Now, decades after the wave of decolonization of the mid-20th century, we still see clear colonial divisions in the contemporary world order: in terms of ongoing settler colonial projects; in political economy, wealth and poverty; in war and militarism; in international political order and organizations; and in knowledge production. There is always a vital need for conceptually and empirically informed decolonial scholarship to address all of these complexities, and we hope that the series goes some way towards contributing to this already rich, vibrant area of social scientific inquiry.

In its essence, this series looks for a world of many worlds.

List of Figures and Tables

Some of the figures are available in colour at: https://bristoluniversitypress.co.uk/critical-racial-and-decolonial-literacies

Figures

5.1	'We'll name this point of land "Dawes Point"'	68
5.2	'To the new colony!'	68
5.3	'Kill! Kill! Kill the white man'	69
5.4	'This is Mary.' 'This is Jim.' *It's Fun to Read*	70
5.5	'Mother is at home.' '"Look at baby, Jim!"' *It's Fun to Read*	71
5.6	'Father comes home in the bus.' '"Look in my bag, Jim."' *It's Fun to Read*	71
7.1	Four stages of developing racial and cultural positionality: racial literacy praxis in and for teacher education	94
9.1	Fiona Foley, *Annihilation of the Blacks* (1986)	126
9.2	Fiona Foley, *HHH (Hedonistic Honky Haters) I* (2004)	129
15.1	*Incantation* provocations	214
16.1	Illustration of policy document cycle	231

Table

16.1	Racial literacy framework for social policy	241

Notes on Contributors

Debbie Bargallie is a descendant of the neighbouring Kamilaroi and Wonnarua Aboriginal peoples of the Liverpool Plains and Upper Hunter region of New South Wales, Australia. She is an interdisciplinary critical race scholar and is Associate Professor – Principal Research Fellow at Griffith University, Queensland. She works on the critical theorization of race, racism, and racial literacy. Her primary research focus is on the experiences of Indigenous Australian peoples and work. Her book *Unmasking the Racial Contract: Indigenous Voices on Racism in the Australian Public Service* (2020) was published by Aboriginal Studies Press.

Faye Rosas Blanch is a Yidinyji/Mbararam woman from Queensland's Atherton Tablelands who teaches in the topics Indigenous research methodologies, colonial intimacies, the economy and the mathematics of genocide, Indigenous studies, decolonizing institutions, and the Flinders University core topic critical Indigenous pedagogical approaches to preservice teachers. Faye explores rap and hip hop as a tool for teaching with Nunga youth, and is a founding member of Unbound Collective, a group of four Aboriginal academic women from all parts of the country who teach at Flinders University in Adelaide.

Andrew Brooks is Lecturer in Media Cultures in the School of Arts and Media, University of New South Wales. His work investigates policing and abolition, technology and aesthetics, race and anti-racism, infrastructure and inequalities. He is Co-Director of the UNSW Media Futures Hub, a founding member of the Infrastructural Inequalities research network, and a co-editor of the publishing collective Rosa Press. With Astrid Lorange, he is one half of the critical art collective Snack Syndicate. Their book of essays on art and politics, *Homework*, was published by Discipline in 2021. He is also the author of the poetry collection *Inferno*, published by Rosa Press in 2021.

Na'ama Carlin is an uninvited settler living on unceded Bidjigal land. She is an academic in the School of Social Sciences at the University of New South Wales and an award-winning teacher committed to dialogic pedagogy and community-making in the classroom. Her research interests include violence and the social, health and illness, and classical and contemporary social theory. Her work is available in academic and non-academic journals. Her monograph, *Morality, Violence, and Ritual Circumcision: Writing with Blood*, is published by Routledge (2023).

Bronwyn Carlson is an Aboriginal woman who was born on and lives on D'harawal Country in New South Wales, Australia. Bronwyn is a Professor of Indigenous Studies at Macquarie University and is the author of *The Politics of Identity: Who Counts as Aboriginal Today?* (Aboriginal Studies Press, 2016). She is widely published on the topic of Indigenous cultural, social, intimate and political engagements on social media. She is also the founding and managing editor of the *Journal of Global Indigeneity* and Director of the Centre for Global Indigenous Futures.

Madi Day is a descendant of the Kukuyalanji peoples who was born and raised on Dharug Country. They are completing their PhD on the relevance of heterosexuality to white settler violence and Australian settler colonialism. Their areas of research include trans studies, gender and colonialism, heterosexualism and white settler violence online.

Nilmini Fernando is a Sri Lankan Australian interdisciplinary postcolonial/ Black/critical race feminist scholar, educator, writer and consultant. She is Adjunct Fellow at the Centre for Social and Cultural Research at Griffith University. Her interests are in critical intersectional and decolonial feminist praxis and racial literacy in fields of asylum, migration and violence against women. Her performance collective Loving Feminist Literature incants feminist of colour texts to public audiences and her publications include 'Getting close to other others' (*Journal of Intercultural Studies*, 2021).

Fiona Foley is from the Wondunna clan of the Badtjala nation, the region encompassing all K'gari/Fraser Island in the Wide Bay area of Queensland, Australia. Foley is an Aboriginal artist, educator and provocateur who exhibits regularly in Australia and internationally. She is Associate Professor – Principal Research Fellow at the University of Queensland. In 2021, Fiona's publication *Biting the Clouds* won the Queensland Premier's Award for a Work of State Significance at the Queensland Literary Awards. The biography *Fiona Foley Provocateur: An Art Life* offers an in-depth look at what drives the Badtjala artist.

Susan Forde lives and work on Jagera country in Brisbane and grew up in regional Queensland. She is Professor of Journalism and Media at Griffith University and was Director of the Griffith Centre for Social and

Cultural Research. She is author of *Developing Dialogues: Indigenous and Ethnic Community Broadcasting in Australia* (Intellect, 2010), *Challenging the News: The Journalism of Alternative and Community Media* (Palgrave Macmillan, 2011) and *Journalism and Climate Crisis: Public Engagement, Media Alternatives* (Routledge, 2017). Her work focuses on community, alternative and independent media forms. She worked as a journalist in both mainstream and alternative/community media sectors before joining academia.

Maria Giannacopoulos is Associate Professor and Director of the Centre for Criminology, Law and Justice at the University of New South Wales. An interdisciplinary scholar and second-generation migrant from Greece, Maria is a leading scholar in decolonizing approaches to law and criminology. Her work has a sustained and critical focus upon the operations of settler law to reveal its role in maintaining colonial relations of power that most acutely impact Indigenous peoples, refugees, asylum seekers and migrants. In 2020, she received the Vice Chancellor's Award for Excellence in Teaching for the development of a decolonial methodology for teaching criminology. Her book *Colonial Debtscapes: Austerity Sovereignty Law* is under contract with Palgrave.

David Hollinsworth is Adjunct Professor in Indigenous Studies at the University of the Sunshine Coast. David taught sociology and Aboriginal studies from 1978 to 2018. He has published widely on Australian racism and anti-racism, including the first textbook, *Race and Racism in Australia* (3rd edn, Cengage, 2006). David has an international reputation for his work on effective strategies for combating racism. His book *They Took the Children* (2003) won the 2004 NSW Premier's Young People's History Award. David has also undertaken dozens of consultancies for Indigenous organizations, state and federal governments.

Ambelin Kwaymullina is an Aboriginal storyteller and academic who comes from the Palyku people of the Pilbara region of Western Australia. She is currently an Honorary Fellow at the University of Western Australia and tells stories across a range of forms, including poetry, short fiction, essays and speculative fiction novels. Her research interests include Indigenous systems and decolonial futures, and she has written to some of this work in *Living on Stolen Land* (Magabala Books, 2020).

Jyi Lawton is a Bidjara man from Central-West Queensland and was Chief Executive Officer of Triple A, an Indigenous community-controlled multi-media organization and Chief Executive Officer of the Brisbane Indigenous Media Association until early 2024. He is now Chief Executive Officer for the peak body facilitating Indigenous community engagement, enterprise, and economic development within the resources sector, Aboriginal

Enterprises in Mining, Energy and Exploration. He has undertaken tertiary study across a range of areas and has worked as co-project lead on the Lowitja Foundation-funded project 'Harnessing Our Own Voices: Indigenous Broadcasting in Urban and Regional Queensland'. Jyi serves on the Board of Directors for the National Indigenous Radio Service.

Alana Lentin is Professor in Cultural and Social Analysis at Western Sydney University in New South Wales. She is a Jewish European woman who is a settler on Gadigal-Wangal land. She works on the critical theorization of race, racism and anti-racism. Her books include *Why Race Still Matters* (2020), *The Crises of Multiculturalism: Racism in a Neoliberal Age* (with Gavan Titley, 2011), *Racism and Sociology* (with Wulf D. Hund, 2014), *Racism* (2008) and *Racism and Anti-Racism in Europe* (2004).

Helena Liu is an Associate Professor of Management at Bond Business School on the traditional lands of the Kombumerri clan of the Yugambeh language group. Her research critiques the way power sustains our enduring romance with leadership and imagines the possibilities for organizing through solidarity, love and justice. She serves as Associate Editor at *Human Relations*. Her work has also appeared in *Management Learning, Organization, Journal of Business Ethics, Culture and Organization* and *Leadership*. Her first book, *Redeeming Leadership: An Anti-Racist Feminist Intervention*, was published with Bristol University Press in 2020.

Juliana Mohok McLaughlin is Senior Lecturer in the Creative Industries Faculty at the Queensland University of Technology, Queensland, where she teaches critical Indigenous studies in higher education, decolonizing methodologies, research ethics and protocols, and culture studies. Her teaching and research are informed by postcolonialism, critical race and critical theories, decolonization and Indigenous standpoint frameworks. She has supervised international and domestic PhD and professional doctorates from multidisciplinary backgrounds and projects over the last 20 years.

Yassir Morsi is Adjunct Research Fellow at La Trobe University, Melbourne and is also a provisional psychologist at an Islamic academy in Australia. His main area of research is the critical analysis of contemporary racism and Islamophobia and he is the author of the auto-ethnography, *Radical Skin, Moderate Masks: De-radicalising the Muslim and Racism in Post-racial Societies* (Rowman & Littlefield, 2017).

Jennifer M. Nielsen is a lawyer and legal educator at Southern Cross University, Australia and has taught and researched across a range of subjects related to First Peoples and law. With Debbie Bargallie, she contributed a rewritten judgment and commentary of *Aldridge v Department of Corrective Services* in *Indigenous Legal Judgments: Bringing Indigenous Voices into Judicial Decision Making* (Routledge, 2021). In 2014, she contributed a rewritten judgment of *McLeod v Power* to T*he Australian Feminist Judgments Project: Writing and Re-writing Law*.

Joseph Pugliese is Professor of Cultural Studies in the Department of Media, Communications, Creative Arts, Language and Literature, Macquarie University, Sydney. His previous books include *Biometrics: Bodies, Technologies, Biopolitics* (Routledge, 2010), *State Violence and the Execution of Law* (Routledge, 2012) and *Biopolitics of the More-Than-Human* (Duke University Press, 2020), which was awarded the 2022 Transdisciplinary Humanities Book Award by the Institute for Humanities Research, USA. With Suvendrini Perera and a team of international collaborators, he established the website *Deathscapes: Mapping Race and Violence in Settler States*. With Suvendrini Perera, he is co-editor of *Mapping Deathscapes: Digital Geographies of Racial and Border Violence* (Routledge, 2022).

Samantha Schulz is a white Australian living on unceded Kaurna land, and a senior sociologist of education at the University of Adelaide, Australia. Sam's research includes race critical theorizing, Aboriginal and Torres Strait Islander education, gender equity, violent extremism, relational pedagogies and decoloniality. Publications include 'Affect and the force of counter stories: Learning racial literacy through thinking and feeling' (*Pedagogy, Culture & Society*, 2023) and *Unsettling Whiteness* (with Lucy Michael, Brill, 2014).

Parlo Singh is Professor of Sociology of Education in the School of Education and Professional Studies, Griffith University. Her research areas over the past 30 years include: decolonizing theories and practices in education; social justice and equity in primary schools disadvantaged by structural conditions of poverty; cultural difference/identities in curriculum and pedagogic practices; and critical race and new material feminist theories. She has held many leadership positions in the university sector, and is the recipient of numerous excellence in teaching awards for higher degree research education and training.

Sinead Singh is a Wiradjuri woman who was born on Ngunnawal Country (Queanbeyan) and later raised on the Gold Coast and in the Tweed region (Kombumerri and Bundjalung), where she has lived most of her life. She was Research Fellow at Griffith University on the Lowitja Foundation-funded project 'Harnessing Our Own Voices: Indigenous Broadcasting in Urban and Regional Queensland' and is now working as Research Fellow on an Australian Research Council Linkage project examining the Australian local news ecosystem. She has a master's degree in international relations and affairs from Bond University, and worked as a consultant to the Indigenous online news site *IndigenousX*. She is Director of First Nations Start-Up, and offers social media services to Indigenous organizations around Australia.

Christopher C. Sonn is Professor and Research Fellow with the Institute for Health and Sport and Moondani Balluk Indigenous Centre at Victoria University Melbourne. He is research leader for the Community Identity and Displacement research group. His research involves understanding and elevating the voices of individuals and groups who are marginalized or excluded through forms of symbolic violence such as racism and sexism. Christopher has expertise in community and liberation psychology and qualitative and creative methodologies. He is co-author of *Social Psychology of Everyday Life* (first and second editions) and co-editor of *Psychology of Liberation* (2009 with Maritza Montero) and *Decoloniality and Epistemic Justice in Contemporary Community Psychology* (2021 with Garth Stevens).

Mandy Truong is an Adjunct Research Fellow at Monash Nursing and Midwifery, Monash University. Her primary research and teaching areas are racism and anti-racism, cultural safety in healthcare and health equity. Mandy has experience conducting qualitative and mixed methods research with children and adults from diverse cultural, linguistic and religious backgrounds. She is also a registered optometrist with over 17 years of clinical experience.

Jessica Walton is a Visiting Fellow at the School of Communication, University of Technology Sydney. Her primary research interests include transnational adoption, racism, anti-racism and intercultural education with a focus on the experiences of children and young people. Her book *Korean Adoptees and Transnational Adoption: Embodiment and Emotion* (Routledge) was republished as a paperback in 2020. Jessica is also a co-founder of the Australia - United States Korean Rights Group (AUSKRG) that advocates for the rights of Korean adoptees and their families.

Nicole Watson is a Murri academic from South-East Queensland whose family hails from the Munanjali and Birri Gubba peoples. Nicole is Professor in the Faculty of Law, University of Technology Sydney. She has an LLB, an LLM and a DCA. Nicole has published a large body of work on legal issues that are pertinent to Indigenous peoples. Her most recent work examines how the stories of Indigenous peoples can be incorporated into legal decision-making.

Susan Whatman is Associate Professor in the School of Education and Professional Studies at Griffith University, Queensland. Her research interests include critical Indigenous studies, Indigenous education, and health and physical education curriculum. She recently co-edited *Indigenizing Education: Case Studies and Discussions from Australia and Canada* (Springer, 2020), and co-authored *Researching Within and Across Diverse Educational Sites: Onto-Epistemological Considerations* (Emerald, 2024).

Zuleyka Zevallos is a Peruvian-Australia sociologist living on Gadigal land (Sydney) who has worked as an applied sociologist for over 20 years. She has managed and scaled several applied research projects across public policy, small business and the not-for-profit sectors. Most recently, this includes improving employment outcomes for vulnerable people, increasing cyber safety, and enhancing COVID-19 public health procedures. Zuleyka has run OtherSociologist.com since 2011, providing social justice education for the public.

Foreword

Parlo Singh

My name is Parlo Singh. I am a diasporic Punjabi Australian, a professor in education (sociology). I live and work on the unceded lands of the Yugarabul, Yuggera, Jagera and Turrbal peoples, a place now called Brisbane, Queensland, Australia.

My grandfather worked in Australia as an Indian subject of the British colonial empire. Despite the Immigration Restriction Act 1901 and its various amendments, designed to keep Australia white (the 'White Australia' policy), Black or coloured subjects of the Empire were allowed into 'Australia' as they were crucial to clearing bushland and helping to 'settle' the country. My family migrated here in the 1960s. Themselves colonized subjects and the victims of colonial racisms, they became entangled in the formation of the Australian white, colonial settler state, which violently wrested unceded lands from Indigenous Australians.[1]

I have written about my standpoint elsewhere (Singh, 1994, 1997a, 1997b). One of the few women of colour in Australia awarded a PhD in education 30 years ago, my academic writing focuses on how discourses and practices of patriarchy and racisms work to construct my body as 'other', as not belonging in this country. However, in all my writing about institutional racisms and my embodied racialized experiences, I never wrote about my own entangled history in the formation of white settler colonialisms. It is through a true project of solidarity with my colleague, Debbie Bargallie, an Indigenous Australian critical race scholar, that I have been given the opportunity to engage, discuss, think and act with critical Indigenous scholarship.

Taunts as a primary school student, 'Go home curry-muncher', constructed a sense of non-belonging, making me feel like an outsider in the only place I had known as home. As a primary school teacher, taunts such as, 'Ooh Ms Blackie, we have a Black teacher' from 'innocent' school children positioned me as other, less than. After gaining employment in the supposedly progressive higher education sector, I shared the stage as other, as a woman of colour, alongside white women speaking out about patriarchy and its numerous oppressions. White women first positioned me as a racialized subject and then silenced me when I spoke out about their racialized practices (Singh, 1997a), othering both my body and my speech. Early in my career, while precariously employed, I was told that the way I said 'et cetera' grated on the white professor's ears – that I needed to understand that 'et cetera' came from Latin and I needed to enunciate my English properly. This was absurd when I had spent my whole education in Australia in a schooling system that forced me to speak and write only in English and actively discouraged using Punjabi, my home language.

Twenty-five years after I wrote about the racist speeches of the One Nation right-wing populist politician Pauline Hanson – particularly her anti-Asian and anti-Indigenous maiden speech in parliament (Singh, 1997b) – Hanson's re-emergence signalled a decade of trenchant anti-Muslim discourse, and more recently a war on critical race theory and indigeneity.

This book contributes to Australian scholarship on critical race theory, critical racial literacies, critical Indigenous studies and whiteness studies. The chapters include poems, art, academic papers and conversational pieces. It is a must-read for all who work in higher education institutions, not only in Australia, but in all societies where white supremacist ideologies prevail.

I feel deeply honoured to write the foreword for this courageous, powerful and timely book. The editors have brought together a collection of beautiful scholarly writing that compels us to listen and engage deeply with calls for critical racial and decolonial literacies for all, in and beyond the academy. Their collaborative work models possibilities for solidarity across multiple racial locations; what unites them is criticality and a praxis orientation. This book is a gift produced through ongoing struggles, pain and joy, and the desire for long-term change.

The gifts for me are twofold. I have been given a seat at the table to engage in sustained listening and have experienced the gift of solidarity, both of which may share the burden of the heavy lifting through the unrelenting resistance activism and scholarly work of Indigenous Australian peoples. Sustained listening is hearing the silences about race in a settler colonized land such as Australia. This includes the silencing of stories about the ongoing histories of resistance and the battles against the deliberate spread of misinformation and disinformation about Indigenous Australians, as well as those, like me, othered by white supremacist policies and practices.

Sustained listening is hearing how race and racism were and continue to be the foundation of all social systems (legal, policing, education, health, media) forged through the ongoing colonial project. The chapters in this book demonstrate what is heard when we, non-Indigenous Australians, work in solidarity with Indigenous Australian peoples on projects of sustained listening and acting. In them, you hear the voices of Indigenous

Australians and their connections with country and ancestors, with the more-than-human.

The works invite readers to hear and acknowledge the deep theoretical and practical activism work of critical Indigenous, critical race, racial literacy and decolonial scholars and the commitment of non-Indigenous critical scholars to educate and transform the racial colonial matrix. Sustained listening entails reading, citing and building on the profound scholarship around:

- conceptualizing solidarity and communities of critical race and whiteness studies, contributing to building structures and systems so that this work is not done in isolation and alone;
- recalibration of racial regimes (see Chapter 21 in this volume), the possessive logics of white sovereignty – country cannot be possessed, owned, controlled and mastered (Moreton-Robinson, 2015);
- deep embedded systemic institutional racism(s) in Australian higher education institutions and across all disciplinary areas (law, humanities, teacher education, psychology) and the difficult, traumatic struggles of anti-racist scholars in their fights against these racisms; and
- the superficial diversity, inclusion and tolerance measures and practices in the higher education sector that appropriate and usurp the work of Indigenous Australians to meet institutional, neoliberal diversity and performance targets.

The chapters in this edited collection are testimony to the energy and passion for forging change within and against the teaching machine of the neoliberal academy (Spivak, 1993), in and through projects of solidarity.

True solidarity for Gaztambide-Fernández et al (2022: 251) is not a general statement, but a 'set of practices directed towards specific political goals and rooted in the specificities of relationships', intentions and ethical commitments. The scholars, artists, political activists and educators in this volume offer this book as a political project of solidarity, to readers in and beyond the Australian context. White settler colonialisms operate not only at a nation-state level, but across the globe.

This book is a project of solidarity, an event that thinks with the practices of systemic institutional racisms, and in this thinking work, acts to produce new material realities. It ruptures disciplinary fields and practices from within by urging us all to think and act against the racialized logic and practices of the ongoing colonial project.

Note

[1] I use the term 'Indigenous Australian' to refer to both Aboriginal and Torres Strait Islander people (AIATSIS, 2018).

References

AIATSIS (Australian Institute of Aboriginal and Torres Strait Islander Studies) (2018) 'Indigenous Australians: Aboriginal and Torres Strait Islander people', https://aiatsis.gov.au/explore/articles/indigenous-australians-aboriginal-and-torres-strait-islander-people

Gaztambide-Fernández, R., Brant, J. and Desai, C. (2022) 'Toward a pedagogy of solidarity', *Curriculum Inquiry*, 52(3): 251–65.

Moreton-Robinson, A. (2015) *The White Possessive: Property, Power, and Indigenous Sovereignty*, Minneapolis: University of Minnesota Press.

Singh, P. (1994) 'Generating literacies of "difference" from the "belly of the beast"', *Australian Journal of Language and Literacy*, 17(2): 92–100.

Singh, P. (1997a) 'Reading the silences within critical feminist theory', in P. Freebody, S. Muspratt and A. Luke (eds), *Constructing Critical Literacies*, New York: Hampton Press, pp 77–94.

Singh, P. (1997b) 'On speaking as an "Asian" teacher: Gender and cultural inclusion in social education curricula', *Education Links*, 54: 1–15.

Spivak, G.C. (1993) *Outside in the Teaching Machine*, New York: Routledge.

Acknowledgements

Curating and editing this unique and original collection has been a collaborative project of solidarity and joy.

We acknowledge and thank the authors for their remarkable and inspirational contributions and Alana Lentin for her guidance as series editor and contributor.

We are extremely grateful to Bristol University Press and the fantastic support we received from Anna Richardson and Emily Ross. We acknowledge the editorial work and support of Susan Jarvis, whose diligence made the manuscript shine.

We also acknowledge the support we have received from the Griffith Centre for Social and Cultural Research – in particular, Susan Forde – and the Griffith Institute for Educational Research at Griffith University.

Finally, we thank our loved ones – Joko and Sam – for their ongoing support and unconditional love.

We dedicate this book to scholars, educators, students, practitioners, and activists worldwide committed to anti-racism praxis.

1

Introduction: Articulating a Critical Racial and Decolonial Liberatory Imperative for Our Times

Debbie Bargallie and Nilmini Fernando

This book was inspired by research conversations undertaken with scholars and educators of race, racism and anti-racism by Debbie Bargallie with Nilmini Fernando (Bargallie et al, 2023). Conversations extended beyond the research. As our network of educators committed to anti-racist praxis grew, we sensed an urgency to curate and collate the dedicated work being done, often at the margins. For us, this book is a project of solidarity.

Debbie is an Indigenous Australian interdisciplinary critical race scholar. Nilmini is a Sri Lankan Australian critical race feminist scholar, educator and writer. We first met in 2014 at the Australian Critical Race and Whiteness Association (ACRAWSA) conference in Brisbane. We met again when we found ourselves sitting next to each other at our inaugural meeting as new ACRAWSA board members (2018–20). Our research, individually and together, emphasizes that race work must be done at multiple locations and be grounded in praxis that enacts scholarly knowledge in transformative ways.

The 2020 ACRAWSA conference, titled 'Racial Literacies vs White Supremacy: Educating and Researching Together Against Racial Silencing, Racial Violence and Racial Capitalism', was convened by Alana Lentin. Patricia Hill Collins was the international keynote speaker, having just published *Intersectionality as Critical Social Theory* (2019). This conference was primarily the impetus for the term 'racial literacy' gaining traction in Australia. As a travelling concept, racial literacy had earlier emerged in a course at the University of Melbourne titled 'Racial Literacy, Indigeneity and Whiteness', developed and taught by Ballardong artist Dianne Jones from Noongar Country in Western Australia, and Odette Kelada, a senior lecturer in creative writing of Anglo-Egyptian heritage. Influenced by renowned African American Black feminist anthropologist and educator Yolanda T. Moses, Jones and Kelada developed their course around 2010 to redress a 'compelling need for greater racial literacy' in Australia particularly in relation to Indigenous sovereignty (Brown et al, 2021: 83).

In the settler racial-colonial context of Australia, race studies and research have been subjected to institutional neglect. Australia's white supremacist roots and later liberal multiculturalist ideologies have marginalized Indigenous knowledges and subjugated critical voices. Bargallie's (2020) Stanner Award-winning monograph *Unmasking the Racial Contract: Indigenous Voices on Racism*, the first to use race as a key framework to critically examine the racism and discrimination faced by Indigenous employees in an Australian institution, unmasks the Australian racial-colonial contract. Bargallie's work shows how multiple forms of racism work together in colonial institutions to sustain white supremacy. In his endorsement of the book, the late Charles W. Mills wrote:

> Despite a history of conquest, genocide, and expropriation, to say nothing of a multi-decade official 'White Australia' immigration policy, mainstream Australian discourse and scholarship still prefers to conceal the central reality of white racial domination with the evasive and obfuscatory categories of 'diversity' and 'culture'. This courageous and hard-hitting text ... reveals the ugly truth of systemic racial exclusion behind the liberal façade – a lesson not merely in the workings of the Australian Public Service specifically but for the country far more broadly. (Mills, 2020)

Given that denial is a key feature of racism in Australia, and considering the obfuscation of the language of race that permeates our everyday life, how might we do race work more critically? Racial literacy as a decolonial anti-racist praxis offers a first step. It provides the language to identify, name and contest racist experiences and a greater understanding of what racism is, what racism is not, how race works as a technology of power, and the tools to undertake the necessary work to transform the structures of white supremacy (Bargallie, 2020: 258).

This book adopts a critical racial literacy approach and praxis to build anti-racist pedagogy. Our use of the term critical implies a deeper level of scrutiny and evaluation of the underlying systems, structures, and narratives that perpetuate racial injustice and colonial legacies. The roots of racial literacy lie in critical race theory and the legal scholarship of the US civil rights movement. Racial literacy is concerned with unveiling the relationships between race and power, aiming to undo the effects of race and challenge racism by showing how power operates in discriminatory and exploitative ways, both historically and in the present (Guinier, 2004). The recent arrival of the concept in Australia and its metaphorization have moved racial literacy from its original intent (Bargallie et al, 2023). In this book, racial literacy is conceptualized as multiple critical pedagogies and practices (Twine, 2004) that disrupt the aspirational notions of Indigenization of curriculum and the decolonizing of Australian universities when examined against the privileging of curriculum reforms and naive assumptions about the systemic and cultural racisms at play in Australian universities today, which do little to create substantive change in institutions steeped in white supremacy.

Recent moves to Indigenize the curriculum and decolonize the university by neoliberalized Australian institutions have glossed over race and racism, excluding, misrepresenting and devaluing critical voices through epistemic racism. The problem is not the lack of critical scholarship; it has always been *the mere mention of race* within it. The contributions in this book belie the myth that race work is not being done here. Rather, it is driven underground or pushed to the margins, along with the educators who dare to do this work. Many choose to reclaim the margins to which they are banished as sites of resistance.

The contributors to this collection counter the epistemic racism experienced in educating about race and racism in Australia. Together, they illuminate the multiple sites in which they carve out spaces to do their work and the decolonial approaches they deploy to critique the racial status quo and counter the silencing of race and racism that thwarts the acquisition and advancement of critical racial literacy. Unique to this collection is an assemblage of Indigenous and non-Indigenous Australian educators brought together to open a dialogue that advances a paradigm shift towards critical racial and decolonial literacies.

Educators engage with themes, concepts and ideas drawn from critical race theory, race critical theory, decolonial and critical Indigenous studies, and Blak/Black feminist thought as instructive and enacted practices of racial literacy. The term 'Blak' was coined by Indigenous Australian artist and political activist Destiny Deacon in 1991. The term is used to signify the specificity of collective political struggle by Indigenous Australian peoples (Aboriginal and Torres Strait Islander peoples). The book offers a 'both and' (Meghji, 2022) approach that combines critical race theory and critical Indigenous studies without losing the specificity of either. Globally, critical Indigenous scholarship and decolonial approaches to education are growing vigorously; this book fills an important gap by highlighting a range of approaches by Australian scholars and educators who intentionally and innovatively align their decolonial and anti-racism praxis with critical Indigenous perspectives. The approaches to teaching about race and racism in this collection strenuously challenge current legislations, policies and practices articulated through contemporary, neoliberal individualistic discourses of diversity and inclusion, cultural competency, and reconciliation that saturate the corporate academic space. Such depoliticized prescriptive solutions to racism rely on remedies such as unconscious bias training, which delimit anti-racism to the individual level, largely through the white analytic frame. In contrast, race educators in this collection deploy decolonial pedagogies and critical praxis to not only contest the contemporary manifestations of racisms, but also the outcomes of historic and contemporary denial, silencing and misrepresentation of race that continue to serve the racial colonial agenda. Our aim is to articulate these practices as politics of resistance, refusal and defiance of the co-optation and dilution of critical praxis grounded in Black race scholarship we are currently witnessing, and to re-emphasize the importance of widening and deepening this pedagogical work. For actions to be emancipatory, they must work against and unravel the conditions of race in the present and navigate the resistance and backlash along the way.

As Audre Lorde (1984: 110–13) informs us, the master's tools will never dismantle the master's house. Critical race and critical Indigenous studies and pedagogies are brought together in this book to articulate a decolonial liberatory imperative for our times. Taking a tenacious anti-racist pedagogical approach and using decolonial framing creates intellectual space for critical voices to exist amidst sanctioned neoliberal white supremacist ideologies and the backlash against critical race studies, theories and pedagogies in white nation-states globally. Educators both inside and beyond the academy write about 'doing' education about race and racism and what gets in the way, illustrating how critical racial and decolonial theories and praxis can work together as complementary approaches aimed at addressing and challenging the legacies of colonialism, imperialism and structural forms of oppression that persist in society. We do not propose that racial literacy merely replace ineffective forms of anti-racism training. Nor can racial literacy alone end all forms of racism. It must always be accompanied by active struggle (Bargallie et al, 2023, p 5). Critical racial literacy is praxis that evolves through continual learning and unlearning. It demands proactive engagement in dismantling racist systems and ideologies.

This book is a collective project of solidarity, joy and critical hope for transforming educational praxis in Australia and beyond. It is structured in five parts that situate the voices of Indigenous and non-Indigenous scholars from multiple disciplines and spaces.

Overview of chapters

In Chapter 2, Indigenous Australian scholars Bronwyn Carlson and Madi Day explore increasing demands for more rigorous and critical anti-racism approaches to Indigenous pedagogy to combat contemporary manifestations of a decades-old anti-intellectualism and its racist proclivities that shape the settler-colonized white nation.

In Chapter 3, anti-racist scholar-activist David Hollinsworth critically reflects on the writing, teaching, designing and delivery of Aboriginal studies education since the 1970s as 'decolonizing moves'. He argues against the privileging of curriculum reform in isolation from critical race theory and serious forms of anti-racism amidst naive assumptions about the nature of systemic and cultural racisms.

In Chapter 4, sociologist Na'ama Carlin reflects on a teaching pedagogy that challenges students to think critically both *when* using social theory and *about* social theory. Rather than completely doing away with the 'dead white men', understanding sociology's colonial/racial development critically informs our understanding of more contemporary theory.

In Chapter 5, Joseph Pugliese interrogates the pedagogical forces in operation in the construction of his racialized subject positions with the context of the Australian white settler state. Critical examination of two school textbooks that were part of his miseducation trace how these texts pedagogically laboured to inculcate a range of hegemonic values that normalized the racialized settler state.

In Chapter 6, Yidinyji/Mbararam academic Faye Rosas Blanch speaks to Indigenous Australian academics as sovereign beings routinely entering confronting and dangerous settler-colonizing spaces. She 'digs deeper' into a critical anti-racist framework, considering narratives carried into teaching spaces by First Nations academics as 'embodied' literacies. She proffers an 'unbecoming' of racializing assembles of discourse, language, text, film and policies through 'shedding of colonial skin', exemplified in creative anti-racist and decolonization performances of the Unbound Collective Sovereign Sisters.

In Chapter 7, Susan Whatman and Juliana Mohok McLaughlin combine their experiences over 30 years of teaching Indigenous education in universities, providing insights into how racial literacy has (and has not) infiltrated teacher preparation degrees in Australian universities. In a conversational style, they discuss critical race theorists who have shaped their conceptualizations of research and teaching practice, and share their ideas of forms of racial literacy in praxis – although it is rarely called that.

In Chapter 8, Debbie Bargallie and Nilmini Fernando engage in a conversation with Helena Liu about her critiques of how power sustains our enduring romance with leadership and imagines the possibilities for organizing through solidarity, love and justice. Liu speaks about educating on race and racism in the fields of business studies and management, and the inspiration for her unique first book.

In Chapter 9, Badjala Aboriginal artist and educator Fiona Foley reflects on her experiences teaching creative arts in Australian and American universities through two provocative artworks that instigate conversations about race, racism and the legacies of racial superiority. The provocateur as decolonial praxis is vital in teaching to move students and colleagues beyond 'feeling uncomfortable' in Australia, where denial is a key feature of racism.

Decolonial legal scholar Maria Giannacopoulos argues in Chapter 10 that one urgent task of decolonizing curriculum across all disciplines in the imperial university is to expose the role and function of colonial law in performing and maintaining dispossession and racialized violence. As a system of law imposed upon First Laws, colonial law forms a nomopoly that lacks consent and so performs nomocide. Giannacopoulos argues for the necessity of a critical theorization of colonial law and illustrates how such theory can be deployed in pedagogical practice.

In Chapter 11, legal scholar Jennifer M. Nielsen argues that generations of lawyers have learned about law in ways that ignore how race is embedded in legal thinking and practice, committed instead to liberal ideals of equality and the rule of law. She elucidates strategies to build racial literacy through a socio-legal approach that contextualizes why and how law has been shaped by racial logics to demystify the 'rightness' of law and examine law and the Australian legal system as a cultural practice.

In Chapter 12, Christopher C. Sonn, drawing on his transnational experiences as a migrant, researcher and educator, argues that decolonial standpoints – that is, critical engagement with lived experience and subjectivity in and through racialized power relations – along with practices of deconstruction, recovery of collective memory and epistemic inclusion, are vital to anti-racist praxis in Australia to disrupt knowledge production anchored in Eurocentrism, colonialism and white supremacy.

In Chapter 13, Mandy Truong and Jessica Walton, as two 'settler' women of colour, draw on their experiences as academics in higher education to reflect on the challenges, discomforts and uncertainties of working in the fields of racism and anti-racism. They critically reflect on their positionality as Asian women, often caught in the trap of 'model minority' stereotypes and rendered invisible in higher education and racism/anti-racism work.

In Chapter 14, Nicole Watson, a Munanjali and Birri Gubba legal scholar, counters the dominant narrative to show us that in the closing decades of the 20th century, several Indigenous people blazed a trail by enrolling in Australia's law schools. She considers the critical contributions of Indigenous women that have been rendered invisible in Australian legal history, arguing that much can be learnt from the stories of such women who, through their actions, made the law accessible to some of the most marginalized people in Australia.

In Chapter 15, interdisciplinary critical race feminism scholar and educator Nilmini Fernando draws from Black and feminist of colour traditions of writing and performance as vehicles for resistance, insurgency and survival. She illustrates one enactment of collective transnational feminist-of-colour praxis in the Australian settler-colonizing context, which opens channels for multiple loci of listening and enunciation, and fosters the development of critical literacies, imagining, re-existing and solidarity.

Peruvian-Australia applied public sociologist Zuleyka Zevallos reflects in Chapter 16 on her experiences as a Latin migrant woman of colour who has worked across local, state and federal government research teams in Australia informing public policy, procedures and decision-making. She exposes how anti-racism work is suppressed, her unpaid contributions sanitized, backlash and the consequences for her wellbeing and safety.

In Chapter 17, Sinead Singh, Susan Forde and Jyi Lawton show that Indigenous community radio stations and associated social media presence serve a vital function in providing local news, community connection and information, while supporting 'Aboriginal English', Aboriginal language and Indigenous music. This praxis directly decolonizes English as a language, further cementing the audience's perspective on Indigenous broadcasting as a site for decolonizing cultural expression.

Samantha Schulz uses personal narrative, affect theory and critical race scholarship in Chapter 18 to examine significant emotional incidents involving death to contemplate how race scholarship has emergently informed her orientation to teacher education and 'what moves us' to sustain commitments to race criticality within institutions hostile to discussing 'race'. Affective encounters and pedagogies present opportunities for changes in subjectivity that can facilitate racial literacy education and nourish affective collegial bonds that may support academics to sustain their commitments to race scholarship within and beyond the university.

In Chapter 19, Debbie Bargallie engages in a conversation with Yassir Morsi about his work as an academic and lecturer, and as a provisional psychologist at an Islamic academy in Australia. Morsi speaks about the ways he navigates spaces that uphold white supremacy by keeping 'one foot in and one foot out' of the academy and enacting the concept of slow ontology as a praxis of resistance.

Writer, artist and academic Andrew Brooks reflects on Stuart Hall's 1980 essay 'Teaching race' in Chapter 20 to consider the challenges of teaching about race from the settler-colonial context of Australia amid an escalating culture war. The chapter asks what is required for the classroom to be a site that both allows for a confrontation with naturalized manifestations of racism *and* creates the conditions for critical reflection, transformation and anti-racist solidarity.

In Chapter 21, Debbie Bargallie engages in a conversation with Alana Lentin, discussing her international race critical scholarship and teaching work as a Jewish European woman, now a settler on Gadigal-Wangal land.

They discuss the silencing of race, its denial, debatability and the hostilities towards critical race work; together, they impel us to urgently reclaim racial literacy as an act of solidarity and community-building, born of intellectual activism, mutuality, love and care.

In Chapter 22, Ambelin Kwaymullina, an Aboriginal storyteller and law academic, closes this collection with a poem, gifting us a powerful set of protocols for all educators that 'allow two worlds', transforming classrooms into places of possibility that may carry us into decolonized futures.

A note on terminology

The generic term 'Indigenous' is contested and is imposed. There is no universally agreed term referring to the diverse groups of Aboriginal and Torres Strait Islander peoples living across mainland Australia and surrounding islands. We have left it up to contributors to choose their preferred terminology. The terms 'Indigenous' and 'Aboriginal and Torres Strait Islander peoples' are used interchangeably. Aboriginal and Torres Strait Islander peoples often choose to identify through country, nation or clan, which describes the lands, regions, waterways and seas with which they are connected (for example, Kamilaroi and Wonnarua, Munanjali and Birri Gubba, Yidinyji/Mbararam, Wondunna clan of the Badtjala nation).

Aboriginal and Torres Strait Islander peoples in Australia have long identified with the term 'Black', or more specifically 'Blak'. We capitalize 'Black' when referring to Black American, African, and Aboriginal and Torres Strait Islander peoples, acknowledging that the term marks a political history and racial identity. We intentionally do not capitalize 'white' as a racial identification category to decentre whiteness.

References

Bargallie, D. (2020) *Unmasking the Racial Contract: Indigenous Voices on Racism in the Australian Public Service*, Canberra: Aboriginal Studies Press.

Bargallie, D., Fernando, N. and Lentin, A. (2023) 'Breaking the racial silence: Putting racial literacy to work in Australia', *Journal of Ethnic and Racial Studies*. DOI: 10.1080/01419870.2023.2206470

Brown, L., Kelada, O. and Jones, D. (2021) '"While I knew I was raced, I didn't think much of it": The need for racial literacy in decolonising classrooms', *Postcolonial Studies*, 23(1): 82–103.

Guinier, L. (2004) 'From racial liberalism to racial literacy: *Brown v. Board of Education* and the interest–divergence dilemma', *Journal of American History*, 91(1): 92–118.

Hill Collins, P. (2019) *Intersectionality as Critical Social Theory*, Durham, NC: Duke University Press.

Lorde, A. (1984) 'The master's tools will never dismantle the master's house', in *Sister Outsider: Essays and Speeches*, Berkeley: Crossing Press, pp 110–14.

Meghji, A. (2022) 'Towards a theoretical synergy: Critical race theory and decolonial thought in Trump America and Brexit Britain', *Current Sociology*, 70(5): 647–64.

Mills, C.W. (1 May 2020). Endorsement of Unmasking the racial contract: Indigenous voices on racism in the Australian Public Service (Bargallie 2020) to Australian Institute of Aboriginal and Torres Strait Islander Studies (AIATSIS) Aboriginal Studies Press, Canberra.

Twine, F.W. (2004) *A White Side of Black Britain: The Concept of Racial Literacy*, London: Routledge.

PART I

Going beyond 'Decolonize the Curriculum'

2

Being Woke to Anti-Intellectualism: Indigenous Resistance and Futures

Bronwyn Carlson and Madi Day

Introduction

Anti-intellectualism (the opposition or hostility to intellectuals or to intellectual pursuits) is a practice and a stance that continues to plague so-called Australian society.[1] During the years of John Howard's Liberal conservative government (1996–2007), the so-called 'history wars' reflected and defined such anti-intellectualism (Manne, 2009).[2] This stance against Indigenous struggles used oppressive ideologies and sought to strengthen a colonial settler mindset via education and public discourse. The history wars intensified and legitimated the underlying racism that has long structured the national, bringing it openly into mainstream discourse once more (Attwood and Markus, 2007). For scholars of Indigenous studies in Australia, this anti-intellectual project poses significant impediments. Mainstream and social media re-readings or misrepresentations of identity politics have picked apart, debated and interrogated our cultural and other identities (Carlson, 2016). This turning point has had a significant regressive impact on anti-racist and decolonial literacies in all spaces of national public engagement. Despite changes in government, anti-intellectualism and the accompanying racism have not subsided, but rather lent themselves to the co-optation, distortion and redeployment by conservatives of terms originating from the left, such as 'political correctness' or 'PC' and, attacks on critical race theory (CRT). Most recently, they have been encapsulated by the populist mantra of 'anti-woke' culture. The anti-intellectualism of these projects works to distract from and dismiss collective movements that mobilize around demands for change.

Traced to Black American blues singer Huddie William Ledbetter – known as Lead Belly – the term 'woke' appears in a brief discussion that follows their Smithsonian recording of the song 'Scottsboro Boys' in 1938, which tells the story of nine Black teenagers accused of sexually assaulting two white women (Lead Belly, 1936). The warning to 'be careful … stay woke' is a clear directive to Black people regarding the dangers of white supremacy.[3]

The onset of anti-woke culture – that is, opposition to anything perceived as 'woke' – has spread rapidly across campuses and public spaces in the United States, Australia, Canada and Europe (Rhodes, 2021; Pilkington, 2021). 'Woke' has become an insult, a shorthand term to defame anything deemed 'left' and a widely populist chorus of derision sung loudly on social media platforms that silences those who speak out or advocate means of addressing and combating racism. Woke folk are often described as 'ideological', erroneously assuming that the un-woken hold non-ideological positions. Anti-wokeness euphemizes racist opposition to diversity and racial justice. Attacks on those who support such ideas have engendered a form of self-censorship among academics who fear punishment and job loss. Speaking out about social justice, and daring to speak of identity – cultural, social or otherwise – is held up to ridicule, and often abuse, by the very people who will then express their own 'offence' at having their free speech curtailed (Gelber and McNamara, 2013). The social media and cultural landscape is becoming a minefield where emboldened settlers hound and harass Indigenous people. This is particularly the case in critical race studies – or indeed any kind of intellectual endeavour, such as teaching, learning or research, that seeks to draw attention to racism.

In the United States, the culture wars waged by right-wing white supremacist conservatives have focused on CRT, creating a moral panic that has led to numerous states banning the theory in classrooms (Schwartz, 2021; Thiessen, 2021) due to it casting 'America and white people [as] irremediably racist' and CRT as 'woke nonsense' (Markowicz, 2021). While CRT is an academic approach that aims to make visible and challenge systems that reproduce structural racism, the conservative media have presented it as a dangerous ideology that views everything through the lens of identity politics and that attacks Australia as being a racist nation; 'wokeism' is represented as a stifling ideology that interferes with free speech. In 2021, the Australian Senate voted in support of a parliamentary motion put forward by far-right politician Senator Pauline Hanson, leader of the One Nation party, calling for the government to remove CRT from the Australian curriculum, despite it never having existed there as an academic framework. Hanson had been objecting to the inclusion of Indigenous perspectives in the curriculum and had previously put forward a motion that 'it's OK to be white', thus endorsing 'the successful co-optation of a racist white supremacist political project' (Sengul, 2022: 593).

This chapter will trace the origins of anti-intellectualism in the period of the Howard government between 1996 and 2007, its spread within universities and its enduring effects. We pay specific attention to the impact of race and racism on Indigenous struggles. We argue that this period in Australia's history and the 'history wars' reinvoked oppressive racist ideologies through vigorous state-led resistance to advances made through Indigenous struggles with the aim of strengthening a colonial settler mindset. We then discuss how this period affected Indigenous students and the development of Indigenous studies as a concrete arena of intellectual pursuit that 'circulates an ever-expanding corpus of knowledge' (Nakata, 2006: 267) before looking at the efforts of Indigenous practitioners to introduce critical literacies into our pedagogical praxes.

CRT emerged as a specific body of scholarship from within critical legal studies in the US context and later widened to include scholarship no longer uniquely critiquing the US legal system, in particular in the United Kingdom. We engage with it here as a body of work that can be used to interrogate and make visible colonial violence, in addition to its critique of systemic racism, and that offers ways to resist these. In the context of this book, we take a close look at anti-intellectualism's latest manifestation in the form of 'anti-wokeism' as this has emerged and taken hold in the public and private spheres. We think critically about the ongoing struggles we experience online, offline, from the public and from our students. Most importantly, as Indigenous Australian scholars and lecturers positioned in the field of Indigenous studies, we consider Indigenous studies' disciplinary response to anti-intellectualism, our *anti*-anti-woke position, our struggles as scholars and students, and our collective will to continue developing a discipline that will feed into Indigenous futures and a reimagining of what can be. This is an ambitious chapter that will take the form of a discussion that perhaps raises more questions than it answers. What is the basis for anti-intellectualism? What are its manifestations for us as practitioners and activists? What kinds of futures can or do we imagine for ourselves as we develop Indigenous critical literacies, and refuse to be silent? To respond to some of these questions, we briefly outline the pedagogical terrain in which we currently work, its aims, achievements and continued successes, and its calls on our collective efforts to pursue a pedagogy grounded in Indigenous thinking, Indigenous critical literacies and Indigenous futures. It pays to stay 'woke' to your oppressors and detractors.

Anti-intellectualism: whose wars were the 'history wars'?

The so-called 'history wars' had a marked effect on Australian political and cultural life. From the late 1970s onwards, debates on the historical violence of invasion and settlement versus the benefits of settler colonialism featured high on the political agenda and were discussed regularly in newspapers, radio, television and in history departments (Macintyre and Clark, 2013). Ironically, the debates in these 'history wars', although centred on interpretations of the foundations of settler colonialism, were conspicuously bereft of Indigenous voices or scholarship. Despite this absence, eminent historians vigorously challenged the official narratives of national origin, providing evidence of frontier wars and widespread massacres of Indigenous peoples (Reynolds, 1982, 1987, 2001; Evans et al, 1993; Richards, 2008; and see Carlson and Farrelly, 2023 for more recent discussion). Added to the overall national angst inspired by the contestation of dominant narratives, language became a central point of contention; terms such as 'invasion', 'genocide' and 'frontier warfare' were subject to fierce interrogation by those who opposed revisionist rewritings of the invasion and theft of land (McGloin and Carlson, 2013; Kilroy, 2016; Nicholson, 2020).

The rewriting of history posed a threat to the conservative agenda of the Howard government, which emphasized 'Judeo-Christian ethics, the progressive spirit of the enlightenment and the institutions and values of British culture' (Fordham, 2015). From 1996 to 2007, these beliefs were deeply ingrained in schools, public spaces, universities and various societal institutions through discourse, policy and legislation legitimated through John Howard's rejection of what he termed a 'black armband' view of history,[4] which he believed diminished Australia's (predominantly white) pioneer past (Clark, 2002). Howard's belief system fostered a culture of national pride in a history steeped in colonial 'success' that discouraged critical examination of the past, leading to a robust culture of anti-intellectualism and resistance to addressing discrimination or acknowledging historical truths (Curthoys, 2007). Most recently, this anti-intellectualism has been characterized by accusations of 'wokeness' wherever there is truth-telling and resistance to discrimination. At the very moment when Indigenous truths erupted into the national psyche, race-literate and decolonial counter-narratives to the 'peaceful settlement' of Australia came under sustained attack. Howard's reign is remembered as a time when the Australian people were assured that race did not exist, while in fact race was reinstated in liberal right-wing white supremacist discourse. The ideological implications of Howard's conservatism were effective. Despite this, the Howard years were a vibrant and generative time for Indigenous politics and activism. Indigenous people are acutely aware that within oppression there is always space for resistance.

Indigenous studies as a discipline

Ironically, it was during this period of rampant anti-intellectualism and the official denouncement of colonial wars and truth-telling that Indigenous studies began to be established in the academy, fostering[5] a revival of dissent through Aboriginal and Torres Strait Islander activism. The National Inquiry into the Separation of Aboriginal and Torres Strait Islander Children from Their Families was conducted and the subsequent *Bringing Them Home* report (Australian Human Rights Commission, 1997) was released and the High Court's *Wik* decision in 1996 ruled that Native Title could coexist on land held by pastoralists (LeCouteur et al, 2001). At this time, John Howard declared the end of Indigenous self-determination with the abolition of the Aboriginal and Torres Strait Islander Commission, which was considered the last vestige of autonomy within federal governance. This trajectory provides a flavour of the push-and-pull of Aboriginal and Torres Strait Islander activism to achieve degrees of attitudinal and institutional change. Indigenous community-led activism defied the mainstream complacency and the systematic attempts to dumb down intellectual inquiry that is specifically about us, our histories and our struggles since invasion.

Aboriginal studies (or Indigenous studies) developed as a separate, disciplinary field of intellectual inquiry in Australian universities directly from and alongside multiple sites of political activism and community-led militancy across the continent that intervened in the anti-intellectual landscape. Intervention at an official level occurred on many fronts and maintained a groundswell of support at a local level across many Indigenous communities. Yet the trajectory of Indigenous studies as a recognized intellectual field has been arduous; universities, after all, are colonial institutions that have, as in many Western states, been deeply affected by the dominance of neoliberal market ideology and the erosion of the humanities (Brett, 2021). Despite this, Indigenous scholarship has prevailed and flourished. The introduction of bachelor's degrees in Aboriginal studies laid the disciplinary foundations for postgraduate programmes with their own interdisciplinary theoretical rigour, and these produced an increasing number of Indigenous graduates across several institutions. Currently bachelor's degrees in Indigenous studies in Australian universities rewrite and incorporate all Western fields of inquiry, ranging from mathematics to literature, cosmology, environmental studies, law and art. There is no single area of study in which we do not insert our laws, our science, literature, creative pursuits, technologies and knowledge of the world, which has maintained our survival for 60,000+ years.

Indigenous studies has its own rigour. We continue to develop our own curriculum centring Indigenous scholarship, Indigenous teachers and Indigenous pedagogical praxis alongside an incisive critique of settler colonialism, racism and its ongoing effects on Indigenous and other marginalized peoples. Moreover, Indigenous studies focuses on our resistance, agency and determination. It includes practitioners at all levels of study whose practical and theoretical understanding gives rise to an oeuvre of knowledge about us, our histories and lived experiences as racialized beings in a society that continues to practice white dominance. As Nakata et al (2012: 123) assert, Indigenous studies 'engages the politics of knowledge production, the politics of education, and the Indigenous politics of self-determination'. For Indigenous students, and Indigenous studies as a discipline, CRT as an approach to race studies offers a set of tenets and a body of scholarship that lends itself to critical methodologies and theorizations of race that make visible white possession, privilege, systemic racial violence and racism in the Australia settler-colonial context. 'Colonisation morphologises in multiple ways as it continues to operate discursively and materially within cultural formations, institutions and public culture' (Moreton-Robinson, 2009: 11), and for that reason Moreton-Robinson advances the concept of critical Indigenous studies (CIS) to provide political and intellectual theorizing and philosophizing of the contemporary 'postcolonizing world' that Indigenous peoples inhabit, which centre our ways of knowing and theorizing.

CRT, anti-colonial theory and CIS speak back to the anti-intellectualism implicit in the 'anti-woke' project that seeks to undermine efforts to expose the extent of race, gender, sexual and other forms of oppression and discrimination that often play out violently both online and offline. It is a threatening body of work precisely because it comes from a place of radical intolerance for the violences that Indigenous people experience daily in all spheres of activity.

Indigenous studies has, in recent years, embarked on a variety of rigorous practical and theoretical applications that, while specific to Indigenous scholarship, can be encapsulated broadly by CRT. Their purpose is to undermine colonial settler mentalities, dismantle colonial structures and imagine and construct Indigenous futures. Some 235 years of colonial rule have made us adept at dodging and circumventing colonial settler moves. However, we are cognisant that the task facing us is not simple and there are instances of polarization in which marginal groups become more marginalized under a kind of orthodoxy that seeks to regulate and penalize valid questions about cultural identity or issues pertaining to LGBTQIA+ people and communities. Such is the nature of critical race studies that we must be able to respond to questions posed by those to whom CRT initially appears confronting or inexplicable. Our student cohort is diverse and, particularly in this 'anti-woke' moment, we cannot assume that students will understand all the complexities of race as it is experienced in a settler-colonial society.

Anti-racist pedagogy as a decolonial praxis

Anti-racist pedagogy is a decolonial praxis (Bargallie et al, 2023; Gabi et al, 2023). Critical racial literacies attempt in many ways to make sense of the variations in the manifestation of white supremacy that occur at micro and macro levels both offline and online (Bargallie, 2020; Carlson and Day, 2021; Day and Carlson, 2023). CRT in Indigenous contexts provides, as Bargallie et al (2023: 3) note, 'a way of challenging the co-optation and dilution of racial literacy we are witnessing'. Indigenous scholars constantly face resistance to our attempts to change racial colonial structures and make whiteness visible. Race study is hard work: it is mentally demanding, rigorous and often exhausting because it demands asking and answering the same questions again and again and again, as how race is conceptualized, produced and reproduced is constantly shifting. Racial literacies, as Bargallie et al (2023: 6) note, require us to teach the distinctive differences between white conceptualizations of the world and our own, which differ significantly from those held by the nation-state. Attempting to teach the origins of race and racism is crucial to understanding colonization and we must explain the latter to begin discussing possibilities for decolonization. The overwhelming dilemma for educators of anti-racism is time and space; we are at the mercy of short courses devised by the academy to suit its semester sectioning of teaching and learning, and we comply with this in a space where white knowledge and pedagogy continue to prevail and dominate. However, we meet the challenge and continue to provide theoretical and practical ways of understanding and responding to racism. Importantly, in the context of the increasing anti-intellectualism and the current climate of racism – which is particularly evident online (Carlson and Frazer, 2018; Carlson, 2022) – we must ask how we can stop ourselves being reduced to the banalities of the popularized 'anti-woke' mentality when we attempt to defend an anti-racist position.

Sovereignty versus social justice

A key racial/colonial literacy that remains undeveloped and under-theorized is that Indigenous peoples globally are racialized 'others' whose existence is always described, proscribed, regulated and scrutinized by colonizers and settlers who lay claim to sovereignty and absolute authority. As Moreton-Robinson (2021: 319) argues, Indigenous sovereignties are incommensurable with Western concepts of sovereignty (of nation-state formation and rule) that justified the conquest and possession of Indigenous territories and are antithetical to Indigenous traditional philosophies. 'There is an ontological intimacy between race and sovereignty', and the 'racial logics' of patriarchal white supremacy embedded in colonial state law permit the 'continuing disavowal of Indigenous sovereignties' (Moreton-Robinson, 2021: 256). Nation-states and heads of state have a vested interest in maintaining white authority, no matter how much lip service is paid to 'social justice' at official levels – a fact easily observed in Australia, both historically and in recent times, through scattered, sporadic attempts to 'reform' the dire conditions experienced by Indigenous peoples.

In 1967, a referendum to include Aboriginal people in the national census was passed; however, it did not address equal pay or citizenship rights, nor did it address wage rates or personal freedoms.[6] Over 20 years later, the Royal Commission into Aboriginal Deaths in Custody (1991) investigated 99 deaths between 1980 and 1989 and produced 339 recommendations and a swathe of publications that the Australian government and legal system have repeatedly overlooked and bypassed. Astoundingly, a further 540 deaths in custody have taken place since this 'inquiry'. In 1992, in the pivotal, emotional Redfern Park Speech, then Prime Minister Paul Keating stated that 'the plight of Aboriginal Australians affects us all' (Keating, 2011; Clark, 2013). While well-meaning, the speech failed to denote the disadvantages that were, and continue to be, endured by Aboriginal people at the hands of colonizers, which played out in the backlash of the 'history wars' that followed.

In 2007, the federal government temporarily suspended the Racial Discrimination Act 1975 to enable the Northern Territory Emergency Response, also known as the 'Intervention'. The suspension of the Racial Discrimination Act enabled a military deployment into some Northern Territory Aboriginal communities as well as a raft of other paternalistic control measures under the guise of protecting Aboriginal children from widespread abuse. Then, to justify the so-called 'emergency', Prime Minister John Howard weaponized the Northern Territory Government-commissioned *Ampe Akelyernemane Meke Mekarle 'Little Children are Sacred'* report (Anderson and Wild, 2007), which had investigated allegations of sexual abuse in Indigenous communities. In 2008, a formal Apology to Indigenous Australians for forced removals of Australian Indigenous children (the Stolen Generations) from their families by the state by incoming Prime Minister Kevin Rudd was considered by many to be a watershed moment. Yet none of this has resulted in any substantive change or improvement across all aspects of Indigenous life. Even the 2023 Voice to Parliament referendum (Liddle, 2023) was convincingly rejected by the Australian people.

Each of the 'gesture politics' discussed has failed to result in improved outcomes for the lived realities of Indigenous peoples; at each point, an opportunity for truth-telling, rewriting of history and reckoning was whitewashed. As educators, we are accused of being cynical and ungrateful in our readings of these events – as progressive moments that inspire change, 'proof' that white Australia has changed and now 'cares', that racism towards us has finally been addressed at an official level. A key to racial literacy would be to unravel these 'flashpoints' in Australian history that provide, for many of our students, a reassuring panacea that will assuage guilt, shame and an acknowledgement of their continuing role in racism. As Chávez-Moreno (2022) points out, white supremacist literacies are also racial literacies,[7] and whiteness and racial domination are learned through pedagogies of the state and public discourse (Sriprakash et al, 2022). For us as educators, this is where CRT, anti-colonial theory, Indigenous critical racial and decolonial literacies – or whatever we might call the body of work by Indigenous scholars that continues to give substance to our racialized realities – finds a pedagogical home.

An anti-woke awakening

In Australia, the minimal concessions and (broken) promises for land rights for Aboriginal and Torres Strait Islander people during the Hawke and Keating governments inspired backlash and undoing from the Howard government. The rise of the internet and social media from the early 2000s has resulted in global connections and distribution of anti-racist and anti-colonial thinking, yet increased global consciousness of shared issues among Black and Indigenous peoples in settler-colonial nations has also provoked an anti-woke response, as well as police violence in retaliation to movements including Black Lives Matter and localized Indigenous sovereignty movements (Liu et al, 2021). Internet technology has facilitated highly connected, reactive and largely unmonitored far-right cohorts to hand-pick and circulate discourse like never before (Richards, 2019). Percolation of far-right ideology and conspiracies accelerated online during the COVID-19 pandemic through anti-vaccination circles underpinned by older Christian and white supremacist ideologies. Those embroiled in popular online conspiracies such as QAnon[8] refer to this moment of increased awareness of one another and far-right ideology as 'The Great Awakening'. Prior to its use in QAnon, The Great Awakening described the revival of evangelical Christianity in 18th-century Anglo-America. This religious movement was a Protestant reaction, in part to perceived 'moral decline' in the American colonies, and was famous for radical fire-and-brimstone preachers such as James Davenport, who engaged in book burning (Lambert, 1999). The Great Awakening today involves a bricolage of hand-picked Christian, New Age and occultist ideas made available to the masses through the internet, tracing a growth of fascism often presented under the guise of religiosity. Chamila Liyanage (2021) has shown how ideas and beliefs can be rewritten and recycled on the internet using the widely shared Great Awakening Map[9] as a journey across New Age teaching, UFO cults, Satanic, anti-migrant and anti-Semitic conspiracies and into white supremacist digital extremism. Although stemming from Europe and the United States, the ideas and conspiracies connected in The Great Awakening are shared and entertained internationally, particularly among Western nations, where they offer simplified and phantastic alternatives to anti-colonial analysis of neoliberal concentrations of power and capital. The

New World Order conspiracy, for instance, gained significant traction on Twitter (now known as X) in Australia in 2021 when NSW Chief Health Officer Kerry Chant mentioned the term while discussing contact tracing for COVID-19 (Hancock, 2021). Australia was also represented as a trial site for the New World Order in the widely circulated and debunked conspiracy documentary *The New Normal* (Reuters Staff, 2021). New World Order conspiracies predict the implementation of a globalist totalitarian regime overthrowing white and Christian dominance and, although many believers may not be aware of this, have a long history connected to Nazism, the Aryan Nation and the American Militia movement.

In a world where white supremacist ideology and disinformation can be spread and consumed with little effort or thought, amid conditions of growing economic precarity and political upheaval, it has never been easier to hand-pick and adapt anti-woke content to rebuke Indigenous and anti-colonial thinking. Accusations of being 'woke' or 'PC' are frequently directed at Indigenous staff in our department. We can cite several instances where students have vilified staff both at an official and a personal level. In these instances, students claim they are entitled to express views that Indigenous staff identify as offensive and/or racist. Such views include active misinformation and disinformation about Indigenous people, including that we would not have 'progressed socially or technologically without colonization', that we are ourselves 'racist towards white folks', that we receive 'free' benefits, that we are inherently criminal … the list goes on and on. In a complaint to our department, one student cited the article 'Woke madness and the university' (Leroux, 2021) to attempt to put us in our place. The article claims that the woke movement is part of a long tradition 'influenced by Marxism, feminism, relativism and so on … not a scientific approach to reality, but essentially an ideological posture, an attitude, a social movement … academics being hired for their political activism rather than their dedication to science and objective knowledge' (Leroux, 2021: 66).

Such claims position anti-woke culture as objective and scientific. However, our research on white internet cultures indicates that anti-woke and far-right cultures are indeed highly ideologically driven (Day and Carlson, 2023). Moreover, as many of our students are not accustomed to critical analysis, they may serve as foot soldiers reproducing, either consciously or unconsciously, historical colonial and white supremacist ideology. Leroux's (2021: 68) article further claims that 'positive discrimination in favour of protected groups has become a secular religion among the "woke"', and ends with the predictable charge that 'universities have become liberticidal'. Such articles and criticisms proliferate in the public sphere, in our classrooms and across social media platforms. Some, for example, Lillian Andrews' (2022) opinion piece, 'Woke symbolism holds Indigenous Australians back', vilifies 'woke' culture under the guise of its harm to Indigenous people. In an extraordinary tirade, Andrews (2022) claims that the 'woke' – or 'caring class' need Indigenous disadvantage for their 'moral credibility'. In a final sleight-of-hand and hijacking of her own frame of reference to her own advantage, the author declares that 'only when Aboriginal Australians take back their identities from their self-styled defenders, will they finally stop being exploited as tawdry political props' (2022). The novelty of the far right (*The Spectator* is a renowned right-wing publication) speaking up for us and the stereotypical anti-intellectualist vitriol levelled at Indigenous supporters accused of being 'paisley-shirted posers' (Andrews, 2022) would be amusing were it not part of a strategy of the right to undermine anti-racist movements.

Critical literacies and Indigenous futures

Our research on the multifarious manifestations of racism on social media is still in its initial stages, despite a developing oeuvre of publications on the topic; the extent of vitriolic racist bludgeoning on social media platforms is astonishing (Carlson and Day, 2021; Day and Carlson, 2023). The user-generated internet provides endless opportunity for racist abuse, with new technologies and racist ideologies constantly evolving (Carlson and Frazer, 2021). But particular ideas have taken root. Many social media posts and comments recycle the same statements about Indigenous people being 'primitive' or 'stuck in the Stone Age' and 'incapable of functioning in the modern world'. We receive constant directives to 'move on' or 'get over it' – 'it' being colonialism and racism. Indigenous and anti-colonial critical literacies, therefore, are constantly inhibited by prevailing ideologies that construct Indigenous people as static while at the same time needing to 'move forward'. Our work seems to awaken our students from a time loop where they cycle between the constructs of barbaric and sacred, where the ambiguity of the 'Noble Savage' must always be made and remade for us to be classified in any meaningful way in colonial mindsets. White settler psyches are fragile, and are the hardest to liberate from this loop. We have been told by settler students that our 'units are shit' and that we have no right to be 'brainwashing' people with lies about Australia's history or that we are not objective and 'only consider Aboriginal perspectives'. We are continually derided for being 'PC' and 'woke', so it is with a sense of pride that we engage with and develop new critical literacies that refuse to be silenced by our detractors. We engage meaningfully with what has come to be known as 'Indigenous futurisms', a term coined by Anishinaabe cultural critic Grace Dillon (2012), which is far more than just an exploration of what a possible future could look like.

Indigenous futurisms is a movement with foundations in rethinking and reimagining all spheres of our cultural knowledge. It counters settler futurism – which, as argued elsewhere (Carlson and Frazer, 2021: 239), turns on 'the disappearance of Indigenous people ... [Indigenous people's] absence from the future, is necessary for settler futures'. Contrapuntal to the tiresome refrain for us to 'move on', the fact that we have a developed a strategic, cognisant plan for our futures as Indigenous peoples is a disturbance to settler-colonial logic and its plans for the continuity of our regulation and demise. We are inspired by Black politics of critical hope, which:

> refers to hopeful action that is based on the critical analysis of a situation and the recognition that wishing alone is not sufficient to make change. It involves an understanding of the forces that produce injustice and an imagining of what the world without these forces, and without the injustice, might look like. (James et al, 2010: 27)

We are inspired by Black and Indigenous people and critical thinking, our vast knowledge of the physical world and our expertise in the modern domain of technology, and our intervention into all areas of cultural production, both 'real' and imaginative Indigenous futurisms, is a living, breathing body of knowledge and action that 'moves' us beyond the current climate of settler colonialism to a prefiguration of decolonial reality where being Indigenous is a statement of our continued sovereignty. It is not defined singularly, but has inserted, and will continue to insert, itself in the colonial domain where we will denounce and rewrite ourselves and our surroundings. Western and 'westernized' universities are identified as institutions where colonial legacies of knowledge production and racialization prevail, but they are also sites where struggles for justice unfold (Maldonado-Torres, 2007). This takes place daily through the activism of woke teachers, communities, writers and thinkers to bring issues into the public domain where anti-woke politicization continues to script us as ungrateful, disrespectful and ideological.

In this sense, tensions between wokeness and anti-wokeness are differences between looking, inquiring and imagining, and looking away. An anti-anti-wokeness is essential, a double negative that heralds our positivity. Like anti-wokeness, wokeness *is an ideology* and we do not resile from this accusation; a non-ideological position is impossible as we are ideological subjects. Indigenous politics clearly do not regulate settler-colonial nations; rather, our ideological position is based entirely on a belief in a set of ideas, principles and beliefs in the right of Indigenous people to assert sovereignty, defined by Moreton-Robinson (2021: 257) as 'inherent rights deriving from spiritual and historical connections to land', our origins and our creation and our right to dedicate ourselves to the reimagining and rewriting of a future that will restore these.

Indigenous and anti-colonial critical literacies are the very stuff of our awakeness, an exciting, stimulating challenge where our educative efforts reap rewards. Following Daniel Heath Justice (2020), with the priority to 'imagine otherwise' at the fore, our educational endeavours have initiated the Centre for Global Indigenous Futures (CGIF),[10] a network of global Indigenous thinkers brought together through liaison, conferencing, the formal and informal exchange of ideas, Indigenous histories and experiences, and pedagogical approaches to decolonial goals, through collegiality and friendship and a firm solidarity that derives from shared aspirations. We are many and varied. The CGIF is vibrant and grows daily. It offers our educators and students the social capital needed to support learning and career aspirations through a 'who you know' network that prioritizes the support of Indigenous futures. CGIF supports scholarship at all levels, and we learn from each other and thrive in a futurist space unencumbered by settler colonialism. It is a space of immense pride and achievement. In addition, we have developed the first Indigenous queer units in our curriculum, expanding on the traditional syllabus of Indigenous studies teaching (Carey and Prince, 2015; Carlson, 2021). Indigenous queer studies endorses a more nuanced understanding of us as sexualized beings whose lifeways are characterized by diversity at all levels. We also have a strong focus on digital technologies where these affect Indigenous lives and where Indigenous creativity and innovation inspires creation. This research challenges long-held ideas that seek to mould us into the past; we are extremely adept and confident users of digital technologies. Finally, we have developed a comprehensive Indigenous internship programme for our graduate students to provide the skills and support required to thrive in academia in these times when one must master more than research or intellectual rigour to survive the terrain of the contemporary university. This is a smattering of what we do to build racial and decolonial literacies to effect transformative change that will continue to feed our futures and another generation of woke thinkers and troublemakers.

Conclusion

As Indigenous Australian educators whose work is grounded by Indigenous intellectual sovereignty, we are enthused and encouraged by our individual and collective efforts. We look with hope to futures where the tired, old, misused mantra of 'anti-woke' will be confined to its banal place in history and we can get on with the job of developing pedagogies where all students can learn our histories and where our people can continue our survivance and thrive into the coming millennia. Anti-intellectualism will undoubtedly continue to rear its head in these times when the far right's Great Awakening seems to be accelerating. But Indigenous peoples are 'woke' to the dangers that threaten. We are across the terrain of settler colonialism, privy to its intentions, mindful of its violence. To create viable futures, the continued development of CRT, Indigenous and anti-colonial literacies is crucial to breaking the racial silence imposed on us. Additionally, we need solidarity networks and organizations to build a critical mass, providing confidence and determination, and fostering the will to collectively imagine something better.

Notes

1. The term 'so-called Australia' is used to make the point that the nation-state is illegitimate and a claim to ownership is grounded in falsehood despite its existence and acceptance as a country. British colonizers declared *terra nullius* (unoccupied land) and illegally occupied the land; this has since been overturned and it now accepted that sovereignty was never ceded.
2. The Australian 'history wars' refers to a series of contentious media and academic debates and disputes over the interpretation of Australian history that attempted to redefine the historical narrative to downplay the impact of colonialism and dispossession on Indigenous peoples and minimize the significance of past injustices, thereby building a conservative national identity. The Howard government introduced policies and legislative changes that limited the scope of Indigenous land rights (Attwood, 2005) and curtailed the rights and autonomy of Indigenous communities in relation to their traditional lands through its interventionist approach, particularly the Northern Territory Emergency Response (also known as the 'Intervention'), which severely undermined Indigenous self-determination and perpetuated historical patterns of dispossession (Altman and Hinkson, 2007).
3. The influence of this song carries through Black American music into the present in albums that engage playfully with love, genre and racial politics, such as Erykah Badu's *New Amerykah Part One (4th World War)* (2008) and Childish Gambino's (aka Donald Glover) *Awaken, My Love!* (Glover, 2016). The phrase itself was revitalized for protest in the Black Lives Matter movement from 2014 when protesters in Ferguson starting using the hashtag #StayWoke (Romano, 2020).
4. The term 'black armband' history was coined by eminent conservative historian Geoffrey Blainey in 1993 to describe an exaggeratedly negative view of Australia's history regarding the treatment of Aboriginal people, Chinese, Kanakas, non-British migrants, women, the very old, the very young and the poor. See https://web.archive.org/web/20090404113845/http://www.aph.gov.au/library/pubs/RP/1997-98/98rp05.htm
5. Prior to this, higher education initiatives were aimed at supporting Aboriginal and Torres Strait Islander student pathways, retention methods, community consultations and so on, under the framework of Western education. Such attempts to involve Aboriginal and Torres Strait Islander students in learning programs entirely ignored our own worldviews and histories. Indigenous input into all education syllabi was negligible.
6. While many people think the referendum gave Aboriginal and Torres Strait Islander peoples the right to vote, this wasn't in fact the case. Aboriginal people could vote at the state level before Federation in 1901, with Queensland and Western Australia being the only states that expressly prevented Aboriginal and Torres Strait Islander peoples from voting. It wasn't until 1962, when the Electoral Act was amended, that Aboriginal and Torres Strait Islander peoples were given the right to register and vote, but voting was not compulsory. Full voting rights were not granted federally until Aboriginal and Torres Strait Islander people were required to register on the electoral roll in 1984.

[7] As Chávez-Moreno (2022: 481) puts it, '(a) all people make meaning of racial ideologies and are racially literate, including those who adopt and perpetuate racist ideologies, and (b) race-evasive and other racist interpretations are themselves *a kind of racial literacy*, albeit one that perpetuates racism'.
[8] QAnon is a conspiracist movement that began on message board 4chan in 2017 and was initially driven by disinformation regarding US politicians, including Donald Trump and Hilary Clinton. It has since exploded into a global conspiracy connected to populist nationalism in the West as well as far right vigilante violence including the riot at the US Capitol on 6 January 2021.
[9] https://greatawakeningreport.com/the-great-awakening-map
[10] https://www.globalindigenousfutures.com

References

Altman, J. and Hinkson, M. (eds) (2007) *Coercive Reconciliation: Stabilise, Normalise, Exit Aboriginal Australia*, Melbourne: Arena.

Anderson, P. and Wild, R. (2007) *Ampe Akelyernemane Meke Mekarle 'Little Children are Sacred': Report of the Northern Territory Board of Inquiry into the Protection of Aboriginal Children from Sexual Abuse*, Darwin: Northern Territory Government.

Andrews L. (2022) 'Woke symbolism holds Indigenous Australians back', *Spectator Australia*, https://www.spectator.com.au/2022/07/woke-symbolism-holds-indigenous-australians-back

Attwood, B. (2005) *Telling the Truth About Aboriginal History*, Sydney: Allen & Unwin.

Attwood, B. and Markus, A. (2007) *The 1967 Referendum: Race, Power and the Australian Constitution*, Canberra: Aboriginal Studies Press.

Australian Human Rights Commission (1997) *Bringing Them Home: Report of the National Inquiry into the Separation of Aboriginal and Torres Strait Islander Children from Their Families*, Canberra: Australian Government, https://humanrights.gov.au/our-work/bringing-them-home-report-1997

Badu, E. (2008) *New Amerykah Part One (4th World War)* [Album], New York: Universal Motown.

Bargallie, D. (2020) *Unmasking the Racial Contract: Indigenous Voices on Racism in the Australian Public Service*, Canberra: Aboriginal Studies Press.

Bargallie, D., Fernando, N. and Lentin, A. (2023) 'Breaking the racial silence: Putting racial literacy to work in Australia', *Ethnic and Racial Studies*. https://doi.org/10.1080/01419870.2023.2206470

Brett, J. (2021) 'The bin fire of the humanities', *The Monthly*, March, https://www.themonthly.com.au/issue/2021/march/1614517200/judith-brett/bin-fire-humanities#mtr

Carey, M. and Prince, M. (2015) 'Designing an Australian Indigenous studies curriculum for the twenty-first century: Nakata's "cultural interface", standpoints and working beyond binaries', *Higher Education Research and Development*, 34(2): 270–83.

Carlson, B. (2016) *The Politics of Identity: Who Counts as Aboriginal Today*, Canberra: Aboriginal Studies Press.

Carlson, B. (2021) 'Data silence in the settler archive: Indigenous femicide, deathscapes and social media', in S. Perera and J. Pugliese (eds), *Mapping Deathscapes: Digital Geographies of Racial and Border Violence*, London: Routledge, pp 84–105.

Carlson, B. (2022) 'The queen died, colonisers cried and the walls came tumbling down', *Anglistica AION: An Interdisciplinary Journal*, 25(1): 9–21.

Carlson, B. and Frazer, R. (2018) *Social Media Mob: Being Indigenous Online*, Sydney: Macquarie University, https://researchers.mq.edu.au/en/publications/social-media-mob-being-indigenous-online

Carlson, B. and Day, M. (2021) 'Technology facilitated abuse: The need for Indigenous led research and response', in B. Harris and D. Woodlock (eds), *The Routledge Handbook on Technology and Domestic Violence: Victimisation, Perpetration and Responses*, London: Routledge, pp 33–48.

Carlson, B. and Frazer, R. (2021) 'Futures', in *The Practice and Politics of Being Indigenous on Social Media: Indigenous Digital Life*, New York: Springer, pp 237–53.

Carlson, B. and Farrelly, T. (2023) *Monumental Disruptions*, Canberra: Aboriginal Studies Press.

Chávez-Moreno, L.C. (2022) 'Critiquing racial literacy: Presenting a continuum of racial literacies', *Educational Researcher*, 51(7): 481–8.

Clark, A. (2002) 'History in black and white: A critical analysis of the black armband debate', *Journal of Australian Studies*, 26(75): 1–11.

Clark, T. (2013) 'Paul Keating's Redfern Park speech and its rhetorical legacy', *Overland*, 213: 10–17.

Curthoys, A. (2007) 'History in the Howard era', *Teaching History*, 41(1): 4–9.

Day, M. and Carlson, B. (2023) 'Predators & perpetrators: White settler violence online', in D. Callander, P. Farvid, A. Baradaran and T. Vance (eds), *(Un)Desiring Whiteness: (Un)Doing Sexual Racism*, Oxford: Oxford University Press, pp 1–20.

Dillon, G.L. (ed) (2012) *Walking the Clouds: An Anthology of Indigenous Science Fiction*, Tucson: Arizona University Press.

Evans, R., Saunders, K. and Cronin, K. (1993) *Race Relations in Colonial Queensland: A History of Exclusion, Exploitation, and Extermination*, 3rd edn, Brisbane: University of Queensland Press.

Fordham, H. (2015) 'Curating a nation's past: The role of the public intellectual in Australia's history wars', *Media Culture Journal*, 18(4).

Gabi, J., Olsson Rost, A., Warner, D. and Asif, U. (2023) 'Decolonial praxis: Teacher educators' perspectives on tensions, barriers, and possibilities of anti-racist practice-based initial teacher education in England', *The Curriculum Journal*, 34(1): 83–99.

Gelber, K. and McNamara, L. (2013) 'Freedom of speech and racial vilification in Australia: "The Bolt case" in public discourse', *Australian Journal of Political Science*, 48(4): 470–84.

Glover, D. (2016) *Awaken, My Love!* [Album], New York: Glassnote Records.

Hancock, S. (2021) '"New World Order": Conspiracy theorists unite as Australian health chief uses term at press conference', *Independent*, 9 September, https://www.independent.co.uk/news/world/australasia/australia-new-world-order-conspiracies-b1917082.html

James, C., Esta, D., Bernard, W.T., Benjamin, A., Lloyd, B. and Turner, T. (2010) *Race & Well-being: The Lives, Hopes and Activism of African Canadians*, Halifax: Fernwood Publishing.

Justice, D.H. (2020) '"Our stories give us a lot of guidance": Daniel Health Justice on why Indigenous literatures matter', *CBC*, https://alllitup.ca/Blog/2021/Indigenous-Speculative-Fiction-An-Interview-with-Daniel-Heath-Justice

Keating, P. (2011) 'Australian launch of the International Year for the World's Indigenous People', *Indigenous Law Bulletin*, 7(23): 20–2.

Kilroy, P. (2016) 'Discovery, settlement or invasion? The power of language in Australia's historical narrative', *The Conversation*, 1 April, https://theconversation.com/discovery-settlement-or-invasion-the-power-of-language-in-australias-historical-narrative-57097

Lambert, F. (1999) *Inventing the Great Awakening*, Princeton: Princeton University Press.

Lead Belly, H. (rec. 1936) *Scottsborro Boys*, YouTube, Smithsonian Folkways Recording, https://www.youtube.com/watch?v=VrXfkPViFIE

LeCouteur, A., Rapley, M. and Augoustinos, M. (2001) '"This very difficult debate about *Wik*": Stake, voice and the management of category memberships in race politics', *British Journal of Social Psychology*, 40(1): 35–57.

Leroux, R. (2021) 'Woke madness and the university', National Association of Scholars, https://www.nas.org/academic-questions/34/4/woke-madness-and-the-university

Liddle, C. (2023) 'Voices beyond yes and no', *Eureka Street*, May, https://www.eurekastreet.com.au/voices-beyond-yes-and-no

Liu, H., Martinez Dy, A., Dar, S. and Brewis, D. (2021) 'Anti-racism in the age of supremacy and backlash', *Equality, Diversity and Inclusion: An International Journal*, 40(2): 105–13.

Liyanage, C. (2021) 'QAnon and the Great Awakening: How the deep web rewrites ideologies and beliefs', Global Network on Extremism and Technology, 14 June, https://gnet-research.org/2021/06/14/qanon-and-the-great-awakening-how-the-deep-web-rewrites-ideologies-and-beliefs

Macintyre, S. and Clark, A. (2013) *The History Wars*, Melbourne: Melbourne University Publishing.

Maldonado-Torres, N. (2007) 'On the coloniality of being: Contributions to the development of a concept', *Cultural Studies*, 21(2–3): 240–70.

Manne, R. (2009) 'Comment: History wars', *The Monthly,* November, 15–17.

Markowicz, K. (2021) 'Critical race theory is part of woke agenda – parents should fight it', *New York Post*, 27 June, https://nypost.com/2021/06/27/critical-race-theory-is-part-of-woke-agenda-parents-should-fight-all-of-it

McGloin, C. and Carlson, B. (2013) 'Indigenous studies and the politics of language', *Journal of University Teaching and Learning Practice*, 10(1).

Moreton-Robinson, A. (2009) 'Introduction: Critical Indigenous theory', *Cultural Studies Review*, 15(2): 11–12.

Moreton-Robinson, A. (2021) 'Incommensurable sovereignties', in B. Hokowhitu, A. Moreton-Robinson, L. Tuhiwai-Smith, C. Andersen and S. Larkin (eds), *Routledge Handbook of Critical Indigenous Studies*, London: Routledge, pp 257–67.

Nakata, M. (2006) 'Australian Indigenous studies: A question of discipline', *The Australian Journal of Anthropology*, 17(3): 265–75.

Nakata, M., Nakata, V., Keech, S. and Bolt, R. (2012) 'Decolonial goals and pedagogies for Indigenous studies', *Decolonisation, Education & Society*, 1(1): 120–40.

Nicholson, R. (2020) 'Yes, this continent was invaded in 1788 – an international law explains', *The Conversation*, 27 January, https://theconversation.com/yes-this-continent-was-invaded-in-1788-an-international-law-expert-explains-130462

Pilkington, A. (2021) 'Black Lives Matter and the anti-woke campaign in the UK,' in *Effective Elimination of Structural Racism*, IntechOpen, https://www.intechopen.com/chapters/78439

Reuters Staff (2021) 'Fact check: Multiple misleading suggestions made in documentary on the COVID-19 pandemic', *Reuters*, 20 January, https://www.reuters.com/article/uk-factcheck-reset/fact-check-multiple-misleading-suggestions-made-in-documentary-on-the-covid-19-pandemic-idUSKBN29O228

Reynolds, H. (1982) *The Other Side of the Frontier*, Ringwood: Penguin.

Reynolds, H. (1987) *Frontier: Aborigines, Settlers and Land*, Sydney: Allen & Unwin.

Reynolds, H. (2001) *An Indelible Stain? The Question of Genocide in Australia's History*, Ringwood: Penguin.

Rhodes, C. (2021) *Woke Capitalism: How Corporate Morality is Sabotaging Democracy*, Bristol: Policy Press.

Richards, I. (2019) 'A philosophical and political-economic analysis of "Generation Identity": Fascism, online media, and the European New Right', *Terrorism and Political Violence*, 34(1): 28–47.

Richards, J. (2008) *The Secret War: A True History of Queensland's Native Police*, Brisbane: University of Queensland Press.

Romano, A. (2020) 'A history of "wokeness"', *Vox*, 9 October, https://www.vox.com/culture/21437879/stay-woke-wokeness-history-origin-evolution-controversy

Schwartz, S. (2021) 'Map: Where critical race theory is under attack', *Education Week*, 11 June, https://www.edweek.org/policy-politics/map-where-critical-race-theory-is-under-attack/2021/06

Sengul, K. (2022) '"It's OK to be white": The discursive construction of victimhood, "anti-white racism" and calculated ambivalence in Australia', *Critical Discourse Studies*, 19(6): 593–609.

Sriprakash, A., Rudolph, S. and Gerrard, J. (2022) *Learning Whiteness: Education and the Settler Colonial State*, London: Pluto Press.

Thiessen, M.A. (2021) 'The danger of critical race theory', *The Washington Post*, 11 November, https://www.washingtonpost.com/opinions/2021/11/11/danger-critical-race-theory

3

Decolonizing Australian Universities: Why Embedding Indigenous Content in the Curriculum Fails That Task

David Hollinsworth

Introduction

In recent years, calls for the decolonization of higher education have become widespread (Arday and Mirza, 2018). These calls do not just reflect the inclusion of diverse, racialized people into the student body and faculty, but also acknowledge that previously ignored and excluded knowledges and perspectives from the 'colonies', including internal colonies in settler societies, have shaped the formation of what is understood as Europe or 'first world' countries (Gopal, 2021).

In most countries, there have been sustained student protests and demands for decolonization of both curricula and (less so) pedagogy. As an Australian academic, I find this particularly interesting, as here the push appears to have come mostly from academics (Vass et al, 2018). Students in both the Global South and the Global North have criticized the 'ways in which higher education practices have been informed by, and continue to perpetuate, a series of assumptions that favour particular epistemological perspectives' (Morreira et al, 2020: 1). This critique identifies not only curricular but also pedagogic practices and institutional cultures that marginalize and disregard racialized students who then struggle to achieve their academic ambitions and have lower completion and higher attrition rates. In Australia, the slow and mixed success in increasing Indigenous[1] participation in higher education has raised all those questions and more.

Drawing from a range of Australian examples and first-hand reflections from my journey of writing and teaching on anti-racism within higher education since the late 1970s, this chapter provides an overview of my involvement in efforts to design and deliver Aboriginal higher education and Aboriginal studies, and critical anti-racism curriculum and policy as 'decolonizing' moves. I argue against the privileging of curriculum reform in isolation from critical race theory and serious forms of anti-racism, amid naive assumptions about the nature of systemic and cultural racisms in Australian universities today. Several pitfalls are highlighted, including a lack of attention to power and governance, culturalist and essentialist representations of Aboriginal people, tokenism, what makes a university a safe and welcoming place for Aboriginal students, racial taxation on Aboriginal staff and becoming an accomplice rather than an ally. These failures point to a range of critical racial and decolonial literacies necessary for the task of decolonizing.

Higher education continues to be an unwelcoming place for many Aboriginal and Torres Strait Islander students despite significant rises in the numbers attending universities over the last 20 years. Indigenous Australians continue to be under-represented in universities, comprising 1.9 per cent of the domestic higher education student population, compared with 3.3 per cent of the total Australian population, and 2.3 per cent of the domestic higher education student population aged 25–34, compared with 3.4 per cent of the Australian population of this age (AIHW, 2021). While recruitment increases, completion rates do not. University completion rates for domestic commencing bachelor's degree students over the nine-year period 2012–20 were 49.4 per cent for Indigenous and 72.2 per cent for non-Indigenous students. First-year attrition rates for domestic commencing bachelor's degree Indigenous students in 2019 were 22.8 per cent compared with 12.1 per cent for non-Indigenous students (Productivity Commission, 2022: outcome area 6).

Studies on Indigenous attrition in universities have frequently noted the dominance of deficit discourses that explain poor student performance and attrition in terms of a lack of academic skills and Western cultural capital (Burgess, 2017). It can be especially challenging for Australian Indigenous students who are more likely than their non-Indigenous peers to be first in their family to attend university (Behrendt et al, 2012). Asmar et al (2011) found that only 58 per cent of Indigenous students were enrolled in full-time, on-campus mode, compared with 74 per cent of non-Indigenous domestic students.

My journey in Aboriginal higher education

My initial experience designing and delivering Aboriginal studies courses was at the Flinders University of South Australia where, from 1973 to 1975, the awkwardly named Aborigines in Australian Society course was offered as a multidisciplinary unit within the politics degree and co-taught by non-Aboriginal academics with local Aboriginal guest speakers. From 1978 to 1980, I taught on the second Aboriginal-specific programme in Australia at the then South Australian Institute of Technology as a casual lecturer (the first being the Townsville College of Advanced Education's teacher education course in North Queensland). The programme, called the Aboriginal Task Force (Anderson, 2015), recruited students from all over Australia to Adelaide to study two main programmes: business administration and community development. My job was to completely replace the mainstream sociology courses, with which the Aboriginal students didn't engage, with a culturally and politically relevant two-year curriculum.

I then shifted to the Adelaide College of the Arts and Education (now the University of South Australia, or UniSA) in Adelaide, where many non-Aboriginal teacher trainees included Aboriginal courses in their programmes, aiming to teach in Aboriginal schools in remote and regional areas.

In 1978, an Associate Diploma in Aboriginal Studies was accredited as the first ever stand-alone Aboriginal studies award. It uncomfortably sought to serve two radically different student cohorts: mature-age Aboriginal people (mostly women) who hadn't completed high school, and were allowed entry without matriculation; and non-Aboriginal graduates (often professionals working with Aboriginal communities) whose degree programmes had no Aboriginal content. Designed to meet the needs of the second cohort, the content was heavily oriented to 'traditional' communities in South Australia's north-west and included compulsory courses in Pitjantjatjara language. Part of my role was to introduce politics and sociology content that more closely reflected the lives of urban Aboriginal people, placing greater emphasis on post-invasion history, on legislation and policies, on urbanization and cultural changes, and, critically, on racism.

A source of tension among staff was the deficit discourse (Fforde et al, 2013) towards urban Aboriginal people, often described (including by themselves) as 'mixed race', 'detribalized' and 'lost between two worlds' (Langton, 1981). Aboriginal staff and students resented such terms and felt 'shamed' when non-Aboriginal people could speak fluent Pitjantjatjara while they couldn't, all the while painfully aware their own local languages had literally been beaten out of their grandparents and parents by missionaries and other settlers.

To address this tension and foreground racism, in 1981 we accredited a Graduate Diploma in Aboriginal Studies to siphon off the non-Aboriginal professionals, another first in Australia. The degree had three components: Aboriginal (post-contact) history and contemporary society; racism in Australia; and a dissertation. Critically, both awards were available through distance education with comprehensive books of readings sent out to students across all states in Australia, and learning enhanced through tele-tutorials and residential workshops (budget-permitting) in major cities.

The first three-year Bachelor of Arts (Aboriginal Studies) in Australia was introduced in 1984, retaining the core curriculum of the Graduate Diploma and 'special entry' pathways for non-matriculated students via the Associate Diploma and transition with credit to the Bachelor of Arts. The final initiative at UniSA was a Master of Arts degree that built on the Graduate Diploma.

Beyond content, a key initiative was to establish full-time study centres with local staff in Alice Springs and Cairns in the mid-1980s. These enabled students to remain in their communities while receiving government financial support and, critically, study full-time – which greatly improved completion rates. Further, semester-break workshops and local graduation ceremonies demonstrated the possibilities of success at university to Aboriginal communities.

Collectively, the creation of a new academic discipline (centred on racism) aimed to provide a decolonizing and subaltern curriculum. Beyond the new curriculum, the programme involved articulated undergraduate and postgraduate awards, entry for non-matriculants, distance education including full-time remote study without residency requirements, inclusive and critical pedagogies, and accountability to Aboriginal communities, in recognition that curriculum renewal on its own is insufficient to enable liberation and address racial justice.

Defining Aboriginal studies and directional divergences: Indigenizing staff

This consolidation of Aboriginal Studies and Aboriginal education generated tensions between those who felt that the only goal was the rapid qualification of as many Aboriginal and Torres Strait Islander students as possible in a diverse range of professional programmes, and those who equally valued the task of educating non-Aboriginal and Aboriginal students in the study of Australian racism and anti-racism.

Overlaying this was a struggle to Indigenize all teaching and research staff; senior management had been Aboriginal for years. By 1990, many Aboriginal staff and most non-Aboriginal and Aboriginal students were challenging the appropriateness of non-Aboriginal staff teaching Aboriginal studies (Morgan, 1991; Hollinsworth, 1993, 1995). My response to this challenge was conditioned by my definition of Aboriginal studies as largely disinterested in the reconstruction of pre-invasion societies, and rather focusing on shared histories and racism in all its forms as profoundly generative of contemporary Aboriginal lives, and the formation of Australia as a racial state (Goldberg, 2002).[2] In other words, is Aboriginal studies about Aboriginal peoples and cultures exclusively or is it a principal way of decolonizing Australia for all of us through truth-telling, as invited by Aboriginal and Torres Strait Islander peoples in the Uluru Statement from the Heart in 2017?[3] Should all Australian university students, in all degrees, study Aboriginal studies to enable them to understand their own positionality as 'raced' and learn to unlearn their white privilege and white supremacist assumptions?

One of the first official recommendations to this effect was Recommendation 295 of the 1991 Royal Commission into Aboriginal Deaths in Custody (2018),[4] which reads:

That:

a. All teacher training courses include courses which will enable student teachers to understand that Australia has an Aboriginal history and Aboriginal viewpoints on social, cultural and historical matters, and to teach the curriculum which reflects those matters;
b. In-service training courses for teachers be provided so that teachers may improve their skill, knowledge and understanding to teach curricula which incorporate Aboriginal viewpoints on social, cultural and historical matters; and
c. Aboriginal people should be involved in the training courses both at student teacher and in-service level.

Such intentions were reiterated in relation to the history of the Stolen Generations in the 1997 *Bringing Them Home* report (Australian Human Rights Commission, 1997):[5]

9a. That all professionals who work with Indigenous children, families and communities receive in-service training about the history and effects of forcible removal.
9b. That all under-graduates and trainees in relevant professions receive, as part of their core curriculum, education about the history and effects of forcible removal.

To race or not race the curriculum

Since then, national Aboriginal (and later, Indigenous) education policies have urged some compulsory Aboriginal studies components, but almost from the beginning the debate was caught up with culture wars and attacked as 'black armband' history or as divisive (McKenna, 1997; Macintyre and Clark, 2013). This is one of the core contradictions in the celebration of multicultural Australia. We are happy to appropriate more than 60,000 years of Aboriginal cultural survival but loathe to address the racist dispossession and abuse of Aboriginal rights that have occurred in the last 236 years.

Despite acceptance of the need for compulsory Aboriginal studies courses, conflicts over curriculum content prevail. Students, some faculty and most administrators are very attracted to so-called 'cultural' content, including Dreaming stories and notions of (remote) Aboriginal people as innate conservationists and 'custodians' (rather than owners) of the land. Such content often operates around colonial notions of 'authentic' Aboriginality, where the vast bulk of the 700,000 plus people who identify as Aboriginal are somehow 'not quite' Aboriginal enough (Carter and Hollinsworth, 2009; Hollinsworth, 2016a). This last assumption is seen in anonymous student evaluations of Aboriginal staff teaching Aboriginal studies, where abhorrent racist slurs are thrown at light-skinned, urbanized Aboriginal staff (Bennett, 2014; Justine Grogan, personal communication, 2013–17).

There is some acknowledgement by academic managers of the need for historical accounts of racism and violence (especially frontier violence) by settlers towards Aboriginal people in Aboriginal studies courses. A key strategy for denying racism is distancing ourselves from its practices (Lentin, 2018). This can be done by outright denial (think ex-Prime Minister John Howard), by deflection from the mainstream (just a few rotten apples and bigots), geographically (the Northern Territory is terrible but here on the Sunshine Coast …) or temporally (that's all in the past, we're multicultural now).

Cowlishaw provides us with an excellent account of how such sensationalism and historicizing ends up absolving us of racial violence and our positioning within the racial state:

> These histories seem to present with ease a view of our own past that fills us, as readers, with horror at the same time as it distances us from it. How is it that in reading these accounts we position ourselves on the side of the Aborigines and identify our forebears as the enemy? These violent and racist men could be our grandfathers and they certainly left us something, if not the land they took or the wealth they made from it, then the culture they were developing. … Our disgust and horror at the violence and abusive racism means we are absolved. (Cowlishaw, 1992: 27)

To discomfort the descendants of those who did the dispossessing requires serious time and assessment tasks on the critical study of racism in all its forms, especially systemic racism in compulsory Aboriginal studies courses. This has never been popular either with managers or many students (Gair, 2016; Hollinsworth, 2016b), but some recent shifts in Indigenous higher education policy have made the challenge even harder.

How embedding Aboriginal and Torres Strait Islander perspectives fails

One key directive in Australian higher education has been the adoption of policies and expectations that Aboriginal and Torres Strait Islander perspectives should be embedded within the general curriculum and a best practice framework for doing this (Universities Australia, 2011). This apparently progressive injunction has an inherently regressive tendency to essentialize Aboriginal and Torres Strait Islander cultures, through exclusive focus on the acquisition of cultural competency by non-Indigenous peoples (Hollinsworth, 2013, 2016a). As Fredericks and Bargallie warn:

> Considering the diversity of Aboriginal and Torres Strait Islander cultures in Australia, it is unrealistic to think that cultural competence could be measured or attained through ad hoc Indigenous cultural competence training courses, in a country where idealized and homogenised visions of Indigenous culture are the object that oversimplifies Aboriginal and Torres Strait Islander cultures and reinforces negative stereotypes. (Fredericks and Bargallie, 2020: 295–6)

Many universities responded to calls for the embedding of Aboriginal and Torres Strait Islander knowledge and perspectives with a single week's topic in one or more courses that may not necessarily be assessed. These initiatives were occasionally accompanied by a stand-alone semester-length course or a short online generic course.

This response falls well short of the Universities Australia's (2011) best practice recommendation for a multi-year stand-alone progression plus embedded undergraduate and postgraduate curriculum content (Hollinsworth, 2016a: 35). It also allowed faculties and schools worried about loss of revenue from a leakage of equivalent full-time student load to abandon service teaching by expert Aboriginal studies staff within existing stand-alone courses that previously were mandated across many different programmes (Aberdeen et al, 2013). In my own university, this resulted in an overall reduction in dedicated Aboriginal studies content and, in particular, in coverage of Australian racism, colonialism, white privilege and white supremacy.

Alongside these changes was a demand that only Aboriginal staff teach courses named as Aboriginal studies. This expectation has been around for decades (Hollinsworth, 1993, 1995). While often well motivated, it can result in the few Aboriginal staff at a university being pigeonholed as only able to contribute to these areas (Asmar and Page, 2018). For example, an Aboriginal colleague was compelled to teach generic Aboriginal culture and history courses when her passion and qualifications were in literary studies, narrative and semiotics. This exclusionist position denied the great potential of multiracial teaching teams that have been shown to be especially effective in managing student resistance and in shielding Aboriginal staff from racist or threatening student pushback (Gollan and O'Leary, 2009; Dank et al, 2015; Gatwiri et al, 2021). It also encouraged management to purge non-Aboriginal contract staff who had been teaching critical race theory within Aboriginal studies programmes for years (in my case, decades). This drive to recruit Aboriginal staff, especially in highly visible 'Aboriginal-related' areas, often resulted in tokenism, racial taxation and culturally unsafe employment (Joseph and Hirshfield, 2011; Thunig and Jones, 2021). It also fed into common assumptions that Aboriginal staff were employed for their Aboriginality rather than their expertise, and for universities to virtue-signal or meet quotas.

The combination of the inadequate and untheorized embedding of Indigenous content and the removal of many non-Aboriginal teachers has led to a more 'cultural' approach that focuses on Aboriginal narrative/voices/successes rather than on structural oppression and especially systemic racism (Pybus and Moore, 2019). As Terry Moore (2011, 2020) has documented over more than a decade, dominant discourses of Aboriginalism have failed to acknowledge diversity or intersectionality, with disastrous results for both policy and Aboriginal studies. While the addition of many new Aboriginal voices has enriched and enabled new conversations and innovations in the design and teaching of Aboriginal studies, it has been accompanied by the loss of critical voices, which used their positionality to effectively analyse and educate about white privilege and settler racism. I argue that this amounts to a fundamental diminution of the original promise of Aboriginal studies.

An intimately related conflict surrounds whose expertise and which epistemologies, knowledges and perspectives should or should not contribute to Aboriginal (increasingly called Indigenous) studies. The National Aboriginal Education Committee declared that Aboriginal studies should be compulsory for all school students and for higher education students in programmes whose graduates would work with Aboriginal and Torres Strait Islander peoples. The definition put forward by the Commonwealth Aboriginal Studies Working Group report to the Australian Education Council in 1982 reflected the changing agenda in relation to understanding Indigenous Australia:

> Aboriginal Studies is the study of the history, cultures, languages and lifestyles of Aboriginal and Torres Strait Islander peoples, both prior to and following European colonization in a context which places emphasis on understanding of issues central to Aboriginal and Torres Strait Islander contemporary society and on their relevance to the total Australian community. Its contents are the descriptions, insights and

explanations of human experience derived both from Aboriginal *and from non-Aboriginal sources.* (Hill, 1986: 1, emphasis added)

To deny students insights, explanations and critical thinking from non-Aboriginal scholars is just as unreasonable and counterproductive as the denial of Aboriginal knowledges and perspectives in the past.

Cultural competency or racial literacy?

Similarly disastrous is the culling or cherry-picking of the full suite of changes required to achieve 'cultural competency' in Australian higher education. Cultural competency is a seriously flawed aim, as is suggesting that mastery is possible or desirable (Hollinsworth, 2013; Hollinsworth et al, 2017). What we need can be termed racial literacy (Bargallie et al, 2023).

The 2011 Universities Australia Best Practice Framework did not recommend inclusion of Aboriginal and Islander knowledge and perspectives into the curriculum in isolation:

> Embedding Indigenous cultural competence requires commitment to a whole of institution approach, including increasing the University's engagement with Indigenous communities, Indigenisation of the curriculum, pro-active provision of services and support to Indigenous students, capacity building of Indigenous staff, professional development of non-Indigenous staff and the inclusion of Indigenous cultures and knowledges as a visual and valued aspect of University life, governance and decision-making. (Universities Australia, 2011: 48)

The framework was based on five guiding principles:

1. Indigenous people should be actively involved in university governance and management.
2. All graduates of Australian universities will have the knowledge and skills necessary to interact in a culturally competent way with Indigenous communities.
3. University research will be conducted in a culturally competent way in partnership with Indigenous participants.
4. Indigenous staffing will be increased at all appointment levels and, for academic staff, across a wider variety of academic fields.
5. Universities will operate in partnership with their Indigenous communities and will help disseminate culturally competent practices to the wider community.

This whole-of-institution approach depends on all aspects being addressed simultaneously. Many universities have tried to do this, but most have failed to deliver across all objectives, partly because of the impact of funding cuts and loss of revenue due to COVID-19 (Hollinsworth et al, 2017). In my own experience as the Embedding Aboriginal and Torres Strait Islander Knowledges and Perspectives team leader for the University of the Sunshine Coast, after a two-year process of co-design, senior management lost its nerve to drive systemic change in the face of against some staff resistance and rejected a university-wide applied research project to embed Aboriginal and Torres Strait Islander knowledge and perspectives across all schools that had support from leaders in each of those schools and would have cost almost nothing to implement.

Research by Bodkin-Andrews et al (2019) shows significant variation in the processes of embedding Aboriginal and Torres Strait Islander content across disciplines, and the resulting impact on student attitudes with positive, negative and contradictory results. Their 'findings strongly suggest that any commitment to embedding Indigenous Graduate Attributes must be monitored very carefully' (2019: 232). A related article offers a

> critical evaluative framework through which both Indigenous Graduate Attributes and the content within the teaching and learning of Australian Indigenous Studies may be evaluated. This includes an acute awareness of imposed colonial narratives, a critical awareness of one's own positioning, engagement with Indigenous voices, knowledge of Indigenous Research Methodologies, and more meaningful levels of Indigenous engagement through Indigenous ethics and protocols. (Bodkin-Andrews et al, 2022: 96)

Highlighting the crucial interconnections between decolonizing curriculum, human resource management, Indigenous research capacity and external community engagement within the 2011 Universities Australia Best Practice Framework, Locke et al (2022: 1) document racist behaviours towards Australian Indigenous early career researchers who describe their position within universities as 'unicorns, cash cows and performing monkeys'. Their interviews record how many non-Indigenous academics and the institutions themselves resist the genuine inclusion of Indigenous knowledges and worldviews.

In a parallel body of work Trudgett et al (2021) note the common practice of universities appointing a single senior Indigenous academic leader, and the challenges for recruitment and for those selected in the absence of serious anti-racism policies and practices. They also record the demanding expectations of non-Indigenous staff, who often assume that all the work of decolonizing higher education should fall to Indigenous staff (Coates et al, 2022).

High-level senior appointments are no substitute for serious support and promotional opportunities for Indigenous staff at lower levels who often continue to be employed on short-term contracts (NTEU, 2017).[6] A significant number of Indigenous staff are employed in Student Support Centres with limited possibilities to transition to teaching and research roles and/or permanent positions. In 2018, the National Tertiary Education Union (NTEU, 2018) conducted its second survey of Aboriginal and Torres Strait Islander staff, finding that 75 per cent experience racism and discrimination in the workplace, up from 71.5 per cent in 2011. The survey further found that 66 per cent of Aboriginal and Torres Strait Islander staff experienced lateral violence[7] from Aboriginal and Torres Strait Islander colleagues, up from 60 per cent in 2011 (NTEU, 2018: 4). A sustained, leadership-driven, whole-of-institution campaign to create an anti-racist university (Law, 2017) is required to ensure cultural safety for all Aboriginal and Torres Strait Islander staff and students, and to reduce racism and lateral violence.

Conclusion

As argued by Universities Australia (2011, 2022), Australian universities must decolonize not only curriculum and pedagogy, but also governmental, administrative and funding legacies from entrenched racisms that continue to reproduce lower representation and poorer retention and completion rates for Indigenous students (Rochecouste et al, 2017). This requires Indigenous-specific anti-racism strategies, not just training for cultural competence (Universities Australia, 2022: 46–9). Hollinsworth et al (2021) argue that dominant misrepresentations of Aboriginality in Australian higher education can impact academic success and attrition. Universities need to abandon rigid culturalist constructions of Aboriginal and Torres Strait Islander students' identities, and expectations that these can be codified and regulated through generic Indigenous policy. Together with non-Indigenous and Indigenous staff who collaborate to teach, research and act in anti-racist ways, this can make universities a welcoming and culturally safe space for Aboriginal and Torres Strait Islander students (Carter et al, 2018).

Such collaboration is often difficult because of real and imagined racism, microaggressions and lateral violence. I found it hard not to be protective – even defensive – about my own curriculum development and pedagogical style, whether the criticisms came from resistant students (Hollinsworth, 2016b), management (Aberdeen et al, 2013) or Aboriginal and non-Aboriginal critics (Hollinsworth, 1992, 1993, 1995). I have learned to listen and critically reflect and work through my own anxieties, but am still learning about being an accomplice rather than an ally.

While the slogan is now spreading in anti-racism circles, there is not a lot of scholarly work on what I think is a crucial element within a whole-of-institution campaign for an anti-racist and culturally safe university (Carroll et al, 2020). Perhaps the original provocation is the article *Accomplices Not Allies: Abolishing the Ally Industrial Complex*, published by Indigenous Action Media (2014).

An insight from the article that has a special importance for the current malaise in non-Indigenous support for Indigenous peoples and knowledges in Australian higher education declares under the heading 'Acts of Resignation':

> Resignation of agency is a by-product of the allyship establishment. At first the dynamic may not seem problematic, after all, why would it be an issue with those who benefit from systems of oppression to reject or distance themselves from those benefits and behaviors (like entitlement, etc) that accompany them? In the worst cases, 'allies' themselves act paralyzed believing it's their duty as a 'good ally'. There is a difference between acting for others, with others, and for one's own interests, be explicit.
>
> You wouldn't find an accomplice resigning their agency, or capabilities as an act of 'support'. They would find creative ways to weaponize their privilege (or more clearly, their rewards of being part of an oppressor class) as an expression of social war. (Anonymous, cited in Indigenous Action Media, 2014: 6)

This provocation makes real sense to me as, since the late 1960s, I have had an agenda of studying, teaching about and fighting racism, in particular that faced by Aboriginal people. I have always been cognisant of my white, male, middle-class privilege – partly because of my feminist academic older sister Jan Pettman (1992). I have always tried to use my positionality to acquire and teach critical racial and decolonial literacies to challenge racist structures and decolonial practices. As an activist and university employee, I have mostly had the benefit of Aboriginal bosses and friends and enemies who were very willing to point out my errors. Consequently, I argue that accountability is the co-requisite of agency.

The rise of identity politics and the fractious nature of the politics of Aboriginal higher education have challenged this standpoint, but I remain convinced about the need for non-Aboriginal accomplices and amplifiers. I am also glad to have finally left university employment, having seen over the decades the defunding and managerialism of neoliberalism (Connell, 2013) undermine the possibilities of critical race teaching of Aboriginal studies.

Notes

[1] In Australia, official policy and data refers to both Aboriginal and Torres Strait Islander peoples collectively as Indigenous. Many Aboriginal people dislike the term, but it is impossible to disaggregate most data, so it remains unavoidable. At other times in this chapter, I will refer to Aboriginal people as preferred by those students.

[2] Goldberg (2002: 271) defines a racial state as 'one where a racially (self-)conceived group (usually the one controlling the terms of ... definition) dominates the power, resources, and

3   'The Uluru Statement from the Heart is an invitation to the Australian people. We ask Australians to accept our invitation to walk with us in a movement of the Australian people for a better future. We call for the establishment of a First Nations Voice enshrined in the Constitution and a Makarrata Commission to supervise a process of agreement-making and truth-telling about our history.' See Uluru Statement from the Heart (2017). The statement was agreed after years of community consultations involving many thousands of Aboriginal and Torres Strait Islander people. At the time of writing, the Australian government was due to hold a referendum to approve the Voice in the constitution – it failed badly, with more than 60 per cent of Australians voting No.

4   The Royal Commission into Aboriginal Deaths in Custody was convened between 1987 and 1991 to investigate the underlying causes of 99 Aboriginal deaths in custody. It made 334 recommendations, some of which are still not fully implemented. Aboriginal incarcerations rates have actually increased since the Commission and are among the highest in the world. See https://www.niaa.gov.au/sites/default/files/publications/rciadic-review-report.pdf

5   The *Bringing Them Home* report estimated between one in three and one in ten children were forcibly removed between 1900 and 1970. See https://humanrights.gov.au/our-work/bringing-them-home-appendix-9-recommendations

6   This is an international issue in settler societies: see Henry et al (2017) regarding Canada.

7   Frankland et al (2011) define lateral violence as 'the organised, harmful behaviours we do to each other collectively as part of an oppressed group: within our families; within our organizations and within our communities. When we are consistently oppressed we live with great fear and great anger and we often turn on those who are closest to us'.

References

Aberdeen, L., Carter, J., Grogan, J. and Hollinsworth, D. (2013) 'Rocking the foundations: The struggle for effective Indigenous studies in Australian higher education', *Higher Education Review*, 45(3): 36–55.

AIHW (Australian Institute of Health and Welfare) (2021) 'Indigenous education and skills', *Australia's Welfare*, https://www.aihw.gov.au/reports/australias-welfare/indigenous-education-and-skills

Anderson, S. (2015) 'Aboriginal Task Force', *Australian Aboriginal Studies*, 2: 24–32.

Arday, J. and Mirza, H.S. (2018) *Dismantling Race in Higher Education: Racism, Whiteness and Decolonising the Academy*, Basingstoke: Palgrave Macmillan.

Asmar, C. and Page, S. (2018) 'Pigeonholed, peripheral or pioneering? Findings from a national study of Indigenous Australian academics in the disciplines', *Studies in Higher Education*, 43(9): 1679–91.

Asmar, C., Page, S. and Radloff, A. (2011) *Dispelling Myths: Indigenous Students' Engagement with University: Australasian Survey of Student Engagement (AUSSE)*, Canberra: Australian Council for Educational Research.

Australian Human Rights Commission (1997) *Bringing Them Home: Report of the National Inquiry into the Separation of Aboriginal and Torres Strait Islander Children from Their Families*, Canberra: Australian Government, https://humanrights.gov.au/our-work/bringing-them-home-report-1997

Bargallie, D., Fernando, N. and Lentin, A. (2023) 'Breaking the racial silence: Putting racial literacy to work in Australia', *Journal of Ethnic and Racial Studies*. DOI: 10.1080/01419870

Behrendt, L., Larkin, S., Griew, R. and Kelly, P. (2012) *Review of Higher Education Outcomes for Aboriginal and Torres Strait Islander People*, Canberra: Commonwealth of Australia.

Bennett, B. (2014) 'How do light-skinned Aboriginal Australians experience racism? Implications for social work', *AlterNative: An International Journal of Indigenous Peoples*, 10(2): 180–92.

Bodkin-Andrews, G., Page, S. and Trudgett, M. (2019) 'Working towards accountability in embedding Indigenous studies: Evidence from an Indigenous Graduate Attribute evaluation instrument', *Australian Journal of Education*, 63(2): 232–60.

Bodkin-Andrews, G., Page, S. and Trudgett, M. (2022) 'Shaming the silences: Indigenous graduate attributes and the privileging of Aboriginal and Torres Strait Islander voices', *Critical Studies in Education*, 63(1): 96–113.

Burgess, C. (2017) '"Having to say everyday … I'm not Black enough … I'm not white enough": Discourses of Aboriginality in the Australian education context', *Race Ethnicity and Education*, 20(6): 737–51.

Carroll, S.M., Bascuñán, D., Sinke, M. and Restoule, J.P. (2020) 'How discomfort reproduces settler structures: Moving beyond fear and becoming imperfect accomplices', *Journal of Curriculum and Teaching*, 9(2): 9–19.

Carter, J. and Hollinsworth, D. (2009) 'Segregation and protectionism: Institutionalised views of Aboriginal rurality', *Journal of Rural Studies*, 25(4): 414–24.

Carter, J., Hollinsworth, D., Raciti, M. and Gilbey, K. (2018) 'Academic "place-making": Fostering attachment, belonging and identity for Indigenous students in Australian universities', *Teaching in Higher Education*, 23(2): 243–60.

Coates, S.K., Trudgett, M. and Page, S. (2022) 'Islands in the stream: Indigenous academic perceptions of Indigenous senior leadership roles', *Higher Education Research & Development*, 41(5): 1451–67.

Connell, R. (2013) 'The neoliberal cascade and education: An essay on the market agenda and its consequences', *Critical Studies in Education*, 54(2): 99–112.

Cowlishaw, G. (1992) 'Review article: The Aboriginal experience, a problem of interpretation', *Ethnic and Racial Studies*, 15(2): 304–11.

Dank, D., Grogan, J., Hollinsworth, D. and Syron, M. (2015) 'What contributions can non-Indigenous staff make to Indigenous content in education? White privilege and partners in anti-racism pedagogies', *Indigenous Content in Education Symposium 2015*, University of South Australia, 21 September.

Fforde, C., Bamblett, L., Lovett, R., Gorringe, S. and Fogarty, B. (2013) 'Discourse, deficit and identity: Aboriginality, the race paradigm and the language of representation in contemporary Australia', *Media International Australia*, 149: 162–73.

Frankland, R., Bamblett, M. and Lewis, P. (2011) '"Forever business": A framework for maintaining and restoring cultural safety in Aboriginal Victoria', *Indigenous Law Bulletin*, 7(24): 27–30.

Fredericks, B. and Bargallie, D. (2020) 'An Indigenous Australian cultural competence course: Talking culture, race and power', in J. Frawley, G. Russell and J. Sherwood (eds), *Cultural Competence and the Higher Education Sector: Australian Perspectives, Policies and Practice*, Singapore: Springer, pp 295–308.

Gair, S. (2016) 'Critical reflections on teaching challenging content: Do some students shoot the (white) messenger?', *Reflective Practice*, 17(5): 592–604.

Gatwiri, K., Anderson, L. and Townsend-Cross, M. (2021) '"Teaching shouldn't feel like a combat sport": How teaching evaluations are weaponised against minoritised academics', *Race Ethnicity and Education*, 27(2): 139–55.

Goldberg, D. (2002) *The Racial State*, London: Blackwell.

Gollan, S. and O'Leary, P. (2009) 'Teaching culturally competent social work practice through Black and white pedagogical partnerships', *Social Work Education*, 28(7): 707–21.

Gopal, P. (2021) 'On decolonisation and the university', *Textual Practice*, 35(6): 873–99.

Henry, F., Dua, E., Kobayashi, A., Janes, C., Li, P., Ramos, H. and Smith M. (2017) 'Race, racialization and Indigeneity in Canadian universities', *Race Ethnicity and Education*, 20(3): 300–14.

Hill, M. (1986) *Aboriginal Studies in Tertiary Education: Project Report*, Canberra: Committee to Review Australian Studies in Tertiary Education.

Hollinsworth, D. (1992) 'Discourses on Aboriginality and the politics of identity in urban Australia', *Oceania*, 63(2): 137–55.

Hollinsworth, D. (1993) 'Who should teach Aboriginal studies?', in D. Coghlan, R. Craven and N. Parbury (eds), *Aboriginal Studies: A National Priority, Volume 2*, Sydney: University of New South Wales, pp 247–58.

Hollinsworth, D. (1995) 'Aboriginal studies: An epistemological no-go zone?', in P. van Toorn and D. English (eds), *Speaking Positions: Aboriginality, Gender and Ethnicity in Australian Cultural Studies*, Melbourne: Victoria University of Technology, pp 90–9.

Hollinsworth, D. (2013) 'Forget cultural competence: Ask for an autobiography', *Social Work Education*, 32(8): 1048–60.

Hollinsworth, D. (2016a) 'How do we ensure that the aim of Indigenous cultural competence doesn't reinforce racialized and essentialised discourses of indigeneity?', *Journal of Australian Indigenous Issues*, 19(1–2): 33–48.

Hollinsworth, D. (2016b) 'Unsettling Australian settler supremacy: Combating resistance in university Aboriginal studies', *Race Ethnicity and Education*, 19(2): 412–32.

Hollinsworth, D., Carter, J., Gilbey, K. and Raciti, M. (2017) 'Indigenous cultural competence in Australian universities: Challenges and barriers', *Journal of Australian Indigenous Issues*, 20(3): 27–44.

Hollinsworth, D., Raciti, M. and Carter, J. (2021) 'Indigenous students' identities in Australian higher education: Found, denied and reinforced', *Race Ethnicity and Education*, 24(1): 112–31.

Indigenous Action Media (2014) *Accomplices Not Allies: Abolishing the Ally Industrial Complex*, Flagstaff, AZ: Indigenous Action Media, http://www.indigenousaction.org/accomplices-not-allies-abolishingthe-ally-industrial-complex

Joseph, T.D. and Hirshfield, L.E. (2011) '"Why don't you get somebody new to do it?" Race and cultural taxation in the academy', *Ethnic and Racial Studies*, 34(1): 121–41.

Langton, M. (1981) 'Urbanising Aborigines: The social scientists' great deception', *Social Alternatives*, 2(2): 16–22.

Law, I. (2017) 'Building the anti-racist university: Action and new agendas', *Race Ethnicity and Education*, 20(3): 332–43.

Lentin, A. (2018) 'Beyond denial: "Not racism" as racist violence', *Continuum*, 32(4): 400–14.

Locke, M., Trudgett, M. and Page, S. (2022) 'Australian Indigenous early career researchers: Unicorns, cash cows and performing monkeys', *Race Ethnicity and Education*, 26(1): 1–17.

Macintyre, S. and Clark, A. (2013) *The History Wars*, Melbourne: Melbourne University Publishing.

McKenna, M. (1997) *Different Perspectives on Black Armband History*, Canberra: Parliamentary Library, https://www.aph.gov.au/About_Parliament/Parliamentary_Departments/Parliamentary_Library/pubs/rp/RP9798/98RP05

Moore, T. (2011) 'Misadventures with Aboriginalism', *Social Identities*, 17(3): 423–41.

Moore, T. (2020) 'Governing superdiversity: Learning from the Aboriginal Australian case', *Social Identities*, 26(2): 233–49.

Morgan, B. (1991) 'Some thoughts on Aboriginalisation in higher education', *Journal of the Aboriginal Studies Association*, 1(1): 7–9.

Morreira, S., Luckett, K., Kumalo, S.H. and Ramgotra, M. (2020) 'Confronting the complexities of decolonising curricula and pedagogy in higher education', *Third World Thematics: A TWQ Journal*, 5(1–2): 1–18.

NTEU (2017) *How Secure Do You Feel?* https://issuu.com/nteu/docs/howsecuredoyoufeel

NTEU (2018) *I'm Still Not a Racist, But …: 2nd Report on Cultural Respect, Racial Discrimination, Lateral Violence & Other Policy at Australia's Universities*, https://issuu.com/home/published/im_still_not_a_racist_but

Pettman, J. (1992) *Living in the Margins: Racism, Sexism and Feminism in Australia*, Sydney: Allen & Unwin.

Productivity Commission (2022) 'Closing the gap information repository. Socioeconomic outcome area 6: Aboriginal and Torres Strait Islander students reach their full potential through further education pathways', https://www.pc.gov.au/closing-the-gap-data/dashboard/socioeconomic/outcome-area6

Pybus, C. and Moore, T. (2019) 'White guilt, Aboriginal culturalism and the impoverishment of tertiary education in Australia', *Journal of the European Association for Studies of Australia*, 10(1): 59–77.

Rochecouste, J., Oliver, R., Bennell, D., Anderson, R., Cooper, L. and Forrest, S. (2017) 'Teaching Australian Aboriginal higher education students: What should universities do?', *Studies in Higher Education*, 42(11): 2080–98.

Royal Commission into Aboriginal Deaths in Custody (2018) *Review of the Implementation of the Recommendations of the Royal Commission into Aboriginal Deaths in Custody*, Canberra: Department of the Prime Minister and Cabinet, https://www.niaa.gov.au/sites/default/files/publications/rciadic-review-report.pdf

Thunig, A. and Jones, T. (2021) '"Don't make me play house-n*** er": Indigenous academic women treated as "black performer" within higher education', *The Australian Educational Researcher*, 48(3): 397–417.

Trudgett, M., Page, S. and Coates, S.K. (2021) 'Talent war: Recruiting Indigenous senior executives in Australian universities', *Journal of Higher Education Policy and Management*, 43(1): 110–24.

Uluru Statement from the Heart (2017) https://www.referendumcouncil.org.au/sites/default/files/2017-05/Uluru_Statement_From_The_Heart_0.PDF

Universities Australia (2011) *National Best Practice Framework for Indigenous Cultural Competency in Australian Universities*, Canberra: Department of Education, Employment and Workplace Relations, https://www.universitiesaustralia.edu.au/uni-participation-quality/Indigenous-Higher-Education/Indigenous-Cultural-Compet#.VCylEL6QcyE

Universities Australia (2022) *Indigenous Strategy 2022–2025*, https://www.universitiesaustralia.edu.au/wp-content/uploads/2022/03/UA-Indigenous-Strategy-2022-25.pdf

Vass, G., Maxwell, J., Rudolph, S. and Gulson, K. (eds) (2018) *The Relationality of Race in Education Research*, London: Routledge.

4

Let's Get Critical: Thinking with and beyond the 'Dead White Men' of Social Theory

Na'ama Carlin

Introduction

I write this reflection as an early career academic and lecturer in sociology, and as an Ashkenazi Jewish Israeli settler scholar who immigrated to this land in her twenties and has been an uninvited settler colonizer ever since. My lived experience and academic training underpin my commitment to anti-racism in the classroom and teaching practice. Racism is a lived reality for many, and discussions about race and racism permeate sociological scholarship. As I write, a neo-Nazi mob crowds Parliament House in Melbourne, Victoria. Over the last few years, the alt-right has become more mainstream, galvanized by political success. In the United States, anti-critical race theory (CRT) measures have been introduced in 49 states at either state level or municipality, or by a local school board (Alexander, 2023). Australia's conservative class keenly imported the latest US moral panic, with commentators, think tanks and politicians cautioning that teaching race in schools is 'divisive indoctrination' (Murray, 2022).

While CRT critically analyses systems of racial oppression and power to understand and dismantle them, conservatives dismiss CRT as 'indoctrination' and claim that simply speaking to young people about race and privilege can have negative consequences, such as making young people feel ashamed or guilty. On *Sky News*, educator and commentator Kevin Donnelly[1] is quoted as saying, 'You should not have to go to school to be told that you're racist, that you're a white supremacist, that somehow you're guilty of oppressing others' (*Sky News*, 2021a). The underlying assumption is that conversations about race and privilege are actually about assigning individual blame rather than engaging in critical debate about structures of power, oppression and domination, how they impact people and how we can challenge, critique and dismantle them. Right-wing commentator Andrew Bolt referred to CRT as 'racial vengeance' (*Sky News*, 2021b),[2] and others have used the term 'anti-white racism' (in Pearson, 2021) and referred to CRT as 'ideology' (*Sky News*, 2020) and 'indoctrination' (Murray, 2022).

It requires critical racial and decolonial literacies to unpack Bolt's claim that CRT is 'racial vengeance' as it operates on two levels: first, it audaciously subverts (ignorantly or wilfully) power structures to position racialized people as having the political and social capital to enforce violence towards white people. I use 'subvert' deliberately because racism is embedded in settler-colonial history. One only need to look at rates of Indigenous incarceration, deaths in police custody and rates of Indigenous children removed from their families to get a sense of how forcefully Aboriginal and Torres Strait Islander people are policed in contemporary Australia. Second, the statement contains implicit acknowledgement that racialized communities experienced such levels of violence to justify 'revenge'. So, the claim that CRT is 'racial vengeance' serves at once as an admission of a violence so extensive, so oppressive and so ongoing that it *warrants* retaliation, while at the same time positioning Bla(c)k folks – the targets of this persistent violence – in a position of social, cultural and political power to exact vengeance.

Within this context, I have worked to reconfigure my teaching away from an all-white curriculum. In doing so, I learnt a couple of things: first, as an institution, the modern university claims commitment to 'diversity and inclusion' while not materially investing in labour or the workforce; second, despite what the right-wing commentariat would like you to think, young people don't feel harassed or alienated by these learnings. Rather, they *crave* them.

My work involves teaching sociology undergraduate courses, including a core course on social theory, which is the focus of this chapter. These next few pages offer a reflection on teaching classical and contemporary social theory to undergraduates, and on the question of what work a discipline considers *classical*, or foundational. What are the implications of elevating some forms of knowledge over others? In other words, what works serve as a discipline's foundations of knowledge and knowing, and what knowledge is sidelined or erased in the process? To be clear: what I do in my classroom isn't unique or exceptional. It is, in fact, the bare minimum, incremental and far from radical. That said, this chapter draws attention to the complexities of doing race critical work within an institution that doesn't offer standardized or material support, meaning that this work is often done in isolation and in ad-hoc ways. In other words, doing race critical work in education remains largely an individual endeavour. It is true that as teachers we are largely responsible for our curriculum, but it is frustrating to see institutions advance a discourse of 'tolerance' and 'embracing diversity' while at the same time avoiding investment in racial literacy in a meaningful sense, such as through support of staff, training and recruitment of Indigenous staff.

This chapter reflects on teaching classical and contemporary social and critical theory to undergraduates at a time when race and critical studies are under attack. Detractors of CRT and other critical studies claim that these fields are brainwashing students, encourage violence and alienation, and are responsible for young people feeling disenfranchised. But my experience as an educator is the opposite: I found that students crave conversations about race, racism and identity in sociopolitical contexts. They crave these conversations because they *know* what it is like to move around the world feeling – whatever their ethnicity might be – racialized. They experience life through a racial lens and in positions of relative power or disempowerment. Race already shapes social structures. Race, for example, is a factor influencing health outcomes such as whether your pain is taken seriously (Hoffman et al, 2016) or how likely you are to be misdiagnosed by your medical team (Institute of Medicine (US) Committee on Understanding and Eliminating Racial and Ethnic Disparities in Health Care, 2003) or have your diagnosis delayed (Shahid et al, 2016). Crucially, it is not *race* that puts people at heightened risk of illness; rather, it is *racism* that influences how seriously a person's concerns are taken.

Not only do students appreciate these conversations, but they are also positively challenged by them and feel seen in texts that explore the lived impact of race, racialization and power. In this next section, I begin with some context for my teaching, and continue by examining the privileging of *whiteness* in sociology, and how to move beyond and against a Western, Eurocentric tradition of social theory in the classroom.

Teaching during global upheaval

In June 2020, I was a few months into my first continuing academic position after five years of precarious employment. I mention this because academic precarity is a significant structural impediment to curriculum change. Precarious workers are on strict and limited contracts with restricted duties, meaning they receive minimal workload allocation and funds to restructure and design course curricula.

The year started off gently and continued with a bang: global pandemic unleashed, international borders closed, local perimeters defined, Zoom accounts created. With students who struggled with isolation, loss of work and some with needing to move back into the family home, the teacher's role took on heightened pastoral dimensions. Black Lives Matter protests swept the United States and then spread across the globe: Colombia, South Africa, Indonesia and Australia, among others. People took to the streets protesting the devastating intersection between police brutality and racism. In the colony we call Australia, Black Lives Matter protests brought thousands of people to the streets, calling for an end to Aboriginal deaths in custody and devastating policing of First Nations communities. Since the 1991 Royal Commission into Aboriginal Deaths in Custody, as of 2023 over 544 Indigenous people have died while under the 'care' of the justice system in the various jurisdictions around Australia.[3] We walked with comrades, colleagues, friends, students and strangers. Thousands of people marched and chanted and demonstrated and raged and demanded better.

Months later, the university for which I work (like most other universities in Australia) used COVID-19 as a catalyst for restructure, which is an excuse to lay off staff and cut costs. My university recorded the highest number of staff cuts in the country, with 726 fewer full-time equivalent jobs in 2021 than the previous year, representing a 10 per cent drop in employees (White, 2022). Fortuitously, I held onto my role. At the same time, the university held a panel discussion on racism and the Black Lives Matter movement in an Australian context, under the auspices of the Equity and Diversity Unit, yet there was no consideration as to how the gross loss of staff might impact socially marginalized students, and in particular how it might impact their safety and progress in academia, as losing trusted teachers can disrupt student progress and learning. As Bargallie et al (2023: 11) argue, 'Indigeneity is comfortably used in academia as data, course material, and soft voices, but there is resistance to employing Indigenous epistemologies, ideas, and skillsets in ways that undermine whiteness and the ideas and institutions it is embedded in'. In a bitter irony, given the continued exhortations of the value of diversity, the university's only centre for Indigenous programmes saw its funding diminished.

I include these details to emphasize rhetorical dissonance and frustration: the institution (a statement that applies broadly to universities in Australia) has no qualms about promoting itself as a place of progress, while making little positive material difference for Indigenous students and staff. To the contrary, up until the time of writing this piece, my institution has made no commitment to a target of Indigenous employment, despite naming the 'recruitment of new Indigenous staff' as a priority in its Indigenous Strategy. The absence of tangible or material support and guidance (such as acknowledgement in workload allocations, guidelines, funds for research assistants to aid curriculum development) for staff wanting to take a race critical approach in their classrooms means that these approaches are often haphazard and ad hoc. Change can be meaningful or tokenistic, and while teachers mean well, we participate in critical labour without necessary institutional support. Put differently, diversity becomes about public relations, with little accountability.

The dead white men of social theory

During this turmoil of 2020 and on the tail-end of mass redundancies, I took custodianship of a social theory course. The brief was as follows. This is a sociological theory course, and it lays theoretical foundations for students to utilize in their respective degrees. It is a core course, and a requirement in all our school's programs, meaning that there's a range of students enrolled (that is, not just sociology students). Conventionally, theory courses open with 'classical' theories and conclude with critical/contemporary texts. This course was structured in the same way: the 'classical' texts from the 'dead white men' of social theory provided a foundation for students' critique, while critical texts were fixed at the tail-end of student learning.

With this in mind, I set out to do two things: incorporate texts by theorists who were not white; and flip the conventional order and assign the 'classical' texts at the end of the course. My plan was to open the course with Frantz Fanon, Edward Said and Audre Lorde so students might scaffold their learnings by engaging with race and gender critique first, with these learnings foregrounding any subsequent critique of the 'dead white men' of social theory. But in a conversation with a senior colleague, I was given the instruction that while I may modify the content, it must still function as a core course in sociological theory, and the first few weeks must introduce students to the *foundations* of sociological theory. This meant that to get to Fanon, Said and Lorde, we must first go through Marx, Weber and Durkheim.

There was leeway in the ways I might consider introducing students to Marx, Weber and Durkheim, but the underlying message was clear: this was a foundational course in sociological theory, and these were foundational thinkers. They were the entry point to sociological thinking and students needed to encounter their work at the outset. As an early career academic in my first year in a continuing position, I avoided pushing the envelope and dropped my plan to 'reverse' the curriculum and place Black and Arab scholars at the foundation of our learnings. But why is it that sociology is so reluctant to question the primacy of the 'dead white men' of social theory? In *Decolonizing Sociology*, Ali Meghji asks:

> How have we got to the point where students see it as a moral obligation to read Marx, Weber and Durkheim? How have we got to the point where those who are not familiar with these three thinkers are construed as having some form of sociological deficiency? Why is the sociological canon composed as it is, and what does this tell us about the dominant vision of sociology? (Meghji, 2021: 15)

To answer this question, Meghji traces the colonial history and development of the discipline of sociology, which underpin its Eurocentric logic today.

Meghji argues that sociology's Eurocentrism constrains the limits of *valid* sociological knowledge. Traditional sociological epistemology prioritizes whiteness as its key frame of seeing, knowing and experiencing the world. I am careful to say *traditional* because, of course, there have been and are now Bla(c)k theorists writing with and against this white Eurocentric frame. Yet the dominant mindset is that sociology *starts* with the 'dead white men', and other writing departs from (and against) these works.

My aim in teaching sociology is to demonstrate the varied ways in which the 'sociological imagination' (Mills, 2000) – a way of thinking that allows us to understand relations between individual and society characterized by an ability to think of things socially and take on alternative viewpoints – helps us analyse social structures, institutions, policies and politics. Put another way, a 'sociological imagination' allows us to think about and understand personal biography in the context of a broader historical context, and their intersection vis-à-vis social structures (Mills, 2000: 143). It enables us to understand history (such as colonialism and nationalism) and biography (experiences of being racialized) and their intersection within a society (social structures and institutions such as a legal system that discriminates against Black, Indigenous and other negatively racialized people).

In class, I facilitate opportunities for students to make these connections – between history, personal biography and society – and reflect on their own lived experience in relation to the social theories we study. To do so, I follow principles of dialogic learning as a way of forging a community of learners (Lyle, 2008; Wolfe and Alexander, 2008; Boyd and Markarian, 2011; Alexander, 2016). I seek for our learnings to 'cultivate curiosity' for students, and for the classroom to be a space for students to experience moments of discovery and newfound knowledge of the world.

This approach positions students as active participants in their learning experience rather than passively being lectured at, as the dialogic system promotes communication through authentic exchanges and meaning is built collectively (Lyle, 2008: 225). But dialogic learning is more than talk – this method of teaching takes a dialogic approach to learning and social relations. I see dialogic learning as emphasizing collectivity in the classroom. As teachers, we are responsible for creating productive learning environments for students where they feel encouraged to engage in dialogue not only with the lecturer, but also with each other and with themselves.

Classrooms are sites for discussion, facilitating and fostering essential critical inquiry skills among the student cohort (Mercer and Littleton, 2007; Wolfe and Alexander, 2008; Boyd and Markarian, 2011). Studies show the effectiveness of dialogic teaching in improving critical thinking disposition among undergraduate university students, as well as enhancing social interaction between students and between students and teachers (Bekirogullari and Hajhosseiny, 2012). Dialogic teaching is so effective because it encourages active participation and knowledge-making through dialogue, questioning, exploration of ideas and student engagement.

The value of dialogic learning is that it creates conditions for students to think critically and challenge assumptions. In lectures and tutorials, students listen to and learn from each other. This happens through a shared sense of responsibility for what happens in the classroom, and through students seeing each other as part of a community of learners. By being open to hearing each other's views, students can see that people have different approaches to knowledge, different standpoints. Here, students develop their sociological imagination and take on different viewpoints and perspectives by having them reflect on their commitments, values and experiences. It is important to see the curriculum as a tool that can sharpen and deepen our students' minds, but also serve as a mirror, reflecting our students' life experiences back to them.

The problem is that so much of the core sociological curriculum, at least as it is taught in Australia, is dominated by white scholarship. Marx, Weber and Durkheim are the entry point into sociological knowledge, but it doesn't end there: we have Mills, Goffman, Foucault, Smith, Arendt. The knowledge we preference in our classroom is knowledge we legitimize, often as a source or site of critique. What message do we convey (either intentionally or without intention) when we affix Indigenous and Black scholarship – often about race, gender and class – as *supplementary* or *auxiliary* knowledge? When this writing is often accessed through specific Indigenous studies units, rather than broader disciplinary programmes such as sociology? What is this writing supplementing, and who is it supplementary to?

The answer is, of course, that Eurocentric epistemologies (ways of knowing and making knowledge) dominate sociology and shape much of how we think about the social. Theorizing in sociology is associated with a particular sociological canon, starting with Marx, Weber and Durkheim and moving through Mills, Goffman, Bauman and Foucault. The problem, as Santos (2015: 15) articulates it, is that 'we know Marx, even though Marx may not know us'. 'We' and 'us', in this context, names communities who have traditionally been excluded from the Western sociological tradition. Santos continues:

> We know Gandhi, and Gandhi knows us. We know Fanon, and Fanon knows us. We know Toussaint L'Ouverture and Toussaint L'Ouverture knows us. We know Patrice Lumumba, and Patrice Lumumba knows us. We know Bartolina Sisa, and Bartolina Sisa knows us. We know Catarina Eufémia, and Catarina Eufémia knows us. We know Rosa Parks, and Rosa Parks knows us. But the large majority of those who know us are not well known. We are revolutionaries with no papers. (Santos, 2015: 15)

To be sure, I'm not trying to do away with Marx, or argue that there is no (or limited) value to reading the 'dead white men' of social theory. Many of these ideas have been instrumental in the ways we understand and critique social forces, colonialism, race and capitalism. We only need to turn to Aileen Moreton-Robinson's (2006) analysis of Foucault with respect to legal decision-making about Indigenous sovereignty, native title and land rights, or Frantz Fanon's (2004, 2008) reading of Hegel, Marx and Sartre to understand that the canon of 'dead white men' is central to meaning-making and critique of racial regimes.

Rather, my concern with teaching sociology in a way that maintains fidelity with the conventional 'entry point' into sociological knowledge as being the 'dead white men' of social theory is that this approach can elevate Eurocentric epistemologies and alienate students. As explained earlier, in my teaching I have done the bare minimum – introduce Black critical texts, but also maintained the space for conversations about power, identity and race.

Challenging the foundation

The knowledge we cultivate in our classrooms is the knowledge that we privilege. It is an acknowledgement that ways of knowing and being are diverse, that lived experience is at the core of meaning-making in the world, and that none of this is neutral – knowledge is power, and power can legitimize or delegitimize, uplift or diminish.

Students by and large welcomed engaging with theorists such as Fanon, Said and Lorde, noting in their feedback that the content was interesting and diverse. Importantly, students stated that our critical conversations in class challenged and shifted their views and noted that they found value in hearing other students' perspectives. I also found that teaching about race (via Fanon, Said and Lorde) to students who had experienced racism could be rewarding to them, as they learnt and acquired the intellectual tools to name their experiences.

One example comes from lecture on Edward Said. We had been watching an excerpt of a video of Said talking about *Orientalism* in his own words when a student sent me a private message on Zoom. The personal nature of the message took me by surprise – the student effectively thanked me for including Said in the course curriculum, saying that they felt represented and seen. Our discussion centred on *Orientalism* (Said, 1979) and specifically on how media representation portrays an unrealistic, violent, fetishized and racialized imagery of the Orient vis-à-vis an image of the Occident as egalitarian, morally correct or superior, and gallant. Through his analysis of the Orient/Occident division, Said argues that this division isn't neutral or natural, but rather rooted in racist and colonialist structures.

The student's message made me pause, and two things became clear: first, this student had clearly been navigating the world as a racialized *othered* subject; and second, encountering Said's work gave them the language and tools to name their experiences. It also provided the reassurance that, in a world where 'neutrality' is seen as a scholarly virtue – at least by non-academic commentators – these experiences can legitimately be discussed in an academic context. I read the student's message as being written with sense of relief, of connection.

Following Said, who argued that 'the relationship between Occident and Orient is a relationship of power, of domination, of varying degrees of a complex hegemony' (1979: 6), we could say that power underpins our social, lived and material conditions. I take this further to claim that violence is at the core of the human condition. Violence and identity converge when we, following Ricœur (2011: 84), experience the other as a menace. This sense of menace is derived from our encounter with the other: 'It is a fact that the other, because she or he is other, comes to be seen as a danger for true identity - our collective identity as much as my own identity' (Ricœur, 2011: 84). Ricœur is suggesting here that the other poses a threat to the 'true' nature of our identity. This not unlike Said's work on the 'subjugation' of the 'Orient' by an empowered, dominant 'Occident', in which Europeans maintain their dominance and control.

Identity is not apolitical: class, gender, ethnicity, religion, sexual orientation, the ways in which we navigate and exist in the world, the ways in which we are seen and known by others, are all tied up in politics. As Olúfẹ́mi O. Táíwò (2022: 6) reminds us, even the term *identity politics* is political, first popularized by queer, Black, feminist socialists in the United States in 1977 to foster solidarity and collaboration, and now used to flatten conversations on power, identity and inequality.

It was in this context that I reflected on my student's message. Identity is political, but so is education – deciding what to include in or exclude from our curriculum is a charged decision. Learning is not a neutral activity. If Foucault was right, and knowledge is intrinsically linked to power, then learning reproduces systems of power, oppression and privilege.

A year later, in June 2021, Senator Pauline Hanson, the founder and leader of the right-wing populist party One Nation, introduced a motion into the Australian Senate, calling on the federal government to reject 'critical race theory' from the national curriculum. The national curriculum is developed by an independent statutory body, the Australian Curriculum, Assessment and Reporting Authority, with extensive stakeholder consultation. The proposed curriculum, last reviewed in 2014, set out to portray a more accurate reflection of the historical record of Aboriginal and Torres Strait Islander people's experience with colonization. One key example is the inclusion of the word 'invasion' when talking about Australia's colonial history. In response, then-Education Minister Alan Tudge said he was 'concerned' about the use of the word 'invasion' (quoted in Zhou, 2021). Tudge further said that he didn't want 'students to be turned into activists. I want them to be taught the facts. And they should understand and be taught the facts as it related to Indigenous history from an Indigenous perspective as much as from a non-Indigenous perspective' (quoted in Zhou, 2021).

Tudge's claim represents how European/white histories are seen as neutral, objective and depoliticized. Importantly, they are hegemonic, taught in schools, at home and as part of the state's national narrative. Conversely, anything that calls this reality into question is deemed an outlier, a danger, a provocation – in other words, activism. One right-wing think tank went further and claimed that '[s]chooling should be about teaching students how to read, write count and think, not used as a tool to politicize them' (d'Abrera, 2021a). But of course, knowledge is political. Decisions about including and excluding narratives, facts and content are political. It is only because we think about European/white histories as dominant, neutral narratives that any deviation is framed as indoctrination.

Continuing their tirade against the proposed curriculum changes, the Institute of Public Affairs, a right-wing non-profit policy think tank, stated that 'Australians are rightly saying no to Critical Race Theory. They are egalitarian and do not support divisive ideologies in the classroom' (d'Abrera, 2021b). Putting aside the fact that the proposed curriculum changes do not fall under CRT, I have found the total opposite of the Institute of Public Affairs' claims in my classroom.

While I don't teach CRT *per se*, discussions on race, power, identity and intersectionality underpin classroom discussions. I have found, over and over, that students are *hungry for* these conversations. Much like my student's message mentioned earlier, students often feel *seen* and *represented* by critical texts on race and gender. Theories of race and racism operate as a window through which students' experiences are reflected. We can access this window through fostering a learning community where we are open to hearing from others about their experiences in a non-judgemental manner, and able to engage critically with ideas – not only the texts, but students themselves, are sources of learning.

Conclusion

Cultivating a critical space in our classrooms is a vital part of an educator's work. By treating the classroom as a community of learners where the starting point is often the student's lived experience, students learn that they each come with a different vantage point and can ask questions of themselves and each other. By studying works about race, and experiences of racism and power, students can reflect critically on the world around them and make connections between the historical, personal and social, and challenge – or affirm – their viewpoints in an invigorating and critical environment. As educators, we must provide them with these opportunities.

Notes

[1] Kevin Donnelly is a former academic and conservative commentator who contributed to Australia's education policy. Along with Kenneth Wiltshire, Donnelly authored the review of the Australian National Curriculum in 2014.
[2] Indeed, this phrase is employed by conservative alt-right aligned figures, such as Michael Rectenwald (2021), and Pat Robertson and Tucker Carlson (Cheney-Rice, 2021).
[3] See https://www.aic.gov.au/sites/default/files/2023-05/Deaths_in_custody_in_Australia_Q1_2023_Summary.pdf

References

Alexander, R. (2016) 'Dialogic teaching', *Robin Alexander* (blog), http://www.robinalexander.org.uk/dialogic-teaching

Alexander, N. (2023) 'Efforts to ban critical race theory have been put forth in all but one state – and many threaten schools with a loss of funds', *The Conversation*, 7 April, http://theconversation.com/efforts-to-ban-critical-race-theory-have-been-put-forth-in-all-but-one-state-and-many-threaten-schools-with-a-loss-of-funds-200816

Bargallie, D., Fernando, N. and Lentin, A. (2023) 'Breaking the racial silence: Putting racial literacy to work in Australia', *Ethnic and Racial Studies*. DOI: 10.1080/01419870.2023.2206470

Bekirogullari, Z. and Hajhosseiny, M. (2012) 'International Conference on Education & Educational Psychology (ICEEPSY 2012): The effect of dialogic teaching on students' critical thinking disposition', *Procedia – Social and Behavioral Sciences*, 69: 1358–68.

Boyd, M.P. and Markarian, W.C. (2011) 'Dialogic teaching: Talk in service of a dialogic stance', *Language and Education*, 25(6): 515–34.

Cheney-Rice, Z. (2021) 'The right's new reason to panic about "critical race theory" is centuries old', *Intelligencer*, 30 June, https://nymag.com/intelligencer/2021/06/the-white-panic-behind-critical-race-theory.html

d'Abrera, B. (2021a) 'Deranged theory', *IPA – The Voice For Freedom* (blog), 10 June, https://ipa.org.au/ipa-today/deranged-theory

d'Abrera, B. (2021b) 'Mainstream Australians reject identity politics in the classroom', *IPA – The Voice For Freedom* (blog), 21 May, https://ipa.org.au/curriculum/mainstream-australians-reject-identity-politics-in-the-classroom

Fanon, F. (2004) *The Wretched of the Earth*, trans. R. Philcox, New York: Grove Press.

Fanon, F. (2008) *Black Skin, White Masks*, New York: Grove Press.

Hoffman, K.M., Trawalter, S., Axt, J.R. and Oliver, M.N. (2016) 'Racial bias in pain assessment and treatment recommendations, and false beliefs about biological differences between Blacks and whites', *Proceedings of the National Academy of Sciences of the United States of America*, 113(16): 4296–301.

Institute of Medicine (US) Committee on Understanding and Eliminating Racial and Ethnic Disparities in Health Care (2003) *Unequal Treatment: Confronting Racial and Ethnic Disparities in Health Care*, ed B.D. Smedley, A.Y. Stith and A.R. Nelson, Washington, DC: National Academies Press.

Lyle, S. (2008) 'Dialogic teaching: Discussing theoretical contexts and reviewing evidence from classroom practice (cover story)', *Language & Education: An International Journal*, 22(3): 222–40.

Meghji, A. (2021) *Decolonizing Sociology: An Introduction*, Chichester: John Wiley & Sons.

Mercer, N. and Littleton, K. (2007) *Dialogue and the Development of Children's Thinking: A Sociocultural Approach*, London: Routledge.

Mills, C.W. (2000) *The Sociological Imagination*, Oxford: Oxford University Press.

Moreton-Robinson, A. (2006) 'Towards a new research agenda? Foucault, whiteness and Indigenous sovereignty', *Journal of Sociology*, 42(4): 341–448.

Murray, P. (2022) 'Teaching critical race theory in schools is "divisive indoctrination"', *Sky News Australia*, 20 October, https://www.skynews.com.au/opinion/paul-murray/teaching-critical-race-theory-in-schools-is-divisive-indoctrination/video/50aae922a28f8444b68d9f5a53d55c0e

Pearson, L. (2021) 'The rise of "the rise of anti-white racism" in Australia – Luke Pearson', *Indigenous X*, 7 July, https://indigenousx.com.au/the-rise-of-the-rise-of-anti-white-racism-in-australia

Rectenwald, M. (2021) 'Vengeance and sacrifice: Whiteness as scapegoat in critical race theory and critical whiteness studies', *Text. Mises Institute*, 26 April, https://mises.org/wire/vengeance-and-sacrifice-whiteness-scapegoat-critical-race-theory-and-critical-whiteness-studies.

Ricoeur, P. (2011) 'Fragile identity: Respect for the other and cultural identity', in C. Yates and N. Eckstrand (eds), *Philosophy and the Return of Violence: Studies from This Widening Gyre*, trans M. Gedney, New York: Continuum, pp 81–8.

Said, E.W. (1979) *Orientalism*, New York: Random House.

Santos, B. de S. (2015) *Epistemologies of the South: Justice Against Epistemicide*, London: Routledge.

Shahid, S., Teng, T.-H.K., Bessarab, D., Aoun, S., Baxi, S. and Thompson, S.C. (2016) 'Factors contributing to delayed diagnosis of cancer among Aboriginal people in Australia: A qualitative study', *BMJ Open*, 6(6): e010909.

Sky News (2020) 'Far left ideology is "based on a lie"', 28 June, https://www.skynews.com.au/opinion/outsiders/far-left-ideology-is-based-on-a-lie/video/5e9e78131c92403b3c7a342ea480bea6

Sky News (2021a) 'It's "shocking": New ABC documentary promotes critical race theory in schools', 21 September, https://www.skynews.com.au/opinion/peta-credlin/its-shocking-new-abc-documentary-promotes-critical-race-theory-in-schools/video/92cb9d64058dd3874c931ffbf382820f

Sky News (2021b) 'Race guilt and race shame are now "taking hold" in Australia: Andrew Bolt', 10 June, https://www.skynews.com.au/opinion/andrew-bolt/race-guilt-and-race-shame-are-now-taking-hold-in-australia-andrew-bolt/video/f8bd82789bd62e070e8cc8ab28e6ef94

Táíwò, O.O. (2022) 'Introduction', in *Elite Capture: How the Powerful Took Over Identity Politics (And Everything Else)*, New York: Pluto Press, pp 1–13.

White, D. (2022) 'Academics sound alarm after NSW universities scrap thousands of jobs', *Sydney Morning Herald*, 10 April, https://www.smh.com.au/national/nsw/academics-sound-alarm-after-nsw-universities-scrap-thousands-of-job-20220310-p5a3e1.html

Wolfe, S. and Alexander, R. (2008) 'Argumentation and dialogic teaching: Alternative pedagogies for a changing world', *Beyond Current Horizons*, http://www.robinalexander.org.uk/wp-content/uploads/2012/05/wolfealexander.pdf

Zhou, N. (2021) 'Australia's school curriculum: What are the proposed changes, and what's the fuss about "invasion"?', *The Guardian*, 30 April, https://www.theguardian.com/australia-news/2021/apr/30/australias-school-curriculum-what-are-the-proposed-changes-and-whats-the-fuss-about-invasion

5

(De)constituting Settler Subjects: A Retrospective Critical Race-Decolonizing Account

Joseph Pugliese

Introduction

What pedagogical forces were operative in the construction of my racialized subject positions within the context of the Australian white settler state? In this chapter, I begin to answer this question by deploying critical race-decolonizing theories to trace a genealogy of forces that operated in the constitution of my subjectivity. In the first instance, I proceed to unravel a genealogy that preceded my family's migration to the Australian colony. I work to reconstruct this genealogy in order to materialize the prior forces of settler colonialism and race that already inscribed me as a subject and which were instrumental as push factors in my family's migration. I then proceed to unpack the racialized pedagogy of the white settler state that I was compelled to experience as a non-Anglo diasporic-settler child. My personal account is located in the practice of '[c]ritical race theorists [who] use storytelling and counter-storytelling through personal stories … as a critical method to recount … experiences with racism' (Bargallie, 2020: 85). By examining two school textbooks that were part of my miseducation, I (autoethnographically) trace how these texts pedagogically laboured to inculcate a range of hegemonic values that normalized the racialized violence of the settler state.

In the course of my miseducation at primary, secondary and tertiary levels, I was never exposed to critical race or decolonizing theories. Rather, my critical education took place in an autodidactical manner, despite the institution of formal education, through my reading of such foundational writers as Frantz Fanon, Ruby Langford Ginibi, Jackie Huggins, bell hooks and so on. Through my reading of the works of decolonizing and critical race theorists, I began to acquire a vocabulary that enabled me to name and identify the constituent parts of the settler state that effectively guaranteed its racialized maintenance and reproduction. My own embodied experience of racism, in the context of Anglocentric-assimilationist culture, now found a grammar that rendered culturally intelligible the enmeshed operations of racism and settler colonialism. Ever since, I have worked to transpose the liberatory and transformative power of decolonizing and critical race theories to the pedagogical context within which I work: the university classroom.

Other histories of race and colonial settlerism

What role does a prior, other-than-Australian history of racialized settler colonialism play in the formation of an Australian diasporic-settler subject? I broach this question to begin to unfold the matrix of forces that operate in the constitution of settler subjectivity. In what follows, the mapping that I unfold of a range of prior forces that attended my own settler subject construction pivots on two points of intersection: a personal attempt to unravel how I became a settler subject within the Australian settler state and the imperative to materialize the *transnational* forces of settler colonialism, empire and race that have been constitutive of my (dis)located subjectivity.[1] I emphasize the *transnational* dimensions of subject constitution in order to problematize approaches that present non-Anglo migrants who become settlers in colonies such as Australia as types of *tabula rasa* – that is, as blank, ahistorical slates that abruptly become inscribed by race and settler-colonial values only on their entry to Australia. The power of such categories as race and settler colonialism is underpinned by transnational networks of transference and exchange. It is this transnational mobility and transferentiality that invests these categories with the capacity to be contingently inflected by, and adapted to, diverse embodied locations.

I am Calabrian by birth. In other words, I come from the southern part of the Italian peninsula. From the moment of Italian unification in 1861, Southerners were largely framed as neither white nor Italian as they were 'unrelated to Latinity because of their sullied admixture of Arab and African ancestry' (Germinario, 1999: 110). And I refer here to role of racial scientists in buttressing the racial hierarchies and politics of the Italian state in both the internal Italian context and the external context of the colonies (Teti, 1993). Marco Levi Bianchini (1906), for example, described the particularities of what he termed the '*razza calabrese*': 'The historical and anthropological primitiveness of contemporary Calabria is constituted by "curious habits and social institutions that appear not dissimilar to those observed in the peri-equatorial populations of Central Africa that today represent that rudimentary state of civilization that Europe left behind millennia ago'" (quoted in Giacanelli, 1999: 394).[2] Scripted as analogous to Central African populations, Calabrians are here rendered as racially and culturally Black.

Lorenzo Veracini (2018: 17) demonstrates how these internal racial hierarchies were tied to the Italian state's external projects of colonial conquest: 'When the government had begun talking about acquiring possessions in Africa at the end of the nineteenth century, the oppositions had admonished that "Italy already had Africa at home," in the underdeveloped regions of Italy.' In the context of Italian unification, the South was viewed as Italy's Africa: a *terra incognita* that compelled the national government to deploy a colonial model to civilize this barbaric region by establishing 'special careers with certain advantages like the House of Indian Affairs in England' (Petraccone, 2000: 101). Articulated here is a double modality of anti-Blackness that encompasses both internal (the South) and external (Africa) racial registers. Binding this double modality is a multispectrality of anti-Blackness that marks its historical expansiveness and its mutability as a racial category.

From the late 19th century onwards, policies of 'bloody internal repression' in the South and the violent 'external expansion' in East Africa were used to legitimate the nation's colonial projects. For example, Sicilian rebels, protesting their dire economic conditions, were framed by the Italian state as equivalent to 'rioting Africans to be easily "pacified" and brutally put down' (Triulzi, 2005: 155–6). The militarized systematicity of this internal repression operated as a 'type of colonial war that anticipated, through its unprecedented violence and contempt for its opponents, those wars that were conducted in Africa' (Del Boca, 2005: 57). The South thus operated as a colonial template and a testing ground for the larger violence that was to be unleashed by the Italian state in its external colonies.

Once Mussolini's fascist movement installed itself as the Italian state's government in the 1920s, it established a position on the South that was constituted by a double move. On the one hand, there was the denial of the Southern Question (concerned, among other things, with the endemic poverty and unemployment in the South) and its series of unresolved differences that were simply expunged in order to project an image of national unity. These unresolved differences pivoted on the asymmetries of economic power that were cemented post-unification; these 'reduced the South to a "colonial market" that was interdicted from having any relationship – of exports and imports – with outside states and that was compelled to consume expensive northern manufactured goods' (Barbagallo, 1973: 57). On the other hand, Italy's internal differences were whitewashed through the project of external colonization. To advance this project, the regime mobilized its propagandistic apparatuses to annul the nation's 'internal alterity [the South]' while simultaneously working to distance the nation from its 'external alterity [its colonies] recognizing in this a dangerous proximity that had to be exorcised and transformed into difference' (Triulzi, 2005: 169).

Italy's settler-colonial wars

Nowhere were these aggressions more violently manifest than in the fascist regime's colonial wars in Africa. The expansive frame of these colonial wars implicates the South. The colonial history of exporting Southern Italian migrants to Italy's North African colonies became one way to address the Southern Question. As Ali Abdullatif Ahmida (2009: 141) contends, '[s]ettler colonialism became a solution to the problems stemming from late industrialization and social conflict in Italy'. The Italian colonies that the fascist regime planned to create in Africa were seen as providing the solution to 'the Southern Question by allowing the expropriation of land not from Italian landowners, but from African peoples judged incapable of properly cultivating the land' (Re, 2003: 178).

In the context of its African colonies, between 1936 and 1937, the fascist regime issued a number of apartheid decrees that forcefully evicted hundreds of thousands of Indigenous Africans from their urban quarters and replaced them with Italian settlers and their institutions and infrastructure (Dogliani, 2014: 291, 293). This all aligns perfectly with the settler-colonial paradigm in which the twinned operations of the *elimination* and *replacement* of the Indigene constitute the foundations of this colonial modality (Wolfe, 2006: 387–409).

Frontier wars by other means

The exacerbation of the destructive effects of the unresolved Southern Question generated by the fascist settler-colonial wars exacted an enormous toll on the South. The fascist regime's commitments to its settler-colonial wars in Africa resulted in the 'the subtraction from the southern regions of the meagre capital that the regime normally invested there' (Del Boca, 2001: 749). Post-Second World War, the profound economic asymmetry between the South and the North was amplified by this fascist legacy. It produced, as Francesco Barbagallo (1973: 180, 252) sardonically remarks, an 'economic miracle' in the North, while simultaneously generating the 'Southern miracle': mass unemployment and mass migration, with over four million Southerners migrating between 1951 and 1971. The structural impoverishment of the South that was left in the wake of the demise of the fascist regime impelled my family to migrate to 'so-called Australia' (Day, 2021: 10). These prior historical factors topologically bind my family to the Australian settler-colonial state.

My family migrated from Calabria to Australia in 1960. As postwar migrants, we arrived in the backwash of another series of colonial wars: the

Frontier Wars, which secured the establishment of the Australian settler state by violently wresting unceded lands from the Indigenous peoples of the continent and its islands. As such, the term 'postwar migrants' resonates in a register that captures, despite itself, another history largely effaced and denied by the settler state. Postwar migrants were crucial to the success of what I would term 'frontier wars by other means': even as they did not participate in the frontline battles of the historical Frontier Wars, their labour – across the agricultural, pastoral, building and manufacturing industries – contributed to the consolidation of the wealth and power of the Australian settler state. Through these lateral wars, postwar migrants, as accessories after the frontline fact, played – and continue to play – a key role in the process of settler accumulation founded on the expropriation of Indigenous lands and resources and the consequent generation of Australia's colonial 'debtscape' (Giannacopoulos, 2019: 11).

In articulating these nested levels of settler-colonial wars and the imbrication of non-Anglo migrants within these violent formations, I do not mean to collapse the differentials that accrue to the categories of Anglo 'settler' and non-Anglo 'migrant', but rather to draw attention to the substructural continuities that subtend both categories once they are situated within the matrix of racial-colonizing-extractive-capitalism – as the operational matrix that governs the Australian settler state and connects it back to its transnational affiliations. Furthermore, the category of non-Anglo 'migrant' needs to be evaluated against the embodied differentials that inflect diasporic subjects within the corpus of the white Australian racial state. For example, the postwar Calabrese migrant, in the context of the 'White Australia' policy, was never simply viewed as white; rather, an equivocal racial history attended this subject who was seen as either not quite white or, alternatively, as not white at all. Southerners experienced racism both outside the Australian nation, at migration recruitment and certification points, and within the nation, in the very civic spaces they inhabited after their arrival (Pugliese, 2002; Andreoni, 2003; Ricatti, 2018). Moreover, they were often viewed as distinctly undesirable immigrants who would compromise the purity of the white nation. However, after the abolition of the 'White Australia' policy in the early 1970s and the entry of previously debarred Black people and people of colour, Southern Italians were recalibrated up the white supremacist racial hierarchy and consequently inducted into the category of whiteness. This recalibration, it must be noted, continues to operate in a corporeally contingent and heterogeneous manner, precisely because of the embodied differentials of certain southern Italian subjects who fail 'phenotypically' to qualify as white.

Growing up in assimilationist Australia during the 1960s and 1970s, I experienced both physical and symbolic racist violence, which achieved two significant outcomes: it produced a counter-discursive corporealized literacy that attuned me to both the brutal and nuanced dimensions of racism, and it established the embodied foundation for my anti-racist and decolonial scholarly activism.

Pedagogies of Australian settlerism

I have spent some time mapping the prior racialized settler history that inscribes my family's diasporic journey to demonstrate that non-Indigenous Australian settler subjects are not blank slates that abruptly, on arrival, become targets of racialized settler inscription and constitution. Rather, in my case, a matrix of transnational forces of racialized settlerism was not only already operative in the constitution of my own family history, but was pivotal to driving my family to become migrants who would contribute to the project of Australian settler colonialism. As we were book poor, I held onto many of the textbooks that were part of my primary school miseducation. I still possess two of them. In what follows, they will be used as primary evidence in my counter-story of settler pedagogy and subject constitution.

One of my textbooks is from the series The Australian Children's Pictorial Social Studies and is titled *The First Fleet* (Australian Children's Pictorial Social Studies, 1958). The discipline of social studies instructed students in the settler history and culture of Australia. After offering a synoptic background to as to why the First Fleet sailed for Australia, the textbook focuses on its arrival at Warrane (Sydney Cove) and the colonial renaming by Captain Arthur Phillip of the key landmarks of the Gadigal people (Figure 5.1).

'We'll name this point of land "Dawes Point".' Thus begins the toponymic process of settler *terra nullius*, with its systematic erasure of prior Indigenous ownership of the lands colonized by the British and the consequent effacement of the names that inscribed the lands occupied by the Gadigal people. Phillip is shown naming and taking possession of Gadigal lands, as three shadow-like Indigenous figures are represented as mere spectators to the expropriation of their lands. This *terra nullius* pedagogical process of wilful forgetting and erasure would be crucial in shaping my whitewashed understanding of Australian history.

The next page of my textbook celebrates the raising of the British flag at the newly named 'Port Jackson' and the toasting to the foundation of the colony (Figure 5.2). Nowhere are the Gadigal people to be seen. They have been visually eliminated from their own lands – a graphic metaphor for the physical process of settler elimination that was to follow the establishment of the colony.

After many pages that celebrate the labour of building the colony, representations of Indigenous people finally reappear. In the latter part of the textbook, the aftermath of the kidnap of Bennelong by Phillip is seen to play out. After his forced capture by Phillip so he could be pressed into service

Figure 5.1: 'We'll name this point of land "Dawes Point"'

Source: Australian Children's Pictorial Social Studies (1958) *The First Fleet*, Volume 11, Sydney: Australian Visual Education. Image reproduced with permission.

Figure 5.2: 'To the new colony!'

Source: Australian Children's Pictorial Social Studies (1958) *The First Fleet*, Volume 11, Sydney: Australian Visual Education. Image reproduced with permission.

Figure 5.3: 'Kill! Kill! Kill the white man'

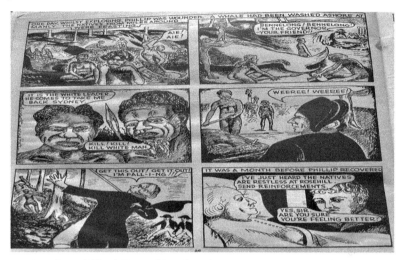

Source: Australian Children's Pictorial Social Studies (1958) *The First Fleet*, Volume 11, Sydney: Australian Visual Education. Image reproduced with permission.

to make contact with the Gadigal people, Bennelong managed to escape. The textbook shows Phillip's subsequent sighting of Bennelong at 'Manly' as he and his relations are feasting on the carcass of a whale (Figure 5.3).

Realizing that Phillip will once more kidnap him, the illustration shows a companion saying to Bennelong: 'Kill! Kill! Kill the white man' (Australian Children's Pictorial Social Studies, 1958: 26), with the subsequent spearing of Phillip. On their first appearance in the textbook, Indigenous people are represented as mere shadowy figures who have no substantial agency or presence in the context of the foundation of the colony. On their second and last reappearance, they emerge as violent killers. This sets the frame for the pedagogical inculcation of the bipolar settler stereotype: the figure of the 'vanishing Aborigines' – as mere insubstantial spectres doomed to be extinguished – is simultaneously bound to the figure of the violent savage. The contradictions of the racial stereotype are succinctly embodied in these two bipolar representations. They can be seen to reproduce the following settler logic: as they were violent and uncivilized savages, Indigenous people were destined to disappear, both from settler histories and their own lands. A retrospective decolonizing reading offers a diametrically opposed reading: in the articulation of 'Kill the white man' and the spearing of Phillip, Indigenous resistance is powerfully materialized and the incipient violence of the Frontier Wars is anticipated.

A second primary school textbook that I still possess is titled *It's Fun to Read* (Infants' Reading Committee, 1957). It was my first 'learn how to read' book. The conceptual fabric of the book is underpinned by three institutionalized forces of settler governmentality: the 'possessive logic of patriarchal white sovereignty' (Moreton-Robinson, 2004), 'heterosexualism and the colonial/modern gender system' (Day, 2021: 1) and the policy of Anglocentric assimilation (Pugliese, 2002). The textbook's pedagogical power resides in its exclusive use of simple declarative sentences that speak to the factuality of what is being represented. The use of declarative sentences functions to produce the enunciation of ontological facts. The gendered ontology of the textbook's declarative sentences is informed by the 'colonial/modern gender system' that 'is organized around sexual dimorphism, patriarchy and heterosexuality' (Day, 2021: 5).

The gender binary system reproduced by the use of declarative sentences is visually reinforced by the textbook's illustrations (Figure 5.4). The factuality-effect of the declarative sentences is further amplified by the heterosexual gender stereotypes that shape the children's activities and toys: Mary is figured as a mother in-waiting as she pushes a pram with a doll, while Jim strides across the page flying his toy plane. Encapsulated here are those reiterative performatives that work to constitute both gendered identities and space. Mary will be circumscribed to the role of patriarchal reproduction and confined to the unpaid domestic space of the home, while Jim will be pursuing his paid career in the larger external world of the colony.

In the textbook, Mary and Jim's respective futures are already embodied by their parents. On her first appearance in the textbook, their mother is shown holding a baby and framed by the delimiting boundary of their home's front verandah (Figure 5.5). The father, dressed in business suit and carrying a briefcase, arrives home from work on a bus to greet the children (Figure 5.6). As Madi Day (2021: 6) remarks: 'Heterosexualism ascribes

Figure 5.4: 'This is Mary.' 'This is Jim.' *It's Fun to Read*

Source: Published by the State of New South Wales (Department of Education) in 1957, public domain. Image reproduced with permission.

Figure 5.5: 'Mother is at home.' ' "Look at baby, Jim!" ' *It's Fun to Read*

Source: Published by the State of New South Wales (Department of Education) in 1957, public domain. Image reproduced with permission.

Figure 5.6: 'Father comes home in the bus.' ' "Look in my bag, Jim." ' *It's Fun to Read*

Source: Published by the State of New South Wales (Department of Education) in 1957, public domain. Image reproduced with permission.

white women sexual passivity and purity, and smallness and weakness of body and mind. In this dynamic, white men protect white women as a means of control of (re)production.'

By drawing on Maria Lugones' work, Day (2021: 6) discloses how colonial 'heterosexualism is racialized and [how] race and racial difference are articulated through gender and sexuality'. In my textbook, the settler disposition of space is controlled by the subject-constituting system of the heteropatriarchal binary that works hand in hand with the power of whiteness as property. The book is set in a white middle-class suburb in which the houses, situated on their quarter-acre blocks, are bounded by the fabled white-picket fences of the 'White Australia' policy – a policy that was still very much in place at the time of my miseducation.

My settler primary school miseducation took place at St Vincent de Paul Church School, Redfern. It took place, in other words, in an epicentre of Indigenous culture: the Block was just a stone's throw from my school. Bill Simon (in Simon et al, 2009: 115) writes: 'The Block has been the hub of urban Aboriginal life since the days of the Great Depression. Many Aboriginal people came to find work at the Eveleigh Railyards and settled in the small community bounded by four streets.' Reading my textbook retrospectively, I am compelled to think through the disjunction of living in the midst of a rich and vital Indigenous community and the total absence of any Indigenous people in the whitewashed pages of the textbook.

The textbook's act of wholesale whitewashing worked to deny and erase the existence of the Indigenous people of the Redfern community where I grew up *and* to secure and reproduce the larger regime of the white settler state that underpins and animates every line of text and every illustration in the book. Aileen Moreton-Robinson (2004: 2) states: 'The possessive logic of patriarchal white sovereignty operates to discriminate in favour of itself, ensuring it protects and maintains its interest by continuing denial and exclusion of Indigenous sovereignty.' In discriminating in favour of itself, the patriarchal white sovereignty that underpins this textbook reproduces a form of settler self-referential epistemology that is racialized as white, gendered as heterosexual and grounded in the possessive logic of patriarchal white sovereignty – precisely in order to 'naturalize the nation as a white possession' (Moreton-Robinson, 2004: 2).

Sanitized of all the racial detritus that haunts the Anglo settler imaginary, the textbook presents the vision of a normative white banality that is, in fact, underpinned by an unrepresentable, yet foundational, racialized violence. The suasive power of the textbook resides in the very banality of declarative whiteness that governs its illustrations, with their assimilationist agenda of settler property ownership and heteropatriarchy. My juvenile induction into the world of Anglo assimilationism, however, was marked by a sort of system failure that resulted from the lived disjunction between two dissonant realities. This lived disjunction was embodied through quotidian racial slurs ('dago', 'greasy wog') articulated by both Anglo students and teachers. I remember my commerce teacher, Mr Woods, demanding that I walk up to the classroom dais after I had asked what he perceived to be a particularly impertinent question. Pointing to me, he spat out the following words that still ring in my ears: 'You migrants came to this country morally, culturally and economically bankrupt. And you will amount to nothing!'

My lived disjunction was also physically felt through practices of race-hate violence. Here are three examples: Anglo neighbours standing on the roof of their backyard shed, throwing empty beer bottles at us and attempting to 'wash clean the dirty dagos' with their garden hose – an exemplary act of what I would now term *vernacular racism*; Anglo students and their ritualized after-school bashing of wogs in the train station's underpass close to my school; and the time when the Anglo neighbour's children threw a piece of brick at my head as they chanted 'dirty dago'. I required stitches to suture the gash and they left a permanent scar. Occasionally, I trace the contours of the scarred ridge at the back of my scalp with my fingers. It retains a perverse sort of mnemonic power as it continues to reiterate a moment of race-hate violence that has been dermographically inscribed on my body.

I never could quite resolve the faultline between my lived exterior reality and the racially homogenized and seemingly benign interior world of my primary school textbook. Only much later in life would I finally find the critical vocabulary to name and identify this form of racialized cognitive dissonance.

Towards decolonized futures

The school textbooks examined in this chapter have travelled with me over the course of half a century. I do not view them as anachronistic artefacts that can now be relegated to the dustbin of history. On the contrary, I view them as pedagogical agents of the white supremacist settler state that, in terms of the vectors of power that produced them, have lost little of their formative agency: in the contemporary context, the text and the iconography have superficially changed, but the foundational values of the settler-colonial racial state remain largely intact. The decolonizing and critical race theories that I was fortunate to acquire outside of, and despite, the various educational institutions that I attended have enabled me to shine a light on my prior, other-than-Australian histories that continue to inscribe me. These critical theories have enabled me to stage a retrospective analysis focused on naming and identifying the interlocking forms of racialized power that inscribed my school textbooks and that were instrumental in interpellating me as a settler subject. The concept of 'retrospectivity', however, needs to be problematized. My backward-looking analysis is, *ipso facto*, ineluctably situated in a settler present that has hardly been overcome or vanquished. Its presentist ground continues to be animated by the still-formative power of its past. My retrospective analysis is, in other words, very much *of* the present – even as it is simultaneously *about* the past.

Crucially, the transformative power of decolonizing and critical race theories lies beyond acts of naming and identifying, and beyond the contestation of the declarative power of the state's onto-epistemologies as they interpenetrate all levels of settler culture and rigidify into the material doxa of seemingly unassailable 'facts'. The crux of their transformative power lies in their promise to abolish the very structures that constitute the racialized matrix of the settler state and thus to realize decolonized futures.

Notes

[1] For a detailed discussion of the matrix of race, settler colonialism and the Global South in the context of Italian fascism, see Pugliese (2022).
[2] All translations from Italian are by the author.

References

Ahmida, A.A. (2009) *The Making of Modern Libya*, Albany: State University of New York Press.

Andreoni, H. (2003) 'Olive or white? The colour of Italians in Australia', *Journal of Australian Studies*, 28: 248–71.

Australian Children's Pictorial Social Studies (1958) *The First Fleet, Vol. 11*, Sydney: Australian Visual Education.

Barbagallo, F. (1973) *Lavoro ed Esodo nel Sud, 1861–1971*, Naples: Guida Editori.

Bargallie, D. (2020) *Unmasking the Racial State: Indigenous Voices on Racism in the Australian Public Service*, Canberra: Aboriginal Studies Press.

Day, M. (2021) 'Remembering Lugones: The critical potential of heterosexualism for studies of so-called Australia', *Genealogy*, 5(71): 1–11.

Del Boca, A. (2001) *Gli italiani in Africa Orientale*, Milan: Oscar Mondadori.

Del Boca, A. (2005) *Italiani, brava gente?* Vicenza: Neri Pozza Editore.

Dogliani, P. (2014) *Il fascismo degli italiani*, Novara: De Agostini Libri.

Germinario, F. (1999) 'Latinità, antimeridionalismo e antisemitismo negli scritti giovanili di Paolo Orano (1985–1911)', in A. Burgio (ed.), *Nel nome della razza*, Bologna: Il Mulino, pp 105–14.

Giacanelli, F. (1999) 'Trace e percorsi del razzismo nella psichiatria italiana della prima metà del Novecento', in A. Burgio (ed.), *Nel nome della razza*, Bologna: Il Mulino, pp 389–405.

Giannacopoulos, M. (2019) 'Debtscape: Australia's constitutional nomopoly', *Borderlands*, 18: 1–16.

Infants' Reading Committee (1957) *It's Fun to Read*, Sydney: NSW Department of Education.

Moreton-Robinson, A. (2004) 'The possessive logic of patriarchal white sovereignty: The High Court and the *Yorta Yorta* decision', *Borderlands*, 3(2): 1–11.

Petraccone, C. (2000) *Le due civiltà*, Rome: Laterza.

Pugliese, J. (2002) 'Race as category crisis: Whiteness and the topical assignation of race', *Social Semiotics*, 12(2): 49–68.

Pugliese, J. (2022) 'Unsettled spectres of Italy's settler colonial wars and a genealogy of Italian anti-Blackness: A diasporic perspective', *Voci: Annuale di Scienze Umane*, 29: 55–77.

Re, L. (2003) 'Alexandria revisited', in P. Palumbo (ed), *A Place in the Sun: Africa in Italian Colonial Culture from Post-Unification to the Present*, Berkeley: University of California Press, pp 279–98.

Ricatti, F. (2018) *Italians in Australia: History, Memory, Identity*, Cham: Palgrave Macmillan.

Simon, B., Montgomerie, D. and Tuscano, J. (2009) *Back on the Block*, Canberra: Aboriginal Studies Press.

Teti, V. (1993) *La razza maledetta*, Rome: Manifestolibri.

Triulzi, A. (2005) 'Adwa: From monument to document', in J. Andall and D. Duncan (eds), *Italian Colonialism*, Bern: Peter Lang, pp 143–63.

Veracini, V. (2018) 'Italian colonialism through a settler colonial studies lens', *Journal of Colonialism and Colonial History*, 19(3): 1–30.

Wolfe, P. (2006) 'Settler colonialism and the elimination of the native', *Journal of Genocide Research*, 8(6): 387–409.

PART II

Being in the Classroom

6

Shedding the Colonial Skin and Digging Deep as Decolonial Praxis

Faye Rosas Blanch

Introduction

Indigenous Australians continue to be viewed within a racialized lens that too often keeps our bodies out of the 'norm' of academic teaching and learning spaces. As Indigenous academics, we are too often relied upon to bring Indigenous knowledge into tough and confronting spaces in which 'race' as a theoretical and methodological concept is never really named or spoken about. As sovereign beings, we enter confronting and dangerous spaces of settler colonialism with a strong desire to disrupt and change that damaged landscape. This raises the question of our bodies as damaged landscapes, especially in the sense of what work we do as sovereign bodies in the context of landscape/bodies when blood is spilt (McKittrick, 2021). 'Race' in Australian coloniality was advanced through an oppressive lens, merging with the development of racist ideological literacies and policies, legislated to deny Indigenous people's rights to land and culture. The process of colonization continues to structure Australian society and privileges whiteness in the racialized entangled assemblages that shape the teaching environment in Australian universities. Racialization and the impact of colonization on our lives have resulted in events, practices and segments that make up the assemblages that force Indigenous peoples to conform to the dominant hegemonic values considered 'normal' (Blanch, 2016: 50). Yet the study of race is omitted from the agenda as instrumental in curriculum development or as a central theme to adhere to within the teaching space. In academic teaching and learning, race only appears in the curriculum when Indigenous people teach it, or when non-Indigenous allies willingly undertake the responsibility to develop topics that explore race as a social construct and deconstruct what this may mean in their own teaching journey.

This chapter digs deeper into a critical anti-racist framework that advances a process of decolonization while teaching in those difficult and dangerous spaces. I draw from the seminal Australian and international critical Indigenous, critical race and decolonial scholarship of Aileen Moreton-Robinson, Sylvia Wynter and Katherine McKittrick to further contextualize the realities of raced bodies and racial literacies. We are more than what we are told and read about in the racial grammar of the settler-colonial state that represents us as abject and that deems us non-human, and that informs knowledge production. I consider how narratives carried into teaching spaces by First Nations academics are 'embodied' literacies and argue that the decolonial process cannot really happen until we (educators and knowledge producers) see that all literacies about us (the racializing assembles of discourse, language, text, film, policies and so on) are 'raced'. I add to the conversation an 'unbecoming' via a 'shedding of colonial skin' through the creative works of the Unbound Collective Sovereign Sisters to add deeper critical analysis of anti-racist and decolonization performance while in those difficult and dangerous teaching and performance spaces. The Unbound Sovereign Acts Collective, an all-First Nations women academic/creative collective, is located within a university within South Australia, where we work together in spaces that can at times be dangerous, inflexible and rigid to be in (Blanch, 2016; Bunda and Phillips, 2018). Contributing the theoretical concepts of unbecoming and sovereignty, I argue, fosters expansiveness of First Nations humanness in the teaching space, both inside and outside the university.

Anticolonial and decolonizing frames

Citing Sylvia Wynter (2006), Katherine McKittrick (2021: 36) unravels and conceptualizes this lack of understanding of how race borders the very being of Black/Indigenous people in knowledge production as 'discipline is empire'. I concur with both Wynter and McKittrick and suggest here that to acknowledge and understand that 'discipline is empire' in Indigenous studies, like Black studies, is coded with racism and racial violence (McKittrick, 2021: 36); therefore, whiteness is not seen. 'Discipline is empire' permits a deeper analysis of the entangled relationship between racial literacy and the construction of the Indigenous subject when a 'sovereign' body enters the socially constructed space of education. I argue that the entanglements of colonialism continue in the learning landscape in various ways to visually represent our 'raced' bodies as abject beings.

As embodied literacy, we (Indigenous people) are the texts that tell the stories of Country and culture, and this is not absent from our bodies (Blanch,

2016: 54). We bear the weight of racial literacy and the silencing of race in academia (Bargallie, 2020) that comes with what Sara Ahmed (2004) calls a 'stickiness'. Ahmed (2004) conceptualizes emotions as affective, as living entities that move through our bodies and minds. The stickiness of the violence is felt and expressed on the skin, circumscribed by the knowledge paradigms and worldviews that frame the racialization that continues to dehumanize First Nations people. How do 'we work through those thorny racial privileges and biases that animate this field' (McKittrick, 2021: 1)?

Ahmed (2004: 90) states that 'perhaps stickiness becomes disgusting only when the skin surface is at stake such that what is sticky threatens to stick to us'. The stickiness happens when we move out into 'dangerous spaces' like the pub, a wedding, the classroom, when racism takes on a life of its own. The stickiness is their racism. I feel disgusted by the racism. The disgust burrows into my body and mind. The stickiness does not affect me until two weeks later, when I am quiet and away from it all. I am vomiting, crying, tossing, turning in my bed. That is the violence of the stickiness.

'Man' or 'the Human', according to Fanon (2008: xv), has been brought into being not objectively, but as constructed, classified and institutionalized through Western world systems in a hierarchically racial order as generically and racially inferior, as subhuman due to Black skin/Blackness (Wynter and McKittrick, 2015: 55). In the knowledge-producing spaces that we First Nations academics/scholars navigate daily, the stickiness of the silencing of race, the unsureness, the unable-ness to commit to Indigenous understanding by non-Indigenous academics, moves through our bodies and minds as affective economies and leave us at times battling fight-or-flight syndrome, gasping for space to breathe. We suffer the racialized tagging of our bodies and minds, we get burnt out, we become almost lifeless; the trajectory of naming the importance of First Nations understandings and ways of being borders the privilege of Western thought, the Western canon of education. We feel this bordering through the skin. Trying to insert Indigenous ways of knowing into the educational system not only evokes a 'deafening' silence about race, but also understanding and acknowledgement that Indigenous intellectual life is tied to 'the corporeal and affective labor – the flesh, brains, and blood and bones, hearts, souls' (McKittrick, 2021: 6) of Indigenous bodies. This is the very DNA that is who we are as sovereign bodies in such burdensome spaces. How must non-Indigenous educators work with this?

Investigating how a process of deconstructing and unpacking the concept of race to reimagine 'race' as literacy can, through a critical anti-racist framework that resists and challenges racist hegemonic practices (Sefa Dei and McDermott, 2013), offer a process of decolonization and digging deep to articulate the various ways that racial literacy as an embodied concept is taken into classrooms. I take into the teaching space copies of my great-grandfathers' and great-grandmothers' application to be exempt from the

Aborigines Protection and Preservation Act 1939 in order to leave the mission. I ask the students to critique the racialized languages in policies that construct Aboriginal peoples as less-than-human (for example, is he intelligent? Are they full blood?) (Blanch, 2022).

Embodied literacies: we are the text

> Disciplines stack and a bifurcate seemingly disconnected categories and geographies; disciplines differentiate, split, and create fictive distances between us. (McKittrick, 2021: 37)

In writing back to the empire of disciplines that are coded and disconnected to the relationality of First Nations people within the epistemological realm of such disciplines, I argue that knowledge of First Nations people is layered. The layered movements and moments occur when First Nations people want truth, want the deconstruction and the challenge for how racism propelled violence that is intimate in its performance (McKittrick, 2021; Blanch, 2022). What this means is moving 'towards a decolonizing epistemology … inclusive of a new language of educational critique and transformation, a new way of thinking about knowledge and a new way to frame conversations about how we process an ongoing process' (McLaren, 2011: viii) that contextualizes and involves 'writing forward, writing back and writing Black' (Worby et al, 2014: 1–3).

While understanding as a First Nation person/academic the palimpsest of our relationality to this country named Australia, we/this appears as invisible to the non-Indigenous colonizing settlers (McKittrick, 2021: 36–7), like objects on the landscape (Moreton-Robinson, 2015). Hence, support is required for Indigenous educators in complex teaching spaces.

Carrying 'Country' is the embodied literacy that I take into the classroom; 'Country' is carried wherever I am, and as Moreton-Robinson (2015: 14) states, 'a relationality exists between Indigenous people by descent, country place or shared experiences'. In the concept of a praxis of decolonization, there must be an acknowledgement that whiteness pervades the institution of education; seeing and deeply acknowledging that whiteness and Indigenous are socially constructed as 'raced' encourages a critical analytical discourse for new ideas, new thoughts and theories (Blanch, 2016: 54). My praxis explores the possibility of storying embodied literacies that centre First Nations voices as a decolonizing praxis. I share family embodied literacies that evoke McKittrick's (2021: 5) perspectives of racialized assemblages as entangled and connected to the weight (pull of gravity) and measure (the mathematics of our engagement) in teaching and learning that seek our continuities and rupture the connection to our intellectual sovereign being. Through providing and inserting my Indigenous feminist standpoint

(Moreton-Robinson, 2013), I locate my human as praxis into this text through unravelling the entanglement that connects non-Indigenous people and Indigenous relationship. I instil the narratives of family into the text to situate myself, as is always done within the context of teaching and learning. I concur with McKittrick (2021: 5) that 'black people are interdisciplinary actors, continually entangling and disentangling varying narratives and tempos, and hues that, together, invent and reinvent knowledge'. I further concur that 'naming demands that we ask about the unnamed and honor the unnamable' (McKittrick, 2021: 31) with the understanding that I am a sovereign person in those dangerous racialized spaces of teaching and knowledge production. As Watego (2021: 7) says, 'we don't need more texts that teach whitefullas about us on their terms … We need stories that are written by us and for us, that challenge us and nourish us – exclusively.'

Mother's story

As a starting point, I offer a conversation between my mother and myself. The conversation adds an important and insightful perspective to our time together and conveys remembering, belonging and intimacy with Country (Bunda, 2007; Moreton-Robinson, 2007, 2015). I offer the telling of our conversation as important because I had no idea that my mother was ever interested in the concept of sovereignty or had any desire to speak about or share knowledge of her language group. In speaking back to the fragments of memory (Carby, 2019), my mother always appeared busy with life, working and raising a family, which expresses to me how our lives have been shaped by institutions and structures that have maintained control over them (Alexander, 2002: 85). To add the concept of embodied literacy in this context, I engender Toni Morrison's praxis of 'literary archeology' to identify and grasp my mother's desire to return to her 'Country':

> The emotional memory or what the nerves and the skin remembers as well, as how, it appears and a rush of imagination is our 'flooding', a kind of literary archaeology, where the information and guesswork journey us to a site to see what remains were left behind and to reconstruct the world that these remains imply. (Morrison, 1990: 302)

As Miranda states, we carry this also as emotional fatigue:

> [O]ur bodies and hearts carry a deep sting, an engulfing shame and a contrary assertion of survivance, which all stem from the fact that our identities and cultures – our hearts – sprang from this land, from a place stolen, defiled, yet still present beneath our feet every day of our lives. (Miranda, 2002: 193)

There are many layers to my mother's life, and not all are mine to tell. Gloria Ladson-Billings (1998) and other feminist activist women of colour, such as Trinh T. Minh-ha (1989) and Toni Morrison (1993), identify the importance of centring life stories as a process of positioning that allows for disrupting the master script. I take a breath here as I speak back to the 'fragments of memory' (Carby, 2019) of my mother.

We all remember our mothers' and grandmothers' stories. As Phillips and Bunda (2018: 3) show, First Nations women's activism, feminism, energies, affective, emotional respect and ethical care are ways in which we 'communicate what it means to be human, that tells of relational tragedies, challenges and joys of living'. Our bodies perform our stories through activism as a process of decolonization. 'Stories are spoken, gestured, danced, dramatized, painted, drawn, etched, sculpted, woven, stitched, filmed, written and any combination of these modes and more' (Phillips and Bunda, 2018: 3). I provide a script:

Mother: So what is this sovereignty thing? … So, can you tell me?
Me: [I wasn't sure that she was serious, however, I needed to respond.] Well, sovereignty is about this country, Australia, and the British Empire; and the belief that Britain had sovereignty over all its lands/Country that was invaded and the citizens of those countries.

Conceptualizing sovereignty can be problematic and is contested; as a legal concept, I wasn't sure that I fully understood the theoretical dynamics of sovereignty. Therefore, how did I give her an answer that provided opportunity for her to know? How did I give her what she was seeking? I told her about *terra nullius*,[1] but I was not sure I was answering her question. Her wanting to know had put me on the spot. Returning to that moment, I now wish I had Aileen Moreton-Robinson's (2015) book *The White Possessive: Property, Power and Indigenous Sovereignty*. Moreton-Robinson provides a provocative insight into the ways in which Britain conveys itself as settled and belonging within the Country/s of Indigenous peoples. In Moreton-Robinson's (2015: 4) words, 'the British Empire established itself through colonization and the concomitant waves of migrants from British shores to colonized ones'. Jacqui Alexander (2002: 85) offers further insight, stating that although we have been impacted by structures, we must 'use flesh-and-blood experiences to concretize a vision'. I contend that *in the asking* my mother was [envisioning] visualizing her right to know about the word sovereignty, and define what it meant for her, her land and Country. She was engaging with her own embodied literacies that spoke to her Country. My mother was progressing towards movement to Country.

While this conversation lies within the discursive (wanting to know what sovereignty means), traumatic and emotional experiences of racism and sexism were fundamental to how my mother manoeuvred through her world on a daily basis. Along with others, I have also experienced racism and sexism (Blanch, 2013). While racism, sexism and silence were pivotal to our oppression (hooks, 1987), we nevertheless resisted and refused to be contained within a framework that denied us our human rights; embodied sovereignty is a critical decolonial literacy. Furthermore, while we operated by the rules of behaviour dictated to us by white Australia, my mother's generation had to strategically manoeuvre, negotiate and work out how to create zones that would be safe for us, as well as equip us – their daughters – with strategies to keep our own bodies safe. My mother and I are sovereign in our ways of making alternate meanings, our embodiment and how we move through coloniality.

Hairdressing story

The violent intimacy of collecting hair as data and sampling hair connection to other colonized countries was and is a potent racial/colonial tool in the construction of Indigenous otherness. Biological data and scientific study play a significant role in literacy and texts, both written and performed. From 1938 to 1939, Norman Tindale and Joseph Birdsell (1941), funded by Harvard University and the University of Adelaide, gathered the DNA from hair samples in their scientific studies into bodies of First Nations groups on missions and reserves throughout the Cairns hinterland, a vast area of land in Queensland. Speaking back to the violent and monstrous intimacies of the technologies of scientific study, I offer my second family story, about hair.

> I have to be at peace with my crisp curly hair. In this performance of a family tale, the emotional affect and entanglements around hair and Black bodies are deconstructed and unpacked and show how a hairdressing space often viewed as white space becomes Black space.
>
> My sister and I sat in the hairdressing salon waiting for her hair to get a dye and myself a conditioning treatment. We went to this hair salon because our niece worked there. She is a fantastic hairdresser, and all family members go that salon to get haircuts, treatment, dyes, etc. This day, my niece noticed I had a book in my hand and wanted to know what I was reading. The book was Katherine McKittrick's (2006) *Demonic Grounds: Black Women and the Cartographies of Struggle*. My niece, who was applying colour to my sister's hair, then asked what it was about. I proceeded to give her information. My response was to relay what I was reading. McKittrick (2006) writes about spaces and contextualizes understanding around spaces. She argues that Black women create and maintain Black feminist spaces wherever we travel, wherever we are. To give further

understanding to this, I presented this scenario. I use Aboriginal English to situate my relationship with each of my family member.

Me:	See this hairdressing salon, well this is space, and for a long time we've [Indigenous women] have always known it to be Migaloo [white] space. We've been at times scared to enter this space, maybe because we weren't sure if white hairdressers could cut our [curly] hair or would even like to touch our hair, or if we had enough money to get our hair done.
Sister:	Mmmm.
Me:	Well in thinking about space and Black woman space, the past has changed. We come into this hairdressing salon and we take over, we are cracked [funny, humorous] in this space. Do you want to know why?
Sister and Niece:	Yeah.
Me:	Mim [our niece] changed the space. She doesn't realize it, but she is the entry point for us to make it Black space. This salon is Black feminist space because Mim works here and, because she works here, we come into the space and [de]colonize the space. We feel safe, we act silly, we laugh loudly, we are not afraid of who is looking at us or watching us. We own this space, we are confident in this space. This is our space when we are all here, we claim the space simply because our niece works here. It is Black space when we come here. This is a powerful concept. Our hair is cared for; it's loved because she [our niece] knows our hair. We trust her with our hair and, whether she is aware or not, she tends lovingly to our hair. By trusting our curly hair with our hairdresser niece, we are empowered and transformed in those known white spaces. I am reminded of McKittrick's (2006) writing on geographical terrains and the movement between timespace and spatiality for Black movement.

Using the metaphor of the hair salon as white space, and past relationship to Indigenous women to the hair salon as contemporary Black space, I draw from McKittrick (2006: xix), who states that 'spatial acts can take on many forms and can be identified through expressions, resistances and naturalizations … these acts take place and have place'. Thus, within the Black space of the hair salon, we connect to our own Blackness/Indigeneity and feminist activism; we relate stories, we tell jokes, we gossip; every component of this space informs our wellbeing, and we leave full – we are happy. And so our hair intimately connects us to place, space, family, culture and belonging.

Becoming/unbecoming

According to Mark Rifkin (2011) and Jodie Byrd (2011), our bodies as First Peoples have undergone a process of all being the same. They argue that we have become reduced to a population of 'Aborigines' and 'Indigenous' through the lens of the settler states. Rifkin's (2011) and Byrd's (2011) clear articulation of this process seek to disrupt this, replacing First Peoples as having clear understanding of who we are as peoples. This provokes the question of what it means when we, as a population, 'become' a certain type of person, a certain group of people, and why and who is this for. Byrd (2011) suggests that we become 'woman', 'Indian/Aboriginal' and 'native' within the perception and representation of the settler-colonial state. I argue that the conceptualization of 'becoming', as articulated by Rifkin and Byrd, is a negative (form of violence) in terms of how the stereotypical dispositions rub up against each other. If we are becoming, then how do we 'unbecome' and just *be*? Becoming in such negative and stereotypical naming in racist and violent ways manifests in colonial spaces and canons of knowledge production, and denies our humanness.

In relating these stories, I deliberate that the 'becoming' can infer an 'unbecoming', theoretically conceptualized with a framework of decolonization and critical anti-racism process. I turn to the social, emotional and political performance of the Unbound Collective to denote how racial silence is performed through the bodies of the Unbound Collective, which bear witness to unbecoming.

Unbound Collective

How do we bear witness to unbecoming? Where is the loophole of retreat (Campt, 2019) when those stereotypical dispositions (woman, Aborigine, Indian/native, Indigenous) rub up against each other? How do we, as First Nations activists, claim our sovereignty, our human as praxis, our refusal and our resistance to connecting with the intersectionality of commitment, expressions, experiences, ideology, integrity, rights, quiet and sacredness that come together (Quashie, 2004)? Unbecoming, as articulated by Helen Vosters (2019), lies in the examination of memory, violence, performance, activism and nationalism. In exploring the notion of unbecoming, I am arguing that the work of the Unbound Collective – performance and research – allows for the navigation of the traps of 'settler-colonial toxic representations' (Vosters, 2019: 20) of our bodies and our minds to enact a process towards being human as praxis by 'unbecoming'. For her, 'unbecoming' as a 'descriptor, refers to that which detracts from or renders less attractive one's image or reputation' as well as a process to unpack and deconstruct 'situated practices and projects that work to unsettle, decolonize, dismantle or unbecome settler-colonial nationalism' (Vosters, 2019: 9).

I assert that through the collective works of the Unbound Sovereign Acts Collective, as First Nations academics and through the performance of activism, politicization and scholarly works, and First Nations women descendants of four different nations in this country, Australia, our voices go together in complementary ways.

Engaging as a collective strengthens our relationship with each other and asserts our right to be in the spaces of the knowledge production, such as universities and schools. We work together across the institutional spaces of the university, teaching, supporting and creating knowledge that offers each of us the chance to engage in research that empowers us. As Mirning academic Ali Baker (2018a: 92), in her role as curator and member of the Unbound Collective in our performances, postulates, 'we wanted to (re)turn the gaze onto the white watcher, research the researcher'. We enact an ethical consciousness and responsibility to each other, grounded in cultural ways of knowing and respect. Our engagement as a collective qualifies shared stories, our voices and our trust for each other, as well as a trust in the knowledge we each bring to the spaces of research, our creativity and performance; we allow ourselves the crafting of ideas, thoughts and methodological engagement with research (Baker et al, 2015; Fine et al, 2008) to centre Indigenous feminism and activism, sovereignty, humanness and refusal. Furthering the crafting and creation of ideas, we allow for difficult conversations that shift us from the margins to the centre (hooks, 2000; Harkin, 2017; Baker, 2018b). Our collective activism positions our ontological, axiological, epistemological and methodological approaches that inform our performances in spaces that, in past proceedings, revealed a sense of invisibility. As bell hooks (2000: xvi) notes, 'living on the edge, we developed a particular way of seeing reality. We looked from both the outside in and the inside out … focused our attention on the centre as well as the margin … we understood both'.

Located within a site where the production of knowledge has done profound harm to Indigenous communities as 'objects' of curiosity and study, engaging in decolonizing and anti-racist educational strategies situates the Unbound Collective and many Indigenous scholars locally, nationally and internationally as both insiders and outsiders (hooks, 2000). Our voices and bodies undertake performances that engage in a process of decolonization as acts of resistance and refusal; this shifts the gaze to make visible the history of oppressive regimes on Aboriginal bodies and lands, and the colonialism that continues to affect our lives (Baker, 2018b). Our voices and our bodies engage decolonization processes in contested and hard spaces that might not necessarily see the historical aspects of our world. We perform the shedding of the colonial skin; we reinterpret the world through each of our own lenses to bring forth new ways of thinking; and we refuse to be denied our right to be who we are. If we are strong as individuals, as a collective we become even stronger and more powerful (Quashie, 2004: 5), a force to be reckoned with. We speak back to the power of the institutions that produced knowledge of and about us (Mohanty, 2003; Fine et al, 2008), and we engage in the politics of refusal (Simpson, 2014).

The Unbound Collective's performances turn the gaze back and refuse to be othered; we flip the master's script (Baker et al, 2015). We take an Indigenous feminist/activist standpoint, and the insertion of key ideas and themes associated with our ontological worldview are employed as a guide towards an Indigenous feminist activist manifesto. We represent and express this through the naming of ourselves:

> [W]e are, Antikirinya/Yankunytjatjara, Mirning, Yidinyiji/Mbabaram and Narungga, we share a legacy of colonial categorization-containment-archivization ... and all that was carried on tall ships across rolling seas ... this intergenerational effect of living under *Aborigines Acts* of the state. We want to share the weight of the colonized burden to lighten this load ... we are sovereign women, we choose to act, speak, look ... give back in critical-performative ... ways we sing, we weave, we project, we disrupt in order to transform we connect to multiple sites of past-present-future and we share this space with you ... with love we are on Kaurna land. (Baker et al, 2015)

The Unbound Collective is morally and ethically connected to ensuring that our research embodies our individual and shared communities and all literacies that come with that. We all tell parts of our story and can't tell it all on our own. This is the disruption and challenge that comes with us arriving, entering, performing and leaving: we leave behind traces of ourselves and the literacies entailed in the message.

I again turn to McKittrick and her insightful words that provide strength she says that the 'Earth is always skin, humanness is always geographical ... writes the land a map that does not follow easily the existing cartographic rules, borders and lives' (2006: ix). 'My skin speaks, My skin hears, My skin feels, My skin breathes. My skin is marked ... My skin pushes the boundaries, My skin searches for my freedom' (Bunda and Blanch 2005, in Blanch, 2009). We engage in quiet sovereignty, that is loud.

Conclusion

To conclude, I have drawn from Wynter, Fanon, McKittrick and Moreton-Robinson to articulate the social construction of the 'human' through how whiteness defines who is and who is not human and how the Indigenous body is viewed within teaching and learning spaces. I have argued that First Nations scholars' embodied literacies are carried into colonial spaces to disrupt Western knowledge production that is silent in naming racialization and makes invisible the knowing of First Nations people to the inner seeing eye, even while First Nations bodies continue to inhabit such harsh and dangerous spaces. I evoke McKittrick's (2021: 33) words that 'the materiality of intellectual inquiry – the ideas we share, the counsel we give each other is an ongoing referential conversation about black humanity ... is a referential conversation that begins from black livingness'. In this context, our First Nations livingness must be recognized and acknowledged within those colonial knowledge-producing spaces. I argue that a decolonial praxis, embedded in an anti-racist framework that articulates the literacy of storying and creative performance, brings to the centre First Nations sovereignty, being and belonging.

Note
[1] *Terra nullius* was the legal concept defined as 'land belonging to no one' that was used by the British government to justify the occupation of Australia.

References

Ahmed, S. (2004) *The Cultural Politics of Emotions*, London: Routledge.

Alexander, J. (2002) 'Remembering this bridge, remembering ourselves: Yearning, memory and desire', in G. Anzaldua and A. Keating (eds), *This Bridge We Call Home: Radical Visions for Transformation*, London: Routledge, pp 81–103.

Baker, A.G. (2018a) 'Sovereign goddess: Looking for Gumillya the Bound and the Unbound', PhD thesis, Flinders University.

Baker, A.G. (2018b) 'Camping in the shadow of the racist texts', *ArtLink*, 38(2): 14–21.

Baker, A.G., Blanch, F.R., Harkin, N. and Tur, S.U. (2015) *Bound and Unbound: Sovereign Acts Act I*, https://www.flinders.edu.au/content/dam/documents/colleges/hass/unbound-act1-catalogue.pdf

Bargallie, D. (2020) *Unmasking the Racial Contract: Indigenous Voices on Racism in the Australian Public Service*, Canberra: Aboriginal Studies Press.

Blanch, F.R. (2009) 'Nunga rappin: Talkin the talk, walkin the walk: Young Nunga males and education', MA thesis, Flinders University.

Blanch, F.R. (2013) 'Encountering the Other: One Indigenous Australian woman's experience of racialisation on a Saturday night', *Gender, Place and Culture: A Journal of Feminist Geography*, 20(2): 253–260.

Blanch, F.R. (2016) 'Teaching Indigenous studies: Considering racialized assemblages and the Indigenous educator's body in tutoring spaces', *International Journal of Critical Indigenous Studies*, 9(1): 49–51.

Blanch, F.R. (2022) 'What is this sovereignty thing? Intimate connection to Country', PhD thesis, Flinders University.

Bunda, T. (2007) 'The sovereign Aboriginal woman', in A. Moreton-Robinson (ed), *Sovereign Subject: Indigenous Sovereign Matters*, Sydney: Allen & Unwin, pp 75–85.

Bunda, T. and Phillips, G. (2018) *Research through, with and as Storying*, Abingdon: Routledge.

Byrd, J. (2011) *Transit of Empire: Indigenous Critique of Colonialism*, Minneapolis: University of Minnesota Press.

Campt, T.M. (2019) 'The loophole of retreat: An invitation', *e-flux Journal*, 105.

Carby, H. (2019) *Imperial Intimacies: A Tale of Two Islands*, New York: Verso.

Fanon, F. (2008) *Black Skin, White Masks*, rev edn, New York: Grove Press.

Fine, M., Tuck, E. and Zeller-Berkman, S. (2008) 'Do you believe in Geneva?', in N.K. Denzin, Y.S. Lincoln and L.T. Smith (eds), *Handbook of Critical Indigenous Methodologies*, Thousand Oaks: SAGE, pp 157–80.

Harkin, N. (2017) 'I weave back to your archival-poetics for the record', PhD exegesis, University of South Australia.

hooks, b. (1987) *Ain't I a Woman: Black Women and Feminism*, London: Pluto Press.

hooks, b. (2000) *Feminist Theory: From Margin to Centre*, 2nd edn, Boston: South End Press.

Ladson-Billings, G (1998) 'Just what is critical race theory and what's it doing in a nice field like education?', *International Journal of Qualitative Studies in Education*, 11(1): 7–24.

McKittrick, K. (2006) *Demonic Grounds: Black Women and the Cartographies of Struggle*, Minneapolis: University of Minnesota Press.

McKittrick, K. (2021) *Dear Science and Other Stories*, Durham, NC: Duke University Press.

McLaren, P. (2011) 'Towards a decolonizing epistemology', in E. Malewski and N. Jaramillo (eds), *Epistemologies of Ignorance in Education*, New York: Information Age, pp vii–xvii.

Minh-ha, T. (1989) *Woman, Native, Other: Writing Postcoloniality and Feminism*, Bloomington: Indiana University Press.

Miranda, D. (2002) 'What's wrong with a little fantasy? Storytelling from the (still) ivory tower', in G. Anzaldua and A. Keating (eds), *This Bridge We Call Home*, New York: Routledge, pp 192–201.

Mohanty, C.T. (2003) *Feminism Without Borders: Decolonizing Theory, Practicing Solidarity*, Durham, NC: Duke University Press.

Moreton-Robinson, A. (2007) *Sovereign Subjects: Indigenous Sovereignty Matters*, New York: Routledge.

Moreton-Robinson, A. (2013) 'Towards an Australian Indigenous women's standpoint theory: A methodological tool', *Australian Feminist Studies*, 28(78): 331–47.

Moreton-Robinson, A. (2015) *The White Possessive: Property, Power, and Indigenous Sovereignty*, Minneapolis: University of Minnesota Press.

Morrison, T. (1990) 'The site of memory', in R. Ferguson, M. Gever, T. Minh-ha and C. West (eds), *Out There: Marginalization and Contemporary Cultures*, Cambridge, MA: MIT Press, pp 299–324.

Morrison, T. (1993) *Playing in the Dark: Whiteness and the Literary Imagination*, Cambridge, MA: Harvard University Press.

Phillips, G.L. and Bunda, T. (2018) *Research Through, With and as Storying*, London: Routledge.

Quashie, K. (2004) *Black Women, Identity and Cultural Theory: (Un)Becoming the Subject*, New Brunswick: Rutgers University Press.

Rifkin, M. (2011) 'The erotics of sovereignty', in Q.-L. Driskill, C. Finley, B.J. Gilley and S.L. Morgensen (eds), *Queer Indigenous Studies: Critical Interventions in Theory, Politics and Literature*, Tucson: University of Arizona Press, pp 172–89.

Sefa Dei, G. and McDermott, M. (eds) (2013) *Politics of Antiracism Education in Search of Strategies for Transforming Learning*, Dordrecht: Springer.

Simpson, A. (2014) *Mohawk Interruptus: Political Life Across Borders of Settler States*, Durham, NC: Duke University Press.

Tindale, N. and Birdsell, J. (1941) 'Results of the Harvard–Adelaide Universities Anthropological Expedition, 1938–39', *Records of South Australian Museum*, 7: 1–9.

Vosters, H. (2019) *Unbecoming Nationalism: From Commemoration to Redress in Canada*, Winnipeg: University of Manitoba Press.

Watego, C. (2021) *Another Day in the Colony*, Brisbane: University of Queensland Press.

Worby, G., Tur, S.U. and Blanch, F. (2014) 'Writing forward, writing back, writing Black: Working process and work-in-process', *Journal of the Association for the Study of Australian Literature*, 14(3): 1–14.

Wynter, S. (2006) 'On how we mistook the map for the territory, and re-imprisoned ourselves in our unbearable wrongness of being, of deserter: Black studies toward the human project', in L.R. Gordon and J.A. Gordon (eds), *Not Only the Master's Tools: African-American Studies in Theory and Practice*, New York: Routledge, pp 107–69.

Wynter, S. and McKittrick, K. (2015) 'Unparalleled catastrophe for our species? Or, to give humanness a different future: Conversations', in K. McKittrick (ed), *Sylvia Wynter: On Being Human as Praxis*, Durham, NC: Duke University Press, pp 9–89.

7

Racially Literate Teacher Education: (Im)possibilities for Disrupting the Racial Silence

Susan Whatman and Juliana Mohok McLaughlin

Introduction

We decided to present this chapter as a conversation between us, as non-Indigenous educators with 20 years of teaching critical Indigenous studies within university programmes. Most of this conversation is derived from a research yarn conducted at the beginning of 2023 between us and the editors of this book. While yarning is much more than a research method, it has increased in popularity and recognition as a qualitative method thanks to works by Martin (2008), Bessarab and Ng'andu (2010) and Walker et al (2013).

We first met as colleagues at the Oodgeroo Unit, an academic support centre for Aboriginal and Torres Strait Islander (First Nations) students at the Queensland University of Technology in Meanjin (Brisbane), Australia in 2004. Susan (Sue) Whatman (she/her) is a non-Indigenous woman with Welsh, Scottish, Irish and English ancestry, living and working on Kombumerri People's land on the Yugambeh nation (Gold Coast) in Australia. Juliana (Julie) McLaughlin (she/her) is from Manus Island in Papua New Guinea, currently living and working on the lands of the Turrbal and Yuggera peoples of Meanjin (Brisbane North). We employ a four-step racial and cultural positionality framework elaborated by H. Richard Milner (2007), which serves to model a process of racial literacy praxis, underscored by tenets of critical race theory (CRT). This four-step racial and cultural positionality framework provides some limits to the many hundreds of examples we could share from decades of teaching critical Indigenous studies in university programs, mostly in teaching, arts and health education.

Figure 7.1: Four stages of developing racial and cultural positionality: racial literacy praxis in and for teacher education

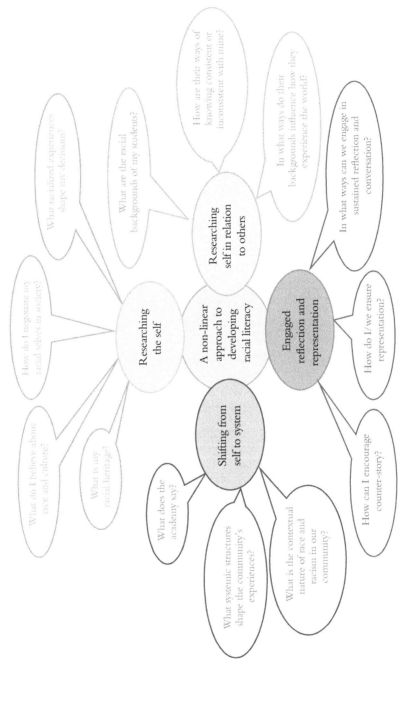

Source: Adapted from Milner (2007: 395–7)

First, Milner's (2007: 395–7) non-linear framework acknowledges the breakthrough work of Gloria Ladson-Billings and William Tate (1995) in applying critical race theory (CRT) to education. Milner concurs with Adrienne Dixson (2006) that teacher education, together with the curriculum, policies and texts it comprises, operates on the assumption that most teachers are white. In taking up Derrick Bell's (1980) explanation of interest-convergence, this means that in teacher education, 'the interests of white teachers take precedence over teachers of color' (Milner, 2007: 394). Milner articulates a four step, non-linear process for developing racial and cultural positionality, primarily as a tool for researchers. He argues that developing researcher positionality negates the unhelpful binary of 'who' should research 'whom' to focus more strategically on developing 'deeper racial and cultural knowledge about themselves' (Milner, 2007: 388) in order to engage with systemic racism in any given setting.

In guiding teachers and students through a series of reflective and dialogic tasks from cultural ignorance to anti-racism, we elaborate by inserting prompting questions that provoke students to critically reflect at each of the four-step cultural and racial positionality framework. Based on our combined pedagogical experiences, we propose that this non-linear framework can shape what Bargallie et al (2023: 1) describe as 'critical, anti-racist pedagogical praxis', a praxis for developing racial literacy in the midst of decolonizing higher education (McLaughlin and Whatman, 2011: 370) (see Figure 7.1).

Researching the self

In this phase of developing racial literacy, teachers and students are required to come to know, or to research, the self (Milner, 2007: 395). This is a step for both Indigenous and non-Indigenous people as Milner (2007: 395), invoking Cornel West (1993), explains that one cannot emancipate others if one has not emancipated oneself. Researching the self enables unconscious, hidden or unanticipated matters in education to come to the fore and provides a natural and controllable starting point for the development of racial literacy.

In this conversation thread, we reflected upon how it was that we became aware of our identity as non-Indigenous educators in relation to Indigenous colleagues and students, and non-Indigenous students and colleagues through our work in the Oodgeroo Unit.

SW: I came to know what it means to be a settler-colonizer through working in the Aboriginal and Torres Strait Islander (Indigenous) student centre at our university. I was employed to provide academic, personal and cultural support to Indigenous students enrolled at our university and to teach into the Indigenous studies minor in the arts and education degrees.

I wrote about this growing awareness of my settler-colonizer self in the *Springer Encyclopedia of Teacher Education* mainly because I felt that the articulation of this evolving awareness is essential for all teachers and should form a core feature of your teaching philosophy (Whatman, 2020). It took me several years of acknowledging Country, the Traditional Owners of Meanjin (Brisbane), in my work to wonder whose Country I had been born onto and grew up upon. It was Minjungbal, inside what settler-colonizers call the Tweed Valley in Northern New South Wales.

JMM: I brought a postcolonial stance to my work in the same university centre, having completed a postcolonial investigation into the practices of the Australian/Papua New Guinean secondary school students' project for my PhD (McLaughlin, 2002). I thought I had a much better understanding of racism than most academics until I joined Indigenous colleagues at the centre. Working with Indigenous people in their struggle for recognition, for sovereignty, for human rights, for the right to insert what Karen Martin (2008) describes as their ways of knowing, being and doing into higher education, showed me that even as an academic/teacher of colour, there was much more for me to learn regarding how to do this work, to become adept at decolonizing education.

SW: You and I have written before (McLaughlin and Whatman, 2011) that this decolonizing project is both political and deeply personal. Indigenous colleagues who take up the challenge of decolonizing university programmes are acutely aware that they must not only teach but live these contestations. It is our job as non-Indigenous educators to show students and other non-Indigenous academics their role in this. It is also interesting how the language around what we do changes with greater awareness, internationally, of each other's struggles and local theorizations about decolonizing. Racial literacy was never a concept we employed, but we have started to see it being used more frequently in critical Indigenous studies (cf McDonald, 2003; Hart, 2005; Vass, 2015).

JMM: Yes, those of us involved in teaching Indigenous studies are aware of racial literacy, but it's not the label used here in Australia. It is what individual academics do when they have some form of critical frameworks but, as far as I can remember, it is not something that is valued as much here. It is more accidental that individual scholars will bring understandings of racial literacy to their teaching spaces, maybe acquired from their own undergraduate or master's education. There was only one person in Australia who taught anything to me in my own postgraduate studies that could have related to racial literacy and that was Anne Hickling-Hudson (2011), who was my PhD supervisor. Teaching racial literacy is not something that gels within the Australian higher education context. It takes scholars who seem to have in fact been impacted by race who would talk about that stuff in their conversations, and at the same time that informed their scholarship in terms of research and publishing, and eventually that filters into the classroom settings. It is not something that is common, or easily fits within the teaching and learning spaces in university.

SW: I think the reason I've heard of it is from working in an Indigenous education unit, where people articulated and spoke about race all the time. My colleagues in the unit also introduced me to Maya Angelou, Frantz Fanon, bell hooks, Lisa Delpit and Gloria Ladson-Billings. Whereas if I had been working in a school of education as I am now, I wouldn't have had it as much, and I certainly wouldn't have seen it in the teaching practices of my colleagues. I'm remembering me as an undergraduate, as I also studied with Anne Hickling-Hudson, and she was the only lecturer I ever had in my undergraduate preparation who did bring in postcolonial theory and talked about race. She talked about racism against Indigenous Australians and that was the only time in my experience as someone studying to be a teacher that I had anybody introduce it.

JMM: We have Indigenous colleagues who would ensure there's theorization about race and anti-racism within their theoretical frameworks embedded in the work they do. We also have scholars from other parts of the world, particularly scholars of colour like Anne, scholars from former colonized places and non-Indigenous Australians who resonate with race and racism in Australian history. Otherwise, you don't have everyone talking about race issues, or how race and racism is applied in what they do in terms of the health services that's offered, the education system, the business sector or whichever discipline.

SW: One of the standout exercises for researching the self was in our compulsory Indigenous studies course for undergraduate (or preservice) teachers. We asked them to name their ancestors, and say where they were born and what racial identity they would identify with. This was a thorough exercise – first, middle and last names, family names before marriage, year of birth, places of birth, where they got married. Detailed family tree stuff. The number of 18- to 20-year-olds who had no idea what their grandmother's family name was, or where they came from, was mind-blowing. Conversely, students who would otherwise not engage with racially identifying as anything other than 'Australian' would start to reveal what they might call their cultural heritage. They found this subject the only one where they had permission to express an identity that wasn't white Australian. This by itself was no guarantee of developing racial literacy, but it first opened up students' minds to the existence of multiple racial identities existing within schooling and, second, made them realize that this could be important for what and how we all learn. I actually did this activity recently with a group of researchers in health and physical education (HPE) at an international conference workshop for the same reason – to illuminate the racial resources we have in HPE if we only take the time to put them in the centre and to reflect together on how these can and should shape what we do in our field.

To summarize this phase, we have illustrated in this conversation how 'researching the self' prompted self-awareness as a starting point for racial literacy. This stage interrogated our previously held knowledge, our vision of support for Indigenous students at our university and our understandings of social justice. Indigenous and scholars of colour, with knowledge and experiences of race and racism as a form of colonial power and its persisting legacies through education and cultural superiority, remain a minority in the Australian education system. Our engagement with these knowledges and experiences neutralized our sense of knowing and inspired us to engage transformative learning opportunities for Australian students to recognize and challenge the status quo.

Researching self in relation to others

The second step towards developing racial and cultural positioning is to research the self in relation to others (Milner, 2007: 395). This means to consider the communities to which your students belong and your own community. This step requires teachers to consider the 'multiple roles, identities and positions' that we bring to the classroom and to identify situations in which teachers' interests align or conflict with those of students as well as community interests (Milner, 2007: 395). It is perhaps the first time teachers become aware that their ways of 'knowing, being and doing' (Martin,

2008) are not universal, and are perhaps vastly different from the onto-epistemologies and axiologies of others (Whatman and McLaughlin, 2024).

SW: Yes. I would say less now than when we taught Indigenous studies at QUT [Queensland University of Technology]. That was because of the design of the courses was to do that work of people pulling out themselves in relation to others and systems – that was the deliberate pedagogical design of the course. So it made people reflect on individual things and make them pull them out and look at them, and you then had to have the ability to help them understand that in the moment. Because you never knew what people were going to come out with. One example that comes to mind was that I had this woman ... we were talking about public spaces, and we were talking about the naming of the streets around Brisbane being called Boundary Street, why they got their name and that sort of thing. And the history of the laws around being in public are all based around laws of managing who can be in a public space and who's made to feel safe in a public space ... and this middle-aged woman in the class said, "Yeah, but those laws are there for all of us. I wouldn't feel safe if I saw a bunch of people drinking in the park." Then I went, "who said anything about drinking in the park?" And she said, "Oh, that just popped out of my brain." I said, "Yeah it's in your brain, isn't it?" She said, "It just popped up. I don't even know where that came from." She's flustered. Yeah, this is it, this is what's in your brain, this is what's actually defining how you relate to people. We weren't talking about drinking in the park but that's where your brain ran to, that's where your mind ran to. Even then in that moment ... I'm being more direct here than when I was with her. You've got to be able to help them to hang on to that moment of realization in what could otherwise turn into a really defensive and a really humiliating moment as well, and say, "Well what have we all learned from that?" and attend to this learning moment for everybody.

SW: It comes back to the politics Julie and I talked about before. I think a lot of people would say standpoint theory has everything I need to be able to teach, and you can stand on that. But, it's like saying that you don't need to engage with anyone else's ideas, and I think that fundamental intention of being an educator or even being in higher education is you can say, no, my culture prepared me for everything I need to know to teach you. But then once you engage with other people's ideas like you've got to do it.

In summary, this reflection upon teaching incidents indicates critical pedagogical moments when students unlearn the knowledge they bring with them into our teaching spaces. Cultural interface as a site for tension, resistance and contradictions (Nakata, 2007) is evident when students unconsciously draw on societal norms and perceptions of the world around them. For non-Indigenous Australian students, recognition of artefacts around them – for example, names of places – is a powerful learning resource in that instant juxtaposition of Indigenous presence. The realization of other ontologies and axiologies specifically entrenched in the physicality of place and space is a powerful learning moment, allowing students to recognize other perspectives in contesting Australia's colonial history, dispossession of Aboriginal lands and racial supremacy of the colonial enterprise.

Unpacking racial and cultural positionality in relation to other knowledges and perspectives does not imply that non-Indigenous students agree with the presence of Indigenous standpoints and knowledge systems; however, the experiences of unpacking previously held knowledges of others motivate students to critique their own positionalities and open up opportunities to learn. 'It is ... comforting ... for non-Indigenous people to see the realization and acknowledgement of our 'differences' as being the destination of our critical repositioning ... rather than the starting point of a lifelong series of new, uneasy realizations within every personal, social, professional and political interface/context' (Phillips and Whatman, 2007: 4).

Engaged reflection and representation

Engaged reflection and representation (step three of developing racial and cultural positionality) requires teachers and students to engage in reflection together, to think through what happens in learning and teaching, schooling and education more broadly by placing race and culture at the centre (Milner, 2007: 396). Scholars such as Ladson-Billings (1998, 1999), Ladson Billings and Tate (1995) and Solorzano and Yosso (2001) have described this as engaging in narrative and counter-narrative and dealing with the tensions that arise in situ. We have drawn connections before (cf McLaughlin and Whatman, 2011) between this step and what Torres Strait Islander Professor Martin Nakata (2007) has theorized as the cultural interface, a place of agency and tension where Indigenous and non-Indigenous knowledges interface, conflict and/or align.

SW: I have taught subjects in the Arts Faculty (humanities), in the Health Faculty, and in education and the way you taught racial literacy was discipline-specific. It did differ a lot between how you introduce the idea of racism. In education it was so 'gently, gently, let's not upset anybody' kind of approach in education. Whereas in the Arts Faculty, in the humanities Australian studies strand, the students who were in that degree were already far more politically aware and activist. They were quite happy to have the kinds of open conversations that you would have about racism. ... They had a better 'starting' racial literacy already than the students did in the Education Faculty. So, all your work with teaching in education, which is still how I do it now in my health and physical education subjects, is you're trying to *not* let them enact their white privilege umbrella straight away, to not to reject what you're going to tell them. So, the way that you bring their awareness of race and as raced educators into their professional awareness is where it is different. It's because of the types of people who choose to be teachers, and who all the other teacher lecturers are who are working alongside you. You do it differently because of the cloak of white privilege they have.

JMM: So, we also have students coming from all disciplines. It's only when they can find an elective in their programme or if they have spaces to include a minor, then they can invest to do it in Indigenous studies or Indigenous knowledges – that's what we call it. So, race theories run through the units that we teach in the Indigenous knowledges minor. The thing that makes our life a lot easier is that the students want to be there. And because of that, our numbers are small; it's because the students elect to study Indigenous studies. So we don't have the same experience of resistance to the kinds of knowledge that we engage them in. Therefore, we can unpack their sense of privilege, we can look at critical race theory and its origins. And we get students to analyse what they need from an Indigenous perspective, or whatever it could be. What we try to do here is to link *the unpacking of the systems of privilege* with recognizing that our work on a *professional basis*, after they graduate from university, *is racialized*, whether it's health services, whether it's law and justice, whether it's education, or media and communication. And so, in that case, we don't hold back because we already have a clientele that's willing to engage.

SW: And it is not typical to have race theory running across all courses. So, how do you do it?

JMM: I teach *with* Indigenous colleagues. I know I'm not Indigenous and therefore I don't have that lived experience to teach from. I cannot make the connection to the direct impact of colonization in this country from my lived experience as a scholar from Papua New Guinea (McLaughlin and Hickling-Hudson, 2005). What I find useful in terms of racial literacy and using critical race framework is that it allows for a non-Indigenous person to be able to see the contradictions, the impacts of colonization and to critically reflect on Indigenous people's lived experiences and the legacies of colonization. So therefore, as a non-Indigenous Australian, I have an appreciation for what a theoretical framework can do to allow students to understand. We can look at experiences and implications for Indigenous and non-Indigenous people. It is too easy to say, 'Oh, that's just an incident that happened.' Using critical race theory, we can trace it back, and we begin to understand the underlying ideologies that led to that 'incident' and realize it is not accidental.

SW: Thinking of an example from our Indigenous studies class with preservice teachers, I want to share the 'gently, gently' approach we took with preservice teachers in engaged reflection and representation, which provided the counter-narrative to something they thought they knew something about: the Stolen Generations (HREOC, 1997). Most white Australian students accepted the lie that Indigenous children were removed from their parents and communities 'for their own good'. There was nothing in teacher education that disrupted the colonial narrative of white benevolence (Moreton-Robinson, 2004) to counter this narrative with what it was: genocide. The preservice teachers were asked to read or watch *Rabbit Proof Fence* (Pilkington, 2002) before a particular class about halfway through the semester. Then we watched the ABC's *Blackout* documentary *Best Kept Secret*, which was ostensibly about Archie Roach's life. And then we watched and listened to his song 'Took the Children Away'. I would start that workshop by putting a tissue box at the front of my desk, closer to the students, and invite anyone who needed them to come and grab some. I would tell them that I would need the tissues as well, as no matter how many times I have watched the documentary or listened to the lyrics of the song, I would cry too. Maybe my memories of which class said what are a bit mixed together now, but invariably it would range from unabated tears combined with 'I never knew' to outrage: 'How dare you make us cry in class – it's unprofessional!' So, my next question would be something like, 'Is it unprofessional to cry as a teacher? Why? Should we never, ever teach or talk about things that are terrible? Or feel emotion?' Archie asked us just 'to feel' in the documentary – that's all he wanted, for white Australians to feel something about what had happened and continues to happen to Indigenous children and their families (Reisz and Cleaver, 1991). It provided what Phillips (2012: 2) calls the 'relational dimensions of Indigenous people's experiences in Australian society that stem from, but are not consigned to, the past'.

JMM: I recall a time when we were walking through the Queen Street Mall and a former student came up to us. She said, "Julie, do you remember me? I was in your Indigenous studies class." We got talking about what she had been doing since graduating, which had been about five years earlier, and whether she was still teaching. She said she stopped teaching – she realized it wasn't for her. And that she couldn't really remember much of her teaching degree. But she said, "I will never, ever forget what we learned in your class. It is the only class I can remember. It will stay with me for the rest of my life." And I thought, yes. We don't know what kind of an impact we will have when our students leave us at the end of the semester, or the degree, but we do know that laying the foundation for racial literacy allows our students to continue engaging in reflection and developing over time, well into the future.

To summarize this phase of the cultural and racial positionality, we indicated teacher educators' knowledge of student cohorts and their ability to couch racial literacy in teaching and learning. Teacher acceptance of student assumed knowledge of Indigenous Australia is central in their learning contexts, so during study, students were exposed to key concepts that interrogated how this knowledge was learnt and the ideologies that endorsed it in the first place. Acknowledgement of colonial discourses against a broader CRT framework allowed the students to interrogate the invisibility of white privilege and accept ownership of mitigating white privilege in both personal and professional capacities.

Our experiences also identified the receptiveness of these phases by students from diverse disciplines – for example, the preparedness to engage by humanities students, the willingness of multidisciplinary students in the Indigenous knowledges minor, or the curiosity of students taking 'one-off' electives in Indigenous studies. A driver of their engagement in these units was the professional expectations through established standards for their various degrees – for example, professional standards for graduate teachers (AITSL, 2023) – and how university education is meant to prepare students for the real world of racism. The students brought different aspirations to this knowledge, or 'coming to know', from the various disciplines including the humanities, differentiating opportunities to learn and knowledge development in contrast to vocational training. This phase of engaged reflection has a lifelong impact, particularly when graduates later decide to change professions, taking the values cultivated in the critical Indigenous studies classroom with them.

Shifting from self to system

This fourth, non-linear phase is all about grounding personal, expanded consciousness in relation to 'historic, political, social, economic, racial, and cultural, realities on a broader scale' (Milner, 2007: 397). It means moving away from personal reflection, 'a-ha' moments and the like to consider systemic issues. CRT assists here with dispelling the myth that racism equates with individual, irrational acts. In our teaching, we might call this decolonizing, or critical pedagogies. In Australia, we have not always employed the language of CRT or racial literacy, but it functions in similar ways. Milner (2007) stresses that although this may seem like a penultimate phase, students move back and forth between understanding themselves and thinking systemically – it is not a lockstep sequence. And nor do students (or teachers, or academic colleagues) who begin to think systemically stay there – regression often happens.

SW: We could have been working within the unit with Indigenous colleagues and talking about standpoint and also developing racial literacy from students from that standpoint, and not calling it critical race theory and not tagging into that bigger international body of literature. But that's what you've done by bringing your lived experiences as a Black scholar, as a postcolonial scholar, inside that Indigenous education space. You've said, 'Look at all of these people who have been developing tools' that help you further this agenda and develop racial literacy. And CRT doesn't fight against an Indigenous standpoint, it doesn't work against an Indigenous standpoint. CRT just gives you more tools and gives you more of a language around how you're describing this (for example, systemic racism) and helping people to see all those things as social, political, cultural arrangements that lead to supposedly random racist incidents. I think that's what has been your giant contribution to this field – even in Australia, which is reluctant to embrace CRT, to say, 'Look, bring it in, look at it, take it, work with it.' Use what you want out of it, and it helps you achieve the same objective.

JMM: Teaching critical Indigenous studies is political. It's never easy. This is how we as non-Indigenous educators can engage with Indigenous knowledges and communities. It is a whole-of-community process of engagement with Indigenous Australia. When you're trying to challenge your own way of knowing Indigenous Australia, it is a very emotional journey. It is a very political form of engagement. And therefore you can … like we do now in Indigenous studies, you have students who would like to teach critically. But, I would say, not everybody. A lot of them will say to us, why didn't we know about this? So, in this case, what I find is good for critical race frameworks is that when you start to use language that is not confronting and makes sense to them, language that is globally applicable and is delivered in an approachable and culturally safe way, students do engage. We are all here because we are part of the complex layers and web of the colonial project. So, without this acknowledgement, we fall onto the default position of feeling guilty about the atrocities of the colonial past. But I found that, with CRT and its potential for transformative learning, we accept and realize that this (the colonial project) is a global phenomenon, its translation and impact in Australia are unique. So, we can become aware through global movements about Black Lives Matter, but then start to think, what about Black deaths in custody in Australia? Tenets of CRT help students to research and understand that statements such as 'we have no experience of slavery' in Australia, as another example, are simply not true.

As our yarn progressed, Sue had cause to reflect on the way she was currently teaching – in HPE curriculum and pedagogy in a mainstream education faculty. In response to a question about why she kept referring to examples from past teaching, Bargallie put it to Sue that there was no reason why critical literacy couldn't be the point of HPE.

SW: It's because I'm not putting those pedagogical moments into my weekly content, each week, because I've got this disciplinary overlay. 'Here are the teacher professional attributes you have to reach in bah blah blah', and they don't let me put in all of the teacher attributes around Indigenous studies. This is one of my real bugbears with the university. If you say that you want to bring in Indigenous knowledges – whether it be through readings, through deliberate content through topics – but then, on the course profile system you say that you're a non-Indigenous person delivering it, then they say, 'No, you're not delivering Indigenous perspectives.' Which is true. I am non-Indigenous, but I want to deliver Indigenous content and knowledges. And, I think that you could absolutely say that race and racism aren't one of the options, not one of the attributes that my professional accreditation bodies are asking me to say that I'm delivering in HPE. They're asking me, 'Oh, do you deliver valuing and appreciating Indigenous cultures?' And then if I say I am, they'll say, 'Are you Indigenous?' No, I'm not. Okay, you can't be valuing Indigenous histories and cultures because you're not Indigenous again. Well, what if I'm bringing in all of these opportunities to learn from other people through materials? So, it's a weird conceptualization of what Indigenous knowledge is, and I think the university's bottom line is it's Indigenous perspectives, and if you're not Indigenous then you're not putting in an Indigenous perspective. I think that's the framing of it.

JMM: I think because Aboriginal content … what needs to be understood is that race is not only an Indigenous issue *per se*. Because race, as far as I'm concerned, is everybody's business. Racism is embedded in all structures. Because even teaching Indigenous knowledge is racialized, because if you're not Indigenous, how can you teach Indigenous studies … race and racism. It's weird.

SW: They like us to keep everything in its disciplinary lane, so it's reinforcing that hegemonic right of white people to decide what's in the lane and what's not in the lane. That is part of the problem of disrupting it. And, I'd have to say I … I'm not doing it anywhere near as well. And I'm not because I'm working alone. I'm not working in a team of Black scholars anymore daily, and part of working with a team of Black scholars in that space is where you can create opportunities for learning that I can't do by myself. Well, I try to do some of it by myself, but I can't do what I used to be able to do when I taught with you and our colleagues in the Oodgeroo Unit.

Our conversation for stage four of developing cultural and racial literacy positionality alerts us to the power dynamics that authorize what *can* be taught and how this *is* taught in higher education in Australia. Our engagement through working with Aboriginal and Torres Strait Islander staff and students in student support, teaching and research encouraged and motivated us to explore theoretical frameworks that enabled us as non-Indigenous academics to decolonize curriculum and pedagogies (McLaughlin and Whatman, 2007). Much of this work was located within institutional directives and their commitments to reconciliation between Indigenous and non-Indigenous Australians, based on social justice agenda. To an extent, decolonizing curricula and pedagogies within institutional and professional regulatory bodies is messy, as priorities may not necessarily gel with Indigenous ways of knowing, doing and being.

Conclusion

Our conversation in this chapter has attempted to illustrate our adaptation of CRT into critical Indigenous studies in Australian higher education, particularly teacher education, as non-Indigenous educators. Our engagement with and deployment of key concepts of CRT, modelled through the four stages of developing racial and cultural positionality (see Figure 7.1) enabled us to unpack our own positionalities while concurrently moving our students through stages of emerging racial self-awareness and positionality, allowing learning to transpire in a personalized way.

CRT in Australia has not enjoyed the same uptake in the academy as theory about race and racism in Australia. It is often seen as a foreign theory that applies to foreign contexts, but we disagree. This is about developing tools to 'talk productively about racism' (Bargallie et al, 2023: 15). As racial literacy as a concept grows, and to counter the misapplication of the concept, we support its grounding within critical Indigenous studies as a powerful way to 'revitalize a critical, anti-racist pedagogical praxis' (Bargallie et al, 2023: 15). We believe from our many years of praxis that the tenets of CRT sit comfortably within critical Indigenous studies, organized by a decolonizing imperative driven by Indigenous scholars. Indigenous theories such as the cultural interface (Nakata, 2002, 2007) and Indigenous women's standpoint theory (Moreton-Robinson, 2013) have revealed how Indigenous knowledges and perspectives are in constant contestation with dominant Eurocentric knowledge systems, but are also agentic.

As non-Indigenous educators, our commitment to decolonizing education (McLaughlin and Whatman, 2011), to developing racial literacy through critical Indigenous studies and to sharing our pedagogical praxis (Whatman and McLaughlin, 2024) remains even though we have moved out of the Oodgeroo Unit, as a service, teaching and research centre for Aboriginal and Torres Strait Islander students at university. Now working in health and physical education, and creative industries, we know we must take the natural opportunities that arise to decolonize, to widen the 'crack in the pavement' (McLaughlin, 2013: 249) through our political and moral praxis. And we know that we continue to work on ourselves, as settler-colonizers who continue to benefit from the dispossession of Australia from its rightful owners.

References

AITSL (Australian Institute for Teaching and School Leadership) (2023) *Australian Professional Standards for Teachers: Graduate Career Stage*, Sydney: AITSL, https://www.aitsl.edu.au/standards/graduate

Bargallie, D., Fernando, N. and Lentin, A. (2023) 'Breaking the racial silence: Putting racial literacy to work in Australia', *Ethnic and Racial Studies*. DOI: 10.1080/01419870.2023.2206470

Bell, D. (1980) 'Brown versus Board of Education and the interest-convergence dilemma', *Harvard Law Review*, 93: 518–33.

Bessarab, D. and Ng'andu, B. (2010) 'Yarning about yarning as a legitimate method in Indigenous research', *International Journal in Critical Indigenous Studies*, 3(1): 37–50.

Dixson, A.D. (2006) 'What's race got to do with it? Race, racial identity development, and teacher preparation', in H.R. Milner and E.W. Ross (eds), *Race, Ethnicity, and Education: The Influences of Racial and Ethnic Identity in Education*, Westport: Greenwood Press, pp 19–36.

Hart, V. (2005) 'Teaching Black and teaching back', *Social Alternatives*, 22(3): 12–15.

Hickling-Hudson, A. (2011) 'Teaching to disrupt preconceptions: Education for social justice in the imperial aftermath', *Compare*, 41(4): 453–65.

HREOC (Human Rights and Equal Opportunity Commission) (1997) *Bringing Them Home: National Inquiry into the Separation of Aboriginal and Torres Strait Islander Children from Their Families*, Canberra: Australian Government.

Ladson-Billings, G. (1998) 'Just what is critical race theory and what's it doing in a nice field like education?', *Qualitative Studies in Education*, 11(1): 7–24.

Ladson-Billings, G. (1999) 'Preparing teachers for diverse student populations: A critical race theory perspective', *Review of Research in Education*, 24: 211–47.

Ladson-Billings, G. and Tate, W. (1995) 'Toward a critical race theory of education', *Teachers College Record*, 97(1): 47–67.

Martin, K. (2008) *Please Knock Before You Enter: Aboriginal Regulation of Outsiders and the Implications for Researchers*, Brisbane: PostPressed.

McDonald, H. (2003) 'Exploring possibilities through critical race theory: Exemplary pedagogical practices for Indigenous students', paper presented at the joint NZARE/AARE Conference, Auckland, NZ, http://www.aare.edu.au/03pap/mcd03504.pdf

McLaughlin, J. (2002) 'The outcomes of the Australian/Papua New Guinean secondary school students' project: An analysis from a postcolonial perspective', PhD thesis, Queensland University of Technology.

McLaughlin, J. (2013) '"Crack in the pavement": Pedagogy as political and moral practice for educating culturally competent professionals', *International Education Journal*, 12(1): 249–65.

McLaughlin, J. and Hickling-Hudson, A. (2005) 'Beyond dependency theory: A postcolonial perspective on educating Papua New Guinea students in Australian high schools', *Asia Pacific Journal of Education*, 25(2): 193–208.

McLaughlin, J. and Whatman, S. (2007) 'Embedding Indigenous perspectives in university teaching and learning: Lessons learnt and possibilities of reforming/decolonising curriculum', in *Proceedings 4th International Conference on Indigenous Education: Asia/ Pacific*, Vancouver, https://eprints.qut.edu.au/10350/1/10350.pdf

McLaughlin, J. and Whatman, S. (2011) 'The potential of critical race theory in decolonizing university curricula', *Asia Pacific Journal of Education*, 31(4): 365–77.

Milner, H.R. (2007) 'Race, cultural, and researcher positionality: Working through dangers seen, unseen and unforeseen', *Educational Researcher*, 36(7): 388–400.

Moreton-Robinson, A. (2004) 'How white possession moves: After the word', in T. Lea, E. Kowal and G. Cowlishaw (eds), *Moving Anthropology: Critical Indigenous Studies*, Darwin: Charles Darwin University Press, pp 219–32.

Moreton-Robinson, A. (2013) 'Towards an Australian Indigenous women's standpoint theory: A methodological tool', *Australian Feminist Studies*, 28(78): 331–47.

Nakata, M. (2002) 'Indigenous knowledge and the cultural interface: Underlying issues at the intersection of knowledge and information systems', *IFLA Journal*, 28(5–6): 281–91.

Nakata, M. (2007) *Disciplining the Savages, or Savaging the Disciplines?*, Canberra: Aboriginal Studies Press.

Phillips, J. (2012) 'Indigenous knowledge perspectives: Making space in the Australian centre', in J. Phillips and J. Lampert (eds), *Introductory Indigenous Studies in Education*, 2nd edn, Sydney: Pearson, pp 9–25.

Phillips, D.J. and Whatman, S. (2007) 'Decolonising preservice teacher education: Reform at many cultural interfaces', in *Proceedings: The World of Educational Quality. 2007 AERA Annual Meeting*, Chicago.

Pilkington, D. (2002) *Rabbit-Proof Fence*, London: Hyperion.

Reisz, R. and Cleaver, L. (1991) *Best Kept Secret – Archie Roach*, Sydney: ABC, www.youtube.com/watch?v=OpL1R1U1JFo&t=15s

Solorzano, D.G. and Yosso, T.J. (2001) 'From racial stereotyping and deficit discourse toward a critical race theory in teacher education', *Multicultural Education*, 9: 2–8.

Vass, G. (2015) 'Putting critical race theory to work in Australian education research: "We are with the garden hose here"', *Australian Educational Researcher*, 42: 371–94.

Walker, M., Fredericks, B., Mills, K. and Anderson, D. (2013) '"Yarning" as a method for community-based health research with Indigenous women: The Indigenous Women's Wellness Research Program', *Health Care for Women International*, 35(10): 1216–26.

West, C. (1993) *Race Matters*, New York: Vintage Books.

Whatman, S.L. (2020) 'Disruption and understanding in professional teaching contexts', in M.A. Peters (ed), *Encyclopedia of Teacher Education*, Singapore: Springer, pp 509–515.

Whatman, S. and McLaughlin, J. (2024) 'Indigenist research practices to support Indigenous pre-service teaching praxis', in S. Whatman, J. Wilkinson, M. Kaukko, G. Warvik Vedeler, L.E. Blue and K.E. Reimer (eds), *Researching Practices Within and Across Diverse Educational Sites: Onto-epistemological Considerations*, Bingley: Emerald, pp 93–111.

8

In Conversation with Helena Liu: Redeeming Leadership – a Project of Critical Hope

Debbie Bargallie, Nilmini Fernando and Helena Liu

DB and NF: Could you tell us about your understanding of racial literacy and how you might educate on race and racism in your teaching?

HL: I've never heard the term 'racial literacy' used before, but I immediately feel an affinity with it. The way it lands with me is just like how we'd talk about financial literacy in the business school, where it's about one's understanding of money, financialization and financial institutions. So when I hear the term 'racial literacy', I imagine it involves one's social, theoretical and critical understanding of race, racialization and systems of racial power.

That said, racial literacy can be a hard sell in the business school. There is a rich history of presenting business and its attendant neoliberal, capitalistic norms as politically neutral. It is not uncommon for business students to start and end their degrees believing that they are simply learning the 'true' reality of the world rather than a specific ideology that promotes performance, productivity and profit.

I think critical race theory is so vital to anyone working in and around organizations, and that's why I teach it to my students who are current and future professionals. Not all universities will take this kind of work seriously. And if it is even brought into a curriculum, there are the dangers of being co-opted by those who may take a groundbreaking concept like intersectionality and dilute it down to be about how 'everybody has different identities'. So there are countless opportunities for domestication and co-optation with anti-racist education.

Anti-racist work is constantly facing resistance from people who think, 'Why the hell do we have to learn this?' and potentially become even more stubborn about their racism because it seems like there's some sort of managerial mandate to learn critical race theory. Some of my recent experiences suggest that there is great promise in creating spaces in the margins of the academy, or beyond the academy altogether.

DB and NF: The doubling down and stubbornness to which you refer have also been noted by a rise in politics of white grievance and whitelash against efforts to uproot the racist and colonial roots of academic disciplines, as critical race and whiteness scholars in the United States – also a settler colony – as Kimberlé Crenshaw and colleagues (2019) and Georgy Yancy (2018) have discussed. Yet, if organizations intend to fulfil the aspirations to tackle institutional racism as many have done since the murder of George Floyd in 2020, it seems absolutely vital that current and future professionals who work and lead organizations are racially literate. Could you tell us more about which subjects you have taught that include race, and your approach to educating on race, racism and anti-racism?

HL: I've taught a range of different subjects in business schools over my career. I've taught diversity, equality and inclusion (DEI), where race might be expected to be a key focal point. I've also taught other more general business subjects such as leadership, strategic management, managing change, human resource management and the future of work. As race and racism are so important to my research, I can't really teach without shining some light onto anti-racist thought and practice. In the past, I have dedicated an entire week to race and white supremacy when I taught management strategy. Race was contextualized within a critical analysis of the interlocking systems of oppression that inform business so that in the week before, I teach gender and sexuality under patriarchy, and then in the week after, we look at culture under imperialism.

My experience is that even in subjects geared towards DEI, business students aren't used to talking about anti-racism. In conventional business thinking and practice, DEI is by and large framed via liberal, conservative notions of increasing representation and promoting tolerance with an overwhelming focus on gender. And, of course, when they're talking about gender they're often only thinking about elite straight cisgender middle-class white women securing the same power as their partners, fathers, brothers and sons.

My teaching traces the colonial and white supremacist roots of capitalism to place business management in its sociological context. I invite students to interrogate how the very logics of conquering economic markets and controlling workers to contribute more and more cost-efficient labour are grounded in colonial practices. We examine how much of our conventional wisdom around the management of workers was derived from the management of slaves.

By naming the ideological roots of business management, I hope to unshackle students from the idea that conventional business practices are somehow fixed, universal, and ultimately morally righteous. I wish for them to question the oppressive nature of capitalism and reimagine ways of living and being in the world. Perhaps some of my students will nevertheless reach the conclusion that capitalism is the best system we've got and still choose to 'play the game' when they enter managerial practice. My aim is not to convert anyone to anti-capitalist politics but is driven instead by a sense that I have a moral obligation to say what is too often made unspeakable.

I have an integrative framework that I use teach management students starting from the position that they're almost all familiar with interpersonal racism. When most of my students hear 'racism', they imagine someone walking up to a person of colour, shouting a racial slur and then walking away. I acknowledge that explicitly and explain how rarely that happens in the workplace. If you're a human resource manager and you think that's all racism is, you're not going to be documenting many cases of that. What's more powerful is letting people name the types of harm. So, I talk about systemic and structural racism, the institutional racism, which might emerge as organizational gaslighting when targets of racism don't get to name racism and complaints get dismissed. We also discuss internalized racism and the ways racial violence in organizations may be implicitly accepted and tolerated by people of colour. As though they come to believe, 'That's what I deserve. I don't want to make a complaint. I don't want to rock the boat. Nothing's going to change.' As current and future managers, I encourage my students to be alive to the multilayered, insidious nature of racism in organizations.

NF: I have noticed just that in my consultancy work, and educating professionals in women's services, domestic and family violence and not-for-profit organizations, direct resistance comes from senior and executive leadership, along with deeply embedded and rigid 'diversity and inclusion' processes and practices that refuse to see race or whiteness. We are curious about how your students respond to the degree of criticality you take in your teaching. Have you found differences across your undergraduate/postgraduate levels and cohorts?

HL: I was aware that by bringing in explicit discussions of race and racism to business school classrooms would ruffle a few feathers, but the nuances of how it does that ruffling have surprised me over the last six years. The biggest shock to me was how many of my students love learning about critical race theory and using that framework to interrogate management theories and practices. I introduce white supremacy in my subjects by first acknowledging how its lay uses may refer to extremist movements like neo-Nazis or the Ku Klux Klan, but clarifying that in its theoretical definition, white supremacy is the water in which Western businesses swim. So, in other words, almost all of us work for white supremacist organizations and live in white supremacist countries. When I introduce this concept, the penny drops for most of my students, who immediately embrace this powerful way of seeing the world and its attendant systems of oppression.

Even my Master of Business Administration (MBA) students, who often have extensive work experience as senior managers in organizations, are stirred by anti-racism in the best ways. They frequently tell me, 'We're not allowed to say this stuff aloud in our organizations. Thank you for creating a space where I get to name this itch underneath my skin that has been bothering me for years.'

There's a stereotype of the woke undergrad who loves talking about race and racism, and makes everything about identity politics, but my undergraduates have surprised me in their diversity. I do meet many undergraduate students who feel liberated about having honest and raw political discussions in class. But a lot of my undergraduate students, depending on their upbringing, are not accustomed to talking about race and racism. Every now and then, I'll find one or two students in the end-of-semester student evaluations complain how I 'crammed anti-racism down their throats' or 'played the race card' in my subjects. Some students maintain that 'racism doesn't exist – just look at our multicultural country'. So I do tend to meet a few students who are very uncomfortable and don't know how to process their discomfort.

For some of my students, it's also about fear. Some undergrads hold the belief that to be successful in a subject means that they have to parrot what the lecturer says. More of my postgrads tend to feel they can openly disagree with me politically and we will still respect each other. They trust that I'm not teaching with the aim of creating an adoring crowd who hang on my every word, and that I will grade them fairly as long as they justify their arguments. More undergrads struggle with the fear that 'if I disagree with you, you're just going to fail me'.

After years of gaining these insights into my students' denial, anger, shame and fear (alongside their joy, delight, relief and enthusiasm) via student evaluations and feedback, I try to address these feelings head on at the start of semester. I make it plain to students that they will likely encounter ideas that are challenging, that may unseat their previously held values and assumptions. I explicitly tell them that I don't expect them to agree with how I see the world, but I am giving them the intellectual tools to better understand (and therefore justify) their own beliefs. I remind them to take care of themselves if they notice feelings of denial, anger, shame and fear come up. Providing these explicit signposts early on and throughout the semester has helped my students navigate tricky political discussions with more openness, reflexivity and compassion.

In my experience, the more resolute resistance to anti-racist education tends to come from within the faculty. Even if staff and administrators may outwardly advocate anti-racist values or promote the goals of social justice, some of the people who are most threatened by anti-racist teaching are those who fear that they are somehow being called out for being racist when a colleague talks about race and racism in organizations in general. Directly and indirectly, I've been confronted with suspicions like, 'Is this lecture secretly about me? Are you accusing me of being a racist? Are you telling everybody that our university is racist?' This shame can be so powerful and painful that someone who feels threatened often projects their own discomfort onto students and insists anti-racist education is disruptive, even in the face of overwhelmingly positive student feedback. They may earnestly defend themselves while exaggerating and personalizing anti-racist work: 'You know me, *I'm* totally down. *I* think what you do is so valuable and important, but I think you'll upset *students* if you go around calling white people Nazis.' It takes a courageous and principled administrator who is secure in their own sense of their moral goodness to support meaningful anti-racist education.

DB and NF: Your classroom pedagogies are, we are certain, unique in your field and so much align with something we often discuss, which is bell hooks' (2000) work on love as a practice of freedom. That sense of inspiration, the thrill of hearing such pedagogies enacted in the classroom, comes through powerfully in your account, and somehow carries the spirit and genealogy of Black- and race-critical feminism right through your research as well. We first encountered your work in your book on anti-racist feminist leadership, a rare volume in the Australian context. Could you tell us more about that?

HL: My book, *Redeeming Leadership: An Anti-Racist Feminist Intervention*, was published in 2020. A paperback edition was released in 2021, which features an extra preface by me and a special foreword written by Stella Nkomo that I feel so incredibly privileged she agreed to provide. *Redeeming Leadership* is the culmination of my previous five years of research in the social construction of leadership in organizations. In it, I try to show how 'leadership' has always been a love song to whiteness and imperialism. The earliest formations of leadership took shape around the values of the European Enlightenment where, at the centre of leadership theory, stood the figure of the autonomous European man from whom leadership gloriously emanated. He represented 'orderliness, rationality and self-control' while the racial others he colonized and enslaved represented 'chaos, irrationality, violence, and the breakdown of self-regulation' (Kincheloe et al, 1998: 5).

Since its inception, leadership studies has been infused with idealizations of white men's moral and intellectual superiority that granted them the birthright to govern others. Popular leadership development programmes likewise venerated ideals of individual heroism, self-assurance and social impact, compelling its participants to fashion themselves after such fantasies of white masculinity.

In the spirit of Aileen Moreton-Robinson's (2000) *Talkin' Up to the White Woman*, I also critique the business handbooks by high-profile 'She-E-Os' such as Sophia Amoruso's (2015) *#GIRLBOSS*, Katty Kay and Claire Shipman's (2014) *The Confidence Code* and Sheryl Sandberg's (2015) *Lean In*. These handbooks, which call on women to 'forge a path through the obstacles, and achieve their full potential', tend to dismiss structural sexism and racism as something ambitious women professionals can choose to overcome. At the heart of this discourse is the valorization of an elite white femininity that perpetuates the wilful ignorance of systemic injustice.

My book is ultimately a project of hope. While the first half is focused on deconstruction, the second half turns to radical dreaming (Nash, 2019) of the liberatory possibilities of leadership. I theorize a framework for anti-racist leadership directed towards the dismantling of interlocking systems of imperialist, white supremacist, capitalist, ableist, cis-heteronormative and patriarchal oppression.

NF: Helena, would you expand on what you might consider anti-racist, decolonial praxes of solidarity? Why do we need it, and how might we more actively work in solidarity in the neoliberal university – those of us who are non-Indigenous women of colour? We also wondered if you receive negative responses to criticality in your work by other people of colour?

HL: Taking seriously Arundhati Roy's call to understand the pandemic as a portal, I have spent the last three years experimenting with ways to cultivate solidarity with others during lockdown. Through my website *Disorient*, I have connected with so many extraordinary anti-racist scholars and educators working across disciplines, approaches and sectors – building these bridges with each other that affirm our existence and fortify our resistance. My website has been a platform through which I've been able to facilitate online workshops for fellow anti-racist scholar-activists.

Nilmini, you put it so beautifully in our initial conversation when you described your work in creating classrooms where they didn't exist, cultivating alternate spaces for teaching. Through my website, I built a container outside my academic job where I could bring a small cohort of clients through producing anti-racist work while finding healing in collective. The participants have included traditional academics who have experienced backlash because of the kind of anti-racist work they do. I also worked with clients outside academia, including a doctor who sought to bring trauma-informed practices into her hospital.

There is tremendous opportunity to take anti-racist education beyond academia. We know from the testimonies of anti-racist scholars that institutions can sometimes seek to control and co-opt justice-oriented work (Andrews, 2018). Institutions may wish to outwardly promote anti-racist initiatives, stamping their name on events and resources as a virtue-signalling exercise while seeking to surveil and censor these initiatives. But when we engage in anti-racist education in the margins, in the grassroots, in the borderlands, among us, we can truly do work on our terms in our joyously resistive ways.

It is a real delight to be part of this volume. In telling our stories as anti-racist scholars and educators with one another, you have all borne witness to my struggles and I bear witness to the struggles faced by my fellow contributors to this volume as well as to anyone who may choose to reach out and share their experiences with me after reading this chapter. When we stand shoulder to shoulder with each other, we all become a little bit stronger. In these solidaristic connections with each other lie the possibilities for critical hope and transformation.

I recall how during my interview, you talked about what a wonderful experience it had been interviewing 30-plus people for your study on breaking the racial silence (Bargallie et al, 2023). When we first spoke, I was travelling through a difficult time in my life, struggling to find strength and hope to keep going. I felt so healed and affirmed by our conversation. I cannot overstate how transformative it is to have a collection of experiences by other anti-racist scholars and educators in Australia.

In the last few years, I've devoured multiple monographs and anthologies including *Complaint!* by Sara Ahmed (2021), *Decolonizing Academia: Poverty, Oppression and Pain* by Clelia O. Rodríguez (2018), *Presumed Incompetent: The Intersections of Race and Class for Women in Academia* by Gabriella Gutiérrez y Muhs, Yolanda Flores Niemann, Carmen G. Gonzalez and Angela P. Harris (2012), *Dismantling Race in Higher Education: Racism, Whiteness and Decolonising the Academy* by Jason Arday (2018) and *The Experiences of Black and Minority Ethnic Academics: A Comparative Study of the Unequal Academy* by Kalwant Bhopal (2016), just to name a few. The stories contained within of the vicious racism faced by scholars of colour are harrowing. When I was going through difficult times, there were days I could hardly bring myself to do anything. But I would read the stories of what other anti-racist scholars have survived, their struggles to teach race and racism, to research race and racism, while being torn to shreds by their institutions. Every story made me feel less alone. Every story gave me just the little bit of strength I needed to keep going.

When I first began my research career over a decade ago, it was not easy to find other scholars of colour who shared my conviction in the importance of anti-racist research and education. When I would present my work at management conferences, it was white scholars in the audience, particularly white men, who were most enthusiastic about my research. Some scholars of colour, especially other East Asian management scholars, would sit with their arms crossed the whole time during my presentation. And it's like their faces were saying, 'Why are you ruining it for us?' Perhaps it's the way some Asian scholars feel trapped within the model minority myth, and we've been told to keep our head down and shut up about racism so we can just all get along. But as the years pass, I've had people reach out and confess, 'Six years ago I gave you the side-eye for a half hour during your presentation and some years after that, I realized that I had a lot of internalized racism. I was so upset with you talking about racism at the time, but I've been doing the work to process my discomfort.' Now that I've been researching and teaching race and racism in business management for a while and I've developed an academic profile in this area, I meet less open resistance. The emerging anti-racist scholars I've had the pleasure of meeting at conferences inspire me so much. They are bolder about questioning, agitating, interrogating and breaking out of the stereotypes that tell them to sit down and shut up. As an East Asian woman of colour living and working on stolen land, there are many ways I've been able to get to this place in my career because of the enormous privileges I hold. People have told me in earnestness that I make 'Black feminism seem less scary' for them, oblivious to the anti-blackness inherent in such 'praise'. I try to centre the knowledge of Indigenous scholars in my curricula. We learn about the logics of possession and the intersection between gender and whiteness through Aileen Moreton-Robinson's books, *The White Possessive* (2015) and *Talkin' Up to the White Woman*

(2000). When teaching leadership, I draw on the work of Michelle Evans. We also explore the racial violence experienced by Indigenous workers and how we might dismantle racism at work through Debbie Bargallie's (2020) book *Unmasking the Racial Contract*. Collectively, the work of Indigenous scholars shows students how business itself is founded on the aims and principles of colonialism.

I am conscious of how the culture and systems of academia can facilitate appropriation and co-optation. I try to engage with the work of Indigenous scholars through quiet listening, decentring myself so that I don't make their inclusion a performance of my own virtue. I'm muddling through and I don't have it all figured out, but I believe the future of my field, business, should be rooted in Indigenous praxis. Only then may we have a hope of transforming the oppressive systems that currently structure our economy and society.

References

Ahmed, S. (2021) *Complaint!*, Durham, NC: Duke University Press.

Amoruso, S. (2015) *#GIRLBOSS*, New York: Penguin.

Andrews, K. (2018) *Back to Black: Retelling Black Radicalism for the 21st Century*, New York: Zed Books.

Arday, J. (2018) *Dismantling Race in Higher Education: Racism, Whiteness and Decolonising the Academy*, New York: Springer.

Bargallie, D. (2020) *Unmasking the Racial Contract: Indigenous Voices on Racism in the Australian Public Service*, Canberra: Aboriginal Studies Press.

Bargallie, D., Fernando, N. and Lentin, A. (2023) 'Breaking the racial silence: Putting racial literacy to work in Australia', *Ethnic and Racial Studies*. https://doi.org/10.1080/01419870.2023.2206470

Bhopal, K. (2016) *The Experiences of Black and Minority Ethnic Academics: A Comparative Study of the Unequal Academy*, London: Routledge.

Crenshaw, K.W., Harris, L.K., HoSang, D.M. and Lipsitz, G. (eds) (2019) *Seeing Race Again: Countering Colorblindness across the Disciplines*, Berkeley: University of California Press.

Gutiérrez y Muhs, G., Niemann, Y.F., Gonzalez, C.G. and Harris, A.P. (2012) *Presumed Incompetent: The Intersections of Race and Class for Women in Academia*, Boulder: University Press of Colorado.

hooks, b. (2000) *Feminist Theory: From Margin to Centre*, 2nd edn, Boston: South End Press.

Kay, K. and Shipman, C. (2014) *The Confidence Code*, New York: HarperCollins.

Kincheloe, J.L., Steinberg, S.R., Rodriguez, N.M. and Chennault, R.E. (eds) (1998) *White Reign: Deploying Whiteness in America*, New York: Palgrave Macmillan.

Liu, H. (2020) *Redeeming Leadership: An Anti-Racist Feminist Intervention*, Bristol: Bristol University Press.

Moreton-Robinson, A. (2000) *Talkin' Up to the White Woman*, Brisbane: University of Queensland Press.

Moreton-Robinson, A. (2015) *The White Possessive: Property, Power, and Indigenous Sovereignty*, Minneapolis: University of Minnesota Press.

Nash, J.C. (2019) *Black Feminism Reimagined: After Intersectionality*, Durham, NC: Duke University Press.

Rodríguez, C.O. (2018) *Decolonizing Academia: Poverty, Oppression and Pain*, Halifax: Fernwood Publishing.

Sandberg, S. (2015) *Lean In*, New York: W.H. Allen.

Yancy, G. (2018) *Backlash: What Happens When We Talk Honestly about Racism in America*, New York: Rowman & Littlefield.

9

The Provocateur as Decolonial Praxis

Fiona Foley

Introduction

Racism continues to be a societal burden in Australia that I have learned to carry – that gaze wrapped up in judgement from a white society and white individuals. It manifests in everyday educational environments, including in my work as an Aboriginal artist-academic-activist. Aboriginal art and politics have had an uneasy relationship in this country. The one-sided colonial narrative continues to silence Aboriginal voices and has far-reaching collateral damage from the academy to wider Australian society. My platform for disrupting the colonial narrative and decolonizing the histories of Queensland is through the visual arts. In this chapter, I reflect on my experiences teaching creative arts in Australian and American universities through engaging two of my artworks, *Annihilation of the Blacks* (Foley, 1986) and *HHH (Hedonistic Honky Haters) I* (Foley, 2004). I engage these artworks to provoke conversations about race and racism, and to explore the legacies of racial superiority. The provocateur as decolonial praxis makes many students and colleagues feel uncomfortable. I argue that critical provocation in teaching is vital and needs to move students and colleagues beyond 'feeling uncomfortable' in Australia, where denial is a key feature of racism. 'The more radical the person is, the more fully he or she enters into reality so that, knowing it better, he or she can better transform it. This individual is not afraid to confront, to listen, to see the world unveiled' (Freire, 2017: 13).

Australian higher education teaching is a highly racialized space for an Aboriginal academic. For most of my art praxis, I've worked alongside universities and within them. I have held two appointments as adjunct professor at the University of Queensland (2011–17) and Griffith University (2003–9), given numerous guest lectures and been a member on staff at each. I've never felt embedded or a sense of belonging in these spaces, but have operated on my own terms largely in the margins through 'research-creation' (Loveless, 2020: xxiv). Unravelling over time, this has been a trajectory where I've learnt to weave my way around conservative restraints of institutional power. In the process, my weaving around power, refusal, resistance and operating at the margins deploying art as critical praxis have lent themselves to developing critical racial and decolonial literacies for students and academics.

Following my first formal appointment in 2003 as adjunct professor at Griffith University, some 20 years later I have not seen adequate change in higher education curricula. Non-Indigenous students continue to lack knowledge about Aboriginal and Torres Strait Islander nations, people and culture. When I enter a classroom, there is a wide chasm in Australia's learning environments. The most basic of questions go unanswered by undergraduates and higher degree research candidates. One must ask why there is a continual silence in Australian universities pertaining to the oldest continuous living culture in the world.

I enhance my teaching in universities by speaking through a visual language. I draw out Australia's hidden histories, encapsulating legislation in Queensland, Indigenous knowledges, museum collections, colonial violence, frontier wars and an array of associated subject matter. I create art for the purpose of communicating with a wide audience. Maintaining research-led practice in the visual arts for the last three and a half decades has allowed me to speak into to the abyss of a raceless Australian education system. Author and biographer Louise Martin-Chew (2021: 123) writes about my art and life: 'Often her work allows an exploration of fixed expectations, an escape from the racist treatment that has impacted her since her earliest school years.'

I choose to use the word 'provocateur' to be provocative. I have been repeatedly scrutinized in social settings through questions loaded with subtext that questions my race and profession simultaneously. For example, 'What type of art do you make?' is really a coded way of asking, 'Are you a *real* artist? Are you a *real* Aboriginal artist?' I refuse to accept this repetitive questioning from non-Indigenous Australians, as whatever answer I give, they would not accept me as a full-fledged artist. I began replying, 'I make provocative art.' It was also a way by which to avoid stereotypical constructions associated with Aboriginal art such as 'dot paintings' and 'political art'. Usually, the conversation would then go cold. Inevitably, someone would try to change the topic. My refusal requires more from non-Indigenous people: to think outside of the box, to reflect on what *provocative art* means in the context of Indigenous Australia. This is critical racial literacy praxis (Bargallie et al, 2023).

Annihilation of the Blacks

I was educated at public schools in Queensland and New South Wales. Scant education was taught in the classroom about Australian Aboriginal people. It was through reading the works of leading historians and from my mother's transfer of knowledge to her children that I gleaned information about our peoples. One oral history account of a massacre on Badtjala Country vexed me. My mother's retelling of the massacre of Badtjala people on the Susan River in Maryborough, Queensland was the impetus for me to animate such a harrowing story into a major sculpture titled *Annihilation of the Blacks*, the image depicted on the cover of this book. This was the first of its kind. While I was at Sydney College of the Arts from 1984 to 1986, there were no Indigenous artists who could act as a role model or mentor, as none existed in the field of tertiary art education at that time. The path through a degree course was navigated by the individual without any support structures in place.

In 1986, *Annihilation of the Blacks* was acquired by the National Museum of Australia, my first institutional acquisition as esteemed Wakka Wakka and Gooreng Gooreng literary scholar Sandra Phillips (2021: 23) notes. By 1986, in contrast to my classmates, my works were shown through invitation in two groundbreaking exhibitions titled *Koori Art 84* and *Urban Koories 86*. At the time, a groundswell of Sydney-based artists was taking place outside of the institution (through Boomalli Aboriginal Artist Cooperative); they created an art movement recognized today as Urban Aboriginal Art. The schism between high artistic achievement and institutional disregard was to become a significant feature of my academic life. The achievement of having my work acquired by Australia's prestigious national museum was not celebrated by the institution and actively went unacknowledged. Multiple harrowing interactions marked my experience as a racialized young Aboriginal student at Sydney College of the Arts. My lecturers were harsh critics, especially at my final examination. Over the full three years of the Bachelor of Arts (Visual Arts) course, I would only ever receive a *pass* grade.[1] I was the only art student in my year studying a double major in the sculpture and printmaking departments. Running concurrently, I similarly experienced racism from my lecturing staff in the printmaking department. I identified these acts of racism as they unfolded and raised my concerns at a meeting with the head of school to no avail. The unique manifestations of the racial ignorance of non-Indigenous lecturers about contemporary Indigenous Australian peoples and cultures became very clear to me. Romanticized assumptions prevailed about the Aboriginal peoples living in the Northern Territory[2] being the only Aboriginal peoples that still practised their art. Urban Aboriginal artists were not deemed to be authentic as artists *or* Aboriginals. This ignorance forced me to educate my educators about urban east coast Aboriginal epistemologies. I will never forget receiving the harshest criticism from staff in the sculpture department; while standing in front of *Annihilation of the Blacks*, my educator's comments at a critique were that my work 'didn't say anything and was just a full stop'. I was wounded and so paralysed that I could not speak back. It was not until I was much older that I found my voice to speak back to what I know now as epistemic violence – the violence of rejection and erasure of Indigenous ways of knowing, being and doing (Martin, 2003). This would not be the last time I would experience overt and subtle forms of racism in the higher education sector.

Today, unapologetically, I engage an image of *Annihilation of the Blacks* (Figure 9.1 in my teaching. Most recently, at the symposium 'Reason and Reckoning: Conversations and Provocations', held at Griffith University in 2022, I spoke to how the sculpture was a way to honour the people killed on the Susan River, decades before the national lexicon of truth telling entered popular discourse. As an Aboriginal academic who has led national and international symposiums, such as 'The Art of Politics/The Politics of Art' and 'Courting Blakness: Recalibrating Knowledge in the Sandstone University' (Foley and Nicoll, 2014; Foley and Martin-Chew,

Figure 9.1: Fiona Foley, *Annihilation of the Blacks* (1986)

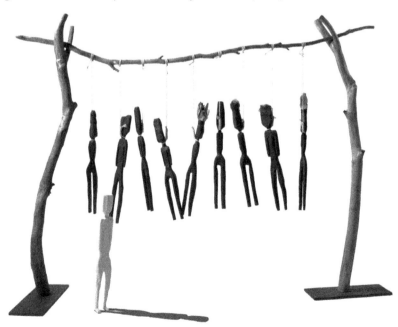

Source: Permanent collection of the National Museum of Australia, Canberra. Image reproduced courtesy of the artist.

2015), I thought my track record had proved my ability to lead a national conversation. It was my impression that I would be supported by my university. However, my symposium 'Reason and Reckoning: Conversations and Provocations' took two years of sheer determination and persistence to realize in the face of passive resistance. I navigated around institutional obstacles by refusing to take no for an answer. In this way, the deployment of an act of refusal is a decolonial praxis.

Griffith University is named after Sir Samuel Griffith. The symposium itself was a provocation to instigate a conversation about whether the name Griffith should be removed from the university altogether (Foley et al, 2023). The symposium coincided with the release of *Griffith Review 76: Acts of Reckoning*. The timing was critical; two separate yet overlapping ventures garnered significant national press attention, including a feature article in *The Guardian* written by journalist Joe Hinchliffe (2022) headlined 'Enabler of massacres: The push to re-examine the legacy of founding father Samuel Griffith'. Various professionals from within and external to the academy were invited to present papers.

Renowned historian and author Henry Reynolds (2021: 220) makes the point that 'colonial politicians … were enablers' and that Samuel Griffith 'actively condoned widespread defiance of the law' because he did not protect Aboriginal people as British subjects or afford them the right to remain on their traditional lands. During his time, Griffith would have been aware of the colonial state apparatus, such as the practices of dispersal enacted by the Native Police Force in Queensland.[3] What conditions made it possible for Griffith not to see Aboriginal men, women and children as human beings and implement laws to stop the indiscriminate killing in Queensland under his leadership? Not to see murder as murder? Despite the role Sir Samuel Griffith played as Premier (twice), Attorney-General, drafter of the Australian Constitution, Chief Justice of the Supreme Court of Queensland and Chief Justice of the High Court of Australia and overseer of Aboriginal massacres in the state of Queensland, should Griffith University change its name?

In *Truth-Telling*, Henry Reynolds (2021: 194) writes: 'For many years the truth was either deftly avoided or consciously suppressed.' Following the symposium, an outcome report largely met with silence by the university. At this point, we have seen no further action. Griffith University is scheduled to go ahead with its planned celebrations of Sir Samuel Griffith in 2025 at the university's 50th anniversary, using an age-old modus operandi of avoidance and suppression. As Richmond and Charnley (2022: 211) argue, 'Whiteness cannot be placated, or made "progressive". It must be abolished through collective action'.

The politics of race is at the centre of my art, research and writing. Aboriginal educator Victor Hart (2003: 15) writes that 'for many Aboriginal scholars and teachers, addressing the first wave of "colonialism" is still an urgent imperative that requires attending to before we indulge a "post" colonial era'. Provoking society to think at a deeper level intertwines with how I speak back to an ever-present colonialist narrative in the academy. Sandra Phillips (2021: 21) also wrote that 'Foley is also deeply rooted in the voices of our lands – voices that assert, beseech, celebrate, proclaim, chastise, encourage, appeal, rail, and rage, and that will never give up until we draw our last breaths'. I employ all these tools to teach in higher education.

Hedonistic Honky Haters: mapping the terrain

In 2004 I was awarded an Australia Council for the Arts artist residency in New York. I arrived in Queens with snow piled high on sidewalks and lived in a one-bedroom apartment for six months. It was an opportunity to engage in a culture and a dialogue as an outsider. Frantz Fanon (2008: 21) writes that '[t]o speak a language is to appropriate its world and culture'. I did appropriate an international language tied to a race hate group situated in the United States. I, like most Australians, am familiar with the Ku Klux Klan through documentaries, cinema, exhibitions, photographs and text. The idea for a series of photographs I created during this time came from one image in an exhibition titled *Only Skin Deep* held at the International Centre of Photography, New York (Fusco and Wallis, 2003). The black-and-white photograph identified a gender through its title that repelled me to think at a deeper level. Taken by artist Andres Serrano, striking in its simplicity the work is titled *Klanswoman (Grand Kaliff II)*, 1990.

As an artist, I could visualize an entirely new proposition: what if the hoods were all black instead of white? What would this group be called? Could the cloaks be made from colourful Kente cloth? I began the process of inversion through daring to take the idea one step further. I created an insignia with the letter H. The group would be known as the HHH. The letters stood for the Hedonistic Honky Haters (Figure 9.2). The actors for this series were a mix of genders predominantly with dark skin from all walks of life. The costumes were made to fit each individual with cloth bought from 125th Street, Harlem. The seamstress measured the circumference of foreheads and distance between eyes. This made the experience very real and conjured up a parallel universe of being measured for the Ku Klux Klan (Foley, 2023).

Before returning to Australia, I held a small exhibition opening at the International Studio and Curatorial Program (New York). The entire series of eight photographs was shown. For me, it was a time to think about race and racism anew. Leading Indigenous Australian educator and scholar Martin Nakata and colleagues write (Nakata et al, 2012: 124) that '[t]here are other

Figure 9.2: Fiona Foley, *HHH (Hedonistic Honky Haters) I* (2004)

epistemologies and other standpoints from which Indigenous people come to know the world and from which we understand and analyse'. Upon my return to Australia in 2004, I didn't know what audiences in this country would make of the new work. The series of photographs was bought along with costumes by the National Gallery of Australia in 2009. A slow burn.

Creating a new photographic series allows for a type of freedom, especially when realized overseas. There are no restrictions when inventing characters, costumes or nuanced cultural markers. Rules can be broken, and the world can be unveiled through new eyes. It is these interstices that make some uncomfortable in their own white bodies. I relish these moments, those awkward silences that permeate Australia's subconscious and consciousness. Often race is not discussed at all in university environments. It is reinforced in a journal article by Australian educators titled 'Affect and the force of counter stories' that '[t]alking about racism within an education system and nation [is] well-known for silencing race' (Schulz et al, 2023: 15).

Bearing witness

The profession of teaching at a university can be exciting for a lecturer when students embark on a new endeavour. It is also fraught by a lack of knowledge gained during the student's former educational years from primary through to secondary schooling.

When I am invited to give a guest lecture to undergraduate students at university, there are often long silences. An unspoken fear permeates this land, located in Aboriginal race murder stemming from a brutal colonial history. As part of my methodology, I don't spoon-feed the class with information but make them be active participants in their own learning and analysis. This means I ask lots of questions. In association with a PowerPoint presentation, I will ask the students to do a reading of something I've written in recent times. Sometimes the student will read this material, but most often they don't. Then we settle into the uncomfortableness of knower and not knowing – a mapping of a historical terrain with which many are unfamiliar because they have either not been taught about Aboriginal or Torres Strait Islander epistemological traditions or there is a reluctance to learn in the first place. Twenty years ago (2003: 15), Victor Hart asked us 'how to engage this resistance in order to transform these silencing frameworks, without reinforcing them'. It is a difficult generational rub that Aboriginal teachers face in the academy. I acknowledge this by bearing witness over the past two decades, where change never seems to arrive.

Courting Blakness

For three years, I worked with Australian academic Fiona Nicoll, who researches in feminism and critical race and whiteness studies as well as theories of intersectionality to realize the project titled *Courting Blakness*. Eight Aboriginal artists were invited to exhibit their work in the University of Queensland's Great Court – the sandstone heart of the university. The exhibition aimed to reclaim this historically elite white space to create a visual dialogue between contemporary Aboriginal art and colonial-inspired architecture (Foley et al, 2015).

An unnecessary problematization for the institution manifested through its own making. A contestation over four flags flying on the Forgan Smith Building galvanized an official resistance from the university to the art installation of Kamilaroi artist Archie Moore. Conceptual artist Moore (2015: 120) writes in the publication *Courting Blakness* that '[f]lags are used to identify sovereignty, imperialism, colonialism, nationalism, exploration, possession, power, protection, law over land and sea, piracy and independence'. Moore's exhibition, titled *14 Nations*, was created from symbols of 14 Indigenous nations imagined and mapped by surveyor and anthropologist R.H. Mathews. Writing about Mathews' account, Moore (2015: 119) asks, 'How tainted was his interpretation of data from a position of racial and intellectual superiority?'

Archie Moore used the symbols found within the map of these 14 nations to make 14 flags in an installation disrupt the dominant narratives of place and nationhood and speak back to incorrect colonially imposed territorial boundaries.

The Forgan Smith Building became the chosen site of contestation two weeks prior to the opening of *Courting Blakness*. The approvals that had been given regarding the use of the flags were then revoked using the following justification: 'The University is also conscious of complying with the National Flag protocols. The flag poles on top of the Forgan Smith Building serve a formal purpose and are reserved for officially recognised flags' (Foley and Martin-Chew, 2015: 16). It was stipulated that no non-official flag was to fly from the Forgan Smith Building at the University of Queensland, so only ten flags were exhibited in the Great Court. Titled *14 Nations* in 2014, this body of work evolved into further iterations in the years that followed. I write in *Biting the Clouds* that 'Australia's accepted standard history is now being challenged as Aboriginal scholars from many nations contest those positions of unfounded historical truths' (Foley, 2020: 112).

One of Moore's flags branded the entire *Courting Blakness* project, but was censored from flying. With such late notification, little could be done as all the branding signage, t-shirts, catalogue and promotional materials had already been released. This was a major blow to the artist and project team, who were never invited to give an explanation about the *14 Nations* installation or its rationale in relation to history. This attitudinal swing undermined the project's success, engagement and innovative pedagogy. The university also pushed back (unsuccessfully) against the invitation for Indigenous Australian Minister of Parliament, the Hon Linda Burney, to open *Courting Blakness*. One must question the motives for such institutional resistance.

As curator of *Courting Blakness*, I offered the UQ Art Museum the first opportunity to buy Moore's *14 Nations*, which was declined. The installation, now titled *United Neytions, 2018*, resides permanently at Sydney Airport's T1 International Terminal.[4] Moore expanded the original 14 to 28 flags for the Sydney commission. It is fitting that residents and international visitors to these shores see the breathtaking conceptual artwork by Archie Moore suspended from the ceiling on their departure.

The lecture room can be a rigid and gridlocked physical and intellectual environment, whereby 'Indigenous academics and non-Indigenous academics make not just educational but political choice' (Nakata et al, 2012: 123). A contestation over flying four flags (from the proposed 14) on the Forgan Smith Building further galvanized another layer of resistance from students, artists and lecturers at the University of Queensland.

After the *Courting Blakness* project made its mark in art, symposia and publication, I am told it is still used in various teachings across the University of Queensland humanities today. Internationally, Fiona Nicoll uses the model created from this project in her teaching at the University of Alberta, Edmonton. It is possible that the slow burn comes after the heat of activism has dropped off.

> There was significant embedding of *Courting Blakness* in the curriculum across the year in at least fourteen different courses. Academics teaching in law, anthropology, studies of religion, political science, cultural studies, linguistics, cultural tourism and event management, psychology, art history, museum studies and education developed assessment tasks based on the art works and the questions they posed about concepts of identity, nation and citizenship. The diverse and creative ways the project was used to reach over 800 students in different disciplines demonstrates the success of *Courting Blakness* as a catalyst for socially inclusive pedagogy. (Foley and Nicoll, 2014: np)

My extensive experience as an Indigenous Australian educator and witnessing the experiences of Indigenous colleagues in the academy attests to the greater demands placed on Indigenous academics than on their non-Indigenous counterparts. I found, as Frantz Fanon (2008: 92) states, that 'I was responsible not only for my body but also for my race and my ancestors'. The environment in which Aboriginal academics are positioned when they enter lecture rooms, staff offices or boardrooms demands that they carry an added weight on their shoulders – history, ancestors and culture – in addition to 'contested knowledge terrains' and being beholden under the white gaze.

Notes

[1] Sydney College of the Arts, Statement of Academic Record, Pass (semester 1 1984 to semester 2 1986).
[2] The Northern Territory is a vast federal territory in the central and central northern region of Australia, which has the highest proportion of Indigenous Australians living in remote or very remote locations. The east coast represents urban population of Indigenous Australians, with the higher populations overall, and includes the major cities of Brisbane, Sydney and Melbourne in the states of Queensland, New South Wales and Victoria respectively.
[3] See https://www.qhatlas.com.au/content/native-police; https://harrygentle.griffith.edu.au/the-queensland-native-mounted-police-research-database
[4] https://thecommercialgallery.com/artist/archie-moore/exhibition/901/archie-moore-united-neytions-public-art-commission

References

Bargallie, D., Fernando, N. and Lentin, A. (2023) 'Breaking the racial silence: Putting racial literacy to work in Australia', *Ethnic and Racial Studies*. DOI: 10.1080/01419870.2023.2206470

Fanon, F. (2008) *Black Skin, White Masks*, New York: Grove Press.

Foley, F. (2020) *Biting the Clouds: A Badtjala Perspective on the Aboriginals Protection and Restriction of the Sale of Opium Act, 1897*, Brisbane: University of Queensland Press.

Foley, F. (2023) 'Disrupting the silence: Australian Aboriginal art as a political act', in G. Hannum and K. Pyun (eds), *Expanding the Parameters of Feminist Artivism*, Cham: Palgrave Macmillan, pp 51–64.

Foley, F. and Nicoll, F. (2014) *Courting Blakness: Recalibrating Knowledge in the Sandstone University: Outcomes Report*, Brisbane: University of Queensland, https://www.academia.edu/37318090/Courting_Blakness_Recalibrating_Knowledge_in_the_Sandstone_University_Outcomes_Report

Foley, F. and Martin-Chew, L. (2015) 'The politics of art and place', in F. Foley, L. Martin-Chew and F. Nicoll (eds), *Courting Blackness, Recalibrating Knowledge in the Sandstone University*, Brisbane: University of Queensland Press, pp 14–21.

Foley, F., Bargallie, D., Carlson, B. and Nicoll, F. (2023) 'Reason and reckoning: Provocations and conversations about re-imagining Samuel Griffith's university', in B. Carlson and T. Farrelly (eds), *The Palgrave Handbook on Rethinking Colonial Commemorations*, Cham: Palgrave Macmillan, pp 263–96.

Freire, P. (2017) *Pedagogy of the Oppressed*, Harmondsworth: Penguin.

Fusco, C. and Wallis, B. (2003) *Only Skin Deep: Changing Visions of the American Self*, Exhibition Catalogue.

Hart, V. (2003) 'Teaching Black and teaching back', *Social Alternatives*, 2(3): 12–15.

Hinchliffe, J. (2022) 'Enabler of massacres: The push to re-examine the legacy of founding father Samuel Griffith', *The Guardian*, 5 June, https://www.theguardian.com/australia-news/2022/jun/05/enabler-of-massacres-the-push-to-reexamine-the-legacy-of-founding-father-samuel-griffith

Loveless, N. (2020) *Knowings and Knots: Methodologies and Ecologies in Research-Creation*, Edmonton: University of Alberta Press.

Martin, K.R. (2003) 'Ways of knowing, being and doing: A theoretical framework and methods for Indigenous and Indigenist research', *Journal of Australian Studies*, 27(76): 203–14.

Martin-Chew, L. (2021) *Fiona Foley Provocateur: An Art Life*, Brisbane: QUT Art Museum.

Moore, A. (2015) '14 Nations', in F. Foley, L. Martin-Chew and F. Nicoll (eds), *Courting Blackness, Recalibrating Knowledge in the Sandstone University*, Brisbane: University of Queensland Press, pp 118–23.

Nakata, M., Nakata, V., Keech, S. and Bolt, R. (2012) 'Decolonial goals and pedagogies for Indigenous studies', *Decolonization: Indigeneity, Education & Society*, 1(1): 120–40.

Phillips, S. (2021) *Sovereign Vision: On Fiona Foley's Veiled Paradise*, Exhibition Catalogue.

Reynolds, H. (2021) *Truth-Telling: History Sovereignty and the Uluru Statement*, Sydney: New South Publishing.

Richmond, M. and Charnley, A. (2022) *Fractured: Race, Class, Gender and the Hatred of Identity Politics*, London: Pluto Press.

Schulz, S., Rigney, L. I., Zembylas, M., Hattam, R. and Memon, N. (2023) 'Affect and the force of counter stories: learning racial literacy through thinking and feeling', *Pedagogy, Culture & Society*. DOI: 10.1080/14681366.2023.2173276

PART III

Doing Race in the Disciplines

10

Decolonizing the Curriculum in the Colonial Debtscape

Maria Giannacopoulos

Introduction

Decolonizing curriculum cannot occur without an intention to dismantle the colonial; its logics and its institutions that stretch across unceded sovereign lands entrenching deep injustice. An urgent task for decolonizing curricula across all disciplines in the imperial university is to expose the role and function of colonial law in performing and maintaining dispossession and colonial violence. As a system of law imposed upon First Laws, colonial law forms a nomopoly (a monopoly of law) that lacks consent and so performs nomocide. Nomocide is the killing function of law that reproduces colonial conditions in Australia (Giannacopoulos, 2021). This chapter argues for the necessity of a critical theorization of colonial law and provides an illustration of how such theory can be deployed in pedagogical practice to foster critical literacies across a range of disciplines.

Much of the thinking in this chapter has occurred over many years on Gadigal, Wangal, Bedegal and Kameygal lands (Sydney) where I was born and on Kaurna Yerta (Adelaide) where I lived and worked for over a decade.[1] It was as a wog[2] on these lands, engaging with Indigenous and wog colleagues, intellectuals and activists, that I was able to think seriously about decolonizing the curriculum and what this means.[3] I was born on Gadigal land to migrant parents from Greece. Mum and Dad's life trajectories were shaped by many intersecting geopolitical forces, but two stand out. The mass poverty in Greece in the aftermath of the Second World War, leading to the exporting of the poorest parts of the population, coincided with the desire of the Australian colony to import people to aid industrialization, white possession and dispossession of Aboriginal peoples. Our ability to build lives and futures on unceded lands was the outcome of an illegitimate process that saw the colonial state enact a migration scheme, granting entry to migrants and providing a birthplace for their future children. But granting access to unceded lands was never within their authority to give. This lack of consent and authority to rule, decide and govern is only partially recognized when acknowledgements of Country assert that sovereignty was never ceded; it is rarely acknowledged that laws stemming from an unceded sovereignty must, logically, also be illegitimate. Aboriginal laws were also never ceded.

Colonialism and the curriculum

At each law faculty where I have worked, the laws that are taught and traded in are not the First Laws of the land. Like all law faculties around the country, including Flinders University, where I worked for over a decade (until the position I held was disestablished in an academic restructure), their core business is to centre colonial law and the scholarship that best allows an inherently racialized law to appear 'race neutral' (Moreton-Robinson, 2004). But this claim to legal neutrality is an exercise in legal supremacy. In such charged locations, 'law' presents and is presented as singular by being stripped of its rightful descriptor, 'colonial'. This is usurpation and epistemic violence at work. Predictably, there are real risks for scholars who pursue decolonizing research agendas, seeking to place the claimed singularity and innocence of colonial 'law' under critical interrogation. This is particularly the case in a period where the citizenry of so-called 'Australia' is being asked to invest in the potential of colonial law to deliver justice for Indigenous peoples. In 2023, an affective investment in colonial law is being invited from the Australian citizenry, the majority of whom are already its beneficiaries. The Australian population (most of whom are not Aboriginal) are being asked to vote in a referendum to make possible a First Nations advisory voice to parliament (Foley and Gibson, 2023). The advisory-only voice model sits in stark contrast to, and seeks to overwrite, the sovereign and self-determined 'law of the land' (Watson, 2017: 218). These critiques of law do not easily find their way into law or related curriculums, so 'law' is spoken of in an undertheorized manner as though its meaning is self-evident. Yet all scholarship that intends to be decolonizing must attend to the colonizing features of law. The stakes are too high when the meaning of concepts and institutions like constitutions, referendums, judiciaries and parliament, and 'law' are taken for granted. As Watson (2017: 218) puts it, 'while First Nations are deemed peoples without law and merely objects of the colonial law, this is not the truth'.

Affective investments in colonial technologies

In 2023, the federal budget allocated AU$364.6 million to the Voice to Parliament.[4] The same year, due to the same budget, the National Aboriginal and Torres Strait Islander Legal Services declared a national funding emergency.[5] This is a clear indication of government priorities: to fund the colonial infrastructure, not those targeted by its carceral and nomocidal features (Giannacopoulos, 2021). In addition, the assurances that a yes vote would not destabilize the constitution or the political order show that this is not a law reform with decolonizing intent or capacity. A yes/no binary flattens and violently displaces the larger questions of colonial debt and decolonization that urgently need to be reckoned with. The technology of the referendum naturalizes the legitimacy of the colonial structure posing the question. Several years ago, I argued that referendums are a technology for the expansion of colonial power (Giannacopoulos, 2017: 33); this remains the case, regardless of a yes or no stance or outcome. This manoeuvre for gaining retrospective consent for a system of law that is founded without consent will see a majority of beneficiaries of colonial law voting to allow for a carefully circumscribed singular Indigenous voice to be relegated to the status of advisor in the Australian Parliament. The Australian constitution forms a nomopoly, an imposed and violent legal infrastructure that seeks to usurp the operation of law pre-existing it (Giannacopoulos, 2019a, 2019b). For a referendum to appear as a legitimate avenue for law reform, the conditions giving rise to the constitution must be removed from view. In this way, the referendum can efface its role in maintaining a colonial debtscape (Giannacopoulos, 2022), concealing 'the foundational debts of dispossession that structure both economy and sovereignty' (Giannacopoulos, 2017: 34). A referendum arising from a legal regime that is non-consensual (Giannacopoulos, 2021) must be thoroughly interrogated as it is a law reform device crafted by a constitution to enable its conservation via alteration. Having been created by the constitution, the referendum performs the role of affirming colonial law as the legitimate starting point and centre of legal authority.

During this historical epoch, legal scholarship and all scholarship in the colony must be asking: What problem is legal constitutional reform seeking to address? The current framing of the campaign suggests that the problem is the lack of representation on Indigenous questions to parliament. Once a singular Indigenous representative voice is enshrined as part of the colonial infrastructure, the idea is that the injustice experienced by Aboriginal people will be ameliorated. But how can this be when then this approach seeking absorption into the colonial structure (Watson, 2009) is an exercise in legal assimilation?[6] Not only does constitutional reform lack both decolonizing intent and potential, but when integrationist logic is at play – as it must be in processes of reform – colonial structures are cemented while the illusion of change prevails (Watson, 2005). Yet First Nations sovereignty and law exist, even if untold resources are poured into denying this truth.

At the time of writing, in early October 2023, an open letter signed by more than 350 historians claims that a yes vote places Australians on the right side of history. The letter states: 'We each support the proposal to amend the Commonwealth Constitution to recognise First Australians and enshrine a Voice enabling representations to be made to the Parliament and the executive government. We will each be voting "yes" at the year's referendum.'[7] Here, among the most educated and informed, is an alarming lack of literacy about the racial features and functions of both constitutions and referendums. Driving this letter is an affective investment and love of law, or nomophilia (Giannacopoulos, 2011), desiring reform but ultimate maintenance of the colonial infrastructure. And herein also sits the desire of the signatories to be seen as not racist and as the agents for progressive change. My research on the coloniality of Australian law across two decades reveals that, far from decentring colonial structures, law reforms function to entrench colonial power. This is not surprising if the colony is understood to always discriminate in favour of itself (Moreton-Robinson, 2004) while remaining in control of the nature and extent of the changes made to itself. Reformed or not, law, the constitution and referendums are mechanisms of colonial law, and they function to displace the First Laws of this land. If sovereignty and law have never been ceded by Aboriginal people – and this is regularly acknowledged and known, including by historians – what is the status and character of the colonial law usurping Indigenous sovereignty and law, which is currently providing the terms for Aboriginal inclusion? There is much at stake in opening the question of sovereignty, so it is systematically kept shut through funding that redirects the national gaze to the constitution and not to the more critical questions of unpaid colonial debts and the persistence of Aboriginal sovereignty.

Academic work and the struggle to decolonize

In 2018, I hosted leading decolonizing criminologist Professor Biko Agozino at Flinders Criminology.[8] During the visit, we had some contentious discussions as Flinders was in the midst of a major restructure. At that time, I spent much time thinking about the law, and in particular the Australian Fair Work Act (FWA), which has undoubtedly generated conditions for the control, containment and punishment of workers. The FWA generates optimal conditions for employers to use restructuring to redefine and reclassify work to reduce labour costs, and the stripping of secure conditions. This is the austerity university, and austerity is always already a colonial device.

During his visit, Agozino (2019: 9) argued that 'that critical scholars are sought-after … because the critical scholars fill a gap in knowledge that is neglected by the majority authoritarian scholars'. This is an important but complex position to hold, especially as many of us currently employed as academics have extensive knowledge of unemployed and underemployed critical scholars and have ourselves been targeted. We hold this knowledge because our workplaces implicate us firmly within the academic class hierarchies structuring the contemporary university. Some of us, in Australia and elsewhere, are currently having to remember and/or experience what academic precariousness feels like as 'secure' employment is being pulled out from under us. In 2021, I was made redundant when my position at Flinders was disestablished. The 'disestablishment' and 'reclassification' of existing positions is a form of 'administrative policing' (Chatterjee and Maira, 2014: 5) and presents real dangers for critical scholars working at the margins of disciplines in ways that do not easily translate into research dollars and industry 'impact'. In the context of university restructuring in the United States, Chatterjee and Maira (2014: 10) ask, 'given that neo-liberal market ideologies now underwrite the "value" of our research and intellectual work, what happens to scholars whose writing directly tackles the questions of US state violence, logics of settler colonialism and global, political and economic dominance?' They argue that the price paid by critical scholars has been 'extraordinarily high', with penalties such as 'denial of promotion to tenure, being de-tenured, not having employment contracts renewed, or never being hired and being blacklisted' (Chatterjee and Maira, 2014: 10).

Law creates a legal foundation for employers to erode basic rights, freedoms and conditions for academic workers. While the FWA does not eliminate unions, it does function to shrink the 'legal' space in which it is possible to resist by designating strict criteria for taking what is termed 'protected industrial action'. Union industrial officers and leaders may be less inclined to countenance industrial action as an option, as it involves considerable work to operate within the legal criteria for such action. By submitting to the legislative will in this way, unions may become complicit with the legalized violence against workers that is licensed at the legislative level.

In the face of the hard material realities stemming from administrative policing, how are we to remain stable and centred in the face of systemic destabilization strategies which amount to the 'policing of knowledge'? (Chatterjee and Maira, 2014: 5). How might academic workers and critical and decolonial thinkers cultivate a belief like Agozino's (2019) that, despite the material conditions of the austerity university, an academic career is possible while producing activist and decolonizing scholarship? Would this require us to inhabit a kind of *tactical* denial of material realities and where might the strength for this come from? These questions form the fundamental challenge that haunts any critical unpacking of the contemporary colonial/

austerity university. Here I can only begin to build on Chatterjee and Maira's (2014: 7) argument that 'the state of permanent war that is core to US imperialism and racial statecraft has three fronts: military, cultural and academic'. Their 'conceptualization of the imperial university links these fronts of war, for the academic battleground is part of the culture wars that emerge in a militarized nation, one that is always presumably under threat, externally or internally' (Chatterjee and Maira, 2014: 7). I attempt to build on these important claims by signalling the colonizing role of *nomos*/laws, particularly the role played by labour and employment laws then used by university management to aid ongoing Indigenous dispossession in the Australian context and beyond. In other words, how do specific workplace laws work to undermine material and employment conditions to structure university contexts in ways that enable or disallow decolonizing and other critical scholarship and related practices?

Across the body of my work, I have argued that it is the machinery of the law that performs a foundational and violent role in dispossession and in ensuring the ongoing operations of colonial power. It is a colonial trick to see law as the innocent, impartial and objective regime that it attempts to represent itself as. To fall for this trick would be to suffer from nomophilia, where a belief in the correctness of colonial law prevents that regime being seen as a system predicated on mass theft and violence against peoples and lands. The immeasurable sovereign debt incurred as a consequence of the theft of land, natural resources and more from First Peoples continues to be actively effaced by governments, corporations, privileged populations and many knowledge producers. Economies like Australia are not really known for their sovereign debt, despite austerity being a key colonial technology. Austerity is a colonial device, where expansion and contraction work in tandem to create poverty. While the colonial state made itself and extended its reach off the back of dispossession, First Nations peoples were made poor by being removed from their own bountiful lands, from which life-sustaining resources could be accessed and their laws sprang and could be practised.

Where do moves seeking to destabilize the connection between scholarly knowledge production and critical teaching practice, which find their expression and legitimation through legal mechanisms, leave us? As we continue to witness universities becoming transactional and consumerist locations, do academics also need to become more cognisant of their status as workers? While there is no doubt that satisfaction and a love of justice motivate critical work, the material demand that we remain employed and employable reminds us that we are/need to be workers to be knowledge producers to make transformative interventions into oppressive disciplines. Yet we are increasingly bound by legal/employment seeking to shape what we can produce. It is true, as Agozino (2019: 6) argues, that 'scholar-activism has succeeded in pushing back the control-freak state in modest ways' and there is no doubt that activist scholarship must continue. But how will we cultivate and/or maintain the requisite beliefs to continue with this if the academic ground from which to work and speak moves from under us? How can we work from within with the boundedness of our employment and shifting class conditions in ways that allow us to produce decolonizing, critical, activist and authoritative disciplinary knowledge? It is a persistent challenge across disciplines in the imperial university to find ways to generate critical legal and critical race literacy about the operations of the law. The 'law' is not one, it is not neutral, and it does not deserve to be blindly loved.

In 2020, a year before I was targeted in the academic restructure, I was awarded the Vice Chancellor's Award for Excellence in Teaching. I conclude this chapter with (an edited) version of my teaching award application, which outlines my decolonial curriculum, as well as letters of support from students and leading scholars in the field that speak to the outcomes of this type of critical decolonial approach. I remain committed to decolonizing legal pedagogy because I know students can think and move with us in decolonizing directions.

Application for Vice-Chancellor's Award for Excellence in Teaching Flinders University: 'Addressing global questions of Indigenous and racial justice'
Awarded 2020

Citation: Decolonizing criminology: The development of cutting edge, research-led curricula demonstrates a command of the field and addresses contemporary, global questions of Indigenous and racial justice.

Context: The rise of the 'true crime' genre in popular culture has contributed to the exponential growth in the discipline of criminology in the last decade. Here at Flinders, this growth is evidenced by high student numbers in the Bachelor of Criminology, introduced in 2017 to replace the Bachelor of Justice and Society and the popular major in Criminal Justice. The insatiable desire to understand crime lures students into the criminology program, keen to explore the psychological and social factors leading to extreme and violent human behaviour. Yet criminality relates to more than the extreme tendencies of some individuals, as recent police brutality worldwide and the entirety of the body of my research reveals.

#BLM: Black lives have always mattered: I teach and research at the intersection of socio-legal studies, law and criminology with a focus on race relations, law and coloniality. As a practitioner who adopts a social constructivist pedagogy, I place equal value on research and teaching. Research conducted by Richardson (2003: 1631) has shown that the constructivist classroom requires 'deep and strong subject matter knowledge'. My advanced knowledge in the emerging sub-fields of border and decolonial criminology, as well as in law and criminology more broadly, is ensured through the rigorous review processes required while publishing the work I deploy in my research-led curricula. In 2020, the course LEGL 2117 Crimes Against Populations could not be more relevant to the global justice issues of racialized police and state violence against Indigenous and black populations. Yet since 2011 I have consciously sought to demonstrate how legal systems with colonial origins are implicated in the perpetration of state crimes against racialized populations, through my teaching at Flinders.

By positioning law in the context of colonialism and by focusing on the critical reflections, and experiences of those targeted and marginalized by the state, my students come to understand the operations of racialized power and the criminality of the state in the present day. This material selection has the added effect of being inclusive of marginalized students. For example: 'As a marginalized and first-in-family student I have often felt further stigmatized or alienated by topic content, but in Dr Giannacopoulos' topics the opposite occurred; I felt engaged, empowered, and "seen" ... of equal importance is the way in which Dr Giannacopoulos shares her knowledge with students. She has mastered the skill of discussing marginalized groups not merely as research subjects, but as valued human members of society' (Letter of support, 15/10/20).

My decolonial approach to criminology is reflected in the constructivist design, which exposes students to uncomfortable truths about the criminal justice system to dismantle established notions of crime that, if left uninterrogated, consolidate colonial thinking and lead to racism and disadvantage. Students are asked to rethink the normative origin story of Australian law and to delve deeply into the taken-for-granted assumptions that underpin state-centric criminology curricula and teaching. Critical questioning in the course allows students to develop a 'metawareness of their own understandings and learning processes' by providing a platform for students to 'determine, challenge, change and add to existing beliefs and understandings' (Richardson, 2003: 1626). Crimes Against Populations asks: If crime is perpetrated by individuals and is punished by the state, what do we make of scenarios where states have caused and cause profound harms against peoples? These are intellectual, ethical and contemporary unfolding societal challenges that build critical thinking capacities of students while fundamentally challenging the logic and racial effects of the criminal justice system and its associated rationale found in the discipline of criminology.

LEGL 1201 Law in Australian Society: In this core first-year course, students are introduced to the main legal institutions and sources of law that operate in Australia, including political institutions, the judiciary, courts, the legal profession, and police as actors who enforce the law. Critically, missing from the material covered in the course were Indigenous perspectives and critiques of sovereignty and colonialism. In 2016, after obtaining convening rights to the topic, I fundamentally transformed the curriculum by integrating my published research on the coloniality of Australian law, specifically on the Apology to the Stolen Generations, the Constitutional Recognise campaign and offshore detention of asylum seekers and refugees. By taking a critical legal approach, I introduce students to highly challenging material from the outset with an emphasis on the colonial foundations of Australia's legal system in their first year. Students are exposed to the idea that law can contribute to social and racial marginalization. This may sound simple, but it is a fundamental challenge to the most deeply held assumptions about law: that it remedies social problems and delivers justice and equality for all. This has had a profound transformational impact on students as they grappled with their newfound understandings and considered how they might effect change in their own careers and futures. For example: 'Before these courses I knew very little in relation to the Indigenous people … and it was thanks to your course and lecturing insights that I have come to have such an appreciation and understanding … This has become an area I'm especially interested in and as such wanted to thank you for introducing these issues to me, as I aim to continue the rest of my Criminology degree in a direction aimed at learning the most I can about the Indigenous peoples, cultures, histories … so that I can hopefully become someone who can help make a difference' (Student email 25/5/17).

Incorporating Indigenous legal knowledge: Following careful redesign, I have also chosen to ground my courses in the work of Irene Watson, arguably this country's leading Indigenous critical legal scholar, and Pro Vice Chancellor Aboriginal Leadership and Strategy at UniSA. The incorporation of Watson's work into the criminology curriculum is crucial, given the absence of Indigenous staff and perspectives in existing curricula. Students find Watson's work deeply challenging to their core understandings of race and identity because, unlike the textbook material to which students are mainly exposed, Watson's work is written in the first person and incorporates personal narrative as part of scholarly research. The importance of this difference in style is easy to miss. Her voice disrupts the appearance of neutrality that is taken for granted in criminology and law literature and requires students to interrogate the features that make something look truer than something else. The challenge for students to think deeply not just about content but about processes of knowledge production through the inclusion of Watson's research is undoubtedly worthwhile, as students 'grew considerably in their ability to engage ... and apply critical thinking skills to their studies of law' (Dr Nerida Chazal, topic coordinator of LEGL 1102 while I was on study leave in 2015).

LEGL 2117 Crimes Against Populations: When I devised this course in the Bachelor of Justice and Society) I did so to fill an important gap in the existing criminology programme. I generated a fresh, contemporary research-led course by drawing on cutting-edge literature, including my own, in the emerging sub-fields of decolonial and border criminology. I sought peer review of my newly devised course guide for Crimes Against Populations from research collaborator and the world's pre-eminent decolonial criminologist Professor Biko Agozino from Virginia Tech. He responded in this way: 'Lucky students. This [course outline] reads like the outline of a book. I suggest you write up your lecture notes with the view of publishing a textbook on such an important topic' (Email 2/3/17).

Crimes Against Populations challenges racism and colonial power dynamics in several ways. It invites students to unpack the criminological knowledge they have already acquired in their study as a way of entering the conceptual world of this course. If students are predominantly taught that crime is perpetrated by individuals and punished by the state, then what, students are asked, do we make of scenarios where states cause profound harms against peoples? The decolonial theory and scholarship with which students must engage as set readings and in group work collaborations and presentations presents a range of critical and ethical questions that lead, importantly, to a critique and 'metawareness' of the discipline in which students are situated. Students commented: 'The biggest take away from this topic for me was the treatment of Aboriginal and Torres Strait Islander peoples. The depth of the problems and pain they feel due to the way they have been treated was something I did not truly understand until doing this topic. Particularly how sacred their land is and what it means to them' (FLO discussion forum 29/10/20). 'The take home from this topic is all based on the severity of the issues that Indigenous people face and how racism is so prevalent in today's society. It was eye opening to learn about what can be done and how we can combat this issue' (FLO discussion forum 29/10/20). 'We found it incredible that the police funding was SO much higher than all other departments. ... What made this even more significant was that public healthcare had the lowest funding rate within the public services displayed in the chart. If as a society we chose not to "model cruelty and vengeance", and instead put funding into education, housing, healthcare, jobs, etc., rates of recidivism and perpetual crime may decrease' (FLO discussion forum, group entry, 27/8/20). 'When we think about the abolition of incarceration, people commonly think it is not a good idea as they are thinking primarily of the safety of society, however after today's lecture it is clear abolishing incarceration can have many positives placing money into other systems such as healthcare and restorative justice, as well as community treatment programs is better to reduce recidivism rates and rehabilitate "criminals". There are many negative aspects of incarceration, today's reading outlines women are commonly sexually assaulted and stripped of general human rights, so other programs instead of incarceration would be a better option' (FLO discussion forum, 27/8/20).

Since 2017, I have strategically included international research by preeminent decolonial criminology scholar Professor Biko Agozino who was the recipient of the Flinders International Visiting Fellowship in 2018. Agozino was recently recognized as the 15th most influential criminologist working in the world today.[9]

The 2019 special issue of Q1 journal *Globalizations* co-edited by Professor Agozino and myself on the theme of 'Law, love and decolonization', features extensively in the course. By including these texts, I have generated spaces for students to communicate directly with the world's leading scholar of decolonial criminology to facilitate their understanding of his pioneering work on the imperial features of criminology as a discipline. As a research-led educator, I was able to set my own well-cited research as core or recommended readings and discussion platforms for this course.

Command of the fields: Critical race theory, decolonial and border criminology

'Dr Maria Giannacopoulos' teaching is distinguished by the manner in which it is critically underpinned and driven by her innovative research' (Joseph Pugliese, Professor of Cultural Studies, Macquarie University).

As my courses are designed around my own internationally recognized and highly regarded critical race research, students are assured of my knowledge and benefit directly from my command of the field. My research standing and continuous engagement on questions of race justice give merit to the inclusion of my work as the basis for curriculum design and as a platform for student critical thinking and analysis. My research expertise in law, cultural studies, socio-legal studies and criminology has consistently been recognized by peers working in these fields. Professor Pugliese stated: 'She grounds her rigorous and original analyses of law in two overlapping fields: Aboriginal sovereignty and refugee and asylum studies … her work across these fields is exemplary and unique.'

In doing this, I continuously offer students the exciting opportunity for critical reflection and learning, precisely by exposing them to new ways of understanding law, processes of criminalization, injustice and justice. This has had a clear impact on students, as evidenced by these student comments: 'Her knowledge and representation of these issues are inspirational. Her classes are not just a series of slides and lecture notes, they are teaching moments where real issues and knowledge regimes are unpacked and analyzed' (Student email 15/10/20). 'The parallels drawn between colonialism in Australia and Greece were of particular interest to me, as I had not previously been aware of such forms of economic dominance over particular populations' (Student email 31/5/17).

My scholarly standing across several criminological sub-fields is further evidenced by several factors. My original research articles are informing curriculum design in the teaching of migration law, border criminology, Indigenous, cultural and media studies at Macquarie University, the University of Technology Sydney and the Sydney, Western Sydney, Melbourne and Wollongong Universities. In 2019/20 my research was used in the teaching of 'Understanding Race' at Western Sydney University with Associate Professor Alana Lentin saying in her lecture: 'The work of scholars such as Suvendrini Perera, Joseph Pugliese and Maria Giannacopoulos in the Australian context … is exemplary of work that shines a spotlight on the complexities and complicities of migrancy and settler colonialism with their sharp focus on the colonial derivations of racial violence as it affects both Indigenous people.'[10]

In 2019, I was invited speaker at the ARC funded Deathscapes project launch in Sydney, where I shared my experiences of teaching critical criminology. I was invited to do so after having incorporated the interactive, analytical website foregrounding deaths in custody of Indigenous peoples and refugees into my topic 'Crimes Against Populations'. In 2018, I decided to replace traditional readings in some weeks with the interactive website, as a way of engaging students around difficult social justice questions visually. At the Sydney launch, I elaborated upon my rationale for using the site as an engagement and methodological tool in the teaching of criminology, and shared student experiences. I learned from the organizers that several scholars in the audience were inspired to adopt similar teaching strategies in their own teaching across the country after hearing me speak. The substance of my talk was andragogical, discussing the complexity but also the necessity of teaching against the grain in criminology, which at times too heavily emphasizes individuals as criminal rather than looking at state harm. My 2020 scholarly article 'Debtscape: Australia's Constitutional

Nomopoly', published in the well-respected journal *Borderlands*, is the resulting publication of this collaboration. It contains a section on teaching criminology at Flinders using the Deathscapes project and has been accessed 486 times, demonstrating widespread reach and impact. So impressed were the CIs with this article that they have recommissioned it for a Routledge book on the Deathscapes project.

In 2020, I was invited guest lecturer in two Indigenous-led Flinders courses: INDG 3001: Colonial Intimacies, the Economy and Genocide of Mathematics (Faye Rosas Blanch) and INDG2004: Reconciliation & Indigenous Knowledges (Dr Christopher Wilson) on the strength of a research paper I delivered at the Critical Race Theory & Resistance Art Conference held at the Flinders Museum of Art in 2019. Students in INDG 2004 take over radio show Nunga Wangga on Radio Adelaide as both their assessment and a way of 'giving back' to Indigenous communities. Students cited my seminal work on law, crime and colonialism during the radio show, demonstrating its relevance and impact on students and contemporary debates on Indigenous justice.[11]

Decolonial curricula: Impact on students: I recently saw a former student, a formerly incarcerated woman who had taken both my topics in recent years. I mentioned that I was applying for a teaching award and she sent a touching letter, speaking of the multiple and empowering impacts of my teaching: 'Given many of the BGL student cohort will be future policy and decision makers or working within justice systems, understanding complex structural issues will not only be invaluable for them and their future employers, but arguably life-changing for the marginalized communities that they will impact. As my undergraduate degree comes to an end at Flinders University, I can honestly say that Dr Giannacopoulos has made the biggest mark on me. Aside from her sharp intellect and wealth of knowledge in this area, her willingness to support and engage with students and discuss serious social issues has been invaluable. As I move into post-graduate studies and seek to use my degree to challenge oppressive systems, Dr Giannacopoulos will be a role model, a woman whose knowledge and writing I will continue to be inspired by' (letter of support, 15/10/20).[12]

Notes

[1] This chapter is drawn from three sources: a keynote address at 'Decolonising the Curriculum: Perspectives on Best Practice' Adelaide University, 8 July 2023. Thanks to Dr Tiziana Torresi and Dr Priya Chacko for their kind invitation to present and to think with excellent scholars engaged in this space, particularly Mr Bernard Kelly-Edwards, Indigenous Art Code, Professor Simone Dennis, Associate Professor Georgina Drew, Professor Melissa Nursey-Bray, Dr Anna Szorenyi and Dr Edson Ziso. The chapter also draws on Giannacopoulos (2019b). Finally, it incorporates the application leading to the award of the 2020 Vice Chancellor's Prize for Excellence in Teaching at Flinders University.

2. 'Wog' is a derogatory term used in Australia to refer to a foreigner or migrant especially from Southern Europe. Many of us subject to this description use it among ourselves to describe an experience and resistance to racialization in the Australian colony.
3. Many of the scholars with whom I have been in dialogue in different contexts are authors in this volume: Dr Faye Rosas Blanch, Professor Bronwyn Carlson, Professor Joseph Pugliese, Professor Alana Lentin, Dr Andrew Brooks, Dr Jennifer Nielsen, Dr Samantha Schulz.
4. https://www.skynews.com.au/australia-news/voice-to-parliament/budget-papers-reveal-the-3646-million-cost-of-delivering-the-voice-referendum/news-story/80a7550b3113a0ff07902cb6da6850e1
5. https://nit.com.au/15-05-2023/5966/funding-crisis-sees-aboriginal-legal-service-freeze-operations-at-13-new-south-wales-courts
6. See Michael Mansell: https://www.youtube.com/watch?v=7U0qrjJLMJ0
7. https://forms.office.com/Pages/ResponsePage.aspx?id=pM_2PxXn20i44Qhnufn7o_GEBPLZjLZMrOJBt3m48BhUMlFCTjhNMk8wQlhCQzQ1TFY5VFRZUEFPViQlQCN0PWcu&wdLOR=cB1AEE12D-00BF-4516-8809-106DF7B01418&mc_cid=c3ae21a277&mc_eid=4d75a65d7b
8. This section first appeared in the *Journal of Global Indigeneity*, 2019, volume 4, issue 1.
9. https://academicinfluence.com/articles/people/most-influential-criminologists-today
10. https://www.alanalentin.net/2019/09/08/colonial-possession-postcolonialism-and-whiteness-studies
11. http://radioadelaide.org.au/program/nunga-wangga/?fbclid=IwAR2hl1n7d731kR7kJyStbimnxQ0nRHbWPzb8q2u-6i4pv781KsPU-BGkxi8
12. This student is now the recipient of a scholarship at the University of New South Wales and I am supervising her doctoral project.

References

Agozino, B. (2019) 'New Zealand and Australia visiting fellowships', *Journal of Global Indigeneity*, 4(1): 1–30.

Chatterjee, P. and Maira, S. (2014) *The Imperial University: Academic Repression and Scholarly Dissent*, Minneapolis: University of Minnesota Press.

Foley, G. and Gibson, P. (2023) 'The use and abuse of history in the Voice referendum debate: An interview with Professor Gary Foley', *Overland*, 2 October, https://overland.org.au/2023/10/the-use-and-abuse-of-history-in-the-voice-referendum-debate-an-interview-with-professor-gary-foley

Giannacopoulos, M. (2011) 'Nomophilia and bia: The love of law and the question of violence', *Borderlands*, 10(1): 1–19.

Giannacopoulos, M. (2017) 'Sovereign debt crises, referendums and the changing face of colonial power', *Continuum*, 31(1): 33–42.

Giannacopoulos, M. (2019a) 'Debtscape: Australia's constitutional nomopoly', *Borderlands*, 18(2): 116–36.

Giannacopoulos, M. (2019b) 'Nomophilia and academic work in the austerity university', *Journal of Global Indigeneity*, 4(1).

Giannacopoulos, M. (2021) 'White law/Black deaths: Nomocide and the foundational absence of consent in Australian law', *Australian Feminist Law Journal*, 46(2): 249–63.

Giannacopoulos, M. (2022) 'The colonial debtscape', in S. Perera and J. Pugliese (eds), *Mapping Deathscapes: Digital Geographies of Racial and Border Violence*, London: Routledge, pp 46–61.

Moreton-Robinson, A. (2004) 'The possessive logic of patriarchal white sovereignty: The High Court and the *Yorta Yorta* decision', *Borderlands*, 3(2): 1–9.

Richardson, V. (2003) 'Constructivist pedagogy', *Teachers College Record*, 105(9): 1623–40.

Watson, I. (2005) 'Illusionists and hunters: Being Aboriginal in this occupied space', *Australian Feminist Law Journal*, 22(1): 15–28.

Watson, I. (2009) 'Aboriginality and the violence of colonialism', *Borderlands*, 8(1): 1–8.

Watson, I. (2017) 'What is the mainstream? The laws of First Nations peoples', in R. Levy, M. O'Brien, S. Rice, P. Ridge and M. Thornton (eds), *New Directions for Law in Australia*, Canberra: ANU Press, pp 213–220.

11

Race-ing the Law

Jennifer M. Nielsen

Introduction

Australian law texts conventionally speak of Australia 'receiving' the British legal tradition and its 'long and distinguished heritage' of rights, freedoms and privileges (ALRC, 2016: para 2.2). They do not dwell on the fact that the British claim over these lands and waterways relied on the fiction that the lands' First Peoples were legally 'no one' – devoid of philosophies, polity, social structures and laws the British considered equal to their superior European ways (Watson, 2014).

As Distinguished Professor Aileen Moreton-Robinson (2021) asks, 'What logics are at play when fiction is accepted as truth?' Indeed, First Peoples could only be considered 'no one' through the European ideas of race that configured them as inferior, entitling the 'superior' British to assume sovereign possession of these lands as 'settlers' – not 'invaders'. This legal fiction has been maintained by colonial and, since then, the Australian courts (Watson, 2014).

Race is a founding logic of Australian law and legal philosophy, and its social, economic and political systems (Moreton-Robinson, 2021). It is evident in the birthing of the nation, distinguishing who belonged and who did not, motivating the new parliament's first substantive laws: the Pacific Island Labourers Act 1901 (Cth) and the Immigration Restriction Act 1901 (Cth), the legal foundations of the 'White Australia' policy (Nielsen, 2016; Moreton-Robinson, 2021). Australian law continues to operationalize race as the status assigned 'to those who are not members of the white race', rendering First Peoples and people of colour hyper-visible yet separate from and 'in contrast to the invisible omnipresent white race within law that defines itself by what it is not' (Moreton-Robinson, 2021). This logic pervades Australian legal, political and social systems as a racial ideology privileging white normativity (Ransley and Marchetti, 2001; Moreton-Robinson, 2021).

Yet race is not talked about – at all or enough – in the teaching and research of the legal academy (Burns and Nielsen, 2018: 2–3). Too few Australian lawyers, judges, academics and researchers demonstrate racial literacy or critique the deployment of race by and in law. Instead, generations of lawyers have learned to ignore the racial logics embedded in legal thinking and jurisprudence (Moreton-Robinson, 2021), duty-bound to the liberal ideals of equality and a colour-blind vision of the rule of law. Law schools and legal education are indeed part of the 'imperial project' (Burns et al, 2018: 13; see also Watson and Burns, 2015).

This chapter contributes to this book's intent to encourage the academy to bring critical attention to race and racism and build racial literacy within Australian tertiary education. I come to this conversation with more than 30 years' experience as a tertiary legal educator. Over time, I have taught a diverse range of core and elective law subjects and collaborated with First Nations scholars to develop curriculum related to First Peoples and the law. My engagement with First Nations scholars, Elders, students and other community members has particularly shaped and informed my experience and practice in encouraging racial literacy within legal education, and I remain indebted for the knowledge and wisdom that has been collectively shared with me (see Nielsen, 2019).

Three other experiences have also been influential. First, for decades I've taught an elective on discrimination and equal employment opportunity law that demands engagement with the concept of systemic racism/bias. Second, I was part of a Southern Cross University team that delivered 'Courageous Conversations About Race', staff training on race and racism based on Glen Singleton and Curtis Linton's (2005) work in the United States. Finally, elsewhere Associate Professor Marcelle Burns and I collaborated to teach and share reflections on our experience with the elective 'Race and the Law' (Burns and Nielsen, 2018).

Drawing on these experiences, my intent is to stimulate dialogue on strategies to promote racial literacy in legal education. I begin by outlining the Australian law curriculum[1] and layers of regulation that inform the 'proper way' law should be taught – often cited as the reason why the law curriculum cannot easily carry social/racial critique. I then look to the potential of a socio-legal approach to teaching law to open up conversations about why and how law and the legal system have been shaped by racial logics. This approach demystifies the 'rightness' of law, opening opportunities to critique the Australian legal system as a cultural practice. To particularize this (within the available scope), I describe two teaching strategies that I believe ground racial literacy in legal learning.

Before I begin, I acknowledge and thank three First Nations scholars in particular – Professor Irene Watson, Distinguished Professor Aileen

Moreton-Robinson and Associate Professor Marcelle Burns – for the deep learning each has provoked me to achieve over years of dialogue; it is difficult not to draw on those conversations and their wisdom while sharing here. Indeed, it is vital for white scholars to build respectful relationships with those who have situated knowledge about race, to ground the work we do in this space. Even so, all errors and misunderstandings remain totally my own.

A regulated curriculum

Australian legal education originates from the system 'exercised by the London Inns of Court and the King's Inns Dublin and the qualification of the legal profession in England and Wales' (Barker, 2012: 1). Colonial legal education was regulated by admission boards, which stipulated educational requirements and that those entering the profession be of 'good fame and character' (Barker, 2012: 4). The emerging antipodean universities established an Australian academic legal curriculum; each had a distinct approach, but all taught the general, civil, constitutional and international laws of England, and the 'classics' – ancient Greek and Roman philosophies and logic (Barker, 2012). No consideration was paid to learning and understanding the even more ancient philosophies, laws and lore that traversed and continue to traverse this country, sustaining First Peoples and their non-human kin for millennia.

Today, the primary objective of the two tertiary law qualifications – the Bachelor of Laws (LLB) and the postgraduate level Juris Doctor (JD) – remains admission to legal practice. Although the pedagogy and philosophical emphasis of each school varies, the law curriculum is relatively uniform across institutions as it remains heavily regulated by admission authorities (Burns et al, 2018: 11–16; CALD, 2020: 1). The first tier of regulation (beyond that of the Tertiary Education Quality and Standards Agency) is set by the requirements for admission prescribed by legislation in each jurisdiction (for example, Sch 1 Pt 2, Legal Profession Uniform Admission Rules 2015 [NSW]). These requirements give primacy to the 'Priestley 11', the legal fields of knowledge considered to be of most importance to legal practice (ALTC, 2010: 13).

The next tier operates at a national level in the Law Admissions Consultative Committee Standards, as promulgated by the Law Admissions Consultative Committee ('LACC'). These reinforce the doctrinal focus of the law curriculum, and mandate matters required for accredited courses, including duration of learning and teaching practices (LACC, 2018).

The final tier is the Australian Law School Standards ('the CALD standards', see CALD, 2020) implemented by the Council of Australian Law Deans (CALD) to describe minimum standards for accredited Australian law schools. They require the curriculum to cover 'all the academic requirements specified for the purposes of admission to practice as a legal practitioner in Australia' (CALD, 2020: Standard 2.3.1, p 17).

An important and recent inclusion in the CALD Standards is that the curriculum should seek to develop knowledge and understanding of 'Aboriginal and Torres Strait Islander perspectives on and intersections with the law' (2020: Standard 2.3.3, p 17). Racial literacy, however, is not mandated separately as part of the knowledge and understanding required. This is of particular concern because, as Burns et al (2019: 21) found, racial literacy supports the development of Indigenous and other forms of cultural competency.

The Threshold Learning Outcomes

CALD responded to the introduction of the Australian Qualifications Framework by adopting disciplinary standards – Bachelor of Laws: Learning and Teaching Academic Standards Statement (ALTC, 2010) and the Juris Doctor Threshold Learning Outcomes (CALD, 2012) ('the TLOs'). These organize the law curriculum around the themes of knowledge; ethics and professional responsibility; thinking skills; research skills; communication and collaboration; and self-management (ALTC, 2010).

The TLOs again reinforce legal doctrine as 'the fundamental areas of legal knowledge, the Australian legal system, and underlying principles and concepts, including international and comparative contexts; the broader contexts within which legal issues arise; and the principles and values of justice and of ethical practice in lawyers' roles' (ALTC, 2010: 8). Like all the other forms of regulation and prescription, they do not mandate racial literacy among the knowledge and skills required by legal graduates.

Legal educators are, nonetheless, encouraged to read the TLOs as capable of supporting a broad set of literacies because TLO 1 requires graduates to understand this 'coherent body' of the 'fundamental areas of law' in the 'broader contexts within which legal issues arise' (ALTC, 2010: 12; CALD, 2012: 3). This reference to 'broader contexts' is anticipated as potentially including 'social justice; gender-related issues; Indigenous perspectives; cultural and linguistic diversity; the commercial or business environment; globalization; public policy; moral contexts; and issues of sustainability' (ALTC, 2010: 13; CALD, 2012: 7). Equally, the CALD standard related to 'Aboriginal and Torres Strait Islander perspectives on and intersections with the law' offers fresh ground to build racial literacy and First Nations perspectives within the law curriculum (CALD, 2020: Standard 2.3.3, p 17).

However, speaking anecdotally, many legal educators use 'easy outs' to avoid doing so. First, a common justification is that the curriculum is already crowded with doctrinal knowledge – 'there's no room'. Second, individuals argue that they lack racial literacy themselves and avoid discussing racial issues so they 'don't get it wrong'; typically, they are also reluctant to address their professional deficits by developing racial literacy, making the problem almost intractable.

Moreover, embedding critical skills and literacies in the core curriculum – the Priestley 11 or other prescribed core subjects (such as Legal Process or Philosophy) – is the only way to ensure graduates gain these skills and knowledge. Elective study can contribute to the development of critical literacies, but at best can only disturb the liberal ideals of equality and colour-blind visions inherent within the law curriculum. And I think it self-evident that more than a single experience of learning about race is required to establish racial literacy. To be most effective, critical racial literacies should be embedded within the LLB's or JD's whole curriculum.

Developing racial literacy: putting race and the law in context

Standpoint

I come to this work as a white woman whose ontological and epistemological worlds are grounded in vastly different realities from those who know the downsides of racism and colonization (Nielsen, 2019: 121–2) – 'the nation's most conscientious students of whiteness and racialisation' – who speak with a body of knowledge (not just perspectives), that resists the hegemony of patriarchal white sovereignty and its assumed privileges (Moreton-Robinson, 2004: 142). My standpoint, being grounded in the legacies of white racial privilege, mediates both my capacity to understand *and* to 'reproduce' what I have learned and know from these experts (Nielsen, 2019).

In my view, when we white folk seek to contribute to the work of racial literacy, we must 'own' our standpoint in the stories of race, work reflexively and beyond our own ways of knowing, and never displace the authority and agency of others to speak for themselves. This demands that that we engage reflexively with our whiteness and privileged position within (and outside) academic spaces (Nielsen, 2019).

Putting race and the law in context

Law operationalizes race through white racial norms that are the natural, neutral and 'universally applicable' character of law; being so 'ingrained' in the common law, the effects of racism are rendered 'ordinary and natural' to those of the dominant culture (Moreton-Robinson, 2021). Teaching racial literacy must therefore reveal *how* law operationalizes race. This cannot be done through the conventional intellectual teaching strategies used to convey legal doctrine. Those strategies apply laws' logics through analyses based fundamentally on the detail of the primary legal sources – parliamentary laws and appellate court decisions. The methods of doctrinal analysis remove social and political reality from consideration through the principle of 'relevance' and the common law's focus on 'material facts' (see Marinac et al, 2018: ch 11). Doctrinal legal analysis thus operates in a vacuum that is decontextualized from factual and personal realities. These realities are discarded because they are deemed legally 'irrelevant', thereby confining legal analysis to a narrow temporal and factual scope (Nielsen, 2008).

Quite different teaching methods are needed to make race 'relevant' and change the conversation about what matters in the application of law. I use 'socio-legal' methods that look at 'the operation of law in a social context, thus underlining the fact that law does not operate in a social vacuum' (Fehlberg, 1997: 11). This frees the learning process from the hold of doctrinal method, making the 'social' (and political, economic, and so on) as important to legal learning as are the specifics of doctrine. In this frame, Australian law is situated as a cultural practice, produced at a particular time within a particular social and political context. This strips common law doctrine of its 'rarefied' character and makes its 'rightness' available for critique.

Indeed, as explained, the TLOs and now the LACC Standards, can be used to ground legal learning in a contextual racial critique and thus build racial literacy and understanding of First Nations' perspectives (Burns and Nielsen, 2018; Burns et al, 2019: 20). Teaching in context transgresses the doctrinal boundaries by restoring 'relevance' to the voices of those who experience law and creating opportunities to analyse the lived impacts of law. Applying a critical race lens in this frame to law foregrounds race and racism, and exposes the raced subjectivity of the social context in which Australian law operates, and the manner by which its liberal 'objective' and 'rational' methods create and secure the dominant racial order (Nielsen, 2019).

However, racial literacy requires more than simply talking about race – the transmission of 'content' is not the objective because learning about race without understanding its human impact is risky (Burns and Nielsen, 2018). By this I mean that the conversation cannot simply transmit the 'detail' and 'fact' of race, but requires understanding the meaning of race *and its effect*. Without that, 'talking about' race risks reinforcing racial stereotypes and reinscribing racist ideology and systems because, by itself, it does not challenge ideology and thinking. A critical understanding of race is essential. This is why the learning should encourage reflectivity, self-growth and humility by challenging students to critique themselves at an ontological level, as well as an epistemological level. The law curriculum tends to emphasize the 'practical' skills needed for law, such as legal reasoning, technical drafting and advocacy. Increasingly, though, the so-called 'soft' skills – emotional intelligence, reflexivity and self-awareness – are being acknowledged as vital to the proper growth of a lawyer's professional development (for example, Field et al, 2019), including building cultural competencies (Burns et al, 2019: 20).

This is why students must be supported to understand their standpoint as it is vital to their learning that they understand that race is about *them – all of them*, not just those rendered racially 'other'. This supports white and other non-Indigenous students to work beyond their guilt and towards accountability for Australia's past and ongoing systems of colonization (Nielsen, 2019).

Within the remaining space permitted, the final two parts of this section describe two strategies I have used that, in my experience, are useful to building the ground needed to develop racial literacy in legal education.

Race-ing the myth of neutrality in equality before the law

Liberal ideals are inherent in common law logic – equality, individuality, neutrality and objectivity. 'Equality before the law', or 'legal equality', is a fundamental common law doctrine 'and a basic prescript of the administration of justice under our system of government' (*Leeth* v *Commonwealth* [1992], cited in Marinac et al, 2018: 256). This basic prescript is practised as 'formal equality', which rests on the Western philosophy that like cases should be treated alike, and unlike cases should be treated differently (Marinac et al, 2018: 255). That is, law is neutral to, but can be moved by, 'difference' – but only when it is relevant.

Indeed, law claims neutrality by regarding difference as 'irrelevant' – despite those differences being meaningful in social and other ways – so that it can treat people as 'relevantly alike' when they are not (Fredman, 2016: 717). Former Australian Human Rights Commission president, the Honourable John von Doussa, gives a neat explanation:

> Assertions of equality usually imply positive connotations, but may disguise hidden vices. Differences of race, ethnicity, religion, sex and economic and cultural circumstances can mean that 'one law for all' protects the values and interests of a majority of citizens at the expense of minorities. It does so by privileging unity and formal equality over cultural diversity and substantive equality. (Cited in Marinac et al, 2018: 260)

Revealing law's racial logics thus starts with debunking the myth of neutrality to reveal law's hidden vices. My contribution to the first-year law text, *Learning Law* (Marinac et al, 2018), has this very purpose. Rather than describing the many ways in which certain groups are 'disadvantaged' by law (an endless project), the chapter 'Equality, difference and law' reorients focus onto the way law is inherently designed *to create* these disadvantages. That work is readily available, so I won't repeat the specifics here. But I refer to it here because, in my view, the crucial starting point to founding racial literacy in law is to unveil law's 'neutrality' and disturb the 'rightness' and purported 'racial blindness' in doctrinal legal logic.

To illustrate, I share the following excerpt from the latter end of the chapter, to illustrate critique directed at what equality at law could mean – not just how it is currently interpreted. This passage is intended to provoke the need to rethink 'our approach to equality in law because some groups will always have separate interests and rights that are deserving of legal recognition and protection':

> To illustrate this, let's revisit our discussion about *Gerhardy v Brown*,[2] and the point we made that the Pitjantjatjara peoples have an immutable and unique connection to their lands. The High Court recognised their right to control access to their land as a special measure. By definition, special measures are expected to be temporary and so must end once they have achieved their purpose – they are not supposed to establish permanent separate rights for particular groups. But the Pitjantjatjara peoples' connection to their country is not temporary and its purpose will continue into the millennia. So, to ensure an adequate protection of Pitjantjatjara peoples' rights to equality we would need to recognise their distinct rights and interests, not just on a temporary basis, but *always*. (Marinac et al, 2018: 281)

From this understanding, attention can be given to the systemic 'inattention, marginalisation, and positioning' of issues of race 'within a deficit narrative' in the law curriculum and connect learning to the way in which doctrinal legal thinking produces 'unequal relationships, access to justice problems, and poor legal outcomes' (Burns et al, 2018: 16).

Experiential learning about systemic racism and privilege

Australian law focuses on the rights of individuals, thereby framing racism as individual acts that impact one individual or a group of individuals. Race as a systemic practice remains unknowable at law, leaving institutional and systemic racism unchallenged (Nielsen, 2008). Racial literacy demands an understanding that racism is an ideological and systemic practice rather than simple and discrete acts of individual bigotry (Moreton-Robinson, 2004).

But systemic racism tends to be invisible to its beneficiaries – the dominant racial group whose interests, values, norms and institutions it tacitly supports. For many of us (and more specifically white Australians), our racialized experience is 'ordinary' and 'natural' as we are socially conditioned not to notice race until we encounter someone with 'it'. We may even choose to overlook 'it' – but our proclamations of race/colour blindness are simply manifestations of our white privilege to choose when and why race matters (Moreton-Robinson, 2004).

But *we do notice*. And I have found that by engaging students in experiential learning, they can connect with what they know in their gut about the effect of race, also creating ground from which they can accept that whiteness (including their own where applicable) has meaning.

The strategy I've used was designed by Singleton and Linton (2006) in their programme, 'Courageous Conversations About Race'. An essential part of their programme is that group participants/students agree to several commitments and conditions, to 'remain connected' by keeping the spotlight on race – while acknowledging other factors cause marginalization, focus remains solely on the function of race in analysing experience.[3]

In my experience, teaching about whiteness theory has always been the more difficult part of this programme, because the members of the mainly white group are finally required to notice that race is about them – and that is not comfortable. Singleton and Linton's exercise is deceptively simple, and offers strong grounds to found this learning. The group members are asked to organize themselves in pairs or small groups. Each pair/group is then assigned a racial identity – that is, 'Aboriginal', 'Japanese', 'Irish', 'white Australian', and so on. I explain that I will present a series of questions and that – thinking from the perspective of a person with that racial identity – they are to position themselves physically on an imaginary continuum to indicate whether each statement applies to them completely (100 per cent) or not at all (0 per cent), or somewhere in between. The following are examples:

- Can you go to a shopping centre by yourself and be confident you won't be harassed or threatened?
- Can you perform well in a challenging task without being told you are a credit to your race?
- When the media report on people from your cultural background, can you be sure their race or colour won't be mentioned?

The exercise creates discomfort and confusion. Participants invariably ask for more direction – 'What gender is the person?', 'Are they poor?', 'What industry?' I simply remind them that our spotlight is on race. I politely decline any further direction and suggest they do what they think most likely. After each question, I ask them to stop, identify who they are (in their assigned racial identity) and notice who is standing where on the continuum. After several rounds, a racial pattern emerges – and that's when I start asking (rhetorical) questions like 'Why did you move to that point – or that one?', 'Why didn't you move much during the exercise?' and encourage them to observe how the pattern of movement demonstrates (as it always does) a hierarchy defined by skin colour. It is at this point that I ask, 'If race doesn't matter [which many of them have said earlier in the session], then why did you move at all?'

Invariably, this final question is met by silence and, for the white participants, very serious discomfort. And that discomfort is deliberate because it creates an embodied shift in their thinking; I then explain that they have enacted whiteness theory – and I didn't tell them to do it; they followed what they know in their gut because, consciously or not, we all notice how race is operationalized every day. From this point, students become open to accepting that race (including whiteness) *does* operate in our society as an ideological system that allocates privilege to some and marginalizes others. For some, this learning is life-changing.

Conclusion

Foregrounding race in our teaching enables legal educators to ask different questions about law by breaching the doctrinal thinking that limits critique to what the law is and says, rather than what law *could or should be*. Putting law in its socio-legal frame allows educators to open different discussions and inspire respect for the authority of those who are the situated knowers of the racialized hegemony of law.

Australian legal educators do not do enough to expose – let alone challenge – the racial ideology infused in Australian law. We may be great at 'doing' the acknowledgement to Country, support our university's Reconciliation Action Plan and turn up for a good feed on Harmony Day, but somehow we collectively tend to avoid critical conversations about race, thinking it is better just not to talk about it. Perhaps these are just the habits of racism and whiteness (Burns and Nielsen, 2018).

In January 2024, the Council of Australian Law Deans promulgated its *Statement on Racism in Australian Law Schools*, endorsing the 'Universities Australia, Indigenous Strategy 2022-2025 and its call for "zero tolerance to racism" in universities' (CALD, 2024).

Importantly, CALD also declared support for 'Indigenous specific anti-racism strategies including an anti-racism statement and actions pursuant to eliminating discriminatory race-based practices' and that work on anti-racism 'be prioritised by law schools' (CALD, 2024).

This signals that it is urgent that legal educators develop racial literacy - if we are true to our word that we intend to dislodge racial privilege and expose and remedy racial injustice, then we must act because *we have an obligation to do this work*.

Notes

[1] Due to limitations of space, my focus will be on legal education in the tertiary setting, and will not discuss a second layer of legal education – Practical Legal Training (see Burns et al, 2018). I also acknowledge that my discussion tends to focus on the experience of white law teachers and students and fails to speak adequately to the experience of First Nations academics and students or academics and students of colour. This reflects the

limitations in my own perspective and knowledge. The chapters by Professor Nicole Watson and Dr Ambelin Kwaymullina, for example, offer informed dialogue on that experience (Chapters 14 and 22).

2   In *Gerhardy* v *Brown*, the High Court decided that land rights legislation breached the principle of formal equality, amounting to direct race discrimination, but was lawful nonetheless as a special measure as defined by section 8 of the Racial Discrimination Act 1975 (Cth): see Marinac et al (2018: 277–8, 281).

3   In addition, the programme anticipates discomfort as 'okay'; engages whiteness theory to see the 'upside' as well as the 'downside' of racial experience; and acknowledges that it is important to speak your truth as we connect through stories and engage multiple perspectives. Finally, this learning is not discrete but an ongoing journey (Singleton and Linton, 2006).

References

ALRC (Australian Law Reform Commission) (2016) *Traditional Rights and Freedoms: Encroachments by Commonwealth Laws*, https://www.alrc.gov.au/publication/traditional-rights-and-freedoms-encroachments-by-commonwealth-laws-alrc-report-129

ALTC (Australian Learning and Teaching Council) (2010) *Bachelor of Laws: Learning and Teaching Academics Standards Statement*, https://cald.asn.au/wp-content/uploads/2017/11/KiftetalLTASStandardsStatement2010.pdf

Barker, D. (2012) '"Colonial gown, cap and wig": The origins of Australian legal education', *Journal of the Australasian Law Teachers Association*, 5(1): 205–18.

Burns, M. and Nielsen, J. (2018) 'Dealing with the "wicked" problem of race and the law: A critical journey for students (and academics)', *Legal Education Review*, 28(2).

Burns, M., Young, S. and Nielsen, J. (2018) '"The difficulties of communication encountered by Indigenous peoples": Moving beyond Indigenous deficit in the Model Admission Rules for Legal Practitioners', *Legal Education Review*, 28(2).

Burns, M., Hong, L. and Wood, A. (2019) *Indigenous Cultural Competency for Legal Academics Program: Final Report*, Canberra: DET.

CALD (Council of Australian Law Deans) (2012) *Juris Doctor Threshold Learning Outcomes*, https://cald.asn.au/wp-content/uploads/2017/11/Threhold-Learning-Outcomes-JD.pdf

CALD (Council of Australian Law Deans) (2020) *Standards for Australian Law Schools*, https://cald.asn.au/wp-content/uploads/2020/07/Australian-Law-School-Standards-v1.3-30-Jul-2020.pdf

Fehlberg, B. (1997) *Sexually Transmitted Debt: Surety Experience and English Law*, Oxford: Clarendon Press.

Field, R., Duffy, J. and Huggins, A. (2019) *Lawyering and Positive Professional Identities*, 2nd edn, Sydney: LexisNexis Butterworths.

Fredman, S. (2016) 'Substantive equality revisited', *I•CON*, 14(3): 712–38.

LACC (Law Admissions Consultative Committee) (2018) *Accreditation Standards for Australian Law Courses*, https://legalservicescouncil.org.au/documents/accreditation-standards-for-law-courses.pdf

Legal Profession Uniform Admission Rules 2015 (NSW).

Marinac, A., Simpson, B., Hart, C., Chisholm, R., Nielsen, J., and Brogan, M. (2018) *Learning Law*, Cambridge: Cambridge University Press.

Moreton-Robinson, A. (2004) 'Whiteness matters: Australian studies and Indigenous studies', in D. Carter, K. Darian-Smith and G. Worby (eds), *Thinking Australian Studies: Teaching Courses Across Cultures*, Brisbane: University of Queensland Press, pp 136–46.

Moreton-Robinson, A. (2021) 'The paradox of race in Australian legal thought: Making the invisible visible', Alice Tay Lecture 2021, https://www.youtube.com/watch?v=frZb1mu2rnY

Nielsen, J. (2008) 'Whiteness and anti-discrimination law: It's in the design', *ACRAWSA e-Journal*, 3(2).

Nielsen, J. (2016) 'Breaking the silence: The importance of constitutional change', in S. Young, J. Nielsen and J. Patrick (eds), *Constitutional Recognition of Australia's First Peoples: Theories and Comparative Perspectives*, Sydney: Federation Press, pp 2–28.

Nielsen, J. (2019) 'The problem with research', in D. Gozdecka and A. Macduff (eds), *Feminism, Postfeminism and Legal Theory: Beyond the Gendered Subject*, London: Routledge, pp 117–36.

Ransley, J. and Marchetti, E. (2001) 'The hidden whiteness of Australian law: A case study', *Griffith Law Review*, 10(1): 139–52.

Singleton, G.E. and Linton, C. (2006) *Courageous Conversations About Race: A Field Guide for Achieving Equity in Schools*, Thousand Oaks: Corwin Press.

Watson, I. (2014) *Aboriginal Peoples, Colonialism and International Law: Raw Law*, London: Routledge.

Watson, I. and Burns, M. (2015) 'Indigenous knowledges: A strategy for First Nations peoples' engagement in higher education', in S. Varnham, P. Kamvounias and J. Squelch (eds), *Higher Education and the Law*, Sydney: Federation Press, pp 41–52.

12

Assembling Decolonial Anti-Racist Praxis from the Margins: Reflections from Critical Community Psychology

Christopher C. Sonn

Introduction

I acknowledge all the people who have come before me, whose stories have been silenced, erased and/or excluded from the archives of South Africa and Australia. I am inspired by Elders, ancestors, contemporary leaders and people in everyday settings who continue to contest this erasure, the result of slavery, colonialism, Apartheid, the brutal practices of land dispossession and the 'culture bomb of whiteness' (Ngugi, 1986). In both countries, this involved the imposition of a hierarchical racial classification system that positioned 'white' people at the top and all other people underneath. I have sought to excavate this history, slowly and carefully, seeking to understand these absences, erasures and denials, recovering the complex and diverse stories of our ancestors – stories buried by colonialism, the violence of Apartheid, white supremacy and the various forms of dispossession and injury that this has entailed.

I was born and raised in South Africa during the Apartheid era in what was designated a 'coloured' community. My parents and two siblings migrated to Australia in the late 1980s, both because of work opportunities and due to the violence of Apartheid. I have lived in Australia since that time. I am a diasporic subject – I belong here and there, like others who have arrived from different shores and who make lives on the unceded lands of First Nations people. I work at Victoria University on the land of the Boonwurrung and Wurundjeri of the Kulin Nation. It is on this land that I, a member of the

African diaspora, have been learning, deconstructing and co-constructing decolonial praxis through liberation and community psychologies.

In this chapter, I reflect on some work done as part of a research network called the Community Identity Displacement Research Network, which we started at Victoria University in 2012. The network's aim was to bring together people from different disciplines into a learning community, a community of practice, through which we could collaborate and collectively construct justice-oriented research and action. A key question is: How do we create and mobilize liberation community psychologies in and outside the neoliberal university to contribute to the empowerment and self-determination of the various communities who suffer the brunt of colonial and racialized structural violence that produce psychosocial suffering? Put another way, how can we create justice-oriented research, research that is responsive to the needs and issues of individuals, community groups and organizations, especially those who are subjected to structural and symbolic violence and who suffer its consequences?

I draw on the tradition of *testimonio* (Reyes and Curry Rodríguez, 2012); this is a form of personal writing used to bear witness to experiences. The method has its roots in Latin and Chicana scholarship and resonates with auto-ethnographic approaches. I use this method to provide a brief overview of my experiences and disciplinary coordinates and to explore the questions outlined through my journey, which has been shaped and textured by encounters in various contact zones born out of the violence of coloniality and racialization: migrancy, Indigenous encounters and whiteness. Informed by Pratt (1991), I view contact zones as sites where 'power relations play out and are contested, remade, or unmade. It is through such shared meaning-making that individuals and communities can define and renew cultural representations that serve identity- and community-making purposes' (Sonn et al, 2014: 554–5). Indigeneity, whiteness and migrant identities can be understood as social locations produced through racial colonial dynamics of power. This conceptualization has helped me to clarify my positioning in relation to the various communities in the broader context of Australia's racial formation and colonial racialized power relations (Moreton-Robinson, 2003; Sonn and Stevens, 2017). By navigating borders with communities, in the flesh and symbolically through areas of inquiry and action, I have engaged in forms of bricolage, a process of stitching conceptual resources as a racial decolonial literacy into a critical reflexive praxis that disrupts structural and epistemic violence (Sonn and Stevens, 2022). The diasporic location produces what Gloria Anzaldúa (Anzaldúa and Keating, 2015) describes as '*mestiza* consciousness', of being in-between and entangled, travelling through different worlds (Lugones, 2003, 2016), understanding oppressions and resistances with an openness; from this it is possible to challenge, resist and enact emancipatory desires. This chapter charts the course of the development of a set of decolonial literacies by a migrating other, and the development of pedagogies and critical praxis approaches to not only counter the contemporary manifestations of racism, but also the outcomes of historic and contemporary denial, silencing and misrepresentation of race that continue to serve the racial colonial agenda.

Stitching a liberating community psychology: engaging from the Australian context

My efforts to engage decolonial approaches for liberation-oriented work are situated within the context of social relations within Australia and the longer history of racialized colonial power relations that have characterized societies in the East and the Southern hemisphere. These relations are inherently racialized and premised on the dispossession of Indigenous people, and the ongoing dynamics of coloniality (Quijano, 2000). As Maldonado-Torres states:

> [C]oloniality survives colonialism. It is maintained alive in books, in the criteria for academic performance, in cultural patterns, in common sense, in the self-image of peoples, in aspirations of self, and so many other aspects of our modern experience. In a way, as modern subjects we breathe coloniality all the time and every day. (Maldonado-Torres, 2007: 243)

Resonant with the South African story, Moreton-Robinson (2015) argues that Australia was founded as a settler-colonial nation on the theft of land, the dehumanization of a racialized 'other' and the simultaneous construction of the myth of a national white identity that has become engrained and reproduced institutionally and culturally. Racism is but one aspect of the colonial matrix of power, which has been described by various feminist and critical scholars (see Hill Collins, 2000; Quijano, 2000). Grosfoguel (2016: 10) offers this summation: 'Racism is a global hierarchy of superiority and inferiority … that [has] been politically, culturally and economically produced and reproduced for centuries by the institutions of the capitalist/patriarchal western-centric/Christian-centric modern/colonial world system.'

Grosfoguel (2016) draws on Fanon's (1982) seminal work to illustrate the creation of zones of being and non-being as positioned within colonial and racialized power relations. The line of the human divides those people above the line as 'recognised socially in their humanity as human beings and, thus, [enjoying] access to rights (human rights, civil rights, women's rights, and/or labour rights), material resources, and social recognition to their subjectivities, identities, epistemologies and spiritualties' (Grosfoguel,

2016: 10). Those below the line are seen as non-human, and thus as undeserving of the same rights, resources and recognition. Fanon (1982) and Césaire and Kelley (2000) provide powerful writing that has largely been absent from Western social and political psychology canons (Abi-Ghannam et al, 2023), expounding the effects of colonialism and racism as experienced by the colonized and sexualized/racialized/class subjects, those in the zone of non-being, below the line of the human.

The Eurocentric underpinnings of Western psychology in Australia grew evident at critical junctures of my academic journey. My doctoral studies on migration in the early 1990s were inspired partly by my own experiences as a person who grew up in South Africa during the Apartheid era, a system borrowed from Queensland, Australia, in a so-called 'coloured' community. My research focus opened a window into acculturation psychology and the many ways in which questions about migration, migrant experiences and settlement were framed through an assimilationist and deficit-oriented lens. At the heart of these approaches were positivist and reductionist understandings of human experience, often stripped of context, history and culture (Shweder, 1990). At the time, no published writing existed in Australian psychology journals on the experiences of migrants of African descent, let alone people from South Africa who were racially classified 'coloured' and Black communities. I quickly learned about the omissions and complicity of academia and psychology in the colonial project and the dominance of the fantasy of the white nation (Hage, 2000), with Anglo Australians perched at the top and Indigenous and multicultural others underneath. These unsettling lessons exposed the limited toolkit of my discipline and its deep foundations in Eurocentrism, along with the raw fact that I was also a racialized 'other' in dominant education institutions in a discipline that ostensibly privileged whiteness or Western Educated Industrialized, Rich and Democratic contexts (Henrich, 2021).

Black psychology and liberation approaches

The writing of scholars advancing critical orientations to race, such as the discipline of Black psychology (Jones, 1990; Azibo, 1994), Steve Biko's (1988) work on Black consciousness (see Mohammed Seedat, 1997) and Hussein Bulhan's (1985) exceptional text on Frantz Fanon and the psychology of oppression, all provided invaluable intellectual pathways to address the enduring effects of coloniality and Apartheid for those negotiating belonging in what was celebrated as 'multicultural Australia'. This Black consciousness scholarship confronts the ontological, epistemological and material dimensions of colonial violence and racism, and provides a counterpoint and countervisions for humanizing and liberating psychologies. As noted by Suffla and Seedat:

> Black consciousness strives to infuse and celebrate black pride and love that is forms of ontic dignity attached to the human-and African-centered notions of self and community where the colonial and apartheid projects of blackness with non-being. ... [I]t calls on the oppressed to recognise the imposition of ontological inferiority by whiteness on the black body and otherness of blackness and the humanity of Africans – where humanity is reduced to an image of whiteness, and whiteness is the epitome of beauty and virtue. (Suffla and Seedat, 2021: 31)

Alongside this work, liberation approaches – which are part of a broader paradigm and expressed in different areas of work – included the critical pedagogy of Paolo Freire, liberation philosophy, sociology and the psychology arm that was articulated in Latin America by Jesuit priest and psychologist Ignacio Martín-Baró (1994; see also Montero and Sonn, 2009). Martín-Baró was critical of psychology, including community psychology, and advocated a new approach with a focus on the needs of people, privileging the voices of the poor and constructing psychology from the vantage point of the oppressed, marginalized and excluded. Some of these ideas and concepts include: a commitment to praxis, which is the synergy between theory and practice; consciousness-raising and de-ideologization, which is problematizing taken-for-granted social realities; the recovery of historical memory; the importance of dialogue and relational ethics; and participatory approaches that engage people in the processes of challenging oppressive social realities. These liberation-oriented approaches resonate with the struggles for self-determination and sovereignty in Australia.

Indigenous knowledges

Travelling into Indigenous worlds involved deconstructing and unlearning taken-for-granted hegemonic knowledge. It meant expanding knowledge about Aboriginal and Torres Strait Islander histories, ways of knowing, doing and being, suffering, oppression, struggle and survival. At Curtin University in 1995–6, I was fortunate to learn with, be welcomed as a racialized 'other' and be mentored by Indigenous colleagues at the Centre of Aboriginal Studies. This vibrant place was 'a third place in a tertiary space', as Dudgeon and Fielder (2006) describe it. It was in this third space, this contact zone (Pratt, 1991), that I was further unsettled and challenged to situate my knowing, to interrogate subject position and psychology's complicity in coloniality and structural racism (Sonn and Green, 2006). Linda Tuhiwai Smith's (1999) *Decolonising Methodologies*, articulations of Aboriginal terms of reference (Oxenham, 2000) and Dudgeon and Oxenham's (1989) writing on the complexity of Aboriginal diversity all draw parallels with the challenges to identity development faced by racialized people in other colonial contexts.

During my journey, I further identified Australian texts that informed my developing decolonial literacy and assisted with the evolving effort of constructing a responsive liberation community psychology. Rigney (1997) articulated three core principles of Indigenist research, as a framework that privileges Indigenous voices, has political integrity and is aimed at resistance to ontological and epistemic violence that is central to emancipation. Karen Martin and Booran Mirraboopa (2003) also emphasized the need to privilege Aboriginal people's realities, honour social mores and practices on Country and lands, and understand context in shaping experiences. This writing articulated different ontologies, cosmologies and ways of being, grounded in relationality and connection between people and the natural world with Country. These scholars and activists were creating counter-settings and spaces for cultural strengthening and the recovery of historical memory, and for healing and responding to the genocidal practices that included dispossession from land and the removal of children from families to be placed in institutions run by missions and churches.

Whiteness studies

I brought these critical, Indigenous and liberation approaches into research and teaching of cultural psychology to ostensibly mostly white Anglo students (see Sonn et al, 2000). Many students found the content unsettling; many arrived at Indigenous empowerment work with a sense of guilt and shame and had limited resources to reflect on their own gendered and raced subjectivities and locations – whiteness in the curriculum and elsewhere is unmarked, unraced and normative (Green et al, 2007). For me and many Anglo students who had an awareness of psychology's complicity in the colonial project, whiteness studies provided a way to shift the gaze towards hegemonic whiteness and to examine the history in the present and the ways in which coloniality continues in various settings. We were cognisant of the critique that this focus may result in recentring whiteness and white subjectivities. Yet, for us, whiteness studies – with its roots in radical Black scholarship (Du Bois, 1994) – brought another lens, a gaze towards power and privilege. It brought concepts and tools to examine operations of power/knowledge in and through dominant discourses and expressions in symbolic and material practices in everyday settings and the process of reconciliation (Green and Sonn, 2006).

For me, this 'world travelling' (Lugones, 1997) of navigating contact zones in research and teaching has been vital to the development of decolonizing standpoints. Reyes Cruz and Sonn (2015: 128) suggest that a decolonizing standpoint is needed to challenge 'essentialist understandings of cultural matters that have served historically to marginalize others. This standpoint brings into clearer view ways in which power/privilege/oppression are reproduced and contested through racialized and ethnicized practices and discourses; that is, how social inequality is maintained and challenged through culture'. Decolonizing standpoints call for a commitment to *create empowering settings*, *relational ethics*, *epistemic justice* and the adoption of a *decolonial attitude* to help rehumanize the world and to produce 'counter-discourses, counter-knowledges, counter-creative acts, and counter-practices that seek to dismantle coloniality and to open up multiple other forms of being in the world' (Maldonado-Torres, 2016: 10).

Travelling with the African diaspora and racialized groups: enacting decolonial and anti-racist community praxis

Our research group has formed university–community partnerships with different cultural and arts organizations over several years, initially through student placements and evaluations of community arts projects (see the discussions of Sisters and Brothers and *amka* that follow) and subsequently through deeper solidarity studies and participatory action research (Fine, 2018). Solidarity work is informed by relationality, sociohistorical consciousness and a desire to support and create of spaces and opportunities in local and global contexts for meaning-making, to remember and tell stories from below, on our/their terms, to contest racialization and coloniality, and to expand our ecologies of being, knowing and doing (Sonn et al, 2022).

Since around 2016, we have been accompanying an emerging collective with a desire to create self-determined community art – art developed for and by young people of colour to promote racial and gender equity. AMKA, for example, was a multidisciplinary performance that explored a third culture story and narratives from the African diaspora through a journey of being, becoming and existence. AMKA (pronounced *um-kuh*) means 'wake up; get up' in Swahili, and its use in most contexts in Swahili culture has a sense of urgency and frankness when articulated. The production explored identity, dispossession and cultural conflict within the African Australian experience, and was performed publicly over two nights at the Arts Centre, a renowned and prestigious arts institution in the centre of Melbourne. The performance combined poetry, music, dance, theatre and projection through a series of individual and ensemble pieces that interpreted stories of the African diaspora in Naarm/Birraranga (Melbourne). Through a process of research accompaniment, an invited dialogical process of listening, bearing witness and imagining (Watkins, 2021), we documented AMKA and used critical narrative analysis (Chase, 2005) to show how the collective is mobilizing art – in this case, theatre – to produce narratives counter to those circulated via mainstream media, academic and political discourse. Through creative practice and artistic expression, the group contested dominant racialized representations of African communities and conveyed their complex subjectivities, aspirations born from their ancestral knowledges and emplaced awareness as settlers on unceded lands (Sonn et al, 2022). As noted by one of the young people:

> I'm identified as African, and I can identify as African. I have no problem with it. But, I think most of the time when people identify you with it they do place a limit and they have a narrow scope with which they look at it from because when I identify as African, I know it's completely different to when my Dad says he identifies as African, and then I also identify very strongly as Black, globally because I'm placed as Black. But then in Australia it's quite tricky, because, like, I'm the type of Black that's got to recognize that I am on stolen land and that I am here potentially as a colonizer if I'm not fully aware of my footprint and what it is I'm doing, so ... that's quite different to being Black elsewhere. (wāni, Bashi Tribe from Walungu; Sonn et al, 2022: 148)

While the group expressed what the project was for them and the African diaspora, the performance resonated with other diasporas, as well as white and racialized communities. The performance was an encounter that opened up opportunities for transformative witnessing by the differently positioned spectators. For some witnesses, it was affirming; for others, it brought into sharper focus the psychosocial distance between them and racialized members of their communities. Using critical whiteness as a lens and critical discourse analysis of textual responses gathered with open-ended audience surveys, Maxwell and Sonn (2020) show how spectators interpret performative counter-narratives. They show how spectators experience the performance as an encounter and that they begin reflecting on their own positions of power and privilege. The performance challenges spectators' hegemonic and overdetermined narratives, those circulating on the outside, and produces feelings of discomfort, guilt and shame, often revealing the taken-for-granted nature of white privilege and ignorance. While the encounter spaces and the dynamics of witnessing may be temporary, the opportunity for facilitating intercultural exchange is significant in that it highlights that 'attending a singular performance is an act of "showing up", supporting, and responsible listening within a lifetime of allyship intentions' (Maxwell and Sonn, 2020: 11) – in essence, igniting the potential for racial literacy for witnesses.

This core group has since developed the collective Next in Colour, which we accompany through evaluation, research and alliance-building. We are committed to practices of knowledge construction that are accountable and responsive to the needs and aspirations of groups, and we seek to expand our sociopolitical ecology of knowledge. That is, we ask critical questions about whose knowledge counts, on whose terms and how we mobilize the resources of the university to support self-determined place-making. In our most recent project (Agung-Igusti et al, 2021), we recorded the narratives of members of the collective, documented their arts and community practice, and analysed their stories using critical narrative analysis and critical race and feminist scholarship. Our collective analysis of the stories provided insights into how the group navigates race and power, and how members understand and enact self-determination. In fact, we understood this as the act of *re-existence* – that is, 'the mechanisms, strategies, and practices that human groups employ against racialization, exclusion, and marginalization, procuring the redefining and resignifying of life in conditions of dignity and self-determination' (Mignolo and Walsh, 2018: 18).

Our analyses revealed the importance of creating homeplaces (hooks, 2015), settings where people can 'confront the issue of humanization' for resistance, away from dominant culture settings. In these homeplaces, the group can reflect, heal and strategize to produce culture and counter-narratives and community-building. As one of the speakers reflected:

[Having a space] It was an important thing because it was about our representation, but also visibility, authentic visibility. Also, it's about having autonomy and self-determination over the work that we do and how we deliver it and providing a reflection of ourselves within the community and letting the broader community know that we are doing these things and we want to do these things for us ourselves as much as everybody else. (Geskeva Komba, quoted in Agung-Igusti, 2022: 93)

One strong narrative produced by the group members through their arts practices of re-existence was based on a deep understanding of their positionality, responsibility and practice of centring Indigenous sovereignty in negotiating belonging and place-making. This was an intentional strategy to engage from place, locally and globally, with Black and Brown diasporas, to reveal the impacts of global coloniality, violence and dispossession, and form solidarities that turn away from white supremacy as a hegemonic discourse that shapes belonging (Moreton-Robinson, 2003). This is reflected in the comments from another speaker:

All of us, Indigenous community, Pasifika communities, we are all looked at from the same lens, from the white perspective. To be able to have that connection with them and being like, 'Hey, you're doing this and we're doing that, let's collab.' Cause if we don't help each other, no one else is going to help us. We have to work through these spaces so that we can give our own communities the same benefits. Being able to link up with Pasifika communities, Indigenous communities is important in the sense that all we have is each other most of the time and we have to work through that for other people. (Anyuop Dau, quoted in Agung-Igusti, 2022: 154)

Agung-Igusti (2022) also showed with further analysis how neoliberal managerialism elevates discourses of efficiency and productivity and flattens difference and context, while perpetuating the hidden dynamics of race that contribute to colour-blind racism. This was expressed by a member of the collective:

[In institutions] people act a certain way. Then when they're out of their suit, they're just people. There's almost a code switch that exists in those institutions and it's so competitive in a way, and that's why these languages exist. Basically, they're just saying the same thing that we would be saying, but in just this very complex English way. It doesn't make sense. It's just a loop that just goes around and around. Then when they use these words. … It's like even their definition … for certain words, it does not talk about the community that they're reaching out to. There's a lot of falsehood in that. There's a lot of promises in the languages that exist. You see a lot of hierarchy. … There's a lot of [superiority] and you can sense that in just how things are constructed because it's an institution … it's just all fictional. (Ruth Nyaruot Ruach, quoted in Agung-Igusti, 2022: 199)

These narratives attest to the critical task of contesting white supremacy and its expression in colour-blind discourses and practices. It also points to possibilities for personal and collective change through alliance-building and solidarity practices rooted in the embodied realities and aspirations of racialized and marginalized communities.

Conclusion

This chapter focused on how we create and mobilize community psychologies in and outside the university to contribute to the empowerment and self-determination of various racialized communities. I have been fortunate to be able to use my location critically and to imagine a decolonial standpoint. This decolonial standpoint weaves liberatory processes for people who engage in contact zones via raised consciousness of our global history of colonialism and coloniality, anchored in dialogical ethics and accountability, and encourages empathy for and appreciation of Indigenous sovereignty and ways of knowing, doing and being.

Through this journey, I have 'stitched' together multiple critical approaches to inform a praxis approach, decolonizing standpoints to tackle coloniality and racialization and to foster re-existence. It is through various strands of work in contact zones, at the borders and in between them, that we are asking questions about how we can produce critical community psychology in support of liberation goals of the communities in local and global contexts that bear the brunt of colonization, racism, sexism and other forms of violence. This important task is also about shifting the gaze from the narrow epistemologies based in Eurocentrism and scientism that produce ignorance, and the discourses of the dominant, and dismantling privileged ideologies in everyday institutions that create harm. For me/us, this orientation is the result of border crossing and boundary spanning; it is a speaking and listening position, our locus of enunciation (Mignolo, 2007) that affords a perspective from which to engage with dynamics of race, coloniality and power/privilege/dispossession.

Liberation-oriented decolonial anti-racist praxis is emergent, critical, contextual and affirming; it advocates for racial literacies (Bargallie et al, 2023). This is a vital praxis for researchers, educators and practitioners to develop. The praxis entails being open to the voices, experiences and standpoints of different groups, to value their lived experiences and ways of doing, being and knowing, to understand our locus of enunciation in the context of local and global history, and to promote dialogical and relational ethics and epistemologies. This approach also means using our privilege as academics/scholars to support and create spaces within and outside the university where people can develop critical racial and decolonial literacies and critically explore – in intentionally carved decolonized 'third spaces' – where their political and cultural identities can re-exist rather than be eroded and diminished.

References

Abi-Ghannam, G., Perkins, K.M. and Fine, M. (2023) 'The comrade on the crossroads of scholarship and struggle: Troubling the exile of Frantz Fanon from social and political psychology', *Social and Personality Psychology Compass*, 17(2): e12727.

Agung-Igusti, R. (2022) 'Next in colour: An alternative setting navigating race and power in the pursuit of self-determination', PhD thesis, Victoria University.

Agung-Igusti, R., Sonn, C. and Du Ve, E. (2021) *Next in Colour: Creating Spaces, Practices, and Processes Towards Self-determined Futures*, Melbourne: Community, Identity and Displacement Research Network, Victoria University.

Anzaldúa, G. and Keating, A. (2015) *Light in the Dark: Luz en lo oscuro – Rewriting Identity, Spirituality, Reality*, Durham, NC: Duke University Press.

Azibo, D.A. (1994) 'The kindred fields of Black Liberation theology and liberation psychology: A critical essay on their conceptual base and destiny', *Journal of Black Psychology*, 20: 334–56.

Bargallie, D., Fernando, N. and Lentin, A. (2023) 'Breaking the racial silence: Putting racial literacy to work in Australia', *Ethnic and Racial Studies*. DOI: 10.1080/01419870.2023.2206470

Biko, S. (1988) *'I Write What I Like': A Selection of His Essays*, Ringwood: Penguin.

Bulhan, H.A. (1985) *Frantz Fanon and the Psychology of Oppression*, New York: Plenum.

Césaire, A. and Kelley, R.D.G. (2000) *Discourse on Colonialism*, New York: Monthly Review Press.

Chase, S.E. (2005) 'Narrative inquiry: Multiple lenses, approaches, voices', in N.K. Denzin and Y.S. Lincoln (eds), *The SAGE Handbook of Qualitative Research*, Thousand Oaks, CA: SAGE, pp 651–79.

Du Bois, W.E.B. (1994) *The Souls of Black Folk*, Mineola: Dover.

Dudgeon, P. and Oxenham, D. (1989) 'The complexity of Aboriginal diversity: Identity and kindredness', *Black Voices*, 5(1): 22–39.

Dudgeon, P. and Fielder, J. (2006) 'Third spaces within tertiary places: Indigenous Australian studies', *Journal of Community & Applied Social Psychology*, 16(5): 396–409.

Fanon, F. (1982) *Black Skin, White Masks*, New York: Grove Press.

Fine, M. (2018) *Just Research in Contentious Times: Widening the Methodological Imagination*, New York: Teachers College Press.

Green, M.J. and Sonn, C.C. (2006) 'Problematising the discourses of the dominant: Whiteness and reconciliation', *Journal of Community & Applied Social Psychology*, 16(5): 379–95.

Green, M.J., Sonn, C.C. and Matsebula, J. (2007) 'Reviewing whiteness: Theory, research, and possibilities', *South African Journal of Psychology*, 37(3): 389–419.

Grosfoguel, R. (2016) 'What is racism?', *Journal of World-Systems Research*, 22(1): 9–15.

Hage, G. (2000) *White Nation: Fantasies of White Supremacy in a Multicultural Society*, London: Routledge.

Henrich, J. (2021) *The Weirdest People in the World: How the West Became Psychologically Peculiar and Particularly Prosperous*, Harmondsworth: Penguin.

Hill Collins, P. (2000) *Black Feminist Thought: Knowledge, Consciousness and the Politics of Empowerment*, 2nd edn, New York: Routledge.

hooks, b. (2015) *Yearning: Race, Gender, and Cultural Politics*, London: Routledge.

Jones, R.L. (1990) *Black Psychology*, 3rd edn, New York: Cobb and Henry.

Lugones, M. (1997) 'Playfulness, "world"-travelling, and loving perception', in D.T. Meyers (ed), *Feminist Social Thought: A Reader*, London: Routledge, pp 148–59.

Lugones, M. (2003) *Pilgrimages = Peregrinajes: Theorizing Coalition Against Multiple Oppressions*, Lanham, MD: Rowman & Littlefield.

Lugones, M. (2016) 'The coloniality of gender', in W. Harcourt (ed), *The Palgrave Handbook of Gender and Development*, Basingstoke: Palgrave Macmillan, pp 13–33.

Maldonado-Torres, N. (2007) 'On the coloniality of being: Contributions to the development of a concept', *Cultural Studies*, 21(2–3): 240–70.

Maldonado-Torres, N. (2016) 'Outline of ten theses on coloniality and decoloniality', Fanon Foundation, 1–37, https://fondation-frantzfanon.com/outline-of-ten-theses-on-coloniality-and-decoloniality

Martin, K. and Mirraboopa, B. (2003) 'Ways of knowing, being and doing: A theoretical framework and methods for Indigenous and Indigenist research', *Journal of Australian Studies*, 27(76): 203–14.

Martín-Baró, I. (1994) *Writings for a Liberation Psychology*, ed A. Aron and S. Corne, Cambridge, MA: Harvard University Press.

Maxwell, C. and Sonn, C. (2020) 'The performative is political: Using counter-storytelling through theater to create spaces for implicated witnessing', *American Journal of Community Psychology*, 68(1–2): 47–60.

Mignolo, W.D. (2007) 'Introduction: Coloniality of power and de-colonial thinking', *Cultural Studies*, 21(2–3): 155–67.

Mignolo, W. and Walsh, C.E. (2018) *On Decoloniality: Concepts, Analytics, Praxis*, Durham, NC: Duke University Press.

Montero, M. and Sonn, C.C. (eds) (2009) *Psychology of Liberation: Theory and Applications*, New York: Springer.

Moreton-Robinson, A. (2003) 'I still call Australia home: Indigenous belonging and place in a postcolonising society', in S. Ahmed, A.M. Fortier, M. Sheller and C. Castaneda (eds), *Uprootings/Regroundings: Questions of Home and Migration*, Oxford: Berg, pp 23–40.

Moreton-Robinson, A. (2015) *The White Possessive: Property, Power, and Indigenous Sovereignty*, Minneapolis: University of Minnesota Press.

Ngugi, wa Thiong'o (1986) *Decolonizing the Mind*, Portsmouth, NH: Heinemann.

Oxenham, D. (2000) *Aboriginal Terms of Reference: A Course Paper for the Indigenous Studies Program*, Perth: Curtin University of Technology.

Pratt, M.L. (1991) 'Arts of the contact zone', *Profession*, 33–40.

Quijano, A. (2000) 'Coloniality of power and Eurocentrism in Latin America', *International Sociology*, 15(2): 215–32.

Reyes, K.B. and Curry Rodríguez, J.E. (2012) 'Testimonio: Origins, terms, and resources', *Equity & Excellence in Education*, 45(3): 525–38.

Reyes Cruz, M. and Sonn, C.C. (2015) '(De)colonizing culture in community psychology: Reflections from critical social science', in R.D. Goodman and P.C. Gorski (eds), *Decolonizing 'Multicultural' Counselling through Social Justice*, New York: Springer, pp 127–46.

Rigney, L.-I. (1997) 'Internationalization of an Indigenous anticolonial cultural critique of research methodologies: A guide to Indigenist research methodology and its principles', *Journal of American Studies*, 14(2): 109–22.

Seedat, M. (1997) 'The quest for liberatory psychology', *South African Journal of Psychology*, 27(4): 261–70.

Shweder, R.A. (1990) 'Cultural psychology: What is it?' in J.W. Stigler, R.A. Schweder and G. Herdt (eds) *Cultural Psychology: Essays on Comparative Human Development*, Cambridge: Cambridge University Press, pp 1–44.

Smith, L.T. (1999) *Decolonizing Methodologies: Research and Indigenous Peoples*, New York: Zed Books.

Sonn, C.C. and Green, M.J. (2006) 'Disrupting the dynamics of oppression in intercultural research and practice', *Journal of Community & Applied Social Psychology*, 16(5): 337–46.

Sonn, C.C. and Stevens, G. (2017) 'Histórias do apartheid, memória e pertencimento entre a população da diáspora sul-africana na Austrália', *Revista USP*, 114: 71–90.

Sonn, C.C. and Stevens, G. (2022) 'Tracking the decolonial turn in contemporary community psychology: Expanding socially just knowledge archives, ways of being and modes of praxis', in G. Stevens and C.C. Sonn (eds), *Decoloniality and Epistemic Justice in Contemporary Community Psychology*, New York: Springer, pp 1–19.

Sonn, C.C., Quayle, A.F., Mackenzie, C. and Law, S.F. (2014) 'Negotiating belonging in Australia through storytelling and encounter', *Identities*, 21(5): 551–69.

Sonn, C.C., Garvey, D.C., Bishop, B.J. and Smith, L.M. (2000) 'Incorporating Indigenous and cross-cultural issues into an undergraduate psychology course: Experience at Curtin University of Technology', *Australian Psychologist*, 35(2): 143–49.

Sonn, C.C., Fox, R., Keast, S. and Rua, M. (2022) 'Fostering and sustaining transnational solidarities for transformative social change: Advancing community psychology research and action', *American Journal of Community Psychology*, 69(3–4): 269–82.

Suffla, S. and Seedat, M. (2021) 'Africa's knowledge archives: Black consciousness and reimagining community psychology', in G. Stevens and C.C. Sonn (eds), *Decoloniality and Epistemic Justice in Contemporary Community Psychology*, New York: Springer, pp 21–38.

Watkins, M. (2021) 'Toward a decolonial approach to psychosocial accompaniment from the "outside"', in G. Stevens and C.C. Sonn (eds), *Decoloniality and Epistemic Justice in Contemporary Community Psychology*, New York: Springer, pp 101–20.

13

Unravelling the Model Minority Myth and Breaking the Racial Silence: A Collaborative Critical Auto-Ethnography

Mandy Truong and Jessica Walton

Introduction

In the wake of the COVID-19 pandemic, the backlash of anti-Chinese and anti-Asian racism and violence in white dominant societies was swift and confronting. This anti-Asian sentiment, which was present prior to the pandemic, continues to impact the lives of Asian people across the world beyond the height of the pandemic. Increases in anti-Asian hate crimes in the United States, Australia, the United Kingdom and Italy have resulted in much harm and even death (Human Rights Watch, 2020; Han et al, 2022; Ballantyne and Giarrusso, 2023; Schumann and Moore, 2023). The pandemic has shown how easily and quickly Asian people can be racially vilified, with any social or cultural traction they may have gained through education and employment being undermined as they are reminded of their marginalized position in a racially stratified society that centres whiteness.

Multicultural settler colonies with white majority populations, such as Australia, have a history of anti-immigration and racist policies towards Asian immigrants. This commonality is reflective of the globalization of whiteness or 'global processes of (neo)colonization whereby apparently separate white nations share common histories of domination over non-white peoples' (Leonardo, 2002: 33). In Australia, people of Asian descent living in Australia have been depicted as the 'yellow peril' at various points dating back to the violent anti-Chinese riots of the gold rush era (Schamberger,

2017) and the Immigration Restriction Act of 1901 (better known as the 'White Australia' policy), which limited non-white immigration to Australia, particularly from Asia.

On the other side of the coin, Asian people are also often praised for their values of hard work and thrift, resulting in academic achievement, economic success and upward social mobility. For example, Asian Australian students are over-represented in high-performing schools, prestigious university courses and professions, drawing admiration and anxiety through two competing discourses: competitive and aspirational versus excessive and threatening (Ho, 2017). This contradiction is explained by the model minority myth concept, which refers to the 'systematic construction of people of Asian descent as representing successful assimilation into a white dominant society' despite persistent racial inequities (Walton and Truong, 2023: 391).

Stereotypes of Asian people as both a model minority and as a threat (for example, in terms of high achievers in education versus 'yellow peril' discourse) serve to obscure the underlying systems of oppression and white domination that marginalize people of colour. Although there is evidence that people of Asian descent continue to experience disadvantage and marginalization (Walton and Truong, 2023), the broader discourse views it as less serious or with reduced urgency due to our perceived status of being model minority or 'honorary white'. In addition, refugees and migrants of colour who make it to Australia are expected to be grateful to have been accepted into the country and told they should 'go back home' to where they came from if they are unhappy (Soutphommasane, 2012).

Despite a sustained historical presence in Australia and increasing numbers of people across Asia migrating to Australia, there continues to be a lack of Asian-Australian representation in the media, politics and leadership positions, which is referred to as the 'bamboo ceiling' (Nunes, 2021). Examples are visible in the corporate world (Nguyen and Lo, 2021) and Asian Australians are severely under-represented in the most senior management positions in Australian universities, with 42 per cent of participants reporting experiences of racism, ethnic stereotyping and marginalization (Oishi, 2017). Although representation is important, it is inadequate in itself if structural change does not occur at the same time (Ahmed, 2012).

Through a critical auto-ethnographic account of our individual narratives, the rest of this chapter explores how we began to question *hegemonic racial literacies*, or 'literacy practices that support making meaning of race and racism through oppressive ideologies and that preserve inequity by maintaining a racial hierarchical structure that advantages whites symbolically and materially over racialized people' (Chávez-Moreno, 2022: 485) exhibited by concepts such as the model minority myth. This account documents a shift along a continuum towards a more anti-racist *counter-hegemonic racial literacy* that 'oppose[s] hegemonic logics of power, language, race, imperialism, and colonialisms' (Chávez-Moreno, 2022: 485) while also recognizing that this process of developing a critical racial consciousness is non-linear.

Background

We first met in 2012 when Mandy was a PhD candidate and Jessica was a research fellow in the same university department. Mandy is a Vietnamese Australian woman who arrived in Australia at the age of four. She began her career as an optometrist and shifted to public health research, then completed her PhD in 2016. Jessica is a Korean adoptee from the United States who studied anthropology, completing her PhD in 2010 and working in interdisciplinary spaces throughout her career. Over time, we collaborated and supported each other as a form of solidarity to resist, question and challenge what we knew about race and racism in our personal and professional lives. Amidst the Black Lives Matter movement, the COVID-19 pandemic and the subsequent anti-Asian hate and backlash, we decided to undertake a project together (Walton and Truong, 2023) as a public record of our experiences during this time and the place we were occupying, visibly and invisibly, in the academy and the public arena.

We write this chapter together to help 'break the racial silence'. We write to critically reflect on our process of challenging and developing racial literacies through navigating racism/anti-racism research on the margins of the academy. We write to stand together with other race and anti-racism scholars and educators by illustrating the importance of collaboration, solidarity and practices of care, especially when faced with the challenge of maintaining presence and integrity in uncertain and often difficult environments.

Critical auto-ethnography as critical methods for doing race

We use critical auto-ethnography as a method of narrative inquiry (Holman Jones, 2016) to interrogate hegemonic racial literacies through the example of the model minority myth concept and how we began to understand our experiences through a counter-hegemonic racial literacy lens (Chávez-Moreno, 2022). This allows collaborative exploration of diversity and identity and the intersecting power dynamics operating within our stories (Boylorn and Orbe, 2020; Iosefo et al, 2020). This method engages critical examination of our individual narratives over time to understand the sociocultural phenomenon of the 'model minority' in the context of higher education and racism/anti-racism work in academic settings (Chang et al, 2013; Ashlee et al, 2017).

Through this collaborative reflective analysis (Ashlee et al, 2017), we seek to explore and make sense of the space as non-Indigenous people of colour conducting racism and anti-racism work within the Australian academy. We found the concept of a continuum of racial literacies helpful in revealing the learning processes in which we engaged to 'make meaning of racial ideologies' (Chávez-Moreno, 2022: 482) and to understand how racial literacies can range from hegemonic oppressive understandings of structural racial ideologies to counter-hegemonic racial literacies oriented towards anti-racism. The following section provides brief narratives of our stories, independently authored, that explore our positionalities as Asian women, often caught up in the trap of model minority stereotypes. We contextualize our experiences as academics, given that Asian women are often rendered invisible in higher education and racism/anti-racism work, and connect our lived experiences with the broader systems of power, integrating conversations we have had on these topics over several years.

Mandy's narrative

My parents fled Vietnam in a boat in the late 1970s and I was born in a refugee camp in Malaysia. I spent much of my early life growing up in the eastern suburbs of Melbourne, Victoria, which back then was predominantly white. I used to watch a lot of television and read a lot of books to keep myself company as my parents worked long hours and I had few extracurricular activities. Growing up, I wanted to be white. I wanted to look like the kids on television and I wanted to be part of a family where the dad told dad jokes and the mum baked cupcakes, and the kids had birthday parties and sleepovers at their friends' houses. Being the eldest of three carried certain expected responsibilities, including understanding and interpreting Australian cultural idioms and norms, translating English into Vietnamese for my parents, babysitting my siblings and being a decision-maker. We were navigating how to live as a family across two distinct cultures. I was also consciously and unconsciously suppressing my Vietnamese and Chinese identity and culture because I did not see it as something that was desirable or valued in the dominant culture. Before I knew the word for it, much of my life has been in pursuit of being a 'model minority', given that I couldn't become 'white'. I wanted to learn and show that I could be as 'Australian' as the next white person – to be an 'honorary white'.

As is common in many Asian migrant families, I was raised to prioritize education above all else; educational success and hard work were going to translate into opportunity and economic security. We were a working-class family and although they rarely talked about it openly, I knew my parents faced discrimination and exploitation. Thus, it was my duty and responsibility to honour their sacrifices by being successful. Feeling this pressure, I worked hard and diligently throughout school and university. The fear of not doing well was omnipresent.

I graduated from university to begin a career as an optometrist. During my years as a health practitioner, I noticed that at times I felt inadequately equipped, uncomfortable and uncertain working with patients/clients from non-English speaking backgrounds. I had experienced first-hand the challenges of navigating the Australian health system when it was different to one's country of origin and English was not my primary language, but now I was experiencing the cross-cultural disconnect and barriers on the other side – as a healthcare practitioner. Not everyone was fitting into the convenient categories and boxes that I had been taught; the tools and solutions I had didn't fit everyone's circumstances.

Undertaking a Master of Public Health degree and studying some social health subjects, I finally found words and theories to explain my experiences and thoughts. I realized I had been heavily socialized into the Western biomedical culture and model of healthcare, which was unnamed during my training. This model viewed itself as superior and expected others to fit into it, rather than adapt itself to fit the needs of diverse people. My early research was focused on improving the 'cultural competency' of healthcare professionals and services to address inequities in healthcare provision to people from migrant backgrounds. However, I eventually came to the view that genuine change was not possible unless we centred race and racism. Cultural 'difference' was a more palatable way of saying 'not-white'. The mantra 'we treat all patients the same' has the effect of excusing inequitable care and dehumanizing people, because not all patients *are* the same.

My journey as a researcher, health practitioner, mother and migrant/settler has involved learning about race, racism and colonization, and thinking more critically and reflexively about the world I took for granted and rarely questioned. In other words, my 'racial literacy' shifted towards an anti-racist orientation. This shift included a realization that I was an uninvited guest on unceded Aboriginal land and that people like me were a key part of the settler-colonial project. As a culmination of my experiences, I realized that I wanted to devote my work to racism/anti-racism research and teaching as a contribution to 'paying the rent'.

Despite my determination and motivation, I found that anti-racism and racism work as a settler in Australia is an uncertain and uncomfortable place for someone with an Asian heritage who is viewed as a 'model minority'. It is also an unexpected location for someone like me, both personally and professionally (being part of the health sector and in academia); we are not usually the ones to call out racism. Navigating this space without any formal training in race and racism studies has been challenging as I have had to learn by doing. There has been so much unlearning and learning to be done. I have struggled to find my 'place' in this space – prior to the pandemic and the ensuing anti-Asian hate, racism seemed less explicit than for other racialized minorities. I have grappled with many questions: Am

I culturally Asian enough to be a spokesperson for my ethnic group? Am I too privileged? How do I navigate a space that demands both authenticity and a non-threatening performance to be accepted into the 'in-group'? How do I avoid crossing boundaries because I still need to 'know my place' and ensure that others are given opportunity and airtime? How do I persist in the face of resistance, apathy and critique?

One key lesson I have learnt is that navigating and contributing to racism and anti-racism work in academia are difficult to sustain if undertaken alone. Seeing others in this space being put under a microscope and being attacked (often without institutional support) has made me wary and fearful. Moreover, the competitiveness, precariousness and hierarchical culture of academia can make it challenging to build genuine and long-lasting collaborations. The personal and professional, the heart and the head, become intertwined and I believe there will be a price to pay – emotionally, physically and professionally. Therefore, genuine solidarity and support are critical – no matter what your level of success may be. This chapter has been one of the hardest projects I have undertaken; ultimately, I know that I could not have done it without Jessica.

Jessica's narrative

When I was adopted to the United States as a Korean child, I was remade as Jessica Walton and became part of a white American family. I was taken from my mother's body and permanently separated from my Korean family, culture and history. My Korean self was reduced to a place where I was born, a second middle name that was the Korean name I was given by a social worker, and a smattering of cultural artefacts like the *hanbok*, South Korean flag, fans, dolls and other vaguely 'Oriental' objects. Through this process, my identity became disconnected from my body. I was also no longer a Korean person and was instead faced with needing to integrate a white identity into an Asian body – a form of racialized body dysmorphia – while trying to survive within a white-dominated social structure where looking 'Asian' – that is, 'not white' – was weird, ugly and wrong.

While the world perceived me differently, within my adoptive family, colour-blindness pervaded everything. This view that we are all the same served to silence and deny my experiences as an Asian woman. I was rendered racially invisible but at the same time I was also acutely and painfully racially visible. In second grade, I was racially vilified on a daily basis, not understanding why people I did not know hated me so deeply. My parents told me to 'just ignore them' and I did not feel that I could go to my teachers for support. I was scolded on several occasions by teachers who thought I was sleeping when I was actually just reading a book or doing my work like the other children. As a child, I did not know what I do now about racism, but I did know that my survival depended on my ability to be as 'normal' as possible, which meant not only trying to be white but also believing that my Asian body *was* white – that is, until proven otherwise.

At the time, I did not know what the 'model minority' concept was – although in hindsight, it felt critical to surviving. It was also a myth that had lasting damaging effects. I developed a racial literacy that oppressed me in the belief that I had to be good at everything to be accepted and that my worth was defined by my proximal acceptance in relation to my white friends and family with the pretence that I was racially one of them. At a superficial level, it provided a minimal protective buffer against the exclusion and marginalization felt in other areas of life. Being a 'model minority' required an exhausting amount of effort and constant policing of my own (non-white) body that did little to alleviate the stress and anxiety that came with this. As a transracial adoptee in a white family and white world, I avoided the few other Asian people at school for fear that I would be targeted by association. The constant threat of racist interactions propelled me to reject anything and anyone, including myself, that could be perceived as 'different' or 'not white enough'. The personal costs have meant that I have had to do a lot of work to unlearn the internalized racism and self-hatred and to also understand that it was not me that was inherently flawed but a whole social structure that made my existence unintelligible without being compared to degrees of whiteness. Ultimately, pretending to be a 'model minority' and trying to 'be white' fed into a white supremacist narrative that did more harm to me and other people of colour.

These experiences have stayed with me into adulthood. As a settler and migrant on Aboriginal country, I found myself navigating a racialized landscape in which the mere presence of cultural diversity was heralded as the progressive marker of multicultural success at the expense of silencing and denying Aboriginal and Torres Strait Islander histories and experiences, and where efforts towards counter-hegemonic racial literacies are thwarted by a societal reluctance to talk about how race matters.

Despite my educational qualifications and relative success, stereotypical markers of the 'model minority', I was still located within a white-dominated racially inequitable social structure. My Asian body was still read as an aberration. One day, when I was getting off the tram at the university where I worked, my mundane morning was interrupted when a white student came up and spat in my face. After the initial shock, I somehow had the wherewithal to ask why he did what he did. His response was, "Because I don't like you." In that moment, I became six years old again and I broke down. I was supposed to give a talk that morning at my university as part of a panel on interculturalism and diversity. I told the white organizer that I would not be able to make it because of what had just happened. Her initial response was shock at what had happened, followed by words of sympathy, then an attempt to convince me to still participate because "it would be so relevant to the discussion". I am tired of telling my personal story and reliving personal traumas for the consumption of others, mainly for those who have never had to live with the oppressive weight of racism. How do you describe the deep bodily harm this has on someone, and the deep intergenerational social harms that racism continues to inflict through its structural and institutional embeddedness in everyday life?

Why do I tell of these experiences now? In this context, I am writing the narrative; I am breaking the silence I have held for most of my life to respond to racism with my own truth. I break the silence for the benefit of others who may be able to relate to my experiences so they may also understand how their experiences are structurally embedded in a racialized hierarchy. I do not tell my story for people to feel sorry for me or to feel better about themselves because they have found something within – often sympathy (pity) masked as empathy. I tell my story so people can do better, so they can critically and honestly reflect on their own circumstances so they may interrupt the silence that racist structures feed off, and to do the equity work that is needed, together, while at the same time making space for those who have the knowledge that comes with living injustices every day.

My experiences as a transracial transnational Korean adoptee and in particular those early school experiences, have informed and driven all the research to which I have dedicated myself throughout my academic career. I worked with schools both in Australia and South Korea to examine racial inequality and to amplify students' voices on the margins. I had the privilege of working with teachers to talk together about how my research findings relate to the work they do and where schools could do better. I was able to provide space for other adoptees to tell their truths, to build community connections and to deepen an understanding of what it means to be adopted within and beyond the adoptee community. However, this is not an easy space to be in or to write in. I could only have done this work and most recently, this book chapter with people like Mandy, with whom I can have honest, raw and deep discussions within safe and caring spaces where we support and uplift each other.

Discussion

We have used this collaborative exercise in critical auto-ethnography to reflect on our positionality and learnings around race, racism and racial literacy. This reflection illustrates the power of hegemonic forms of racial literacy that serve to obscure racialized structures through the example of the model minority myth concept, and the need to work in solidarity with others to care for each other and to do the work that is needed to develop anti-racist racial literacies. In this discussion, we explore some of the nuances that differentiated our experiences of Asianness when navigating white-dominated social worlds as well as reflecting on the process of challenging hegemonic racial literacies.

The model minority myth: racial isolation and inferiority

One of the most insidious effects of white supremacy is the power it wields to under-value lives and ways of living that are considered deviations from the dominant norm. Added to this is racial isolation – whether through demographic makeup of neighbourhoods, or schools or family; the dominant message communicated repeatedly is that *you are not enough*. When you do not see yourself represented in popular media, in a range of positions of employment including leadership, or even in the faces of your own family, you are again reminded that *you are an outsider* within a world that does not see you as someone with full human potential. To not be extended by the spaces you are in (Ahmed, 2007), both explicitly and implicitly, says to someone from a young age, 'You are not good enough.'

As faculty members at universities, the culture of academia intersected with a racialized dimension of racial inferiority. Racial microaggressions (Sue, 2010) are actually deeply embedded structural aggressions and manifestations of white supremacy, and include being temporarily confused for another Asian staff member, assuming the ability to read or write in an Asian language that is not always even of our own background (and, in the case of being adopted, assuming a level of knowledge that was not necessarily possessed growing up), being mistaken as an 'international student' who cannot speak English well, being complimented for our English writing skills by anonymous reviewers, or being viewed as not possessing leadership qualities based on stereotypes of Asian women as passive. Each of these everyday moments represents a lifetime of injustices and indignities that accumulate and sediment in our bodies – a burden we are made to shoulder and told we simply must endure.

The model minority myth is an integral part of this insidiousness because it not only masks oppression, but also makes those who are oppressed adopt a hegemonic form of racial literacy that tells them they are only as good as what they are told they are within a delimiting set of parameters. At face value, the model minority myth can be construed positively, with its focus on educational and economic success. However, this success, as it is attributed to some (certainly not all) people of Asian heritage, has negative impacts at all levels, for those to whom it is attributed as well as those for whom it is not. It offers a temporary protective benefit that can provide a buffer for Asian people at an individual level, but it does not protect Asian people from the structural embeddedness of racism (as we saw in the context of COVID-19), and it does not stop Asian people from being killed. The ultimate social cost of buying into the model minority myth is that it obscures inequitable power relations and undermines efforts to challenge societal structures formed and reinforced by white supremacy (Walton and Truong, 2023).

Challenging hegemonic racial literacy

A commonality between our stories is that educational institutions often failed to provide the knowledge we needed to make sense of how racial inequality structures our society, even though we felt this inequality from an early age. Education outside the school walls was also inadequate. More open and critical discussions about race as part of family and peer racial socialization processes would have helped us to understand race beyond an individual level in the sense of feeling inferior within a white social world. Later, at a university level, this education was also inadequate as race was peripheral to our training in non-humanities disciplines. Much of our learning required searching on our own and through discussions with others within and outside the higher education space.

Our racial literacies developed within a deliberate and awkward silence on matters of race and racism; most people are more comfortable talking about 'diversity' and 'culture' (often as a problematic proxy for race) and 'cultural competency' rather than considering the centrality of race (Bargallie et al, 2023). Learning about racism cannot happen in a detached, abstract and disembodied way. It is not simply about memorizing facts about racism, but about understanding how racism intersects across all aspects of society and differentially impacts people depending on how they are racialized within an inequitable social structure. Understanding racism and its impacts is also about knowing when to give and make space to others, particularly by those who are directly disadvantaged. Working towards racial equality, especially as a person of colour, requires support and solidarity with others.

This chapter provides reflections on what it is like to be a settler of colour with Asian heritage in Australia at this time. People of Asian descent and other migrants have benefited from colonization and need to understand the ongoing impacts of racism and settler colonization that impact both Indigenous and non-Indigenous people (Watego, 2021). Collaboration, interdisciplinary work and solidarity in academic institutions, across all disciplines, are critical to breaking the racial silence and moving forward in a meaningful way with courage, persistence, resistance and grace.

References

Ahmed, S. (2007) 'A phenomenology of whiteness', *Feminist Theory*, 8(2): 149–68.

Ahmed, S. (2012) *On Being Included: Racism and Diversity in Institutional Life*, Durham, NC: Duke University Press.

Ashlee, A.A., Zamora, B. and Karikari, S.N. (2017) 'We are woke: A collaborative critical autoethnography of three "womxn" of color graduate students in higher education', *International Journal of Multicultural Education*, 19(1): 89–104.

Ballantyne, G. and Giarrusso, V. (2023) 'Asian Australian experiences of racism during the COVID-19 pandemic in Victoria: A preliminary analysis', *Journal of International Migration and Integration*, 24: 1437–53.

Bargallie, D., Fernando, N. and Lentin, A. (2023) 'Breaking the racial silence: Putting racial literacy to work in Australia', *Ethnic and Racial Studies*, forthcoming.

Boylorn, R.M. and Orbe, M.P. (2020) 'Introduction: Critical autoethnography as method of choice/choosing critical autoethnography', in R.M. Boylorn and M.P. Orbe (eds), *Critical Autoethnography: Intersecting Cultural Identities in Everyday Life*, London: Routledge.

Chang, H., Ngunjiri, F. and Hernandez, K.A.C. (2013) *Collaborative Autoethnography*, Abingdon> Routledge.

Chang, H., Ngunjiri, F. and Hernandez, K.A.C. (2016) *Collaborative Autoethnography (Vol. 8)*, New York: Routledge.

Chávez-Moreno, L.C. (2022) 'Critiquing racial literacy: Presenting a continuum of racial literacies', *Educational Researcher*, 51(7): 481–8.

Han, S., Riddell, J.R. and Piquero, A.R. (2022) 'Anti-Asian American hate crimes spike during the early stages of the COVID-19 pandemic', *Journal of Interpersonal Violence*, 38(3–4): 3513–33.

Ho, C. (2017) 'The new meritocracy or over-schooled robots? Public attitudes on Asian–Australian education cultures', *Journal of Ethnic and Migration Studies*, 43(14): 2346–62.

Holman Jones, S. (2016) 'Living bodies of thought: The "critical" in critical autoethnography', *Qualitative Inquiry*, 22(4): 228–37.

Human Rights Watch (2020) 'COVID-19 fuelling anti-Asian racism and xenophobia worldwide', 12 May, https://www.hrw.org/news/2020/05/12/covid-19-fueling-anti-asian-racism-and-xenophobia-worldwide

Iosefo, F., Jones, S.H. and Harris, A. (2020) 'Introduction: Critical autoethnography and/as wayfinding in the Global South', in F. Iosefo, S.H. Jones and A. Harris (eds), *Wayfinding and Critical Autoethnography*, London: Routledge, pp 1–11.

Leonardo, Z. (2002) 'The souls of white folk: Critical pedagogy, whiteness studies, and globalization discourse', *Race Ethnicity and Education*, 5(1): 29–50.

Nguyen, T. and Lo, J.-Y. (2021) 'Advancing ethnically and culturally diverse representation and inclusive leadership in Australia: Court of conscience', *Race, Law and Equality*, 15: 79–84.

Nunes, L. (2021) 'Lessons from the bamboo ceiling', *Association for Psychological Science Observer*, July/August, https://www.psychologicalscience.org/observer/bamboo-ceiling

Oishi, N. (2017) *Workforce Diversity in Higher Education: The Experiences of Asian Academics in Australian Universities*, Melbourne: Asia Institute, University of Melbourne.

Schamberger, K. (2017) 'Difficult history in a local museum: The Lambing Flat riots at Young, New South Wales', *Australian Historical Studies*, 48(3): 436–41.

Schumann, S. and Moore, Y. (2023) 'The COVID-19 outbreak as a trigger event for Sinophobia hate crimes in the United Kingdom', *The British Journal of Criminology*, 63(2): 367–83.

Soutphommasane, T.E. (2012) *Don't Go Back to Where You Came From: Why Multiculturalism Works*, Sydney: New South Books.

Sue, D.W. (2010) *Microaggressions in Everyday Life: Race, Gender, and Sexual Orientation*, Chichester: John Wiley and Sons.

Walton, J. and Truong, M. (2023) 'A review of the model minority myth: Understanding the social, educational and health impacts', *Ethnic and Racial Studies*, 46(3): 391–419.

Watego, C. (2021) *Another Day in the Colony*, Brisbane: University of Queensland Press.

14

Counter-Storytelling as Critical Praxis

Nicole Watson

Introduction

The late Mohawk scholar Patricia Monture (1990: 185) once described her experiences of law school as a perpetual feeling that she was 'missing something'. Initially, Monture assumed that there was something lacking within, and that if only she changed, then law school would become fulfilling. Later, she realized that the 'greatest obstacle' was not herself, but the 'very structure of the institution and the program' (Monture, 1990: 185). As a young, Indigenous woman pursuing a legal education, Patricia Monture's words left an indelible impression on me. They put into words feelings that, until that point, I had been unable to articulate.

My journey began in 1991 at the T.C. Beirne School of Law at the University of Queensland. As the state's oldest and most prestigious law school, it emanated wealth and power. I was fascinated by the grandiose library, and it was exciting to read judgments whose pages bore the annotations of generations of students. It was also a time of promise. In April, the Royal Commission into Aboriginal Deaths in Custody (1991) had released its ground-breaking treatise on the intersections between Indigenous peoples and the criminal justice system. The following year the High Court had rejected the racist mythology of *terra nullius* in the *Mabo* case (1992) and paved the way for Indigenous peoples to seek recognition of their native title.

But, like Patricia Monture, I soon developed the ever-present feeling that something was missing. Mirroring Monture's experience, it would be some time before I realized that the most formidable barrier was not myself, but an institution that had erased Indigenous people. At the time, Indigenous scholars were yet to secure a foothold in Australia's law schools. Their works never appeared in the prescribed readings for my courses and although we occasionally studied cases that involved Indigenous parties, their stories had been effaced and their names reduced to monikers for legal rules.

This chapter draws upon the work of Wendy Leo Moore (2008) and others who argue that law schools are 'white spaces'. In such locations, Black people are 'typically absent, not expected, or marginalized when present' (Anderson, 2015: 10). While such spaces are usually considered by whites to be unexceptional, they are often understood by Black people to be 'off limits' (Anderson, 2015: 10). I will argue that one means of challenging the whiteness of law schools is to tell the stories of Indigenous lawyers through the lens of a Black historical consciousness. Black historical consciousness has been defined as 'an effort to understand, develop, and teach Black histories that recognize Black people's humanity' (King, 2020: 337). Although the concept relates to African American history, it is a useful device for Indigenous peoples to centre our voices.

Law schools are white spaces

This section of the chapter draws upon the work of American scholars about law schools as white spaces. The racial hierarchy finds resonance in the physical environment and pedagogies that sanitize the law of complicity in slavery and colonization while normalizing the continued marginalization of others. Those arguments will be followed by a reflection on my own experiences as an Indigenous Australian legal scholar. This section will conclude that even though gains have been made in recent decades, Australian law schools – like their American counterparts – continue to be white spaces.

American law schools as white spaces

The environments that house law schools are typically spacious and imposing. The exteriors are ostentatious and the interiors are adorned with monuments to the white men who have shaped both the development of law and how it is taught. While the imagery of eminent jurists is of only passing interest to most students, it is often jarring to those who come from communities with histories of racial oppression. Professor Adrien Katherine Wing (2012) has described the powerful messaging conveyed by the portraits of white men that are routinely hung throughout the hallways of law school buildings. Radiating from such depictions is the message 'We are important. We are the law. This is our world' (Wing, 2012: 359).

The alienation experienced by Professor Wing has been echoed by other Black scholars. In *Reproducing Racism: White Space, Elite Law Schools, and*

Racial Inequality, Wendy Leo Moore (2008: 28) describes how portraits of white male jurists operate as 'racial signifiers of power'. More recently, Bennett Capers (2021: 27) has argued that it is not only the imagery of such individuals that sends 'messages of exclusion'. The names of wealthy donors that are embossed on classrooms, libraries and moot courts also communicate 'who the law school once served, who it serves now' and 'who are its true legatees and beneficiaries' (Capers, 2021: 27).

A racial hierarchy also finds resonance in faculty appointments. Just over 69 per cent of professors are white (John et al, 2022: 2100), and the vast majority are graduates of law schools that are not only highly ranked, but also have small numbers of Black students (2022: 2100). However, the most influential factor in maintaining the dominance of whiteness is neither the physical environment nor the cultural homogeneity of those who inhabit such spaces. Rather, it is 'the law itself' (Moore, 2008: 29).

For hundreds of years law, race and colonization have been inextricably bound. As Christina John and her colleagues (2022: 2097) point out, the American legal system has been the 'engine of white supremacy', via 'conquest, enslavement, and Jim Crow, and later through facially neutral laws that, despite the civil rights movement, continue to maintain disparate White power and wealth'. Despite its long-standing relationship with various forms of oppression, law is taught as though it has no 'specific cultural, political, or class characteristics' (Crenshaw, 1988: 2).

From the earliest days of law school, a student's imagination and intellectual curiosity are harnessed and confined to silos that consist of legal rules and relevant facts. Social context, cultural differences and morality are reduced to irrelevance (Capers, 2021: 36). Legal judgments are to be read as though they were written from positions of neutrality undiluted by bias or sentimentality. Consequently, legal decisions that lead to the entrenchment of inequality on the bases of race, gender and class are viewed as inevitable.

The Socratic method, in which students are randomly questioned about legal principles, can be intimidating and is often sanitized of ethical considerations. In her research on elite law schools, Moore (2008: 57) observed that sarcastic humour is one of the tools used by law professors who embrace the Socratic method. When issues of race are responded to with caustic jokes, one result is the mitigation of the brutalities suffered by victims of white supremacy. Students who have the courage to share their own histories of racial violence grapple not only with power imbalances, but also the risk of having to perform emotional labour (Moore, 2008: 31).

Arguably, the lack of racial literacy in legal education has become even more problematic in recent years, with police officers killing defenceless individuals, such as Breonna Taylor, with impunity (Ossei-Owusu, 2020). On the one hand, students who are Black, Indigenous and people of colour are acutely aware of the realities of a legal system that places little value on the lives of Others. At the same time, they experience pressure to adhere to an 'emotionally desensitized all-sides-matter approach to law' (Ossei-Owusu, 2020). In the end, this conflict can lead to 'spirit murder' (Ossei-Owusu, 2020). The term 'spirit murder' was created by Professor Patricia Williams to put into words the killing of the psyches of others whose humanity is corroded by pervasive racism (Garcia and Davila, 2021).

The Australian experience

Akin to their American counterparts, Australian law schools are awash with representations of white men, and the occasional white woman. While such gestures celebrate the luminaries who have shaped the evolution of Australian law, they also act as 'racial signifiers of power'. Like Professor Wing, I have experienced a visceral reaction to my workplace. In 2016, I became one of a handful of Indigenous scholars to secure employment in Sydney Law School, which sits within Australia's oldest university. Sydney Law School is renowned for its talented scholars and the best and brightest students, who go on to wield power in the legal profession and politics.

When I reflect on the five years that I spent at Sydney Law School, I feel gratitude for colleagues who supported me during my acclimatization to a culture that can best be described as 'sink or swim'. But I also feel sadness when I reflect on surroundings that defined who belonged and who did not. Such exclusivity found resonance in paintings of the professoriate that had been hung in our common room. I got to know some of those in the portraits, who kindly provided me with a sympathetic ear and wise counsel. But I was always unsettled by the lack of Black and Brown faces among the portraits, and the implicit assumption that such absences were normal.

Akin to the American experience, faculty staff in Australian law schools are, for the most part, culturally homogeneous. When I began my academic career 20 years ago, most Australian law schools were yet to recruit an Indigenous academic. Today, I am happy to report that there has been some progress, and we are now a small but growing community. However, most Indigenous legal academics remain the only Indigenous person employed in their institutions. I can speak from first-hand experience of the loneliness that this entails.

Since the early 1990s, scholars have examined the experiences of Indigenous Australian law students. By the end of 1990, only 21 Indigenous people in the entire country had completed their studies, a statistic that Lavery (1993: 4) describes as 'embarrassingly low'. Some explanation for this figure was offered by Banks and Douglas (2000–1: 43), whose research revealed that Indigenous law students experienced profound alienation and were 'systematically disempowered by the structures and processes of law school'.

A more recent study by Hobbs and Williams (2019) revealed that although Australian law schools are yet to become level playing fields, Indigenous people are commencing legal studies and completing their degrees in increasing numbers. There have also been developments in research and teaching. The Tanganekald and Meintangk scholar Professor Irene Watson (2014) broke new ground through work that created space for Indigenous law in Australian legal scholarship. At the same time, the Wiradjuri academic Dr Annette Gainsford (2018) has shown how Indigenous knowledge can be embedded in legal curricula. Despite such milestones, for the most part Australian law schools remain white spaces.

I recognize that there is no silver bullet that will instantly transform law schools into places that nurture, love and celebrate Indigenous scholars and our students. I also acknowledge that substantive change is likely to depend upon an array of tools and the unwavering commitment of generations of warrior scholars. In this chapter, I have identified one means of challenging the whiteness of law schools, which is telling the narratives of groundbreaking Indigenous lawyers.

Indigenous people in the legal profession

There are two sides to the story of Indigenous people's engagement with Australian law. On one side, law is a conduit for colonization. Law was instrumental to the erasure of Indigenous people's rights to our lands, and generations were stripped of personal autonomy under various Protection Acts (Senate Standing Committee on Legal and Constitutional Affairs, 2006). However, Indigenous people are also adept at using law to achieve our goals. In the 1970s, Indigenous activists and their supporters established legal aid services to defend the victims of police violence (Potter, 1974). Two decades later, Indigenous people seized the imperfect tool of the Native Title Act 1993 (Cth) and used it to achieve their own ends. Due to their tenacity, registered native title determinations now cover almost half of Australia's land mass (Federal Court of Australia, 2022). An important but relatively unknown protagonist in this story is the Indigenous lawyer.

It was not until the 1970s that those who would become the first generation of Indigenous lawyers overcame histories of disadvantage and exclusion to pursue legal education. At the same time, law schools began to roll out alternative entry programmes for Aboriginal and Torres Strait Islander people (Banks and Douglas, 2000–1). Mullenjaiwakka, who was also known as Lloyd McDermott, became the first Indigenous barrister when he was called to the New South Wales Bar in 1972 (Pelly, 2008).

Born in the North Queensland town of Eidsvold in 1939 (Harris, 2019), McDermott grew into a talented athlete. While a student of the Church of England Grammar School, McDermott's sporting prowess gave him a degree of equality with his white peers (Harris, 2019). But his beginnings in the profession were marred by racism. In an interview in 2008, he revealed that early in his career, his identity had been questioned by colleagues who believed that Aboriginal people could possess neither a law degree nor a pin-striped suit (Pelly, 2008). Undeterred by such prejudice, McDermott went on to establish a successful career in criminal law, and later became a mentor to young Indigenous lawyers (Fraser, 2019).

The first generation of Indigenous lawyers gained their qualifications during the height of the Indigenous civil rights movement. This was a time when those who marched in the streets were subject to unrestrained police brutality. In capital cities such as Sydney and Brisbane, police would also impose informal curfews on Indigenous people. Anyone caught in public space at night was liable to be arrested (Perheentupa, 2020). So it is unsurprising that many of our early lawyers were motivated by a desire to create a sanctuary from such violence.

The Kuku Yalanji lawyer Dr Pat O'Shane completed her studies at the University of New South Wales in 1976. She worked at Aboriginal Legal Services in Sydney and Central Australia before becoming the first Indigenous magistrate in 1986 (Behrendt and Walsh, 1991). The Wiradjuri man Paul Coe helped to build the country's first Aboriginal Legal Service in Redfern in 1970 (Perheentupa, 2020). In addition to being a trailblazer in the law, Coe was an important figure at the Aboriginal Tent Embassy in Canberra in 1972 and would become a lifelong advocate for Aboriginal land rights. Coe and O'Shane's contemporary, the late Judge Bob Bellear, was inspired to study law after witnessing police violence in Redfern (McAvoy, 2005). Bellear would earn the admiration of his peers as a public defender before his appointment to the District Court of New South Wales in 1996 (Wootten, 2005).

Over 600 Indigenous people have followed in the footsteps of those giants (Allman and Dale, 2021) and, like their forebears, they have been unwavering in their contributions to public life. Aboriginal and Torres Strait Islander lawyers act for native title claimants, represent Indigenous people in the criminal justice system and advise Indigenous corporations. They have also challenged Australians to confront the legacies of colonization by playing leadership roles in groundbreaking inquiries. Together with the late Sir Ronald Wilson, the Yawuru lawyer Professor Mick Dodson conducted hearings in which members of the Stolen Generations told their stories to the National Inquiry into the Separation of Aboriginal and Torres Strait Islander Children from their Families. Some of those testimonies featured in the watershed report *Bringing Them Home* (Human Rights and Equal Opportunity Commission, 1997). It was because of such important work that the voices of those who survived the horrors of child removal policies entered the national consciousness.

Indigenous lawyers such as the Waanyi and Kalkadoon barrister Joshua Creamer have been instrumental in holding powerful institutions accountable for egregious acts of racial discrimination through class actions (Donazzon, 2020). While many have sought to achieve justice by working within the parameters of the law, others have challenged the law to live up to its promise of equality through indomitable activism. Such contributions have been personified by the Palawa lawyer Michael Mansell, who helped to establish the Aboriginal Provisional Government, a body that fights for the recognition of Aboriginal sovereignty (Gregoire, 2022). Recently, Mansell made national headlines by asserting ownership of the yacht *Huntress*, which had been competing in the 2022 Sydney to Hobart race (Moran and Pridham, 2023). The yacht sank and washed ashore on the island of Cape Barren. Mansell argued that under Aboriginal sea law practices, the yacht became the property of the Aboriginal owners of the island (Moran and Pridham, 2023). Although Mansell's advocacy did not prevent the yacht from being salvaged, it brought attention to the rights of Aboriginal landholders.

Today, lawyers such as Professor Megan Davis, Noel Pearson, Dr Hannah McGlade and Teela Reid are among those who are leading the conversation on the constitutional entrenchment of an Indigenous Voice to Parliament. Some have achieved national and international acclaim for their advocacy. For example, the Eualeyai and Kamilaroi lawyer Professor Larissa Behrendt has become a public figure through her willingness to speak out against corrosive policies such as the Northern Territory Intervention, and her support for the families of murdered Aboriginal children who are yet to receive justice (Behrendt, 2014).

While the Indigenous legal fraternity has made significant inroads over the past five decades, we are still a long way from achieving parity in the profession. Although Indigenous people constitute 3 per cent of the population, we represent only 0.8 per cent of Australia's solicitors (Allman and Dale, 2021). Of the 6,000 barristers throughout the country, 20 are Indigenous (Walsh, 2018). The lack of representation in the senior ranks of the Bar and the judiciary is even more stark. Tony McAvoy and Justice Lincoln Crowley are the only Indigenous lawyers to have been elevated to senior counsel (Cheshire, 2018). Fewer than 20 Indigenous people have ever been appointed as either magistrates or judges.

The stories of Indigenous lawyers have been captured briefly in articles published in journals such as the *Indigenous Law Bulletin* (Gallegos, 2014) and the *Law Society Journal* (Williams, 2022). However, the narratives of such practitioners have never been the subject of sustained scholarly analysis. It is time for this to change. Indigenous communities, and indeed all Australians, stand to benefit from the recognition of such pioneers. With a referendum on the Indigenous Voice to Parliament imminent at the time of writing, a revision of our national story is overdue. In any such reimagining, Indigenous lawyers deserve a page of their own. In the final part of this chapter, I will argue that law schools also have much to gain from the narratives of Indigenous lawyers. Such stories have the potential to illuminate systemic racism while also celebrating perseverance in the face of adversity, and demonstrating how law is strengthened through the contributions of outsiders.

Making Indigenous lawyers visible: counter-storytelling

One of the tenets of critical race theory is that much of what we believe to be real is constructed by narratives. Such narratives cloak inequalities on the bases of race, gender and class as inescapable. One means of challenging such narratives is to tell the stories of outsiders. Outsider storytelling is a 'powerful means for destroying mind-set – the bundle of presuppositions, received wisdoms, and shared understandings against a background of which legal and political discourse takes place' (Delgado, 2013: 71). The stories of Indigenous lawyers, when told through the lenses of Black historical consciousness, are a form of outsider storytelling that could expose the whiteness of Australian law schools, while at the same time spurring new and important conversations about how legal education can better serve our entire society.

Black historical consciousness

The concept 'Black historical consciousness' was conceived by Professor LaGarrett J. King (2020: 337) as an approach to teaching Black history that dismantles 'white epistemic logic', which is 'the rationalization of Black historical experiences and ways of knowing/doing through traditional Western European perspectives'. A racial literacy approach predicated on Black historical consciousness recognizes the diversity of Blackness (Simmons et al, 2019) and ignores traditional Western timelines which identify slavery as the beginning of Black history (Simmons et al, 2019). It also examines what it is to be Black, by acknowledging positive Black histories, together with 'people's deficiencies and vulnerabilities' (Simmons et al, 2019: 56).

While it is important to acknowledge the significant differences between Black Americans and Indigenous Australians, Black historical consciousness is a useful device to make the experiential knowledge of Indigenous people visible in legal education. For a start, Indigenous people's engagement with law did not begin with the arrival of the British in 1788. Rather, the beginning can be located thousands of years beforehand, with our own legal traditions. An approach predicated on Black historical consciousness recognizes that Indigenous people have been and remain the victims of disproportionate rates of incarceration. However, it also celebrates the ingenuity of the Indigenous legal fraternity.

Through learning about the triumphs of Indigenous lawyers, students would be prompted to question the negative stereotypes of Indigenous people that are perpetuated by legal judgments that erase the stories of Indigenous parties. They may also begin to recognize that the predominance of whiteness in law schools is not unavoidable. I have identified two additional ways in which legal education may be enhanced through engagement with the narratives of Indigenous lawyers – by raising student awareness of the contributions that outsiders can make to the development of law and equipping law schools to become responsive to the needs of Indigenous lawyers. This is not an exhaustive list of the benefits to be gained from such engagement, but rather the beginning of a promising conversation.

Law is strengthened by outsiders

Law is strengthened by lawyers who are empowered to inflect their work with lived experience of marginalization. In reminiscing about the contributions of Justice Thurgood Marshall to the US Supreme Court, Justice Sandra Day O'Connor (1991–2) describes the impacts of Marshall's life experience on his fellow judges. Stories from Marshall's time as a civil rights lawyer were a reminder to his colleagues of the need for constant vigilance in narrowing 'the gap between the ideal of equal justice and the reality of social inequality' (Day O'Connor, 1991–2: 1218).

Closer to home, the contributions of Indigenous lawyers have impacted the delivery of legal services to the most disadvantaged Australians. When the Aboriginal Legal Service in Redfern opened its doors in 1970, it was a radical creation. The shopfront service was subject to community control, provided its services for free and was a fierce proponent of Indigenous self-determination. It created a benchmark that would later find resonance in legal aid services throughout Australia (Perheentupa, 2020). Through learning about such contributions, students may open their minds to the possibilities of what law can be. Students may also begin to understand that when we treat social context and cultural differences as irrelevant, we dehumanize our fellow citizens and legitimize the poor value that the legal system places on the lives of Others.

Meeting the needs of Indigenous students

Because the stories of Indigenous lawyers have been overlooked by scholars, little is known about how they balance family and community expectations with professional fidelity to a legal system that perpetuates colonization. However, some commonalities may be drawn with the experiences of

Indigenous lawyers in the United States. Fletcher (2006) likens some Native American lawyers to the 'abductee' in Native American mythology. In such stories, a young maiden is kidnapped and forced to adapt to the ways of her captors. When she eventually returns, the maiden has a new gift that is of great use to her people. However, the maiden has been so profoundly affected by her abduction that she can no longer live among them and goes into exile. By way of analogy, Native Americans commonly attend law school with the goal of obtaining skills that are needed by their communities. But instead of being embraced by the latter, Native American lawyers often face distrust and are presumed to have assimilated, so that they have become agents of colonization (Fletcher, 2006).

Scholars are yet to consider whether Indigenous lawyers in Australia experience the alienation described by Fletcher. However, there are obvious examples of situations in which the fulfilment of one's duties as a lawyer could compound the disadvantage that Indigenous people experience in the legal system. Aboriginal and Torres Strait Islander lawyers who prosecute Indigenous people charged with criminal offences, and those who represent powerful interests that are opposed to the recognition of native title, presumably face a moral quandary. By engaging with the narratives of Indigenous lawyers, scholars may learn more about how such dilemmas can be resolved. Such research could be drawn upon by law schools so that Indigenous law students may become better prepared to weather the challenges of serving both their communities and the profession.

Conclusion

For too long, law schools have been white spaces. Thanks to the work of American scholars such as Wendy Leo Moore, Bennett Capers and Adrien K. Wing, we can articulate how whiteness manifests in such institutions. Such dominance resonates in the physical surroundings, faculty appointments and the Socratic method, which treats race as irrelevant.

One means of challenging the whiteness of law schools is by making the stories of Indigenous people's contributions to the development of law and the delivery of legal services visible. Such narratives may prompt students to question the stereotypes of Indigenous people that are perpetuated through the erasure of Indigenous people's stories from legal judgments. Students may also begin to realize that the cultural homogeneity of law professors is not inevitable. Through learning about the creativity and lived experience of marginalization that Indigenous lawyers bring to the law, students may also begin to consider the possibilities for what law can be and who it exists to serve. Finally, it is through engagement with such narratives that law schools could learn how to meet the needs of future Indigenous lawyers, as they prepare to become intermediaries between their communities and the legal system.

References

Allman, K. and Dale, A. (2021) 'The state of the profession 2021', *Law Society Journal*, 9 August, https://lsj.com.au/articles/the-state-of-the-profession-2021

Anderson, E. (2015) 'The white space', *Sociology of Race and Ethnicity*, 1(1): 10–21.

Banks, C. and Douglas, H. (2000–1) ' "From a different place altogether": Indigenous students and cultural exclusion at law school', *Australian Journal of Law and Society*, 15: 42–66.

Behrendt, L. (2014) 'Bowraville murders: After the NSW inquiry, the elusive justice the families seek is one step closer', *The Guardian*, 10 November, https://www.theguardian.com/commentisfree/2014/nov/10/bowraville-murders-after-the-nsw-inquiry-the-elusive-justice-families-seek-is-one-step-closer

Behrendt, L. and Walsh, S. (1991) 'From Cairns to the courtroom', *Polemic*, 2: 161–5.

Capers, B. (2021) 'The law school as a white space', *Minnesota Law Review*, 106: 7–57.

Cheshire, A. (2018) 'Tony McAvoy', *Bar News*, Autumn: 82–3.

Crenshaw, K. (1988) 'Foreword: Toward a race-conscious pedagogy in legal education', *National Black Law Journal*, 11(1): 1–14.

Day O'Connor, S. (1991–2) 'Thurgood Marshall: The influence of a raconteur', *Stanford Law Review*, 44: 1217–20.

Delgado, R. (2013) 'Storytelling for oppositionists and others: A plea for narrative', in R. Delgado and J. Stefancic (eds), *Critical Race Theory: The Cutting Edge*, 3rd edn, Philadelphia: Temple University Press, pp 71–80.

Donazzon, S. (2020) 'Turning trauma into a life of fighting against injustice', *The Standard*, 19 October, https://www.theswinstandard.net/2020/10/19/turning-trauma-into-a-life-of-fighting-against-injustice

Federal Court of Australia (2022) *Annual Report 2021–2022*, Canberra: Commonwealth of Australia.

Fletcher, M. (2006) 'Dibakonigowin: Indian lawyer as abductee', *Oklahoma City University Law Review*, 31(2): 209–36.

Fraser, J. (2019) 'Mullenjaiwakka', *Hearsay*, https://www.hearsay.org.au/author/john-fraser

Gainsford, A. (2018) 'Connection to Country: Place-based learning initiatives embedded in the Charles Sturt University Bachelor of Laws', *Legal Education Review*, 28(2), https://researchoutput.csu.edu.au/en/publications/connection-to-country-place-based-learning-initiatives-embedded-i

Gallegos, R. (2014) 'Paving the way: Indigenous leaders creating change in the legal word', *Indigenous Law Bulletin*, 8(11): 8–18.

Garcia, N.M. and Davila, E.R. (2021) 'Spirit murdering: Terrains, trenches, and terrors in academia', *The Journal of Educational Foundations*, 34(1): 3–13.

Gregoire, P. (2022) 'The weakest proposal for the advancement of Aboriginal people: Michael Mansell on the Voice', *Sydney Criminal Lawyers*, blog post, https://www.sydneycriminallawyers.com.au/blog/the-weakest-proposal-for-the-advancement-of-aboriginal-people-michael-mansell-on-the-voice

Harris, B. (2019) 'Lloyd McDermott: Wallaby No 470 and an inspiration to Indigenous youth', *The Guardian*, 8 April, https://www.theguardian.com/sport/2019/apr/08/lloyd-mcdermott-wallaby-no-470-and-an-inspiration-to-indigenous-youth

Hobbs, H. and Williams, G. (2019) 'The participation of Indigenous Australians in legal education, 2001–18', *University of New South Wales Law Journal*, 42(4): 1294–327.

Human Rights and Equal Opportunity Commission (1997) *Bringing Them Home: The Report of the National Inquiry into the Separation of Aboriginal and Torres Strait Islander Children from Their Families*, Canberra: Commonwealth of Australia.

John, C., Pearce, R.G., Archer, A.J., Camiscoli, S.M., Pines, A., Salmanova, M. and Tarnavska, V. (2022) 'Subversive legal education: Reformist steps toward abolitionist vision', *Fordham Law Review*, 90: 2089–124.

King, L. (2020) 'Black history is not American history: Toward a framework of Black historical consciousness', *Social Education*, 84(6): 335–41.

Lavery, D. (1993) 'The participation of Indigenous Australians in legal education', *Legal Education Review*, 4(1), http://classic.austlii.edu.au/au/journals/LegEdRev/1993/8.html

Mabo v Queensland (No 2) (1992) 175 CLR 1.

McAvoy, T. (2005) 'Obituary: Bob Bellear (1944–2005)', *Indigenous Law Bulletin*, 6(10): 21.

Monture, P. (1990) 'Now that the door is open: First Nations and the law school experience', *Queen's Law Journal*, 15(2): 179–216.

Moore, W.L. (2008) *Reproducing Racism: White Space, Elite Law Schools, and Racial Inequality*, Lanham, MD: Rowman & Littlefield.

Moran, J. and Pridham, B. (2023) 'Salvage fight over Sydney to Hobart yacht, *Huntress* as Aboriginal Land Council claims ownership', *ABC News*, 9 January, https://www.abc.net.au/news/2023-01-09/sydney-to-hobart-yacht-huntress-salvage-fight-indigenous-claim/101836372

Ossei-Owusu S. (2020) 'For minority law students, learning the law can be intellectually violent', *ABA Journal*, 15 October, https://www.abajournal.com/voice/article/for_minority_law_students_learning_the_law_can_be_intellectually_violent

Pelly, M. (2008) 'Black lawyers can raise the bar', *The Australian*, 28 March, pp 33–6.

Perheentupa, J. (2020) *Redfern: Aboriginal Activism in the 1970s*, Canberra: Aboriginal Studies Press.

Potter, C.E. (1974) 'Poverty law practice: The Aboriginal Legal Service in New South Wales', *Sydney Law Review*, 7(2): 237–56.

Royal Commission into Aboriginal Deaths in Custody (1991) *Royal Commission into Aboriginal Deaths in Custody: National Report*, Canberra: Australian Government Publishing Service.

Senate Standing Committee on Legal and Constitutional Affairs (2006) *Unfinished Business: Indigenous Stolen Wages*, Canberra: Commonwealth of Australia.

Simmons, G.D., King, L.J. and Adu-Gyamfi, M. (2019) 'Developing a Black history and Black studies course using a Black historical consciousness framework', *Oregon Journal of the Social Studies*, 7(1): 1–67.

Walsh, K. (2018) 'One barrister's battle to increase Indigenous lawyer numbers: Chris Ronalds AO', *Australian Financial Review*, 1 February, https://fjc.net.au/wp-content/uploads/2018/06/One-barristers-battle-to-increase-Indigenous-lawyer-numbers-Chris-Ronalds-AO-Katie-Walsh.-AFR-Feb-1-2018.pdf

Watson, I. (2014) *Aboriginal Peoples, Colonialism and International Law: Raw Law*, New York: Routledge.

Williams, O. (2022) 'Meet the new kids on the block', *Law Society Journal*, 1 November, https://lsj.com.au/articles/meet-the-new-kids-on-the-block

Wing, A.K. (2012) 'Lessons from a portrait: Keep calm and carry on', in G. y Muhs, Y.F. Niemann, C.G. González and A.P. Harris (eds), *Presumed Incompetent: The Intersections of Race and Class for Women in Academia*, Denver: University Press of Colorado, pp 356–71.

Wootten, H. (2005) 'Robert William Bellear (1944–2005)', *University of New South Wales Law Journal*, 28(1): vii.

PART IV

Building Critical Racial and Decolonial Literacies beyond the Academy

15

Incantation: Insurgent Texts as Decolonial Feminist Praxis

Nilmini Fernando

Introduction

> INCANTATION: chant, intonation, recitation, song, spell, cantillation, cry, slogan, rallying call, war cry, chorus, mantra, ritualistic, repetitive. Saying love out loud. Saying race out loud. Over and over to evoke the energy and spirit of our textual utterances and release their transformational power into unconditioned space. (Fernando and Banks, 2022)

Writing, art and drama have long served as vehicles for intellectual women of colour worldwide to magnetize their psychical and intellectual resistance and theorize their insurgency and survival of imperial domination (Sandoval, 2000). Drawing from this tradition, *Incantation*[1] is a collective decolonial feminist praxis that creates and curates live, multivoiced performances of seminal feminist of colour texts and original creative responses to them by women of colour.

The praxis model for *Incantation* emerged through my doctoral research with a group of women from West Africa 'on their way' through the asylum/migration nexus in the Republic of Ireland (Fernando, 2016a, 2016b, 2021). Instrumentalizing arts-based methodologies of the oppressed (Boal, 1979; Sandoval, 2000), my research examined identity, representation and power through interrogating the poetics (practices that signify/make meaning) and politics (the power dynamics that govern these practices) of participant women's narratives and devised performances of their journeys.

As a diasporic Sri Lankan Australian researcher researching with women crossing multiple geographical, political and cultural Global South–North borders, specific Black/Third World feminist theory and decolonizing epistemologies and methodologies enacted in the Irish context proved invaluable ground for critical decolonial feminist of colour praxis in the contemporary Australian settler-colonizing context. First, the location as academic/artist/activitist, which served as a critical counterpoint through which to interrogate identity, power and representation from 'below'. Evocation of Anzaldúa's (1987) construct of *'mestiza* consciousness' for positionality opened channels for multiple reading/listening positions and loci of enunciation. This, in turn, forged the development of multiple critical literacies necessary to read and decipher the colonizing assemblage of visual, affective, political discourses that entrapped women of colour in postcolonial asylum encounters in the West. The research illustrated how embodied, voiced, live utterances of self-representational texts through performance allowed women at the asylum/migration nexus to disrupt and speak back to the discursive violence of the assemblage of fetishizing gendered/raced representations of Black and Third World women that preceded their arrival, making them hyper-visible but speechless (Fernando, 2016a, 2016b). A crucial learning was that decolonial praxis requires strenuous, intentioned 'backstage' work to decolonize research and performance processes and practices and to carve autonomous spaces where women are protected from state surveillance, fetishization in the media and exploitation by white charitable organizations. The research found that critical decolonial research encounters can foster convivial spaces and conditions for the production of truthful art and speech that replenish agency, creativity and self-regard, even while living in financial precarity and encamped within the privatized asylum incarceration complex (Fernando, 2021).

Ten years ago, I was not aware of 'decolonial' theory and praxis, but was impelled by the theoretical edginess of Indigenous/Native feminist texts within and extant to the genealogies of Black, anti-colonial and postcolonial feminist theory and praxis in which I was steeped. Their concerns with plurality, relationality, contextualized inquiry and critical praxis orientation were indeed foundational elements of decolonial forms of feminism (Lugones, 2010). Travelling as a transnational decolonial praxis from the Republic of Ireland to Australia, this chapter draws from a live outdoor performance of *Incantation* (Fernando, 2022a) on 19 February 2022 as part of the Seat at the Table at the 'TwoSixty' project – an 18-month decolonial/anti-racist feminist residency in Naarm (Melbourne).[2] Designed and curated in collaboration with multidisciplinary African American artist Maxime Banks,[3] the final production featured 12 Indigenous and non-Indigenous feminists of colour of different ethnicities, who read and responded with original poems, spoken word, music and dance to seminal texts by Indigenous Australian feminists Aileen Moreton-Robinson and Jackie Huggins, and African American black feminist icons Toni Morrison, Audre Lorde and bell hooks.

The first section of this chapter addresses positionality, finding our place and naming ourselves as non-Indigenous others on colonized lands, followed by a discussion on decolonial feminisms of colour. Both, I propose, are foundational for 21st-century decolonial feminist of colour praxis. The chapter then presents key decolonial feminist praxes and literacies that informed, were informed by, and emerged through the Incantation project, including:

- 'Wild Tongues and Insurgent Texts';
- polyvocal and intertextual naming and doing;
- deciphering and analyses of listening locations;
- re-existence; and
- playful cosmic travelling in expansive articulations of the 'Sistership'.

Positionality

Finding our place, naming ourselves

> Aileen Moreton-Robinson is on the radio speaking about land, relationality, and sovereignty:
> Her elders taught her to walk lightly on Aboriginal land
> As the land, waters, rocks and all that live on her are sentient.
> An intertextual moment with Yeats –
> 'tread softly for you tread on my dreams'. (Fernando, 2022b)

Returning from the Anglo-Euro context to Australia and entering feminist academic/arts/activist spaces, I needed to re-examine and rearticulate who the 'we' are of a decolonial feminism of colour in settler-colonial land. What do we name ourselves in the complexities and shifting textual landscapes of 21st-century settler coloniality? Solidarity in the decolonial project is to 'form political collectivities that can encompass heterogeneity and multiplicity' (Lugones, 2003: 208–9). What is involved in solidarity building amid the global movement of peoples, the endless proliferation of new others, the rise of white supremacist fascism and capitalist forces that continually seek to fragment and hierarchize we others, and other others? As Moya (2011: 79) tells us, 'who we are and from where we speak' matters; our loci of enunciation have political and epistemic significance for knowledge production and to define where we stand, in what struggles/s and in solidarity with whom.

Feminists of colour in and beyond the academy have traversed the discursive and linguistic shifts that have taken place through evolutions in Black, postcolonial, transnational/intersectional/queer/Indigenous and decolonial feminisms. To name ourselves here, now, we can draw from liberatory energies coded and accumulated through the genealogies of anti-colonial, Third World, postcolonial, intersectional and decolonial feminist movements. As a non-Indigenous woman, I am not politically black, Black or Blak, but an 'other other' arrivant of colour in a settler-colonial multicultural state.[4] Whether then or now, here, there, elsewhere in Asia, or in white/WEIRD[5] spaces, the darkness of my skin and womanity imprint gendered/raced differences (of inferiority) on my body and identity.

While I could self-identify as a brown woman to distinguish that I am raced – but not in the same ways as a Black woman – I prefer the term 'Third World' woman, as it evokes the postwar decolonial spirit and vision of the non-aligned nations at Bandung in 1955.[6] 'Third World women' also theoretically aligns with postcolonial feminist theories of representation and construction of the gendered/raced/colonized other, and the term holds in view transnational gendered/raced division of service labour. 'Third World' also aligns with the genealogy of American Third World feminisms, Chicana feminisms and Womanism (Moraga and Anzaldúa, 1983; Walker, 1983; Mohanty, 2003), and queer Black feminist coalitions such as the Combahee River Collective (1982), which call for Black/brown unity.

The term 'people of colour/woman of colour' has been contested in Australian Indigenous intellectual/activist debates and among non-Indigenous women of colour,[7] and generally signifies a shared political location of being 'othered' in white supremacy – although the impacts are incommensurable and inequivalent in form, degree and impact with Indigenous peoples. My use of the term 'woman/feminist of colour' follows Lugones (2003: 87) to stand for a 'heterogenous collectivity [that represents] a coalition of differences grounded not in coincidences of individual or group interests but in multiple understandings of oppressions and resistances'. Woman of colour feminisms (or *feminisms of colour*) as defined by the Santa Cruz Feminist of Color Collective (2014), recognize and trace 'intergenerational relations of "women of colour" feminists and philosophers who historically have critiqued normative, colonial and modern understandings of knowledge while constructing interdisciplinary and alternative spaces for theorizing and sustaining communities of resistance across constructed borders' (2014: 23). The term refers to being not part of white structural power (Rankine, 2020), a political relationship (not a biological identity) defined by racism, dispossession and imperialism (Kelly, 2016), which serves as a political location that broadens possibilities of solidarity from pluralities against multiple structures of oppression.

Naming ourselves, finding our place, further requires giving an authentic account of the ethics and complexities of doing and being feminists of colour in relation to the incommensurability with Indigenous feminist struggle, but also in relation to the complexities of navigating exclusionary spaces within and beyond the academy where decolonial feminism is 'done' and simultaneously 'undone', including by women of colour, as discussed next.

Savaging Black and feminism of colour theory and praxis

In Australia and elsewhere, critical feminist of colour academics inhabit the borderlands of knowledge production and teaching. In 21st-century settler coloniality, as killjoys (Ahmed, 2023) exiled to the far edges of the academy, critiques typically focus on financial precarity, extractive labour and the general demise of academia as a workplace through neoliberalization and corporatization of the university sector. Of equal or greater concern ought be the excision of our emancipatory knowledges and pedagogies, along with our bodies, from spaces of authority and knowledge production. Even as we inhabit the fringes, our cultural and representational labour continues to be extracted, leaving us 'gasping for breath', as Lobo (2020) puts it. For me, to find breathing spaces, to make room to do critical feminist work, has always meant the creation of my own platforms to offer education and tools for critical and radical thinking and decolonial praxes that many feminists of colour urgently seek but cannot easily find.

Outside of academia, in which I remain an edge-dweller and intermittent interlocutor, my encounters with feminism and women of colour take place through research, education, consultancy and activism. I move through arts spaces, community spaces, domestic and family violence sectors and legal/bureaucratic feminist spaces; needless to say, colonial technologies of oppression intersectionally operate through them all. Straddling the not-for-profit and women's services sectors, my feminist of colour encounters painfully reveal a vast ignorance of race and merciless co-optation of white and non-white women alike into mainstream liberal equality patriarchal feminisms. It is here that we fully face – on a mass, public scale – the consequences of ignorance and miseducation, the ravages of individualized white liberal feminism and decades of multiculturalist policy. Playing havoc with the notion of reflexive positionality, intersectional feminism has descended into an additive, exhaustive exercise, a matter of naming 'traits' of 'difference' or 'diversity' used to legitimize claims of injury, and ultimately to access knowledge, resources, speaking spaces and power for those already at the table.

Intersectionality, savaged as a praxis through primitive and naive applications in white liberal feminisms, has resulted in a disturbing form of 'elite capture' (Táíwò, 2022), where on one layer elite/professional/corporate white women claim identity-based locations of victimhood to the neglect of Indigenous women and women of colour. On the next (lower) layer, elite/professional/corporate women of colour and their organizations use multicultural/diversity labels to gain (conditional) entry to rooms, seats at the table and state funds and contracts (for which they compete with white established organizations). Meanwhile, the grim conditions for those most marginalized (incarcerated as Indigenous peoples or as non-Indigenous in asylum detention or houseless) remain unseen and unheard (Táíwò, 2022). And this is quite apart from efforts to 'co-design' and 'consult' with 'lived experience', which are poorly renumerated and often re-exploitative.

Persard (2021: 18) warns that intersectionality, a feminist analytic framework that serves as a 'vehicle for feminist praxis' has become 'translated into a descriptive (that is, "intersectional")' and this ontological shift makes intersectionality theoretically become 'not something one does, but something one is'. The genealogy of critical resistant knowledges and Black feminist thought (Hill Collins, 1990, 2019) is disappeared in favour of 'intersecting' social identities. Similarly, 'decoloniality' is increasingly deployed as feminist currency to stand for anything to do with women of colour, at the risk that we 'proceed with decolonising everything without decolonising anything and obscure the violences of coloniality' (Persard, 2021: 19). Decoloniality is 'not a radical method of inclusion', and we must not confuse what we name ourselves politically and analytically with our identities (2021: 19).

How, then, do we build coalitions and alliances that are not mediated by whiteness and white feminisms? Should we adopt women of colour feminist praxes that centre, listen to and follow the decolonizing struggles of Indigenous women and feminisms? What theoretical attention and praxes of political solidarity do we need in order to listen, learn and unlearn? To unsettle, and attune to the shifting contours of plural locations/loci of enunciation, without disturbing the shared ground on which we stand? *Incantation* as a praxis was devised through asking these very questions and attending to these nuances throughout the project.

Refusing the shallow, narrow terms of such politics, *Incantation* provided a rare occasion for a simultaneous intercentric[8] staging – not of our differences (from each other or the dominant white norm), but of spaces we inhabit. An articulation of what is created in and through the 'vitality of human and more-than-human power that struggles but emerges from the cracks, fissures and margins to seed plural becomings' (Lobo, 2020: 576), and forms and modes of belonging. A grounding decolonial praxis in Australia, following Ahmed (2023), is 'to make Indigenous sovereignty a first principle' and to change how we relate to history and to land by hearing what race critical Indigenous scholarship such as the white possessive (Moreton-Robinson, 2015: 11) teaches us.

One must be cognisant of an alternative ontology, epistemology, worldview in which the land, spirit, cosmology, theorizations of the interdependency of human and non-human life are inextricable from Indigenous political/intellectual/territorial struggle and futurity (Moreton-Robinson, 2015; Watson, 2015). We must revive and rearticulate the genealogies of critical feminist of colour thought. To be in decolonial movement with Indigenous feminisms, we advance rigorous praxes of naming and finding our place that refuse cursory, performative acknowledgements of living on stolen land and listing off privileges, as (some) white feminists have learned to do, only to proceed with business as usual.

Decolonial feminisms

Incantation follows Vergès' (2019: 65) understanding of decolonial feminisms as part of 'the long movement of scientific and philosophical reappropriation that is revising the European narrative of the world ... [contesting] the Western-patriarchal economic ideology that turned women, Black people, Indigenous people and people from Asia and Africa into inferior beings'. Decolonial feminisms draw on 'the theories and practices that women have forged over time in anti-racist, anti-capitalist, and anti-colonial struggles' and expand theories of liberation and emancipation around the world (Vergès, 2019: 65–6). *Incantation* is aligned with the objectives and aspirations of recent writing by non-Indigenous decolonial feminists of colour in and from the Australian context. An anthology focusing on 'border crossings' by seven migrant women academics from the South (mostly Latin America) to universities in the North (Arashiro and Barahona, 2015) makes a decolonial intervention to 'shift from epistemologies of difference in coloniality to epistemologies of resistances created through the women's movement across borders, through the loss of privileges and the discovery of [their] Otherness in new social hierarchies' (Skachkova, 2017). In that collection, Motta (2015: 90) posits that attention to the bodies of subjectivities in narratives of the self and sharing stories are ways to 'nurture bridges of relationships between other raced and gendered subaltern subjects and communities experiencing the onto-epistemological wounds of coloniality and attempting to heal from these wounds'. With Motta, we sought to tend the common wounds of coloniality, to forge and nurture bridges of solidarity that defy the forced terms of multiculturalism, diversity, inclusion and white feminism against which we railed. To regroup, reconfigure and rearticulate our borderland living in and around the interstitial spaces we inhabit as South-in-North on Aboriginal lands. And in doing so, to go some part of the way to 'construct interdisciplinary and alternative spaces for collective theorizing, resisting, coalition building and solidarity' (Santa Cruz Feminist of Color Collective, 2014: 23).

Delinking from extractive, erasing and recolonizing spaces, practices and processes

As Purewal and Ung Loh (2021: 5) note, 'coloniality regenerates itself through patterns of denial, erasure, extraction and domination'; hence, decoloniality must resist, refuse, oppose and disrupt 'discourses and practices that reproduce interlocking, racial-colonial, hetero-patriarchal and capitalist relations of power and institutions' (Fúnez-Flores, 2023b: np). Importantly, decoloniality is enacted, a praxis that does not separate theoretical analysis and vision from action, but 'undoes, disobeys, and delinks from [the colonial matrix of power] constructing paths and praxis toward an otherwise of thinking, sensing, believing, doing, and living' (Mignolo and Walsh, 2018: 194). Beyond epistemic disruption and relinking with radical Black/Blak feminist texts and thought, the TwoSixty project sought to delink from extractive, erasing and recolonizing spaces, practices and processes typical in state-funded community arts projects. These include conditional, controlled occupation/inhabitation of space; short-term funding where marginalized groups 'take turns'; and administrative 'rules' and restrictions (for example, fixed budget categories, exclusionary eligibility criteria). Two factors enabled the holding of radical feminist space: free, unrestricted long-term studio space and a dedicated project manager fully committed to the task of developing, from the ground up, authentic collaborative decolonial feminist praxis models. When COVID-19 and multiple lockdowns prevented physical occupation of the space, the lead fought for a dedicated online space so unrestricted dialogue, discovery and dreaming on what decolonial feminist praxis could be was not interrupted. These conversations led to funding for *Incantation* through a Merri Bek Flourish Arts Recovery grant, also negotiated by the lead.

This invaluable role shifted to one of role 'mediating whiteness and bureaucracies' and mitigating deeply harmful effects well known to many of us through previous experiences of arts funding for diverse/difficult to reach/marginalized communities. The role required staunch commitment and disobedience/disloyalty to whiteness at times, deep reflexivity as a white woman and the ability to distinguish between mediating and gatekeeping and advocacy. Recalibration of relationships was needed to adjust for the ways we 'troubled' the existing hierarchies and, on occasion, the need to literally put her body in that space and 'take the bullets' spared us the added labour expropriated through racialized/gendered capitalist funding programmes:

> In the past I have felt defeated, shattered by lamestream white colonial culture in the arts, structures that continually box in the actual production. To get the idea over is a fight against capitalism. This is the first time where I haven't had to do advocacy to get endorsement and access from a white institution. First time to step into a collective space as a producer from a decolonial perspective, where it's not my artistic vision that's coming forward in someone else's, I found that power was shared, there was equity, visibility and we were all able to continually build each other up. (Fernando et al, 2022)

Having outlined the central theoretical elements that ground decolonial feminism in the Australian settler context and delinking from exploitative and extractive processes and practices, the second part of the chapter turns to insights into the liberatory and transformative potential of methods/enactments of decolonial praxes and 'incantatory' texts created through and in the afterlife of the performance.

Enacting decoloniality: intertextuality, polyvocality, mapping theory

> Words, images, voices, sounds, spirits are full of energy. Spoken aloud, together, in unison, in praise, we can bring back to life connections that been lost, broken, fractured and INCANT us back into spaces of belonging – to ourselves, to each other, to the universe. (Fernando and Banks, 2022)

A text offers a plurality of meanings, and is also woven out of other words, other utterances, other existing texts, and codes from other texts or discourses. The text is not a unified, isolated object that gives a singular meaning, but an element open to various interpretations. All meanings are made in the interpretation and reinterpretation of texts and involve particular ways of seeing based on power relations, forms of resistance, and being and knowing in the world (Kristeva, 1980). In reading out loud canonical feminists texts and performing our responses, intertextuality within an incantatory assemblage is a form of alchemy where bodies, sounds, flesh, stories, memories, truths, emotions and power comingle onstage (Figure 15.1). In the audience, our friends, families, fans and strangers meet the texts, the readers and one another. Together, we are more than the sum of our parts (Anzaldúa, 1987). We can remake ourselves. Dream ourselves into where we want to go, to be. Words too are materials/matter; once we create them, craft them, then utter them in incantatory fashion, we embody them with energy and meaning and they fire like textual arrows. Words make worlds. As Ahmed (2023) says, we need new words, we need books for our survival, books can be our buildings that we build from the 'fires' of Black feminism and feminism of colour: 'We have to build our own buildings when the world does not accommodate us. Books can be our buildings. We write ourselves into existence. Feminism: we cite each other into existence. But we have to find ways to send the work out so it can be shared, catch fire' (Ahmed, 2023: 184–5).

> Think about the multifarious words and deeds through which the very humanity of women has been questioned, desecrated, denied, vilified, brutalized, monetized, industrialized as well as how it has been exoticized, pedestalized, hypersexualized, celebritized, shero-ized.

I created the word 'womanity' to dispel all the ways our humanity is disavowed.
We deserve an entire category to ourselves.
Womanity has nothing to do with sex or gender.
Womanity avows the fullness, largesse and big badass cosmic explosion that we truly are, beyond-matter, beyond-mind, beyond the tiny spaces in which we are told we can thrive. (Fernando, 2022b)

Figure 15.1: *Incantation* provocations

PROVOCATIONS

Words, images, voices, sounds, spirits are full of energy. Spoken aloud, together, in unison, in praise, we can bring back to life connections that been lost, broken, fractured and INCANT us back into spaces of belonging- to ourselves, to each other, to the universe.
Text is Energy. Words are energy. Writing is a Tool. Text is a Tool. Text is Energy.
THEMES: power, joy, freedom, dreaming, healing, uniting, imagining.
INCANTATION: The overall theme of INCANTATION speaks to the POWER OF WORDS, TEXTS and the ENERGIES they contain.
INCANTATION: chant, intonation, recitation, song, cantillation, cry, slogan, rallying call, war cry, chorus, mantra, ritualistic, repetitive.
Saying things out loud, again and again and over times, and in unison to evoke these qualities and spirits in others and ourselves.
PRAISE POETRY: Many cultures follow traditions of praise poetry: African, Irish, Medieval odes, Japanese Renga. Following traditions of utterances of public praise, we work with the idea that rather that adulation, elevation, pedastalising, flattery, or 'celebritizing' individuals, for us, praise is to honour, to recite texts, create responses that 'spell out' the dreams, visions of seminal Black woman writers.
To evoke their qualities in ourselves and in others.
To write/right ourselves as present/presence into the histories of Black female intellectuals, artists, action-takers, holders and carriers of visions across time, space and generations.
INTERTEXTUALITY: A text offers a plurality of meanings, and is also woven out of other words, other utterances, other existing texts, codes from other texts or discourses. The text is not a unified, isolated object that gives a singular meaning, but an element open to various interpretations. All meanings are made in the interpretation and re-interpretation of texts and involve particular ways of seeing based on power relations, forms of resistance and being and knowing in the world. (Julia Kristeva, Roland Barthes).
POLYVOCALITY: Listen, speak and hear through multiple voices and locations. Each may speak in their own register. Each voice, location and perspective is valued equanimously. This dispels the idea that we must arrive at a unified common view, or ideas about minority/majority voices or representation. Instead, we can stand together and speak

from our multiple locations, as one or as a many. What do we hear when speech and meaning-making are orchestrated along different lines, rules, intentions? When we listen differently?

ALCHEMY: When texts, people, sounds, images, bodies and community gather, there is alchemy. Together we are more than the sum of our parts. We can re-make ourselves. Dream ourselves into where we want to go, to be.

COSMIC/UNIVERSE: Limitless, eternal, orbital, vast, past/present/future interconnected, through and across generations. An underlying/ or overlying theme is also limitless, universal cosmic forces and dreaming that we may access through focus, intention, love and freedom of thought and spirit.

ENFLESHMENT: Your body, your voice as the vehicle through which the text is being articulated. Giving words life, enriched with your experiences, incanting spaces with body, voice, as texts.

MODES OF DELIVERY: You might think about incantation as a literary device (e.g. repetition, recitation, praise) as well as a device of speech or performance style (e.g. A chorus of voices, echoing, mirroring, declarations, provocations, mourning).

Source: Fernando and Banks (2022)

Vergès (2019: 167) holds that writing, for racialized women, departs from the trajectory and process of European feminist writing: '[I]t is not about filling a void, but about finding the words to breathe life into that which has been condemned to non-existence, worlds that have been cast out of humanity.' Writing ourselves in as feminists of colour is itself a critical racial literacy (Bargallie et al, 2023) and a decolonial act of 're-existence', which is not refusal, non-acceptance or resistance, but 'the redefining and re-signifying of life in conditions of dignity. It is the resurgence and insurgence of re-existence today that open and engage venues and paths of decolonial conviviality, venues and paths that take us beyond, while at the same time undoing, the singularity and linearity of the West' (Mignolo and Walsh, 2018: 3, citing Achinte, 2013).

Incantation was performed on a hot summer afternoon in an empty parking lot – a community space in the making; invited audiences and passers-by comingled, some stood to look and listen. The space was 'activated' through live speech, of enfleshed narratives threaded together to tell a collective sounding. Feminist theory has thoroughly addressed speaking locations in terms of speaking for, as and about the other, and representing the other (Alcoff, 1991; Spivak, 2006 [1988]), but less theoretical attention has been paid to *listening positions*. Not only do we speak through a polyvocal voicing, but we also listen and hear from multiple voices and locations. We have many names, many selves. Each may speak in its own register. All voices, locations and perspectives are of equanimous value. This dispels the idea that we must arrive at a unified common view, or ideas about minority/majority voices or representation. Instead, we can stand together and speak from our multiple locations, as one or as many.

The place from where we listen is a crucial notion of literacy in multiculturally fragmented settler-colonizing societies, where we non-Indigenous 'other others' are encouraged to narrowly focus on our own communities. What do we hear when speech and meaning-making are orchestrated along different lines, rules, intentions? When we listen differently? Ambelin Kwaymullina (2020) spells out several such listening positions in her poetic manifesto for non-Indigenous Australians, *Living on Stolen Land*. It is key to 'learn to hear the noise of settler-colonialism inside our head and all around you so you can *hear past* it to understand our voices on our own terms' (Kwaymullina, 2020: 55–6, author emphasis).

Incantation also aimed to re-link with and re-generate traditions of utterances of public praise from our own cultures – of praise poetry, mantra, odes, renga – that serve to deeply honour, not adulate or elevate, pedestalize, flatter or celebritize in the style of white Western feminisms. When we recite texts and create responses that 'spell out' the dreams and visions of seminal Black woman writers, we evoke their qualities in ourselves and in others. We write/right ourselves as present/presence into the histories of Black women/women of colour intellectuals, artists, action-takers, holders and carriers of visions across time, space and generations. The following excerpt from *Incantation* exemplifies a number of writing/performance practices around intertextuality and feminist companion texts that feminist playwright Emilie Collyer (2021: 16) speaks of as 'thinking' by 'poeming' theory, which represents a way to 'map reading, critical thinking, memory and internal dialogue; showing the multiple strands but also, importantly, them being held together on one page'.

> I Invoke Cherie Moraga to theorize from the flesh. I incant Gloria Anzaldua's threshold living, border-dwelling, zing through the interstices across geo space locations. I step through the portal with Arundhati Roy and make my body a divine vessel for insurgent knowledges. I incant Sara Ahmed's bricks, doors, tables, nests, corridors, and institutional walls.
> I am a stand up theoretician, philosophizing from the flesh.
> Here is my powerpoint (point to body/self).
> My work is to dispel dominant ideological forms
> that work against one another
> to ultimately divide our movement from within.
> Through decolonial praxis, targeting and dismantling the colonial matrix of power.

A continuous learning/unlearning
decentring western rationalities and
centring other ways of knowing, being and relating.
I refuse the 'metaphorisation' of decolonial work with Tuck and Yang, and move to restitution, redistribution, reparation.
Decolonial work is NOT just done at the level of epistemology, discourse, theory, ideology but at the level of practice. At the level of affect. At the level of embodiment. At the level of time. Space. Cosmos. (Fernando, 2022c)

Wild tongues and insurgent texts

For Anzaldúa (1987: 54), 'our wild tongues cannot be tamed – only cut out'. Early into my doctoral research, I railed against the force of Western knowledge that disciplined my thinking into disciplines, thereby constraining my outputs. Rather than cutting off my tongue, I sharpened my intellectual teeth and political claws against the textual finery of critical feminist of colour texts – going against the grain of the colonial grinding stone. Without the language or grammar to articulate this (yet), I began the companion practice of 'shadow writing', someone who writes from and in the shadows, about the shadow, from the 'underbelly, under currented cargo' (Fernando, 2022c) of multiple worlds her various parts inhabit, and through which she drinks from the primordial cosmos. Submerging the 'black' part of myself, in shadow writing, free and poetic, interiority and affect could meet intellect and politics. Stemming from adherence to authentic feminist reflexivity in research, these practices became, when working with Black and Third World subjects, writings and resistant knowledges and the evolution of double consciousness, plurality, multiplicity.

Following Mohanty (2003), my earlier work considered the Black and brown female body as a political site, a text on which multiple ideological scripts of race/gender are inscribed and reinscribed in the colonial modern. *Incantation* spelt a vision to re-script and re-embody the body to re-exist by writing back to, and beyond, these violent inscriptions. My research (Fernando, 2016a, 2016b) rearticulated women of colour's bodies in asylum as 'insurgent texts' – that is, bodies and knowledges that speak back to dominant discourses and that recognize agency, power and intellect. Such texts resist fetishizing or appropriating their differences from white women and neither pathologize nor erase their suffering (Boyce-Davies, 1994: 34). Bodies as insurgent texts deploy theoretical, methodological, metaphorical, figurative and material weaponry; through 'building our own houses of thought' (Gordon and Gordon, 2006, cited in Mignolo and Walsh, 2018: 7) to inhabit, we become the change we seek.

Deciphering, woman-as-praxis, re-existence

Incantation as a praxis hoped to recalibrate a vision for feminisms of colour that moved its sights beyond a politics of denunciation, complaint, reviling and replacing; to not only give voice and speak back but to draw our sustained attention to and dwell on/in spaces of feminist life inhabited at the margins, in the interstices, to engrave with our bodies-as-texts alternative domains of intelligibility that defy the narrow discourses and epistemic rigidities that seek to cage us. In other words, it hoped to explore and show how we live our lives as women of colour in coloniality.

Wynter's (2003) decolonial texts are themselves incantatory encounters; one needs to stop every few lines to allow for diffraction, dreaming, deciphering, to catch a glimpse of what is unveiled intertextually. Her work is spellbinding, rich, furtive, fugitive and emblematic of decoloniality, not as an intellectual abstract project, but as embodied living. Decoloniality, for Mignolo and Walsh (2018: 7), is enacted and, at the same time, made possible in the 'interdependence and continuous flow of movement' rooted in the 'praxis of living and in the idea of theory-and- as-praxis and praxis-and-as-theory'. Wynter, reading across texts and genres and disciplines, 'situates herself beyond the crass body politics of colonial knowledge' (McKittrick, 2003: 5). Her concepts of deciphering and being human-as-praxis, of other ways to be 'human' and to reimagine other interhuman worlds, determined my understanding of decolonial praxis. For Wynter, being human *is* praxis – it is a verb, not a noun, and it is from interrogating ways that those cast out as non-human and less than human through racial/colonial knowledge systems inhabit their lives, that we delink and reimagine a way to think about being human anew (McKittrick, 2003: 3). *Incantation* attempted to provide a way to enflesh, articulate and express our being woman-as-praxis, to inscribe our womanity anew, drawing textual and flesh material from the past and incant into the future. For this, we need new words, a new lexicon that is fit for purpose, that articulates our experiences and our imaginaries outside racial/gendered/colonial frames, and a new 'deciphering practice', defined by Wynter (1992) as a reading practice that *notices that the tendency to describe black (as less than human, defective, captive) is not a measure of Black life*. It is a practice that:

> considers multiple social realities and differential psycho-affective fields while also exposing the intense weight of our governing … [colonial] system of knowledge. A deciphering practice recognizes the intense weight and how it induces how we feel and know the world; this recognition, importantly, signals and has the capacity to honor other ways of feeling and knowing the world. (McKittrick, 2022: 9)

The decolonial processes and practices that were anterior, 'backstage', aimed to evoke and elicit forms of agency that ask: What life is lived, outside the spaces of intense 'weight' of oppression? How might we write and perform, imagine and enact an aesthetics of Black life outside the governing system of knowledge? Outside the intense weight of coloniality (McKittrick, 2015: 41)?

> We asked ourselves – constantly, during the making of the work/ world we envisaged – what are we feeling? Are we feeling crushed, feeling pressured by the bureaucracies? Rather than succumbing, we intentionally released that, by breathing, laughing, making time rather than filling it, and refreshing our hearts with the intention to create word in decolonised conditions. (Fernando et al, 2022)

It is this recognition of 'resistant emancipatory intentionality' (in oneself and in others) that Lugones (2003) considers central to coalition-building projects that might succeed against multiple oppressions (in Moya, 2011: 86).

Poetry and playful world/cosmos travelling

> Poetry is a way of knowledge and communication, of a world that is discovered and constructed at the same time … the creation of new relationships between the elements of the universe, or of new nuances in them, but a genuine transfiguration of existence. [Poetic language] is vehicle and substance at the same time. (Aníbal Quijano, 1964, translated by Fúnez-Flores, 2023a)

Poetry, as Lorde (1984) has said, is not a luxury for women of colour but a technology of survival that invokes reserves of creativity and power and more – a decolonial knowledge-producing system when living life in conditions designed to eliminate it. Knowledge is already known, felt, before it is named, thought, said. For Jordan (1995: 3), poetry is a political action of truth that 'means taking control of the language of your life', a feminist of colour praxis of having to 'invent the power my freedom requires' (Jordan, 1985: 100). The praxis of poetry and poetic language as both vehicle and substance create new relationships that genuinely transfigure existence (Quijano, in Funez-Flores, 2023a). A poem is an event of naming/ conceptualizing the world, of reinventing the self as human, an expression of that which does not yet exist (Wynter, 1976).

The themes of travelling – across multiple lands, geopolitical territories, disciplines, temporalities, space, the universe, cosmos (Fernando and Banks, 2022) infused the curatorial concept of *Incantation* to recalibrate the outer edges of possibility, to relink our ontological alignment with limitless thinking. Following Lugones (2003), all forms of border crossings/world travelling need be 'playful' in a loving, tender way. Such playfulness is a 'crux of liberation – both as process and something to achieve … that is tied to risk: we risk our ground as we prepare our ground, as we stand on a ground that is a crossing' (Lugones, 2003: 72). Having prepared the ground, how might we use words to shape things, make things? What forms of textual spaces and figures are created, but also what do geographical/physical and community become when we work this way? Which bodies can inhabit these spaces that otherwise would not be there?

Thinking decolonially with the concept of space – or *Akasha* in Buddhist ontology – I evoked its properties as the fifth primordial element, along with earth with its property of solidity, water and its property of fluidity, fire and its property of heat, and air that has the property of motion. Space is clear, skylike, the container that connects, enables, embraces. It is an unconditioned thing, all-encompassing, boundless, emptiness that is simultaneously fullness. Incanting energies, bodies, words into decolonized/deconditioned space, we dissemble form and matter into formlessness to rematerialize it, reword the world, reworld the world, re-exist. Speaking, moving, creating bodies offer vehicular access to transmit texts and transmute bodies from the present collective and release them – incant them – to serve purposes needing to be served.

Writing poetically during the project and into its afterlife, a number of figures were birthed, which served as thinking platforms, launch pads, loci, whose bodies we may speak through, borrow to travel further. These include the 'stand up theoretician', 'the darkling' and the 'Sistership', which appear in the incantations presented here. I have added these to my intellectual armoury of companion transgressive feminist figures that include *feminist killjoy, fugitive, outlaw, sistergirl, mestiza, Dakini* – such figures delink us from conditioned thought, using words to free us, not sentence us. They make room to contribute our text to the texts that went before, and add to the one big story of womanity. Such forms of feminist or womanist poetical praxis of imagining/imaging, re-existing and inhabiting the freedoms we define can be at once healing, recuperative, oppositional, transgressive, transfigurative. As Mignolo and Walsh (2018: 3) hold, '[i]t is the resurgence and insurgence of re-existence today that open and engage venues and paths of decolonial conviviality, venues and paths that take us beyond, while at the same time undoing, the singularity and linearity of the West'.

In closing, the final incantatory text presents a vision of solidarity as vehicle and substance, both to traverse unconditioned space, as source, as life lived beyond the spaces of the intense 'weight' of oppression.

Sisterships

Can you believe there is a treaty for outer space that included the 'moon and other celestial bodies' but not one for the Aboriginal peoples of Australia?

Sisterships are how we fly through this colossus mollassacular oracalur density
The propensity to love is our vessels fuel

Once we were Queens, some of us lions, elephants
Then undercurrented cargo dirt sweat scum
Then beds and mattressess of pillowy lust
Our labour the fruit of our Lionessence and Elephantry
Our very fur was tickle in the throatlings of the rapelings.

The rapeling babes born of rape are not bastards.
Rapelings are darklings. They are my Creations.
We know how to love them because we bore them.

Once we were Queens, then hospital cleaners, uber drivers, now
We are professors and influencers spreading our wings and Wild
Things. With our tongues we
soothe the pain inflicted by mind poisoners
With our swordwords we slay
those dirty cheap stickfigure ghosts
The chalk men, hollow men
And call in unison
With our brown men: 'I am not your Uber Driver'

I am ink and they the paper. A ligress
I dwell exclusively in those shadows.
How monumental I feel
How vast and vescular,
How drunk on the feed of freedom of the sistership.
And its material manifestation in the cellular is-ness

Air breeze. Leaf. Birdsong. Sunbear. Starlight. Moonbirth.
Flowerful eyesomed and soft, slightly stale sweat and womanessence
Unwashed and ripe. Breathing. Swallowing. Refuelling

Queen bee. Dirty dancer. Star prancer. Loud mouse
Stage stealer. Refuse stick figure white

Hollow no substance dickswinging chest beating whitewash.
Cut that net. Nest in the flesh.

Earth it in the love of your sistership
Who now like DNA are forevermore
imbricated in your futurity

You feed from the well of the oracle.
The vast colossal mollascular is-ness of the such-ness
of the this-ness.
Through the enchantment of words, poets, roses,
From the throats of crowded stars,
The primordial soup that sounds wet, dark, ominous but
Are really protonic fragments, tingle, dancing lightlings.

Daka, sky flower, *Dakini*, dancing light of unconditioned wisdomlove
Lustratory, Lucent, Starlight tracing spintronic currents
Rove toward sistering darkling particles. (Fernando, 2022c)

Notes

1. I am indebted to my co-residents in the Seat at the Table Project, Fjorn Butler, Janelle da Silva, our project manager Karen Anderson, Joseph Norster from Siteworks, the Merri Bek Council for funding us through the COVID-19 Artist Recovery Grant, co-curator and Creator Mlle Maxime Banks and all the artists and crew and audiences who incanted with us at the live performance on 19 February 2022, in Brunswick, Naarm (Melbourne).
2. The Seat at the Table residency provided us (long-term residents) with free, unrestricted meeting space and a permanent desk in a large unused tower room of the local council building, with the expected outcome that we would contribute to the activation of a proposed new community space in a vacant car parking lot at 260 Sydney Road amid a busy alternative arts precinct.
3. Maxime Banks, see https://www.instagram.com/maxime.art.design
4. In the Australian context, 'other others' (Ahmed, 2002) refers to racialized non-Indigenous peoples of colour, the first 'others' being Indigenous. See Fernando (2021). 'Black' and 'Blak' are chosen terms to represent Aboriginal and Torres Strait Islander peoples of Australia, who are collectively represented as Indigenous Australians.
5. WEIRD stands for Western, Educated, Industrialized, Rich and Democratic (Henrich et al, 2010).
6. Sri Lanka (then Ceylon) was one of the 29 non-aligned Asian and African nations that convened at Bandung Indonesia to define an anti-capitalist, anti-militarist global order post-Second World War. In the late Charles W. Mill's words, 'Bandung offered a revolutionary decolonial revisioning of the affective sensibilities, dominant temporalities, and official corporeality of the planetary body politic. It is a vision we urgently need to recover' (Pham and Shilliam, 2016).
7. See https://www.abc.net.au/news/2017-12-01/who-identifies-as-poc-in-australia/9200288#comments
8. Intercentric here refers to race being centralized in critical race theory analysis, while acknowledging that layers of racial subordination are shaped by forms of subordination

based on gender, class, sexuality, language, culture, immigrant status, phenotype, accent and surname (Yosso and Lopez, 2010). Intercentic avoids 'oppression Olympics' (which group is more oppressed) and 'whataboutery' (for example, when talking about race, to deflect the issue and ask, 'What about gender', as if the two are not coexistent and intersectional) and recognizes that racism pervades all Indigenous and non-Indigenous communities of colour.

References

Ahmed, S. (2002) 'This other and other others', *Economy and Society*, 31(4): 558–72.

Ahmed, S. (2023) *The Killjoy Handbook*, London: Allen Lane.

Alcoff, L.M. (1991) 'The problem of speaking for others', *Cultural Critique*, 20: 5–32.

Anzaldúa, G. (1987) *Borderlands La Frontera: The New Mestiza*, San Francisco: Aunt Lute Books.

Arashiro, Z. and Barahona, M. (eds) (2015) *Women in Academia Crossing North–South Borders: Gender, Race, and Displacement*, Lanham: Lexington Books.

Bargallie, D., Fernando, N. and Lentin, A. (2023) 'Breaking the racial silence: putting racial literacy to work in Australia', *Ethnic and Racial Studies*. DOI: 10.1080/01419870.2023.2206470

Boal, A. (1979) *Theatre of the Oppressed*, London: Pluto Press.

Boyce-Davies, C. (1994) *Black Women, Writing and Identity: Migrations of the Subject*, New York: Routledge.

Collyer, E. (2021) 'Exercising the poetic muscle: A creative practice research method', in J. Wilkinson, C. Atherton and S. Holland-Batt (eds), *TEXT*, 25(64). https://doi.org/10.52086/001c.30980

Combahee River Collective (1982) 'A Black feminist statement', in G.T. Hull, P. Bell Scott and B.S. Smith (eds), *Some of Us are Brave*, New York: Feminist Press, pp 13–22.

Fernando, N. (2016a) '"On our way": Identities and representations of African women seeking asylum in Ireland', PhD thesis, University College Cork.

Fernando, N. (2016b) 'The discursive violence of postcolonial asylum in the Irish Republic', *Postcolonial Studies*, 19(4): 393–408.

Fernando, N. (2021) 'Getting close to other others: Doing difference differently', *Journal of Intercultural Studies*, 42(1): 46–67.

Fernando, N. (2022a) 'Incantation 1', Live performance piece, unpublished.

Fernando, N. (2022b) 'Incantation 2', Oral conference presentation, Australian Women and Gender Studies Association (Activist Energies), University of Melbourne, November, unpublished.

Fernando, N. (2022c) 'Sisterships', Live performance piece, unpublished..

Fernando, N. and Banks, M. (2022) '*Incantation*: Provocations and call out', unpublished work, Melbourne.

Fernando, N., Da Silva, J. and Butler, F. (2022) 'TwoSixty: Evaluation report', unpublished, Melbourne.

Fúnez-Flores, J.I. (2023a) 'Poetry: A praxis by Aníbal Quijano (1964)', *Substack*, 26 January, https://jairofunez.substack.com/p/poetry-a-praxis

Fúnez-Flores, J.I. (2023b) 'Aníbal Quijano: (Dis)Entangling the geopolitics and coloniality of curriculum', *The Curriculum Journal*, 35(2): 288–306.

Gordon, L. and Gordon, J.A. (eds) (2006) 'Introduction: Not only the master's tools', in *African-American Studies in Theory and Practice*, Boulder: Paradigm, pp ix–xi.

Henrich, J., Heine, S.J. and Norenzayan, A. (2010) 'The weirdest people in the world?', *Behavioral and Brain Sciences*, 33(2–3): 61–83.

Hill Collins, P. (1990) *Black Feminist Thought: Knowledge, Consciousness, and the Politics of Empowerment*. Boston, MA: Unwin Hyman.

Hill Collins, P. (2019) *Intersectionality as Critical Social Theory*, Durham, NC: Duke University Press.

Huggins, J. (2021 [1998]) *Sister Girl: Reflections on Tiddaism, Identity and Reconciliation*, Brisbane: University of Queensland Press

Jordan, J. (1985) *On Call: Political Essays*, Boston: South End Press.

Jordan, J. (1995) *Poetry for the People: A Revolutionary Blueprint*, New York: Routledge.

Kelly, R.D.J. (2016) 'Black study, Black struggle', *Boston Review*, 1 March, https://www.bostonreview.net/forum/robin-kelley-black-struggle-campus-protest

Kristeva, J. (1980) *Desire in Language: A Semiotic Approach to Literature and Art*, New York: Columbia University Press.

Kwaymullina, A. (2020) *Living on Stolen Land*, Broome: Magabala Books.

Lobo, M. (2020) 'Decoloniality: Seeding pluriversal imaginaries', *Postcolonial Studies*, 23(4): 575–8.

Lorde, A. (1984) 'Poetry is not a luxury', in *Sister Outsider: Essays and Speeches*, Berkeley: Crossing Press, pp 36–9.

Lugones, M. (2003) *Pilgrimages/Peregrinajes: Theorizing Coalitions Against Multiple Oppressions*, Lanham: Rowman & Littlefield.

Lugones, M. (2010) 'Toward a decolonial feminism', *Hypatia*, 25(4): 742–59.

McKittrick, K. (2003) 'Yours in the intellectual struggle: Sylvia Wynter and the realization of the living', in S. Wynter, *On Being Human as Praxis*, Durham, NC: Duke University Press, pp 1–8.

McKittrick, K. (2015) *Sylvia Wynter: On Being Human as Praxis*, 2nd edn, Durham, NC: Duke University Press.

McKittrick, K. (2022) 'Dear April: The aesthetics of Black miscellanea', *Antipode*, 54(1): 1–18.

Mignolo, W. and Walsh, C.E. (2018) *On Decoloniality: Concepts, Analytics, Praxis*, Durham, NC: Duke University Press.

Mohanty, C.T. (2003) *Feminism Without Borders: Decolonizing Theory, Practicing Solidarity*, Durham, NC: Duke University Press.

Moraga, C. and Anzaldúa, G. (eds) (1983) *This Bridge Called My Back*, New York: Kitchen Table Women of Color Press.

Moreton-Robinson, A. (2015) *The White Possessive: Property, Power, and Indigenous Sovereignty*, Minneapolis: University of Minnesota Press.

Motta, S.C. (2015) 'Becoming woman: On exile and belonging to the borderlands', in Z. Arashiro and M. Barahona (eds), *Women in Academia: Crossing North–South Borders. Gender, Race, and Displacement*, Lanham, MD: Rowman & Littlefield, pp 89–116.

Moya, P. (2011) 'Who we are and from where we speak', *Transmodernity: Journal of Peripheral Cultural Production of the Luso-Hispanic World*, 1(2): 79–94.

Persard, S.C. (2021) 'The radical limits of decolonising feminism', *Feminist Review*, 128: 13–27.

Pham, Q.N. and Shilliam, R. (eds) (2016) *Meanings of Bandung Postcolonial Orders and Decolonial Visions*, Lanham, MD: Rowman & Littlefield.

Purewal, N.K. and Ung Loh, J. (2021) 'Coloniality and feminist collusion: Breaking free, thinking anew', *Feminist Review*, 127: 1–12.

Rankine, C. (2020) *Just Us: An American Conversation*, London: Allen Lane.

Sandoval, C. (2000) *Methodology of the Oppressed*, Minneapolis: University of Minnesota Press.

Santa Cruz Feminist of Color Collective (2014) 'Building on "the edge of each other's battles": A feminist of color multidimensional lens', *Hypatia*, 29(1): 23–40.

Skachkova, P. (2017) 'Book review: *Women in Academia Crossing North–South Borders: Gender, Race, and Displacement*', *Hypatia*, https://www.cambridge.org/core/journals/hypatia-reviews-online

Spivak, G.C. (2006 [1988]) 'Can the subaltern speak?', in B. Ashcroft, G. Griffiths and H. Tiffin (eds), *The Post-Colonial Studies Reader*, 2nd edn, Abingdon: Macmillan, pp 66–110.

Táíwò, O.O. (2022) *Elite Capture: How the Powerful Took Over Identity Politics (and Everything Else)*, London: Pluto Press.

Vergès, F. (2019) *A Decolonial Feminism*, London: Pluto Press.

Walker, A. (1983) *In Search of Our Mothers' Gardens: Womanist Prose*, San Diego: Harcourt Brace Jovanovich.

Watson, I. (2015) *Aboriginal Peoples, Colonialism and International Law: Raw Law*, London: Routledge.

Wynter, S. (1976) 'Ethno or sociopoetics', *Alcheringa*, 2(2): 78–94.

Wynter, S. (1992) 'Rethinking "Aesthetics": Notes towards a deciphering practice', in M. Cham (ed), *Ex-Iles: Essays on Caribbean Cinema*, Trenton: Africa World Press, pp 237–79.

Wynter, S. (2003) 'Unsettling the coloniality of being/power/truth/freedom: Towards the human, after man, its overrepresentation – an argument', *CR: The New Centennial Review*, 3(3): 257–337.

Yeats, W.B. (1889) 'Aedh wishes for the cloths of Heaven', in *The Wanderings of Oisin and Other Poems*.

Yosso, T.J. and Lopez, C.B. (2010) 'Counterspaces in a hostile place: A critical theory analysis of campus culture centers', in L.D. Patton (ed), *Higher Education: Perspectives on Identity, Theory and Practice*, Sterling, VA: Stylus, pp 85–6.

16

Race at Work within Social Policy

Zuleyka Zevallos

Introduction

Race is the foundation of invasion and colonial rule in Australia, and is enshrined in laws and social policy. The edict of *terra nullius* (land belonging to no one) legitimized state violence and a British legal framework to take possession of Aboriginal and Torres Strait Islander lands. In the Australian settler-colonial context, racial literacy in social policy requires an understanding of patriarchal white sovereignty, which is, 'a regime of power that derives from the illegal act of possession and is most acutely manifested in the form of the Crown and the judiciary, but it is also evident in everyday cultural practices and spaces' (Moreton-Robinson, 2015: 35). Patriarchal white sovereignty grants white people a sense of social belonging through ownership of property and resources, cultural power and socioeconomic authority. The logic of ownership is established by enforcing racial differences, even while social policies and laws promote individual equality, as conferred through citizenship (Moreton-Robinson, 2015: 52).

Policy makers and academics rarely give critical attention to the processes and politics of the production of policy documents, instead focusing on what the document says. This is one way to maintain racial silence, since each step of policy creation – particularly the production of documents – presents an opportunity to address, or ignore, race. This chapter raises the question of which agents and actors conduct each step of the process and how. How do race relations impact how and when policies are negotiated? I present an analysis of the ways poor racial literacy across the policy cycle weakens the potential for social transformation, particularly in drafting strategies that seek to implement anti-racism.

Racial literacy exposes how race is used to structure 'social, economic and political relations' so groups in power retain their dominance (Guinier, 2004: 114). Race is used to normalize white supremacy by taking attention away from the unequal distribution of power and resources and creating division. Racial literacy can be defined as a way to learn about race, and act on racial inequality (Guinier, 2004: 115). This requires an understanding of how social context shapes how we think, talk and act on race; the role of social forces that impact our ability to make change (agency), such as institutional and environmental factors; and the interplay between race and other forms of social stratification, such as class, geography and gender (Guinier, 2004: 115).

Given its institutional authority, an examination of racial literacy in public policy processes presents a potent opportunity to examine how patriarchal white sovereignty is enacted through institutions, chiefly policy negotiation and documentation.

This chapter presents three case studies of policies I have advised on in one agency within the New South Wales (NSW) state government, on data sovereignty, service delivery and disability-inclusion strategies. While the policies and workforce data discussed in these case studies are public, the sources and the organization are anonymized; the point is not to make an example of the agency and teams involved, but instead to study these to exemplify how the public service as an institution learns about, and uses, anti-racism knowledge. Rather than focus on individuals (who said what and how it made me feel), I use racial literacy to illustrate how policies are created and negotiated, and what happens to anti-racist expertise along the way. I argue that a racial literacy approach helps us to understand institutional racism in four ways:

1. making race relations explicit;
2. targeting structural, rather than individual, inequity;
3. redressing the ongoing impact of colonialism; and
4. eliminating institutional racism.

I will show how state policies have adopted a white supremacist reframing of First Nations scholarship and anti-racism, to fit in with what I term 'hegemonic diversity', and thus maintain patriarchal white sovereignty. I conclude with a discussion of why we need to move away from individualistic approaches to policy and practice using critical racial literacy. Existing understandings of race, diversity and inclusion are inadequate for the task of dismantling institutional racism; analysis of policy documentation exposes how white interests are reproduced through institutional processes, even as organizations seek to address racism, because institutions are not fully committed to radical transformation – which is at the heart of seeing, responding to and redressing racial inequity.

Racial literacy in practice

I am a Peruvian migrant woman of colour and sociologist. I have worked in research leadership roles across federal and state government, the not-for-profit sector and private consultancy in Australia for over two decades. For five years, I worked in a senior management (non-executive) role for a central government department in NSW. I managed research to improve state policies and programmes, predominantly on issues of social disadvantage, and provided policy advice to support executive decision-making.

NSW has the largest population of all states and territories in Australia, with over eight million residents, one one-third (34.6 per cent) of whom were born overseas, making it the third highest proportion of migrants in the country. NSW is also home to 278,000 Aboriginal and Torres Strait Islander people (3.4 per cent), the largest number of First Nations people in any state or territory (Australian Bureau of Statistics, 2021). Yet this racial and ethnic diversity is not mirrored in the NSW public service – the largest employer in the state – which employs 10.4 per cent of all workers in the state, the majority of whom work in frontline services, primarily in healthcare, education and public service centres (NSW Public Service Commission, 2021: 6–11).

Of the 11,500 staff employed in the organization for which I worked, most deliver frontline services and public programmes, and a mere 1 per cent work on research (including my team). Eighty-seven per cent of staff are of white-majority backgrounds ('Oceanian' and European), and just 3 per cent are Aboriginal and Torres Strait Islander people, but few of them work in policy. This is not unique to state government.

Research indicates that the Australian public service more broadly has made little progress in addressing institutional racial justice; glaringly few staff and senior leaders are Indigenous (Bargallie, 2020: 65) and from migrant, non-English-speaking backgrounds (Opare-Addo and Bertone, 2021: 9–11). Race, gender and class inequalities are institutionally reproduced in the public service sector through formal practices (such as policies, recruitment and management) and informal interactions, such as when minorities are sanctioned for speaking up about unfair treatment (see Bargallie et al, 2023). However, the main driver of policy advice is written documents.

Why documents matter

Organizations measure institutional change through the creation of documents; these documents are not static, but rather move as entities through organizations and are worked on by many people from different departments (Ahmed, 2012: 85). Policies become enacted only after they are documented, but before this there are conversations, meetings and numerous associated activities to decide timeframes, what actions need to be taken, how to monitor progress and how success will be evaluated. Decisions are made about how to write the document – definitions of a problem, what content is included, solutions and recommendations. Documents also assign roles and responsibilities of individuals in charge of making the policy work, who holds authority and networks who have input (such as working groups). The policy document cycle is shown in Figure 16.1.

Consultation with experts is a requirement when producing policies, including diversity responses (Ahmed, 2012: 93–4). Figure 16.1 illustrates the process for policy document creation. This is typically triggered by an external event, such as responding to a state priority, legislation, an inquiry, programme or other initiative. One team will lead the response. Documents flow back and forth as relevant agencies negotiate the content. In Stage 6 (Draft) and Stage 8 (Consult) of the policy document cycle, advice to other agencies can be provided in written form, such as responses to ministerial briefs, draft reports, PowerPoint slides and oral presentations. Deadlines for departmental and expert input are short – typically between 24 hours and one week – and senior managers are often asked to provide verbal advice on policies and initiatives without prior planning, often in face-to-face meetings. In either case, we don't always see the outcome. This dynamic operating environment means that policy workers rely on existing expertise. At each stage, if race is not explicitly addressed, the document and subsequent policy actions reinforce the racial hierarchy by prioritizing white interests and ignoring racial justice.

Racial literacy is low in the public service (Bargallie, 2020: 14, 75, 199, 202). This means that policies rarely have race relations at front of mind. Even when anti-racism advice is provided, actions are managed by teams who have insufficient racial literacy, leading to sub-optimal results.

The following case studies show the importance not just of applying racial literacy, but of resourcing and managing these efforts correctly. The first examines racial literacy advice provided on a data strategy and an Indigenous data sovereignty project.

Case study 1: Indigenous data sovereignty

Cross-agency advice concerning statewide policy for data management was sought by a lead government agency during the scoping phase (Stage 5) from several policy managers across government, including myself. The only context provided was that the agency sought to 'improve data collection and governance', and they wanted to 'consider the needs of Aboriginal and Torres Strait Islander clients'. I had no time to prepare and provided advice on the spot. I discussed the impact of colonial history and current policies, giving examples from our sector, such as over-collecting data on

RACE AT WORK WITHIN SOCIAL POLICY

Figure 16.1: Illustration of policy document cycle

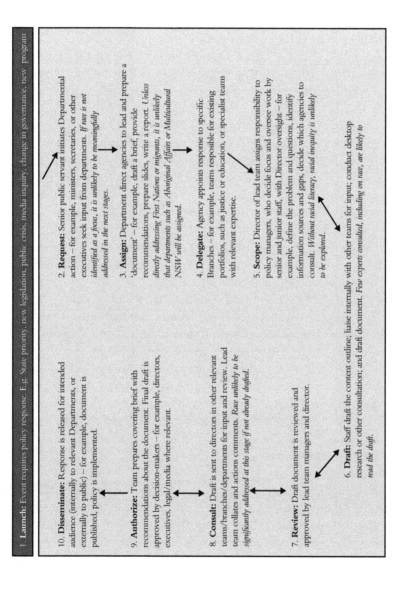

Aboriginal people that is never used or poorly analysed. I further outlined the importance of Indigenous data sovereignty, self-determination, cultural safety, informed consent and ethics in data collection, analysis, reporting and storage. I cited evidence from Aboriginal and Torres Strait Islander scholarly works, provided links to Aboriginal organizations already leading Indigenous data sovereignty projects and recommended the recruitment of Aboriginal experts to lead the work.

As is usually the case, I didn't see the outcome of consultation until about one year later, when the data strategy was published by the agency. I was approached again, to further advise on implementation of the strategy's component on Indigenous data sovereignty. An overview of the published data strategy and the advice I provided is presented in what follows, using a racial literacy framework that exposes the power dynamics of race. The data strategy defines data sovereignty as the right of First Nations people to govern the collection, ownership and use of their data. The strategy distinguishes this from Indigenous data governance, described as the right of Aboriginal people to make autonomous decisions on data collection and use, and to ensure data reflects their priorities, values, cultures, worldviews and diversity. This closely follows one of the references I recommended, the Maiam nayri Wingara Indigenous Data Sovereignty Communique (2018), but without citation. The data strategy also omits other components from the Communique, which seeks for Aboriginal and Torres Strait Islander people to 'exercise control of the data ecosystem including creation, development, stewardship, analysis, dissemination and infrastructure'. The data strategy whitewashes the 'sovereignty' component from Indigenous data sovereignty. Aboriginal scholars define Indigenous data sovereignty as the right to govern data not just about First Nations people and communities, but also lands and resources (Bodkin-Andrews et al, 2019). There is no plan for how control of data, land and resources will be moved from the state to First Nations people. Instead, power is retained by government.

- The published data strategy does not mention race, despite having a section on Aboriginal and Torres Strait Islander people. It does not address other racialized minorities. There is no plan for how to redress how data are used to maintain unequal racial relations.
- The data strategy seeks to 'engage the Aboriginal Community' to ensure research is safe, ethical, respectful and beneficial to Aboriginal people. Aboriginal and Torres Strait Islander people are positioned as individuals who can be consulted, but who do not ultimately lead policy decisions.
- The data strategy does not specify that First Nations communities would review current and historical data collection and use, only that the state will establish a group to consult on data governance in future.

After the launch of the data strategy, another policy officer was tasked with implementing the data sovereignty component. They were in a temporary role and had no funding. A colleague from my team and I provided the following advice:

- *Pay Aboriginal and Torres Strait community-controlled organizations already working on Indigenous data sovereignty to lead this work.* I connected the policy officer with several First Nations experts (with their permission).
- *Provide First Nations organizations with funding for their data infrastructure.* In order to manage their own data, Aboriginal and Torres Strait Islander people need hardware, software and physical sites to house data servers.
- *Address anti-racism, including sovereignty and ethics.* We provided references to national guidelines, privacy laws, data-sharing agreements and frameworks by Aboriginal scholars. We discussed multiple examples of data complexities that need redress – for example, to hand data management over to First Nations groups, an audit of data sources should be conducted to identify what race-related data are being held, consolidate data categories and sources, and review data sources.

At the end of the policy consultation cycle, the funding considerations we raised proved insurmountable. The agency decided to wait to see how other government initiatives for Indigenous Australians (such as Closing the Gap)[1] could be aligned with the Indigenous data sovereignty project, to develop a whole-of-government approach. Progress faltered.

The data strategy and Indigenous data sovereignty project case study makes visible the way institutional racism works; bureaucratic hurdles stall anti-racism actions even when agencies seek to draw on anti-racism concepts. This case illustrates *fracasomania*, an obsession with failure, which typifies data policies (Walter and Suina, 2018: 6–8). Policy makers define problems and create actions to be solved by outside experts (that is, non-Indigenous people). New policies are launched without evaluating previous policy failures. Policy makers accept the lack of progress on First Nations 'disadvantage' as a perennial and unavoidable problem. There are no repercussions to the state for its policy failures.

Case study 2: Service delivery strategy

Around the same time as the data strategy, the institution drafted a strategy to address service delivery for Aboriginal and Torres Strait Islander clients. The draft was sent to several agencies for consultation, including Aboriginal-led teams (noting these teams are a tiny minority and under-resourced). Requesting our team's input at the consultation phase (Stage 8), on the data collection section of the draft, my advice was specifically sought due to previous recommendations provided on the data strategy (which, at the time, I had not seen). The critical racial literacy reading of key issues in the draft service delivery strategy reveals a *whitewashing of First Nations knowledge.*

The draft service delivery strategy did the following:

- Sought feedback from Aboriginal people who were disengaged, to enhance service delivery.
- Incorrectly applied self-determination. This term means political and economic power in the hands of Indigenous communities (Moreton-Robinson, 2015). The draft strategy erroneously defined self-determination as the right for Aboriginal people to live according to their cultural values and beliefs, and to be respected by others; it was positioned as a celebration of Aboriginal strengths and proud heritage. To achieve self-determination, the draft strategy stated that services should be delivered in consultation with Aboriginal people and be responsive to individual needs.[2]
- Cited the need to provide 'culturally safe' services 16 times,[3] but failed to define cultural safety; instead, the draft strategy sought to ensure that Aboriginal people received services in a way that was 'welcoming', so that Aboriginal people would feel 'comfortable and respected'. The draft service delivery strategy promised to achieve 'culturally safe' services by: (1) providing 'cultural awareness' training for all staff; (2) having customer services sites display an Acknowledgement of Country, stating the traditional owners of that land; and (3) corporate branding to incorporate Aboriginal artwork and Aboriginal branding (the latter undefined), which would be 'more relatable … and therefore safer'.[4]

This time, given 24 hours to provide written advice on the draft – which in reality was only one hour, as this came to me in the middle of a packed workday – my advice was, once again, to facilitate First Nations self-determination. I suggested they do the following:

- *Recruit Aboriginal researchers to lead the strategy.* Incorporate First Nations' research frameworks, which seek to decolonize how data are collected, reported and governed. Centre cultural safety, self-determination, truth-telling and healing. Be aware of ongoing and historical distrust of government use of data. Avoid collecting data that are not integral to decisions and solutions valued by the community, as well as other sensitive data.
- *Draw on culturally appropriate data collection.* Use data collection methods based on community-centred approaches.
- *Situate data collection in connection to Country.* Recognize diversity of Aboriginal and Torres Strait Islander peoples. Begin with awareness

of the specific culture and language groups and their history wherever we work, and before beginning data collection. Build sustained trust with community.
- *Draw on communal sense-making.* Use open-ended questions and large-group discussions, and develop consensus with Aboriginal communities over many sessions (rather than relying one-on-one interviews and one-off surveys).
- *Use a consultative approach to reporting.* Aboriginal people often report feeling over-surveyed, and that they gain little from government research. Use action research, which feeds back data analysis to community, and reiteratively seeks input at each stage of drafting. Visit communities multiple times to co-design findings and action community responses, rather than simply making recommendations and publishing reports.

The final published strategy refers to anti-racism concepts and Aboriginal knowledge; however, these terms are poorly applied, and instead reinforce white supremacy. For example:

- *Centring cultural safety* becomes 'create a culturally safe environment'. The actions in the final strategy are to develop a 'cultural capability impact statement' (not further defined) and providing 'cultural capability training' delivered by a non-Indigenous media company. Authentic cultural safety would involve changing service delivery practices with self-reflection on anti-racism.
- There are no actions to address truth-telling, healing and policy practices that impact First Nations' distrust of data collection. The service delivery strategy seeks to have government consultation with the Aboriginal outcomes team, to deliver 'Aboriginal customer-centric' services. This term is not defined, but it suggests that Aboriginal people have value only as individual consumers, rather than as sovereign people, as self-determination establishes.
- There are no actions to recruit Aboriginal researchers, nor to limit data collection, use culturally appropriate methods, situate data to the local context, local community decision-making, and implementing action research. Instead, government will create a new dashboard to collect data on the 'success' of Aboriginal customer engagement.

This case study illustrates how institutions vigorously resist racial literacy, even as they aspire to use anti-racism terms. In a policy guiding services for Aboriginal people, self-determination is tempered, reduced to a positive 'celebratory' framing that non-Indigenous people can control (a celebration of culture) that negates the truth about the ongoing impact of colonialism.

Case study 3: Disability inclusion

This case study emerged through my membership of the organizational disability inclusion steering committee of over 20 members across the organization, which was governed by two senior executives. I was one of only two people of colour on the committee. During the scoping phase of the policy cycle (Stage 5), the committee was planning a draft disability action plan for our sector. In my first meeting, I asked whether our remit might cover intersectionality. *Intersectionality* is a theory to critically understand power relations in society (Hill Collins, 2019). It illustrates how racism, sexism and other institutional discrimination are interconnected, compounding social inequity. I immediately noted the lack of Aboriginal representation on the committee, and how committees tasked with implementing diversity policies lack critical racial literacy to see how they themselves are replicating racial inequities.

Presenting evidence of Aboriginal people carrying twice the burden of disease compared with non-Indigenous people (Australian Institute of Health and Welfare, 2022), I suggested we could invite a representative from the Aboriginal employee group to join our committee (agreed and implemented), and that we have a standing agenda item on Aboriginal disability (not supported). This put the onus on one Aboriginal person to raise Indigenous disability issues, in a packed monthly agenda that allowed no time to address race. This is one of the many reasons why 'representation' alone makes negligible impact on institutional reform and illustrates the limits of diversity approaches.

In the previous decade, the NSW public service had halved its disabled workforce, from 4.2 per cent in 2007 to 2.5 per cent in 2018 (NSW Public Service Commission, 2017: 14; NSW Public Service Commission, 2018: 61). The five-year disability action plan seeks to increase disabled people's employment in public service to 5.6 per cent, to align with the NSW Premier's Priority. This would translate to around 650 disabled staff across the sector, of over 11,500 employees. Without applying racial literacy, these aspirational new disabled recruits would likely mirror our existing workforce, prioritizing white cisgender men.

When asked to develop targets to address intersectionality, I approached this as a social scientist; I drew on scholarly literature, included references and used statistical modelling to devise annual targets. My suggestions on the draft disability inclusion plan included:

- *Ensure that half of the total disability target for our sector are Aboriginal disabled people (2.55 per cent, or around 300 disabled Aboriginal staff)*. This was to account for the fact that Aboriginal people are twice as likely to have a severe or profound disability. Additionally, one in five people in Australia who have a disability are migrants (18 per cent). I recommended that we meet a yearly incremental increase so that 18 per cent of non-Indigenous disabled people at every level are from racial, cultural and linguistical minority backgrounds (at least 47 people). The issue of 'representation' alone to effect institutional change reappears, highlighting the need to problematize the critical theoretical gap between 'diversity' and 'intersectionality' frameworks. A racially literate reading makes aiming for 5.6 per cent 'minority targets' meaningless, as the number of disabled people of colour is so small that 'representation' could never lead to institutional change, especially when policies and systemic patterns are left untouched.

- *Improve data collection and system enhancements to better measure outcomes for disabled people.* For example, I recommended that human resources systems add voluntary opt-in for disabled people to receive alerts on career opportunities, especially tailored to attract disabled people of colour. Additionally, I suggested progressing all Aboriginal and Torres Strait Islander applicants to interview (as they are less likely to be shortlisted) and annually report recruitment outcomes by race, gender and disability to executives.
- *Formalize a paid partnership with race experts*, specifically the First Peoples Disability Network, to co-design a recruitment campaign, develop meaningful career objectives and ensure disability policies and practices are trauma-informed and apply cultural safety. Recommendations included seeking paid expert advice from migrant and refugee groups, professional development for disabled people of colour and a mental health programme that addresses intersectionality (including culturally and religiously appropriate support).
- *Fund new initiatives to support career progression of older disabled people from regional areas, from diverse ethnic backgrounds.* To promote career advancement, the launch of a new programme was recommended, which would pair disabled Aboriginal staff with senior executives who would proactively champion their career progression, in addition to new recruitment strategies and secondment opportunities for transgender people of colour and measures to track recruitment outcomes. Finally, I relayed an additional recommendation from my executive leader, who requested the inclusion of a budget; without funding, the draft disability action plan would not make persistent change.

Most of my suggestions were adopted, although the targets and evaluation recommendations were softened. The final disability action plan currently seeks to 'review' the total number of disabled Aboriginal people in the organization (rather than suggested targets to increase their recruitment). Instead of new initiatives, the final action plan aimed to 'develop a strategy' for disabled people from diverse backgrounds. The funding recommendation was rejected, as the committee had no resourcing.

As a result of my racial literacy input, the final disability action plan has five brief references to intersectionality (where the draft had none); however, intersectionality is substituted for addressing systemic patterns.

As the sole race studies expert on the committee, in an organization that lacks basic racial literacy, I was awarded no institutional authority to further question the final document. Policy documents are a process of consensus, where the lead teams and their executives have the final say. Objections may be noted, but change remains unsupported. This case study demonstrates that even when racial literacy is sought (in this case, specifically about intersectionality), anti-racism action is deemed too difficult, and change is presumed to be cost-neutral. Without targets and resourcing new solutions that address racial disadvantage and other structural inequities and measurable initiatives, it is unlikely that white, cisgender, able-bodied dominance will be disrupted.

Discussion

The three case studies of Indigenous data sovereignty, service delivery and disability inclusion incorporate a limited view of race, exercising what I term *hegemonic diversity*. Hegemony is the rule of one class over others, particularly through ideology. Hegemonic diversity is the ideology that maintains the illusion of progress while upholding white supremacy, by focusing on 'celebrating' individual differences without dismantling interlocking systems of disadvantage, such as racism, sexism and ableism. Individualism is central to this ideology because this maintains the status quo. An organization never has to change if individuals are framed as the problem. In turn, groups that benefit from existing power structures never give up their resources and benefits.

Hegemonic diversity is predicated on ignoring race, so lack of racial literacy maintains white supremacy. Conversely, racial literacy can undo hegemonic diversity, through four principles:

1. make race relations explicit;
2. target structural inequity;
3. redress the ongoing impact of colonialism; and
4. eliminate institutional racism.

First, hegemonic diversity is established by *maintaining the racial order*. For example, in the first case study, the data strategy does not define nor deal with race, even though it has a focus on First Nations people and refers to vulnerable people. Racialized minorities, especially First Nations people, and poor and working-class migrants and refugees, bear the brunt of state data collection. They are more closely surveilled and policed. They are therefore over-represented in datasets, leading to flawed predictions and risk modelling. The state creates new data policies without evaluating past 'social policy disaster' impacting First Nations people (Walter and Suina, 2018: 3). Racial literacy would *make race relations explicit*, ensuring First Nations people and other people of colour lead the planning, measuring and implementation of institutional change.

Second, hegemonic diversity *reduces discrimination to individual experiences*. In the second case study, the service-delivery strategy seeks to 'establish trust' with 'Aboriginal community members' who have 'cultural authority'. This replicates patriarchal white sovereignty, which seeks to eradicate First Nations sovereignty. Hegemonic diversity focuses on culture rather than race because it seeks to reduce collective meaning and action to mere aesthetics, such as 'Aboriginal' corporate branding. Aboriginal people are cast as the problem: they need to be made to feel welcome – on their own Country, no less! Again, this replicates hegemonic diversity, by focusing on individualism (the First Nations person who does not 'fit in'), rather than racial justice (the First Nations who have been dispossessed from their lands – commandeered for profit and use by public services). The service-delivery strategy does not name, nor does it aim to demolish, the systemic conditions that necessitate cultural safety when accessing public services in the first place. Rather than *targeting structural inequity*, racism is reduced to interpersonal impoliteness, so the organization is silent about its role in institutional discrimination.

Third, hegemonic diversity seeks to *whitewash history and distract from increased discrimination*. The data strategy references First Nations concepts, such as self-determination; however, this is diluted into 'celebrating culture', using positive and 'happy' language (Ahmed, 2012) to make racial inequity invisible. The data strategy ignores the definition of self-determination by Aboriginal scholars, which is 'political and economic power in the hands of Indigenous communities' (Moreton-Robinson, 2005). The data strategy champions consultation with First Nations people to collect more data about them – thus serving the state's management of First Nations people. Self-determination cannot be a guiding principle without addressing colonization and, by definition, it cannot be mediated by government.

The Indigenous data sovereignty project faltered by not factoring in funding for First Nations expertise and data infrastructure. Managing property is a hallmark of patriarchal white sovereignty (Moreton-Robinson, 2015). By not funding First Nations' physical ownership of data infrastructure, the state maintains white supremacy. In order to strive for self-determination, the data strategy and Indigenous data sovereignty project would need to *redress the ongoing impact of colonialism*, giving leadership back to First Nations people, with resources available for them to self-govern.

Finally, hegemonic diversity aims to *subsume and weaken the impact of anti-racism*. In the third case study, the disability action plan did not implement targets to increase recruitment of First Nations disabled people, despite the intersection of racism and health inequity, due to colonialism. The disability action plan reproduces hegemonic diversity by positioning intersectionality as symbolic of respect for individual differences, rather than as an analytical tool addressing systemic patterns of race, gender, disability and other social disadvantage. A perverse function of hegemonic diversity is to promote poorly conceived targets and policies that aim for 'inclusion' while doing nothing to remove institutional barriers. Hegemonic diversity discards scholarly definitions advancing racial literacy and scientific methods of anti-racism. It also does not invest money in fixing systemic problems. A racial literacy framework would *eliminate institutional racism* by reviewing policy failures, drawing on First Nations leadership and knowledge, and funding initiatives to address structural barriers. Table 16.1 further summarizes the racial literacy framework, followed by the conclusion.

Conclusion

Race has been an organizing principle in Australian society since British invasion. Race is enshrined in legislation, and it confers power to white people through property and resources. Patriarchal white sovereignty shows how the logic of property ownership relies on notions of racial difference.

The public service maintains racial hierarchies and inequality. Aboriginal and Torres Strait Islander people and migrants make up a small proportion of public servants. Hegemonic diversity is the ideology that organizations can reach equality by making individuals feel welcome, rather than addressing systemic racism. In this chapter, I have argued that racial literacy makes visible institutional disadvantage by:

- making race relations explicit;
- targeting structural inequity;
- redressing colonialism; and
- eliminating institutional racism.

I presented three case studies to demonstrate how institutions incorporate anti-racism concepts without committing to institutional change. First, I showed how a government agency adopted some anti-racism language on the data strategy and Indigenous data sovereignty project without

Table 16.1: Racial literacy framework for social policy

Racial literacy principles	Examples of low racial literacy	Examples of high racial literacy
Make race relations explicit	• No discussion of race, despite seeking to service Aboriginal and Torres Strait Islander people, and 'vulnerable cohorts' (1), aspiration to address racism (2), and referencing intersectionality (3). • Collect data on First Nations and migrants, but no critical thinking about whiteness (1). • Arbitrary diversity targets that don't account for race – for example, no specific plans to increase recruitment of disabled First Nations people and other people of colour; no career progression pathways for disabled people of colour who are LGBTQIA+ or from rural regions (3).	• Consider how race impacts services, such as data collection. • Provide an actionable plan to dismantle racial inequity. • Recruit First Nations researchers to lead strategic planning, using Indigenous research frameworks. • Fund First Nations and other people of colour organizations to lead and implement change. • Use data and scientific methods to plan and measure targets and institutional change, with a focus on racial justice.
Target structural inequity	• Rhetoric of individualism that keeps racialized people as passive consumers – for example, consult, gain trust, make First Nations 'feel welcome' (1, 2); be responsive to individual needs and evaluate disengagement to enhance service delivery (2). • Ignore material conditions of race inequity – for example, the state controls data infrastructure and takes for granted the resources required to achieve Indigenous data sovereignty (2). • Maintain political and economic power imbalance through inaction – for example, waiting for results from other long-term policies (for example, Closing the Gap) before implementing First Nations-led initiatives, such as Indigenous data sovereignty (2). • Cumbersome processes and systems that do not track material progress of racialized and other marginalized groups – for example, poor evaluation of career progression by disabled people of colour (3).	• Ensure collective rights and active decision-making by First Nations and other people of colour. • Prioritize First Nations' peoples' connection to Country in programmes and policies.

(continued)

Table 16.1: Racial literacy framework for social policy (continued)

Racial literacy principles	Examples of low racial literacy	Examples of high racial literacy
Redress the ongoing impact of colonialism	• Whitewashing racial justice with reference to narrow definition of culture – for example, self-determination incorrectly positioned as cultural empowerment (1), as well as cultural values, beliefs, respect by others, and celebrating heritage (2). • Distract from historical and ongoing discrimination – for example, highlight community consultation, rather than how business-as-usual replicates colonial power relations (2). • Maintain conditions that lead to racial inequity – for example, disability policies and practices neglect cultural safety. Race experts have little decision-making power (3).	• Use racial justice to transform policies and services – for example, clear steps for transitioning First Nations data governance. • Provide resources to self-govern. • Paid partnership with Aboriginal community-controlled organizations and racial literacy experts/ • Implement cultural safety – for example, trauma-informed policies and practices.
Eliminate institutional racism	• State's coercive power maintained by defining First Nations people through a deficit lens, and identifying problems and solutions that suit white interests (1). • Misrepresent racial justice concepts – for example, cultural safety replaced with 'culturally safe' services that are 'welcoming', 'comfortable' and respectful, achieved through 'cultural awareness' training and cosmetic adornments, such as Acknowledgement of Country signs, Aboriginal artworks, and other corporate signs (2). • Ignore ethics, procedures and other institutional processes that maintain white supremacy – for example, the state has no centralized audit of what data are collected about First Nations, migrants and other marginalized groups, as well as racialized use of datasets (1). • Tokenistic approach to inclusion – for example, remove race and institutional focus from intersectionality in disability action plan; design inaction through sedentary goals, such as monitoring (but not increasing) the small number of minoritized individuals; and develop a plan to support people of colour in future, rather than pursue current change (3).	• Review past policy failures impacting racial inequity. • Employ First Nations and other people of colour experts to review current and historical data collection and use. • Draw on ethical frameworks by First Nations and other people of colour. • Fund infrastructure and other resources needed to achieve self-determination – for example, hardware, data servers. • Name and eliminate institutional racism. Engage in truth-telling of colonization in organizations. • Implement cultural safety – for example, service providers to self-reflect on race and cultural power relations, and change behaviour, processes and decisions using anti-racism. • Fund novel initiatives informed by racial literacy, to address structural barriers – for example, expand on-the-job training opportunities through secondments in metro agencies for disabled people of colour from rural areas.

Source: (1) Case study 1, Indigenous data sovereignty; (2) Case study 2, service delivery; (3) Case study 3, disability inclusion.

committing to anti-racist action. Both documents refer to Aboriginal scholarship on sovereignty and self-determination, but not as they defined it, and without First Nations people retaining control of their data, decisions and infrastructure. A lack of funding stalled progress on Indigenous data sovereignty.

Second, the service delivery strategy sought to support self-determination and cultural safety, respectively misrepresented as a 'cultural celebration', and making First Nations people 'feel comfortable'. Colonial hierarchies are reasserted as First Nations people are merely customers to be consulted, not sovereign beings with the right to autonomous control.

Third, the disability inclusion action plan shows how intersectionality is modified to make inaction palatable. Recruitment numbers will be monitored, and plans will be developed for review beyond the life of the policy document. Effectively, this ensures that recruitment and promotion of disabled people of colour is not a priority.

This chapter has demonstrated the need to move away from hegemonic diversity, which promotes individual outcomes, and critically interrogate the policy process cycle as reliant on broad consultation and extensive drafting, yet totally bereft of measures to ensure anti-racism and the authentic implementation of First Nations expertise. Thus, social policy needs to be transformed so racial literacy is applied at every step of policy creation, management and evaluation.

My analysis suggests that First Nations people and other people of colour with racial literacy expertise are ideally poised to facilitate transformative policy change by identifying how race dynamics are being neglected, and understanding the impact of this on further entrenching inequity. However, this requires an investment in funding and other resourcing. Consulting with individual First Nations people and other people of colour gives the illusion of fairness, but this work can be, and in the cases presented in this chapter was, easily overlooked at each stage of the policy document process. Instead, First Nations and other people of colour experts need institutional authority to implement and measure novel changes to organizational processes.

Notes

[1] Closing the Gap is the National Agreement to enable Aboriginal and Torres Strait Islander people and governments to work together to overcome the inequality experienced by Aboriginal and Torres Strait Islander people. It has 19 national socioeconomic targets across 17 socioeconomic outcome areas that have an impact on life outcomes for Aboriginal and Torres Strait Islander people. See https://www.closingthegap.gov.au/national-agreement

[2] This point remained in the final published strategy, despite correction.

[3] The final published version retains nine references.

[4] A modified version of these aims remains in the published strategy.

References

Ahmed, S. (2012) *On Being Included: Racism and Diversity in Institutional Life*, Durham, NC: Duke University Press.

Australian Bureau of Statistics (2021) *New South Wales, 2021 Census All Persons QuickStats*, Canberra: ABS, https://www.abs.gov.au/census/find-census-data/quickstats/2021/1

Australian Institute of Health and Welfare (2022) *Indigenous Health and Wellbeing*, https://www.aihw.gov.au/reports/australias-health/indigenous-health-and-wellbeing

Bargallie, D. (2020) *Unmasking the Racial Contract: Indigenous Voices on Racism in the Australian Public Service*, Canberra: Aboriginal Studies Press.

Bargallie, D., Carlson, B. and Day, M. (2023) *Make Us Count: Understanding Aboriginal Women's Experiences in Victorian Public Sector Workplaces*, Melbourne: Commission for Gender Equality in the Public Sector, Victoria State Government, Griffith University and Macquarie University.

Bodkin-Andrews, G., Walter, M., Lee, V., Kukutai, T. and Lovett, R. (2019) *Delivering Indigenous Data Sovereignty*, Canberra: AIATSIS.

Guinier, L. (2004) 'From racial liberalism to racial literacy: *Brown v Board of Education* and the interest-divergence dilemma', *Journal of American History*, 91(1): 92–118.

Hill Collins, P. (2019) *Intersectionality as Critical Social Theory*, Durham, NC: Duke University Press.

Maiam nayri Wingara (2018) *Indigenous Data Sovereignty Communique*, 20 June, Canberra.

Moreton-Robinson, A. (2005) 'Patriarchal whiteness, self-determination and Indigenous women: The invisibility of structural privilege and the visibility of oppression', in B.A. Hocking (ed), *Unfinished Constitutional Business: Re-Thinking Indigenous Self-Determination*, Canberra: Aboriginal Studies Press, pp 61–73.

Moreton-Robinson, A. (2015) *The While Possessive: Property, Power and Indigenous Sovereignty*, Minneapolis: University of Minnesota Press.

NSW Public Service Commission (2017) *State of the NSW Public Sector Report 2017*, Sydney: Public Service Commission.

NSW Public Service Commission (2018) *State of the NSW Public Sector Report 2018*, Sydney: Public Service Commission, https://www.psc.nsw.gov.au/sites/default/files/2020-11/State-of-the-NSW-Public-Sector-Report-2018.pdf

NSW Public Service Commission (2021) *Workforce Profile Report 2021*, Sydney: Public Service Commission, https://www.psc.nsw.gov.au/reports-and-data/workforce-profile/workforce-profile-reports/workforce-profile-report-2021

Opare-Addo, J. and Bertone, S. (2021) 'Slow and uneven progress: The representation of non-English-speaking background employees in the Australian Public Service', *Australian Journal of Public Administration*, 80(3): 385–406.

Walter, M. and Suina, M. (2018) 'Indigenous data, Indigenous methodologies and Indigenous data sovereignty', *International Journal of Social Research Methodology*, 22(3): 233–43.

17

'The Sole Source of Truth': Harnessing the Power of the Spoken Word through Indigenous Community Radio

Sinead Singh, Susan Forde and Jyi Lawton

Introduction

Indigenous community radio stations serve a vital function for their communities – primarily in the provision of local news, community connection, and information about public health initiatives and emergency announcements during natural disasters. However, Indigenous community radio also provides crucial services in terms of language maintenance, along with broader content about Indigenous politics, community achievements, Indigenous music and cultural activities. The power of Indigenous radio reaches remote areas, providing often-isolated communities with access to programming in language and serving as a voice that promotes cultures, traditions and belief systems; the sector also has a strong footprint in urban areas, where the majority of Aboriginal and Torres Strait Islander people now live.

This chapter endeavours to understand the role of Indigenous media – particularly radio stations and their attached digital channels – in the lives of urban and regional Indigenous Australians. We focus the work in this way following an analysis of existing research on Indigenous peoples and media, which uncovers an emphasis primarily on remote communities and media use. The Indigenous Remote Communications Association (2016), for example, conducted a survey to understand the value of Indigenous community radio in remote regions. This research confirmed that remote radio stations are a source of information, entertainment, community connection, and cultural and language maintenance, and that in remote regions, more than 80 per cent of people had tuned in to Indigenous radio in the previous week (see also Indigenous Remote Communications Association, 2017; Social Ventures Australia, 2017; Watson, 2021). What is less understood is urban and regional Indigenous people's media use, and the role of Indigenous radio in their lives. This chapter therefore seeks to fill that gap – an important one, given that the majority of Indigenous people now reside in urban and major regional hubs (Australian Bureau of Statistics, 2016) – and focuses on findings from our research with Indigenous community media services in urban and major regional centres of Queensland.

The Indigenous broadcasting sector

In Australia, Indigenous broadcasting is a well-established sector: 53 Indigenous media organizations are funded to provide broadcasting (radio and/or television, now with attached digital channels) services to metropolitan, regional, rural and remote communities. These 53 licensees are responsible for 214 Indigenous community broadcasting transmission sites. Well-known metropolitan examples of Indigenous radio include Triple A Murri Country in Brisbane; 3KND Kool n Deadly in Melbourne; Noongar Radio in Perth; and Koori Radio in Sydney. In regional and remote areas, organizations such as the Top End Aboriginal Bush Broadcasting Association and the well-established Central Australian Aboriginal Media Association run or support radio stations with retransmission sites throughout many desert regions and remote communities in the Northern Territory.

We use the terms 'community radio', 'Indigenous radio', 'Indigenous broadcasting' and 'Indigenous community media' interchangeably throughout this chapter. While 'broadcasting' refers to television and video as well as radio, the digital era has meant that all radio stations now also produce some video or social media content; in that way, they are more comprehensive media outlets than just terrestrial radio stations. Still, they all started out as radio stations and retain that identity. For this reason, the terms are used interchangeably but all refer to Indigenous-controlled broadcasting, operating with a specialized community radio licence as granted by the Australian Communications and Media Authority. We consider the role of Indigenous radio within the context that Indigenous radio helps to form an 'Indigenous public sphere' within communities – a sphere of conversation, culture, information, language and interaction that, in many instances, sits alongside broader, more mainstream public spheres and forms something of a 'counter-public sphere' (Fraser, 1990). In thinking about Indigenous radio in this way, we draw on the work of African American scholar Catherine Squires (2002: 465), who challenged the notion of a single 'Black public sphere' in the United States and argued that multiple Black public spheres existed to account for a diversity of views and different positionings of African Americans that were, at least in part, determined by class, gender, ethnic and ideological standpoints.

Indigenous radio and creating Black public spheres

Habermas's (1989) original theory of the 'public sphere', in which he enunciates mass media as the contemporary form of the old 19th-century bourgeois coffee houses – facilitating debate, discussion and interaction for the citizenry – is often critiqued for its exclusion of already marginalized groups (Garnham, 1992; Fraser, 1990; Burrows, 2010, 2014). This includes Indigenous peoples, who Burrows (2016: 115) explains are therefore rendered 'unheard and invisible'. Many scholars have since reframed the public sphere as multiple public spheres. In other words, debate plays out across a dominant public sphere and many heterogeneous 'subaltern' public spheres that operate in either isolation from or opposition to the dominant public sphere – for example, Fraser (1990), but also Habermas (1992) and Squires (2002). These subaltern counter-public spheres provide spaces for minority and subordinate groups in society to withdraw, regroup and circulate counter-discourses (Fraser, 1990: 67) and also to enact oppositional – perhaps decolonized – cultural and political identities (Stephenson, 2000: 4). Rather than thinking in terms of a single and all-encompassing public sphere, this chapter continues prior research of Australian community radio in adopting Nancy Fraser's approach to a series of parallel and overlapping public spheres. These public spheres are spaces where participants with similar cultural backgrounds engage in activities concerning issues and interests of importance to them.

Part of what differentiates this work, however, is a narrower focus on Indigenous community radio – and thus on exploring the parallels between the Black public spheres described in the early work of Squires (2002) and the Black public spheres that urban and regional Indigenous community radio stations in Queensland facilitate, create and operate. Like Fraser, Squires (2002: 450) notes that feminist and African American scholars have 'taken the stance that there are multiple public spheres' and suggests it is only possible to understand patterns of public activity in 'actually existing' democracies – where there are long histories of inequality – through the notion of multiple public and counter-public spheres that operate apart from, alongside and sometimes in conversation with a more dominant public sphere. The implication of a single Black public sphere is that 'Black' is a singular identity with a 'single common goal', but the reality is that there are 'existing social cleavages along class and gender lines' (Squires, 2002: 451) that undermine any understanding of a singular Black public sphere. Thus, Squires made the case over two decades ago that, following Fraser's (1990) theorization of multiple public spheres, we think in terms of multiple Black publics and public spheres:

> I propose we speak of multiple Black publics. Thus a Black public is an emergent collective composed of people who (a) engage in common discourses and negotiations of what it means to be Black, and (b) pursue particularly defined Black interests. This definition, although still wedded to the idea that there is a Black social group, does allow for heterogeneous Black publics to emerge, and also for people who do not identify as Black, but are concerned with similar issues, to be involved in a coalition with Black people. (Squires, 2002: 454)

We can see further relevance in Squires' (2002) understanding of multiple Black public spheres for Indigenous Australia. She notes a time in the 1950s and 1960s civil rights period in the United States when political actions were far more coordinated and united in their focus (Squires, 2002: 453). We can find a parallel here in the 1967 Referendum in Australia to recognize Aboriginal and Torres Strait Islander people in the Australian census, which had significant widespread support; and the rise of a coordinated land rights movement of the late 1960s through late 1980s, culminating in the massive street protests at the time of the 1972 Aboriginal Tent Embassy in Canberra, the Brisbane Commonwealth Games in 1982 and the Australian Bicentenary in 1988 (Langton, 1993; Robinson, 1994; Meadows, 2001; Dodson, 2015; Foley et al, 2014). This period was followed by increased recognition of the wrongs of the past, the rise of the Council for Reconciliation, the establishment of the Aboriginal and Torres Strait Islander Commission, then-Prime Minister Paul Keating's famous 'Redfern Speech' and a fragmentation between reformists and more radical calls for sovereign land rights. But this type of fragmentation does not suggest that a Black counter-public no longer exists; rather, as Squires puts it:

> By trying to understand and describe what kinds of activities, discursive and otherwise, are generated by different Black publics and whether these activities nurture or hinder particular Black communities, it is possible to recognize the internal diversity of the larger Black collective. ... The lack of institutional power or widespread coordinated political action becomes a challenge facing these collectives rather than evidence that they do not exist. (Squires, 2002: 453, 456)

Importantly for this study, Squires highlights that stronger public spheres are those 'with ready access to organized forms of association and publicity, such as independent media production', meaning that 'a history of Black public spheres must acknowledge the lack of civil rights as a foundational condition of Black publics, and then interrogate how this affects the development of Black media, political institutions, and tactics' (Squires, 2002: 456–7).

From this, we frame this study of Indigenous community radio in Australia in a way that sees these radio outlets as part of a broader set of Indigenous public spheres – akin to Squires' Black public spheres – that are developed due to the marginalization of Indigenous peoples in broader Australian media discourses. The development of Indigenous media is, at the same time, an attempt to give voice to cultures, politics and experience so that Indigenous peoples are reflected and given voice through media, but also so that this content is available to a broader public wanting to engage with and understand Indigenous communities, culture and politics.

Historical background to Australian Indigenous media

Indigenous community media in Australia has existed in different forms since a group of inmates on Tasmania's remote Flinders Island produced the *Flinders Island Chronicle* in 1836 to make their case for release and human rights to the colonial government (Burrows, 2014). Burrows has since outlined the development of Indigenous media in Australia throughout the 19th and 20th centuries (Burrows, 2004, 2010, 2014, 2016; see also Bayles, 1993; Rose, 1996; Meadows and Molnar, 2002; Dreher et al, 2018). We can also look, for example, at the work of Aboriginal journalist John Newfong, a prominent figure in the land rights movement of the 1970s and beyond, who worked as the communications spokesperson for the famous 1972 Tent Embassy protests that served as something of a trigger and inspiration for subsequent actions. Newfong's work as an Indigenous journalist working both within Indigenous media – as editor of the Aboriginal-led *Identity* magazine – and as a voice in non-Indigenous media for the land rights movement reflected a desire to contribute to public discourse and, eventually, influence public discourse in relation to Aboriginal people (Plater, 1999; Armstrong, 2018). Historically, in the Australian Indigenous media context, the establishment of Radio Redfern in Sydney by activists was an important moment, as was the rise of the aforementioned *Identity* magazine on the back of the 1972 Tent Embassy protests. In Queensland, Cheryl Buchanan's Black News Service published stories of the movement and information about new actions on a regular basis, printed on old-fashioned roneo machines and distributed by hand. The publication of *NQ Messagestick* and the development of Indigenous community radio changed the way Indigenous protest was imagined and presented. Indigenous-controlled media had begun to depict and source stories about the land rights movement from the perspective of Indigenous peoples for the first time, and they were trusted by the protesters far more than the mainstream media of the time.

In the intervening years, more Indigenous journalists have moved into positions in mainstream media but, even today, those journalists recount the difficulties of being the often 'lone' Indigenous voice in an essentially white institution. The importance of Indigenous-controlled and managed media is therefore as important now as it was through the intense days of street protests, and it is for this reason that we set out to explore the role of Indigenous media in the contemporary lives of Indigenous peoples in urban and major regional areas.

Research methods

To understand contemporary Indigenous broadcasting and its 'public sphere' role, we conducted an online and face-to-face survey, attracting 316 responses from across the Queensland capital city of Brisbane and major regional areas such as Cairns and Townsville in North Queensland, Mt Isa in Western Queensland, Rockhampton and Woorabinda in Central Queensland, Cherbourg and other parts of the Wide Bay area, and regional areas around South-East Queensland. We followed this survey with qualitative audience focus groups and station personnel interviews in four towns and cities – Brisbane, Cherbourg, Rockhampton and Cairns – in late 2022 and early 2023. These research methods have been applied before in community media studies, including Indigenous media, and are an established way to access audience views – as well as perspectives from community media sectors about their motivations for and perceptions of their role in the broader media landscape *and* in servicing their communities of interest (Meadows et al, 2007; Forde et al, 2009).

For this work, two Indigenous researchers (Singh and Lawton) collaborated with a university-based researcher (Forde) to design and deliver the project. Lawton, a Bidjara man, is chief executive officer of the Brisbane-based Triple A radio station, operated by the Brisbane Indigenous Media Association. Lawton's[1] organization was established by major contributors to the development of Indigenous media in Australia – Ross Watson, his sister Maureen Watson and nephew Tiga Bayles – who had developed Radio Redfern in Sydney in the 1980s and later 'Murri Hour' on Brisbane's 4ZZZ radio station, which eventually led to the establishment of Triple A, Murri Country in 1993. Sinead Singh, a Wiradjuri woman, worked as the project's research fellow and also provides social media support to Triple A – so brings knowledge of the uses and power of digital and social media to the project, along with an understanding of the Indigenous media sector. Forde is a professor of journalism at Griffith University, and her key research field is community and alternative media, in its many different forms. Together, the three authors designed the survey, focus group and interview questions, and analysed the data.

The research data were gathered and founded on 'Indigenist research methodology', enunciated by Rigney (1997) and deployed by Bargallie (2020) in her examination of structural racism within the Australian public service. Rigney's model identifies three core principles that underpin this project. First, the research is 'undertaken as part of the struggle of Indigenous Australians for recognition for self-determination' (Rigney, 1997: 118); second, it is undertaken to 'responsibly serve and inform the political struggle of Indigenous Australian peoples and communities', which ensures that the researchers remain accountable to the Indigenous community (Rigney, 1997: 118); and third, the research privileges Indigenous voices and 'focuses on the lived, historical experiences, ideas, traditions, dreams, interests, aspirations and struggles of Indigenous Australians' (Rigney, 1997: 119). The research aims to challenge existing knowledge structures and discourses 'through which Indigenous peoples have been framed and known' (Moreton-Robinson, 2016: 5; see also Hokowhitu et al, 2021); in this, there is synergy with the overt aims of Indigenous media.

Findings

Our key findings from this combined quantitative and qualitative work suggest, first, that in some communities Indigenous community radio is considered the 'sole source of truth' and is the most trusted media outlet available to audiences. Second, we found that community radio was valued because it broadcast local information *in local voices*. Third, people told us that hearing Indigenous music, or music that they cannot hear on other stations (such as a specialist country music format), was another main reason for listening to Indigenous radio above others. Finally, we found a significant number of survey respondents identified 'Aboriginal English' or 'lingo' as an additional language they spoke; they felt community radio supported the maintenance of this unique form of English, along with maintaining Aboriginal language in smaller regional or remote communities. This was a particularly important issue in communities where literacy levels were low and so oral language and information received verbally were crucial to community engagement with media.

Overall, the project emphasized the high rates of listenership for Indigenous community radio in major urban and regional communities, and audiences and station workers recounted the significant role their station plays in their lives. In Brisbane, for example, 69 per cent of survey respondents from the Brisbane area had listened to Indigenous radio station Triple A in the past month; this reflects a high level of awareness and also a high penetration of listening within the target audience. This compares with 46 per cent of Brisbane Indigenous respondents who indicated that they had listened to ABC radio in the past month; and 66 per cent who said they had listened to any form of commercial radio in the past month. In Brisbane, then, among the 316 Indigenous people randomly sampled, Triple A was the most listened-to radio station. In an Aboriginal community such as Cherbourg, there was 100 per cent listenership for the local Indigenous radio station, Cherbourg Radio; in comparison, 44 per cent had listened to ABC radio and 49 per cent to commercial radio in the past month in Cherbourg. Even though Cherbourg radio only broadcasts original live content for about three to four hours each morning, with three local community broadcasters running programmes, the station stays on air and broadcasts other Indigenous radio content off the satellite to deliver ongoing Indigenous programming throughout the day and night. In the major regional town of Townsville, listenership to local station 4K1G – a pioneering Aboriginal and Torres Strait Islander radio station – also exceeded listenership to public or commercial radio. There were some towns such as Cairns where audiences were fairly evenly split between Indigenous radio, ABC radio and commercial radio; and in Mackay, while listening to Indigenous radio outweighed Indigenous audiences for the ABC, there was a significant listenership for commercial radio at about 90 per cent of the local population. Still, across the areas we examined, a strong majority of Indigenous radio stations in Queensland were attracting more Indigenous listeners than either the well-resourced commercial radio sector or the public broadcaster, ABC.

We can gain some insight into these listening patterns from the focus group data gathered during fieldwork visits. Participants in the Cherbourg focus group found the local nature of content, and the fact that broadcasters were people they knew from within their community, were a large part of the station's appeal and reasons for listening:

> '[The broadcasters] are not pretending to be anything. And I think that's what people like, is that we're just ourselves. And I think that's the big thing.'

> 'It's like you were saying before about the girls [the broadcasters] speaking from the heart. All of us are in the station, you know, we live in community, so you got to live here and actually go in and go out in the community. It's not for outsiders.'

> '[Other people who might come in] They got no, no bloodline, no connection, you know? So yeah, you got a big community, you gotta live it, you gotta breathe it. You gotta talk into the community. So I feel like they're [the broadcasters] connected. You gotta connect.'

Other participants in the Brisbane focus group, talking about Triple A, identified the news and information from the station as well as the country music format as important reasons to listen:

> 'I think it's the place to go to where you can get information on what is going on in the community and there is knowledge sharing. It's a place to go to hear those yarns. And I think it's because blackfullas love country music as well. It's got a great genre of country and new music.'

> 'They [the community] need to hear their own voice on the radio. Those that live and breathe the community.'

> 'I listen to Triple A to get yarns sometimes, because on other platforms you wouldn't have anybody else talking about grassroots topics or issues.'

The issue of trust in media was one that featured strongly in this project. Across all the Indigenous radio station broadcast areas involved in our survey, the local Indigenous station was the most trusted. This contrasts with broader data about the Australian population, for whom the ABC is the most trusted media outlet (Park et al, 2022: 103). The ABC was also a more trusted source for Indigenous people than commercial radio – but, in all communities, Indigenous radio was the media outlet that people indicated 'I trust them a great deal'. In Brisbane, for example, 65 per cent of survey respondents said they trusted Brisbane's Triple A 'a great deal'; less than half that number – 31 per cent – said they trusted commercial radio, while about 49 per cent trusted the ABC. Similarly, while Cherbourg's radio station had the highest listenership reflected in the survey – at 100 per cent of respondents – it also had one of the highest levels of trust across the state (74 per cent trusted Cherbourg Radio 'a great deal'). Townsville's 4K1G recorded the highest level of trust among its audience, at 84 per cent.

The issue of language was raised in both the survey and focus groups. Participants in the Cairns focus group spoke regularly about the importance of the station (Bumma Bippera, BBM) delivering health messages in 'Aboriginal English' or 'creole', presenting this as an important reason for them to listen to local Indigenous radio. Some related this specifically to information during the COVID-19 period:

> 'I think it's coming across, to get our needles and where to get our needles and stuff like that. They also have it in creole language. The messages we also get from Queensland government [are on BBM].'

> '[One of the reasons I listen is for Aboriginal] language, especially with health messages. People want to hear it in their own language.'

> 'Aboriginal language is the fourth language in my household.'

> 'For me, we speak broken English.'

'There is a lot of broken English, Aboriginal English and Torres Strait, Creole, here.'

Indigenous media, public spheres and decolonizing the airwaves

Research into Indigenous media in Australia has shown over the past 25–30 years that Indigenous community radio is valued by communities for different reasons – most of them related to local voices, local content, highlighting Indigenous issues, playing country music and giving airtime to Indigenous artists and speakers. We sought to find out whether these reasons had shifted in the digital era and at a time when the broader population, along with Indigenous people, had to rely on media messaging to navigate the global COVID-19 pandemic and more frequent natural disasters such as floods and bushfires. Our research found that, in all areas but two, Indigenous broadcasting was the preferred form of media for First Nations people, even when they had many other media options such as commercial and public radio.

A key interest for us was to consider the ways in which Indigenous radio stations – and all their associated digital content, including websites, social media and podcasts – fit within Squires' (2002) theorizing of Black public spheres and, ultimately, Indigenous public spheres. What was clear through our survey and focus group data was that audiences did not expect that their local Indigenous station represented particular politics or points of view, but rather that they prioritized Indigenous voices and issues in their content. Further, they emphasized the importance of providing opportunities for young people and ordinary community members to be trained in media and journalism by the station and/or invited in for interviews, yarns and to give their point of view on current issues. This is consistent with Squires' notion that a single Black public sphere does not exist and, indeed, is not desired. Rather, multiple spheres of discussion exist, sitting outside the dominant public sphere of mainstream media content and directly challenging representations of Indigenous peoples within the dominant public sphere. Indigenous radio provides a forum that sometimes interacts with the broader public sphere – they may cover similar issues and talk about politics that are on the wider public agenda, but this is done by Indigenous voices in an arena that is owned and led by First Nations peoples. This provision of Black public spheres – in Brisbane, Cairns, Townsville, Mt Isa, Cherbourg, Palm Island, Charleville, Mackay and Rockhampton – decolonizes this part of the media ecosystem and, notably through the prioritizing of 'Aboriginal English', Indigenous broadcasting is practising decolonization of language and cultural expression across multiple Indigenous public spheres.

Note

[1] Jyi Lawton was CEO of the Brisbane Indigenous Media Association at the time of writing this chapter; he has since left this position.

References

Armstrong, D. (2018) 'The door John Newfong nudged ajar', *Inside Story*, 21 November, https://insidestory.org.au/the-door-john-newfong-nudged-ajar

Australian Bureau of Statistics (2016) *Aboriginal and Torres Strait Islander Population, 2016*, Canberra: Australian Bureau of Statistics, 31 October, https://www.abs.gov.au/ausstats/abs@.nsf/Lookup/2071.0main+features122016

Bargallie, D. (2020) *Unmasking the Racial Contract: Indigenous Voices on Racism in the Australian Public Service*, Canberra: Aboriginal Studies Press.

Bayles, T. (1993) 'Kicking open doors: The struggle for indigenous media in Australia', *Interadio*, 5(2): 10–11.

Burrows, E. (2004) 'Bridging our differences: Comparing mainstream and Indigenous media coverage of Corroboree 2000', *Australian Journalism Review*, 26(1): 175–90.

Burrows, E. (2010) 'Tools of resistance: The roles of two Aboriginal newspapers in building an Indigenous public sphere', *Australian Journalism Review*, 32(2): 33–46.

Burrows, E. (2014) 'Resisting oppression', *Media History*, 20(3): 221–38.

Burrows, E. (2016) 'Chronicling the land rights movement: The democratic role of Australian Indigenous land rights publications', *Media International Australia*, 160: 1–13.

Dodson, P. (2015) 'Reframing the terms of engagement in Aboriginal affairs', in B. Douglas and J. Wodak (eds), *Who Speaks for and Protects the Public Interest of Australia? Essays by Notable Australians*, Sydney: Australia21, pp 36–7, https://library.bsl.org.au/jspui/bitstream/1/5024/1/DouglasB_Who-speaks-in-the-public-interest-of-Australians_Aust21-2015.pdf

Dreher, T., Waller, L. and McCallum, K. (2018) 'Disruption or transformation? Australian policymaking in the face of Indigenous contestation', in E. Pereen, R. Celikates, J. de Kloet and T. Poell (eds), *Global Cultures of Contestation*, New York: Palgrave Macmillan, pp 215–40.

Foley, G., Schapp, E. and Powell, A. (eds) (2014) *Aboriginal Tent Embassy: Sovereignty, Black Power, Land Rights and the State*, London: Routledge.

Forde, S., Foxwell, K. and Meadows, M. (2009) *Developing Dialogues: Indigenous and Ethnic Community Broadcasting in Australia*, Chicago: University of Chicago Press.

Fraser, N. (1990) 'Rethinking the public sphere: A contribution to the critique of actually existing democracy', *Social Text*, 25/26: 56–80.

Garnham, N. (1992) 'The media and the public sphere', in C. Calhoun (ed.), *Habermas and the Public Sphere*, Cambridge, MA: MIT Press, pp 359–76.

Habermas, J. (1989) *The Structural Transformation of the Public Sphere: An Inquiry into a Category of Bourgeois Society*, Cambridge, MA: MIT Press.

Habermas, J. (1992) 'Further reflections on the public sphere', in C. Calhoun (ed) *Habermas and the Public Sphere*, Cambridge, MA: MIT Press, pp 421–61.

Hokowhitu, B., Moreton-Robinson, A., Tuhiwai-Smith, L., Anderson, P. and Larkin, S. (eds) (2021) *The Routledge Handbook of Critical Indigenous Studies*, London: Routledge.

Indigenous Remote Communications Association (2016) *Remote Indigenous Communications and Media Survey*, McNair Ingenuity Research, https://firstnationsmedia.org.au/projects/indigenous-communications-and-media-survey-2016

Indigenous Remote Communications Association (2017) *Annual Report 2017*, Alice Springs: Indigenous Remote Communications Association.

Langton, M. (1993) *Well, I Heard It on the Radio and I Saw It on the Television: An Essay for the Australian Film Commission on the Politics and Aesthetics of Filmmaking by and About Aboriginal People and Things*, Canberra: Australian Film Commission.

Meadows, M. (2001) *Voices in the Wilderness: Images of Aboriginal People in the Australian Media*, Westport: Greenwood Press.

Meadows, M. and Molnar, H. (2002) 'Bridging the gaps: Towards a history of Indigenous media in Australia', *Media History*, 8(1): 9–20.

Meadows, M., Forde, S., Ewart, J. and Foxwell, K. (2007) *Community Media Matters: An Audience Study of the Australian Community Broadcasting Sector*, Brisbane: Griffith University.

Moreton-Robinson, A. (2016) 'Introduction: Locations of engagement in the first world', in A. Moreton-Robinson (ed), *Critical Indigenous Studies: Engagements in First World Locations*, Tucson: University of Arizona Press, pp 3–16.

Park, S., McGuinness, K., Fisher, C., Lee, J.Y., McCallum, K. and Nolan, D. (2022) *Digital News Report: Australia 2022*, Canberra: News & Media Research Centre, University of Canberra, https://www.canberra.edu.au/research/faculty-research-centres/nmrc/digital-news-report-australia-2022

Plater, D. (1999) 'Obituary: John Newfong, Aboriginal voice', *The Age*, 7 June, p 18.

Rice, E., Haynes, E., Royce, P. and Thompson, S.C. (2016) 'Social media and digital technology use among Indigenous young people in Australia: A literature review', *International Journal for Equity in Health*, 15: 1–16.

Rigney, L. (1997) 'Internationalization of an Indigenous anticolonial cultural critique of research methodologies: A guide to Indigenist research methodology and its principles', *WicazoSa Review Journal for Native American Studies*, 14(2): 109–21.

Robinson, S. (1994) 'The Aboriginal Embassy: An account of the protests of 1972', *Aboriginal History*, 18(1/2): 49–63.

Rose, M. (1996) *For the Record: 160 Years of Aboriginal Print Journalism*, Sydney: Allen & Unwin.

Social Ventures Australia (2017) *More than Radio – a Community Asset: Social Return on Investment Analyses of Indigenous Broadcasting Services*, Canberra: Australian Government.

Squires, C.R. (2002) 'Rethinking the Black public sphere: An alternative vocabulary for multiple public spheres', *Communication Theory*, 12(4): 446–68.

Stephenson, M. (2000) *The Impact of an Indigenous Counterpublic Sphere on the Practice of Democracy: The* Taller de Historial Oral Andina *in Bolivia* (Working Paper #279), Notre Dame, IN: Kellogg Institute.

Watson, H. (2021) *Renewing a Vital Indigenous Voice and Community Asset: The Indigenous Broadcasting and Media Sector*, Canberra: National Indigenous Australians Agency.

PART V

Resistance, Solidarity, Survival

18

Death Can Be Clarifying: Considering the Forces That Move Us

Samantha Schulz

Introduction

Emotions always do things. They may move us and prompt uncomfortable, if necessary, social change. Equally, they may crystallize in 'affective numbness' (Rogers, 2021) – the impulse and capacity to say or do nothing, which is facilitated by race privilege. As Machado de Oliveira (2021: 52) says with respect to those of us who enjoy the relative (if differential) privileges born of modernity, 'despite our transgressions and rebellions and our ideals of revolution, our struggles do not structurally jeopardize our survival: we have a choice to show up or not'. Within the context of Australian higher education, affective numbness manifests most fluidly around and through those of us who are white. It may surface as the failure to raise difficult if necessary workplace conversations which challenge racial bias; to initiate 'taboo' conversations around race with majority white, often resistant learners; or to fail 'to emotionally or "affectively" engage with nondominant experiences' (Zembylas, 2023: 2). Research and teaching on race in white Australia *is* emotional – especially within teacher education, where most preservice teachers are white. Indeed, Australian teachers frequently report being 'scared' (Maher, 2022) if not 'paralysed' (Memon et al, 2023) in their efforts to embrace this discomforting terrain. Yet working with racialized emotions is a part of effective, ethical teaching.

This chapter reflects on the relationship between emotions and race. Specifically, I consider two emotional incidents as a backdrop to my work as a 'white' academic in Australian teacher education. Both incidents invoke death: the first involving a Kenyan village where I was a volunteer teacher – or 'voluntourist' – and the second involving the more recent deaths of my parents. Extreme incidents that surface emotions/affects categorized as exceptional can shift our perceptions to elicit 'deeper analyses of the practices in which we live and work' (Lowe and Galstaun, 2020: 93). Emotional encounters are thus one vehicle for exploring how we are affectively governed, and how racial literacy education may usefully co-opt the body's sensory capacities to engage students in 'affective' learning. The following section starts with a theoretical discussion of the relationships between emotions and race. The chapter then explores the two personal narratives and is offered overall as a resource for racial literacy education that floodlights the emotionality of race.

Affects-emotions, subjectivity and race

Critical studies of affect constitute an expansive field that emerges from poststructuralism, queer theory, feminism and anti-racist theory following the affective turn (Schaefer, 2020). For Clough (2007), the affective turn was impelled by a need to make sense of our increasingly messy worlds, which move through individuals but are nonetheless irreducible to the individual. Broadly speaking, affect theory follows two streams: the psychological and social (Ott, 2017). In this chapter, I pursue a social-relational orientation that emerges from the work of Spinoza and Deleuze and through more recent scholarship of feminist and decolonial theorists (for example, Ahmed, 2008; Leys, 2011). Instead of viewing affects or emotions as psychological states arising from individual bodies, affects are understood as forces that circulate through and between bodies. Subjects are not perceived as self-contained, autonomous machines (Schaefer, 2020: 3), but rather as discursively and affectively produced 'open-ended achievements' (Zembylas, 2017), influenced by and produced through a tangle of forces. From this viewpoint, affects move us. And while emotions may represent threshold points when affects pass through bodies to become momentarily codified, affects might be considered as *emotions on the move* (Boler and Davis, 2018), less defined by the personal and more related to 'public feelings' (Cvetkovich, 2012).

As entangled phenomena, affects-emotions thus permit a reconsideration of subjectivity in the sense that emotions are not neatly inscribed within the boundaries of the individual. Rather, feelings 'spill over' to illustrate 'the thrall in which our relations with others holds us ... in ways that challenge the very notion of ourselves as autonomous and in control' (Butler, 2004: 23). This 'emotional governance' occurs via entanglements between affects, discourse and intra-actions between bodies and a world imprinted with discursive meaning. For example, Ahmed explains that a white racist subject who encounters a racial other may experience an intensity of emotions (fear, hate, disgust, pain). That intensification involves moving away from the body of the other, or moving towards that body in an act of violence, and then moving away. The 'moment of contact' is shaped by past histories of contact, which allows the proximity of a racial other to be perceived as threatening, at the same time as it reshapes the bodies in the contact zone of the encounter. These histories have already impressed upon the surface of the bodies at the same time as they create new impressions. (Ahmed, 2004: 31)

Instead of focusing on what race and racism *are* in terms of fixed social categories constructed through binary logics, an affective orientation hence focuses on what they *do* (Zembylas, 2015). Such an orientation draws attention to what bodies do as a consequence of affective encounters, how these events are entangled in broader structures and how we may avail the conditions of possibility generated by emotional encounters to exercise circumscribed forms of agency. In the following sections, I consider emotional encounters as expressions of our embedment in these relations, and the ways in which affects traverse racial lines to manifest in feelings linked to histories of race and whiteness.

Narrative I: Encountering death

Another unbearably hot afternoon and we are hand-washing clothes to Lingala music when, suddenly, a deep thud, followed by screams. We peel into the glaring sun to see that a *matatu* carrying around 50 people has flipped at speed on the Kisumu–Busia Road. Everyone flies into action; I dash around looking for sheets to be used as makeshift bandages. Amidst the turmoil, I catch glimpses of Black bodies and blood and, in contrast, the motionless white body of a single volunteer. She is a recent law graduate from Canberra and horse-riding enthusiast. She is standing still and staring as though disconnected from the scene unfolding around her. Eventually, the *matatu*, the injured people, and bodies; all of it is proficiently cleared away by local Luo people – I've personally offered nothing useful and wander around clutching bed linen. The rains break and life carries on. That night I try talking to the horse-rider, but she refuses to be drawn out. The next morning she announces her withdrawal from the nine-month volunteer programme, explaining, 'life is too precarious here'.

There are numerous ways to make sense of this encounter. In its immediate wake, if I hadn't already been questioning the legitimacy of my presence in Kenya as a volunteer teacher with no formal teaching qualifications, then the *matatu* accident threw these concerns into stark relief. What was I doing there? If I'd had medical training and been able to offer tangible if short-term assistance in the heat of this particular moment, then my desires to help while experiencing somewhere different might have gone unquestioned. But I was a young, white, female Bachelor of Arts graduate from working-class South Australia with a smattering of sociology; what exactly did I think I had to offer?

In reality, my capacity to participate hadn't required deep thinking. Paying the deposit was enough for the organizing company, and expressing a desire to help those presumably 'in need' was more than sufficient for my predominantly white circle of friends and family. In fact, merely expressing a helping imperative imbued me with a moral pretence that seemed somehow 'beyond critique' (Heron, 2007). Studies in sociology had, nonetheless, equipped me with a tendency to inquire. I'd read about Said's (1979) concept of Orientalism and his theories concerning the power and dominance of Western representation and its effects. Said asserted that the West comes to know and understand itself through the generation of knowledge of the East, with the Western subject hence shaped through an impulse for colonization in the making of white subjectivity. I had also a vague understanding of Aboriginalism, developed to similar effect by First Nations scholars, whereby the 'Aboriginal' emerges as the most enduring 'other' in the remaking of the white Australian (for example, Barney, 2006).

As a white Australian, I was genuinely interested in these relations, but dominant discourses had also imbued me with a *felt* understanding that a Bachelor of Arts degree was somewhat unremarkable – not like the esteemed fields of medicine, engineering or law. I sensed that the things concerning me – like global coloniality – were therefore of lesser importance in the worldly scheme of things. And although I knew that going to university was itself to be prized – especially for someone from a working-class area – less clear was the reality that entering higher education had entered me more fully into a matrix of dividing practices that fragment and rank knowledge, separating 'official' (rational, masculine, white, scientific) areas of inquiry from those of lesser value, thus maintaining global hierarchies rooted in gender, race and class (Stein, 2020). I had a sense of these things, but no language for rendering them real.

So, the horse-rider left to get on with the important work of being a lawyer and I stayed to wrestle with these 'trifling', if genuine concerns. It genuinely concerned me that my task was to teach English to Luo children from a textbook containing words like 'blunderbuss'. I questioned how this was helping when the learning was so disconnected from learner lifeworlds. It concerned me that my white skin would frequently grant me access to spaces from which Luo people were excluded. I felt awkward and discomforted by these encounters and wondered how I was helping when my presence triggered dynamics that seemed to revitalize imperialism. And it concerned me upon returning to Australia to find that, simply due to having participated in development work, I was now being congratulated, especially if my experiences included proximity to danger, privation or death. There emerged myriad ways in which I could cash in on this newly elevated subjectivity and the associated feelings of pride or altruism. It became clearer that I was part of a global system that mediates raced and classed privileges, and that Western education was somehow implicated in its reproduction. But still, I lacked a clear language or framework for analysis.

Making affective-discursive sense

To make deeper sense of these encounters, here I move between personal narrative and affective-discursive analysis, with this micro–macro movement designed to avoid whiteness becoming reified to a single, ahistorical agent. This means that the 'white' (individual) body is also reconceptualized as the white (collective) body – for example, the international volunteer – in this case, *voluntourist* – constitutes a historically white body via which whiteness as a global structure of power is animated. Against the backdrop of the non-white contexts to which voluntourists typically travel, which renders them a body 'out of place' (Tembo, 2021), whiteness as a phenomenon that 'impresses upon spaces as an affective formation of power' (2021: 1) is cast into arguably sharper focus. Examining the patterns and implications of voluntourism thus has relevance for illuminating aspects of teaching in white Australia – a context to which I soon turn, where a majority of white teachers teaching a predominantly Anglocentric curriculum led by a preponderance of white leaders and policy makers typically have minimal to no preparation when it comes to understanding race.

Voluntourism is a contested global phenomenon now widely understood as a form of 'moral' holiday-making that combines organized tours with charity work and 'unskilled, temporally shallow travel' (Jakubiak, 2014: 93). The nine-month timeframe described here is a departure from the contemporary norm; however, it is worth noting that despite grasping a modicum of postcolonial theory and having stayed in the host destination for an extended period, immersion did not imbue me with a racially literate or post-abyssal consciousness (Santos, 2018). Time in a host destination can be important, but is not a panacea, and the patterns to surface in the story speak to aspects of voluntourism broadly. Key among these are flows of interaction between global centre and margin, which circumscribe and constitute the voluntourist as principally a Western individual drawn to popular humanitarianism with sufficient disposable income to participate (Mostafanezhad, 2014). Voluntourism thus reaffirms 'white subjectivities' through reinforcing hegemonic discourses that establish 'who is in need' and 'who should help', thus reproducing the moral rationalization of the civilizing mission (Spurr, 1993).

Voluntourism is also popularly associated with feel-good qualities, with the marketing of voluntourism ventures implanting the 'sensuous, affective and emotional aspects of the experience within altruistic desires by tourists to help "others" represented as in "need"' (Everingham and Motta, 2022: 234). My own initially unexamined impulses to *help* through proximity to *difference* might thus be reread from a perspective of structural inequality, whereby certain desires are made available only to certain subjectivities within specific sociohistorical configurations. Given that participation is determined by the capacity to cross the physical borders of travel, but not invisible borders of culture and race (Gómez-Peña, cited in Townsin and Walsh, 2016), voluntourism also fortifies whiteness under a guise of innocence that enables white subjects to exploit overseas travel for personal benefit. Such benefits nowadays include enhancing one's CV (McGloin and Georgeou, 2016) and social media profile (Schulz, 2019), while 'discovering' oneself as caring or brave (McDonald and Tiessen, 2018). Given the inflated sense of Self that voluntourism facilitates, the voluntourist can consequently comprehend the unearned racial privilege on which their participation rests as a natural 'sign of success' (Shultz, 2007: 252). The desires of voluntourists are thus excised from the contexts that produce them, permitting a sentimental rationality anchored in phenomenological selfhood: the self as asocial, existing outside of racialized histories and relations (Schulz and Agnew, 2020).

Moreover, there are specific implications when overseas ventures involve danger, adversity or death. Shocked by such experiences, the immediate impulse of voluntourists may be to internalize the emotional encounter as a narrative via which they reproduce the host destination in deficit terms: as a dangerous or exotic world that reinscribes a boundary between the safety of the known, against that which is 'too precarious'. When voluntourists exercise discursive manoeuvres of this kind, the effect is to reproduce abyssal lines by disconnecting self from other, as though phenomena such as poverty or precarity are a 'characteristic of the people whose very lives are being limited' by such things, rather than outgrowths of globalized modes of structural inequality from which voluntourists benefit (Heron, 2011: 115). This move to innocence thus reinscribes white hegemony while offering the voluntourist a fleeting, if deeply felt, sense of superiority.

Rethinking emotional encounters

In the years that have followed my experiences in Kenya, I have drawn on as well as developed analyses like the ones presented here to emergently make sense of my location within whiteness and my evolving orientation to teacher education. I use sociological lenses with preservice Australian teachers to illuminate that which often remains invisible to white people, such as the normative association of whiteness with teaching. Schick (2000: 303) explains: 'Because teaching is largely a white-identified profession, and since whiteness is unmarked, the profession presents itself as racially neutral and normal. Because white domination has colonised the definition of what it means to be normal ... a "normal" teacher is white.' Within the contours of white Australia, the normative whiteness of the teaching body is frequently naturalized and unnamed – for instance, in policy documents or everyday talk where 'white' teachers are just teachers while the Aboriginal educator is named as such. Whiteness persists in Australia as 'a socio-spatial process that constitutes particular bodies as possessing the normative, ordinary power to enjoy social privilege' (McLean, 2013: 354), which has deep implications for all aspects of schooling.

Consequently, there is deep value and need for critical reflections of the kind illustrated here, which investigate 'contact zone' encounters (Pratt, 2008) framed by neoliberal fantasies in which the behaviours of altruistic (white) individuals are positioned as 'solutions' to structural problems with deep colonial roots (Jakubiak, 2014). The same cultural logics colonize the ways we are led to understand schooling in Australia, which under neoliberal influence is now one of the most unequal systems in the Organisation for Economic Co-operation and Development (Connell, 2013). Mainstream Australian schooling is a site where a raft of standards and accountability frameworks establish whiteness as a norm against which 'diverse' student cohorts are judged (Vass and Chalmers, 2015). It is a space where the Professional Standards for Teachers 'do not recognise that race and racism are variables that impact on education outcomes' (Moreton-Robinson et al, 2012: 12), and where racism in the form of deficit discourses moves freely through the white teaching body. Thus, while voluntourism is refracted through logics of neoliberalism that reframe questions of structural inequality as questions of individual morality (Mostafanezhad, 2014), white Australian schools and teachers are governed through comparable discourses that reduce 'good teaching' to 'race-neutral' quantifications of highly individualized performance.

Yet, despite the power of race critique to expose these far-reaching injustices, looking back on my time in Kenya I also remain discontented by the ways in which my own critiques now feel somewhat overdetermined. I cannot help but see the overarching message that 'voluntourism, mapped by whiteness, is bad', in the same way that, when applied to schooling in white Australia, the message can be misconstrued as 'mainstream Australian schooling, mapped by whiteness, is also bad'. Put differently, as I revisit my lived experiences and scholarship over 20 years later, I see an impulse to reinscribe overly simplistic binaries at the same time that I seek to disrupt them.

Returning to the *matatu* encounter that first jolted me out of complacency and into deeper analysis, decolonial feminist framings of affect now sensitize me to more nuanced re-readings of these formative events, which realistically should never exist as 'learning events' for white people. Drawing on similar resources, Everingham (in Everingham and Motta, 2022: 233) notes that her embodied positionality as a voluntourist 'was fluid, moving between and within the borderlands of researcher/volunteer/tourist, woman/gringa/ "other". This methodological positionality of in-betweenness led to an analysis attentive to affect, emotions, the body and the importance of partial, or pluriversal analysis'. My own experiences as a white/*mzungu/piranpa* voluntourist/teacher/'other' were (are) equally as evocative, and somehow surface in 'excess' of the analyses laid out previously. What emerges for me now are those moments in which I *feel* unsure or uncertain, and far from moved by an elevated sense of self – for example, when clutching bed linen, questioning my role as an English teacher or closely observing life through the experiences of Luo people. Everingham and Motta suggest:

> Emotions such as awkwardness ... can signal a moment of vulnerability, a moment that opens the possibilities of emergent unlearnings of colonial certainty and confidence that comes from occupying a privileged subjectivity ... *It is critical to make visible these vulnerabilities*, as this is where the possibilities for decolonising transformation emerge: in the relationships of becoming, opening and integrity, which involves a reflexive crossing ... to the borders of self and certainty. (Everingham and Motta, 2022: 231, emphasis added)

Attentiveness to racialized vulnerabilities requires attentiveness to the body, feelings and moments of rupture that destabilize colonial certainties. Applying these sensitivities to my own story as well as to the context of Australian classrooms, I *knew* in an embodied sense that the hierarchical nature of knowledge production in Western universities was unfair, and likewise, particularly following the *matatu* incident, *sensed* that myriad aspects of voluntourism were deeply problematic. Yet I did not have the words to explain these things, and embodied knowing is largely silenced within Western educational practices that value 'mind over the body with a Cartesian division that privileges a rational view of knowledge untainted by the body, its feelings, or emotions' (Garrett and MacGill, 2021: 1223).

'Disembodied' and decontextualized English language imperialism operates daily in Australian classrooms as a form of racialized harm (Bargallie et al, 2023). A clear expression is the dominance of testing instruments, such as the National Assessment Program – Literacy and Numeracy, which, while framed as culturally fair and racially neutral, disavows a diversity of learner lifeworlds and is standardized on whiteness as a norm via which 'good' and 'bad' student bodies are constituted. It is little surprise that those who do well on such high-stakes tests that have become normalized in Australian schooling are thus white bodies, or those who are rewarded for performing whiteness (Vass, 2014: 179).

Performances of whiteness also extend to include mastery of emotional responses, with subversive or extreme emotional expressions habitually labelled by the state and its functionaries as deviant or pathological. For instance, Aboriginal youth and working-class boys are disproportionally suspended or expelled from Australian schools (Llewellyn et al, 2016), which highlights a limited yet dominant way of understanding extreme emotions as located 'in' certain bodies while structural and symbolic forms of violence, including poverty and racism, are habitually overlooked. Lohmeyer (2018: 1075) argues that 'deviance lies not in the act itself, but rather in the reaction to the act by those who have the power to make the label stick'. When racially marginalized students enter white schooling spaces that are culturally unsafe and that devalue their cultural assets, they *know*, but they may have insufficient grasp of the language and culture of power to articulate this knowing. Such students typically are also faced with white teachers and leaders unlikely to have learned *to listen* with a racially literate ear. Hence, affects-emotions as impulses that are historically constituted, embodied and enmeshed with power also materialize as 'felt spaces' that make places like schools feel safe and welcoming to some, but unfamiliar and hostile to others (Ahmed, 2014).

Illuminating these dynamics by working with bodies as legitimate sources of knowledge production and transmission is an act of racialized refusal. One of the aims of this work is to disrupt colonial certainties by allowing moments of vulnerability, which open possibilities of emergent unlearnings. This can include 'embodied' forms of learning that engage future teachers in discomforting emotional experiences supported by productive discussions about emotions, including their entanglements with the structural legacies of colonialism. For example, in my work I discuss 'what painful feelings like guilt or anger "do" in terms of limiting or intensifying our desires and capacities to move towards or away from, be with, learn from, or "hear" others' (Schulz et al, 2023: 13). Yet, under neoliberal and neoconservative forces, this work is admittedly growing harder.

Narrative II: Rethinking death

When I secured a tenured academic position as a teacher educator 15 years on from Kenya, conditions were far from perfect in Australian higher education. However, I was surrounded by a critical mass of critical educators, including a strong cohort of First Nations academics. We had scope to work collaboratively, 'mindful that relegating questions of race or whiteness …

to areas such as Indigenous Education entrenches the covertly racist belief that such issues be ignored elsewhere' (Schulz and Fane, 2015: 137). As time wore on and my previous employer not only endured but enthusiastically embraced an aggressive neoliberal restructure, opportunities to work in critical solidarity sharply declined.

Conceptually, while neoliberalism views the human in economic terms and empties the subject of content, neoconservatism fills this gap 'with normative white hegemony' (Gray and Nicholas, 2019: 272). These dynamics have enabled the rise of far-right groups, including the intensification of neo-Nazism in Australia and, as illustrated throughout the COVID-19 pandemic, an emergent nexus of youth, masculinity and right-wing populism that distillates around notions of white male victimhood. Along with the already problematic aspects of neoliberal educational approaches flagged earlier, these tensions manifest in moral panics over critical race theory that further complicates racial literacy education – an area already relegated to the academic margins.

In practical terms, the neoliberal restructure of my prior institution resulted in the loss of scores of critical colleagues, who were either retrenched or squeezed from positions through industrial spill-and-fills. The First Nations Centre was atomized, the pressure to achieve grant capture amplified and academic research increasingly judged by its amenability to lucrative industry partnerships. Money was poured into upper-management salaries and marketing campaigns, while other areas of the institution were starved – particularly teaching-heavy areas staffed by women or minoritized academics. For those of us left standing, our days were increasingly characterized by intensified teaching and administration workloads, mounting academic burnout, rising frustration and the instalment of a new tier of middle managers whose minds were closed to teaching or research in areas such as race criticality; thus, 'affective numbness' around race was institutionally fortified. I became one of few, if any, education academics teaching race and whiteness, and as the academic treadmill accelerated, death unexpectedly reappeared:

> Mum called at 6.00 am: she'd been trying to revive Dad, didn't know if he was dead; the story spilling out. It was Sunday and I was preparing to get a jump on research, but instead, called 000 and arrived at their house to find paramedics hunched over his body. Between then, and finding Mum three weeks later, I'd worked overtime to prepare classes, chase grants, make funeral arrangements, orchestrate eulogies, care for Mum, and essentially work myself to the bone. Mum pleaded, 'Take time off'. I said that I could not possibly, and despite feeling sick with worry about her, went home to follow deadlines. When I returned the next morning, she was dead.

Death makes it difficult to sustain the neat borders of our lives. Death spills over, it seeps. It is said that being confronted with the materiality of death, especially the body of a family member, is traumatic owing precisely to the fact that it is death infecting life (Felluga, 2015). The shock of finding Mum was intense. It was like walking through glass to find myself in another world in which I was now an onlooker, and my body, on autopilot, simply moved itself away from the world of the academe with its deadlines and pressures and countless invisible harms. Despite deep and ongoing commitments to my work, the workplace I once knew felt hostile, especially in relation to race research or practice, despite a world that was screaming out for it – for example, #BlackLivesMatter movements, mosque shootings, and skyrocketing Indigenous deaths in custody. Moreton-Robinson's (2004) observations of universities not having been designed for women and Indigenous peoples felt suddenly more tangible. Yet it was because of the low-stakes reality of my work and the very grievability (Butler, 2015) of my parents' white lives that, ironically, I *could* momentarily stop. Quite unlike life in the Kenyan village, which had no choice but to carry on, I had a modicum of choice.

When finally I re-entered higher education after a long period of refusal, I quietly recommitted, not to a singular institution so much as to critical orientations to teaching that meant teaching racial literacy. Reorientating my focus to 'spaces in-between' (Everingham and Motta, 2022), I have since tried, where possible, to follow the affective warmth and power of critical intellectual friendships. Stein et al (2020) call this hacking: having one foot in and one foot out of the institution, situating our work within efforts to claim decolonial feminist spaces and connecting across boundaries. While universities remain imperfect spaces for race critical and feminist research or teaching, as academics we are nonetheless capable of reflexively and critically examining our conditions of possibility and creatively resisting or refusing elements of those terms. The encounters with death described in this chapter have not illuminated 'answers' so much as moved me out of temporarily stuck or institutionally 'numbed' states to explore new possibilities while remembering what really matters.

It *matters* that Australian teachers are given opportunities to apprehend life through a racially literate lens. When they are not, dysconsciousness of social relations legitimates their voices 'as individuals' while negating the ties that bind us. Rather than perceiving ourselves as disconnected from 'others over there', race criticality illuminates – among many things – our interconnectedness. Learning racial literacy is thus important for those of us engaged in low-intensity struggles for remembering what is really at stake: 'communities not quite recognized as such, subjects who are living, but not yet regarded as "lives"' (Butler, 2009: 32). Death can be numbing. But death can also shake us from numbness to remind us of these basic lessons. And if schooling and teacher education are not calibrated to bring these basic lessons to life, death can embolden us to ask: what are we really doing here, what the hell is education for?

References

Ahmed, S. (2004) *The Cultural Politics of Emotion*, Edinburgh: Edinburgh University Press.

Ahmed, S. (2008) 'Open forum imaginary prohibitions: Some preliminary remarks on the founding gestures of the "new materialism"', *European Journal of Women's Studies*, 15(1): 23–39.

Ahmed, S. (2014) 'Atmospheric walls', *Feminist Killjoys*. https://feministkilljoys.com/2014/09/15/atmospheric-walls

Bargallie, D., Fernando, N. and Lentin, A. (2023) 'Breaking the racial silence: Putting racial literacy to work in Australia', *Ethnic and Racial Studies*. DOI: 10.1080/01419870.2023.2206470

Barney, K. (2006) 'Playing hopscotch: How Indigenous women performers resist Aboriginalist constructs of race', *Crossings*, 11(2): 1–45.

Boler, M. and Davis, E. (2018) 'The affective politics of the "post-truth" era: Feeling rules and networked subjectivity', *Emotion, Space and Society*, 27: 75–85.

Butler, J. (2004) *Precarious Life: The Powers of Mourning and Violence*, London: Verso.

Butler, J. (2009) *Frames of War: When Life is Grievable*, London: Verso.

Butler, J. (2015) *Precariousness and Grievability: When is Life Grievable?* London: Verso.

Clough, P. (2007) 'Introduction', in P. Clough and J. Halley (eds), *The Affective Turn: Theorizing the Social*, Durham, NC: Duke University Press, pp 1–33.

Connell, R. (2013) 'The neoliberal cascade and education: An essay on the market agenda and its consequences', *Critical Studies in Education*, 54(2): 99–112.

Cvetkovich, C. (2012) *Depression: A Public Feeling*, Durham, NC: Duke University Press.

Everingham, P. and Motta, S. (2022) 'Decolonising the "autonomy of affect" in volunteer tourism encounters', *Tourism Geographies*, 24(2–3): 223–43.

Felluga, D. (2015) *Critical Theory: The Key Concepts*, London: Routledge.

Garrett, R. and MacGill, B. (2021) 'Fostering inclusion through creative and body-based learning', *International Journal of Inclusive Education*, 25(11): 1221–35.

Gray, E. and Nicholas, L. (2019) '"You're actually the problem": Manifestations of populist masculinist anxieties in Australian higher education', *British Journal of Sociology of Education*, 40(2): 269–86.

Heron, B. (2007) *Desire for Development: Whiteness, Tender, and the Helping Imperative*, Ontario: Wilfrid Laurier University Press.

Heron, B. (2011) 'Challenging indifference to extreme poverty: Considering Southern perspectives on global citizenship and change', *Ethics and Economics*, 8(1): 109–19.

Jakubiak, C. (2014) 'Moral ambivalence in English language voluntourism', in M. Mostafanezhad and K. Hannam (eds), *Moral Encounters in Tourism*, Burlington: Ashgate, pp 93–106.

Leys, R. (2011) 'The turn to affect: A critique', *Critical Inquiry*, 37(3): 434–72.

Llewellyn, L., Lewthwaite, B. and Boon, H. (2016) 'Culturally responsive classroom management strategies: What Australian Indigenous students and parents have to say', American Educational Research Association. https://researchonline.jcu.edu.au/44474/1/1059806.1.pdf

Lohmeyer, B. (2018) 'Youth as an artefact of governing violence: Violence to young people shapes violence by young people', *Current Sociology*, 66(7): 1070–86.

Lowe, K. and Galstaun, V. (2020) 'Ethical challenges: The possibility of authentic teaching encounters with Indigenous cross-curriculum content?', *Curriculum Perspectives*, 40(1): 93–8.

Machado de Oliveira, A. (2021) *Hospicing Modernity: Facing Humanity's Wrongs and the Implications for Social Activism*, Berkeley: North Atlantic Books.

Maher, K. (2022) 'The Aboriginal and Torres Strait Islander histories and cultures cross-curriculum priority: Pedagogical questions of country, colonialism and whose knowledge counts', *The Social Educator*, 40(2): 3–17.

McDonald, K. and Tiessen, R. (2018) 'Introduction to special issue: The practice, politics and possibilities for globally engaged experiential learning in diverse contexts', *Journal of Global Citizenship and Equity Education*, 6(1): 3–17.

McGloin, C. and Georgeou, N. (2016) '"Looks good on your CV": The sociology of voluntourism recruitment in higher education', *Journal of Sociology*, 52(2): 403–17.

McLean, S. (2013) 'The whiteness of green: Racialization and environmental education', *The Canadian Geographer/Le Géographe canadien*, 57(3): 354–62.

Memon, N., Schulz, S., Kelly, S. and Chown, D. (2023) 'Schools, religion, and affect: Unpacking Australian educator discomfort', *Asia-Pacific Journal of Teacher Education*, 51(3): 266–82.

Moreton-Robinson, A. (2004) 'Whiteness, epistemology and Indigenous representation', in A. Moreton-Robinson (ed), *Whitening Race: Essays in Social and Cultural Criticism*, Canberra: Aboriginal Studies Press, pp 75–88.

Moreton-Robinson, A., Singh, D., Kolopenuk, J. and Robinson, A. (2012) *Learning the Lessons? Pre-service Teacher Preparation for Teaching Aboriginal and Torres Strait Islander Students*, Melbourne: Australian Institute for Teaching and School Leadership.

Mostafanezhad, M. (2014) *Volunteer Tourism: Popular Humanitarianism in Times*, Burlington: Ashgate.

Ott, B. (2017) 'Affect in critical studies', in *Oxford Research Encyclopedia of Communication*. https://doi.org/10.1093/acrefore/9780190228613.013.56

Pratt, M.L. (2008) *Imperial Eyes: Travel Writing and Transculturation*, 2nd edn, London: Routledge.

Rogers, T. (2021) 'Knowing how to feel: Racism, resilience, and affective resistance', *Hypatia*, 36: 725–47.

Said, E. (1979) *Orientalism*, New York: Vintage Books.

Santos, B. (2018) *The End of the Cognitive Empire: The Coming of Age of Epistemologies of the South*, Durham, NC: Duke University Press.

Schaefer, D.O. (2020) 'Whiteness and civilization: Shame, race, and the rhetoric of Donald Trump', *Communication and Critical/Cultural Studies*, 17(1): 1–18.

Schick, C. (2000) 'White women teachers accessing dominance', *Discourse: Studies in the Cultural Politics of Education*, 21(3): 299–309.

Schulz, S. (2019) '"Beating their unclad chests": Voluntourism, international service and the place of critical pedagogy inside the neoliberal university', in S. Riddle and M. Apple (eds), *Re-Imagining Education for Democracy*, London: Routledge, pp 224–38.

Schulz, S. and Fane, J. (2015) 'A healthy dose of race? White students' and teachers' unintentional brushes with whiteness', *Australian Journal of Teacher Education*, 40(11): 137–54.

Schulz, S. and Agnew, D. (2020) 'Moving toward decoloniality in short-term study abroad under New Colombo: Constructing global citizenship', *British Journal of Sociology of Education*, 41(8): 1164–79.

Schulz, S., Rigney, L.I., Zembylas, M., Hattam, R. and Memon, N. (2023) 'Affect and the force of counter stories: Learning racial literacy through thinking and feeling', *Pedagogy, Culture & Society*. https://doi.org/10.1080/14681366.2023.2173276

Shultz, L. (2007) 'Educating for global citizenship: Conflicting agendas and understandings', *Alberta Journal of Educational Research*, 53(3): 248–58.

Spurr, D. (1993) *The Rhetoric of Empire: Colonial Discourse in Journalism, Travel Writing, and Imperial Administration*, Durham, NC: Duke University Press.

Stein, S. (2020) 'A colonial history of the higher education present: Rethinking land-grant institutions through processes of accumulation and relations of conquest', *Critical Studies in Education*, 61(2): 212–28.

Stein, S., Andreotti, V., Susa, R., Amsler, S., Dallas, H., Haruko, O., et al (2020) 'Gesturing towards decolonial futures: Reflections on our learnings thus far', *Nordic Journal of Comparative and International Journal*, 4(1): 43–65.

Tembo, S. (2021) 'Bodies out of place: Affective encounters with whiteness', *Emotion, Space and Society*, 41: 1–8.

Townsin, L. and Walsh, C. (2016) 'A new border pedagogy: Rethinking outbound mobility programs in the Asian century', in D.M. Velliaris and D. Coleman-George (eds), *Handbook on Study Abroad Programs and Outbound Mobility*, Hershey: IGI Global, pp 215–47.

Vass, G. (2014) 'The racialised educational landscape in Australia: Listening to the whispering elephant', *Race Ethnicity and Education*, 17(2): 176–201.

Vass, G. and Chalmers, G. (2015) 'NAPLAN, achievement gaps and embedding Indigenous perspectives in schooling: Disrupting the decolonial option', in B. Lingard, G. Thompson and S. Sellar (eds), *National Testing in Schools*, London: Routledge, pp 139–51.

Zembylas, M. (2015) 'Rethinking race and racism as technologies of affect: Theorizing the implications for anti-racist politics and practice in education', *Race Ethnicity and Education*, 18(2): 145–62.

Zembylas, M. (2017) 'The contribution of non-representational theories in education: Some affective, ethical and political implications', *Studies in Philosophy and Education*, 36: 393–407.

Zembylas, M. (2023) 'The resilience of racism and affective numbness: Cultivating an aesthetics of attention in education', *Critical Studies in Education*. https://doi.org/10.1080/17508487.2023.2171452

19

In Conversation with Yassir Morsi: Slow Ontology as Resistance

Debbie Bargallie and Yassir Morsi

Dr Yassir Morsi is a lecturer in social inquiry and a provisional psychologist at an Islamic academy in Australia and author of the auto-ethnography *Radical Skin, Moderate Masks*, on Islamophobia and racism in Australia.

DB: Yassir, what is your understanding of racial literacy as a concept?

YM: Many of us use the term 'racial literacy'. I have heard it in the context of anti-racism used by people trying to build both a coalition and a mobility and culture of activism against racism, to speak about one of the obstacles that we face. It refers to the level of knowledge, understanding of the history of how racism works, evolves, how it plays out in various arenas, at the state level. Importantly, here in a white settlement, it's about how race shaped and still shapes the lives of Indigenous folk, immigrants, people of colour, and of course, white people. So I see it as a term that we use to measure how well we, in a public debate, understand racism, the way it works and its foundations.

DB: So, Yassir, what academic disciplines or fields do you teach in?

YM: I initially began in politics. I stayed there for a little while. My PhD was in politics. I expanded to the field within Islamic studies that focuses on politics with respect to Islamophobia and anti-Muslim racism. And then, without my permission, the next thing I knew I was a race scholar. And I say 'without my permission' because of both the institution and environment of the day; publicly and otherwise, I was continually called upon as a Muslim scholar – but not paid for it – to deal with the harms of racism and the impact to my community, and others. So I slowly found myself getting involved in cultural studies in the broad sense and ended up in a gender and sexuality role and in the diversity department of a university. I have come to be known for my expertise in racism and coloniality. But, as I mentioned, I did not really make that choice.

DB: It is interesting how negatively racialized academics are positioned and pigeonholed that way to fit the system. In your book *Radical Skin/Moderate Masks* (Morsi, 2017), you draw on the work of Frantz Fanon – the Marxist, French West Indian psychiatrist and political philosopher, radical intellectual and revolutionary from the French colony of Martinique. Your title extends on his first book *Black Skin, White Masks* (Fanon, 1952). What led you to Fanon and what other disciplines or theories do you draw on in your teaching?

YM: Fanon was and is a major influence on me. Initially, I learned a lot from the 'trinity' of post-colonial scholars – Edward Said, Gayatri Spivak and Homi Bhabha. I found myself getting more and more involved in cultural studies. Stuart Hall became an incredible influence, and I started reading Alana Lentin quite early, who was influenced by Hall and others. Reading Lentin, it opened up a whole different literacy on race and racism. I closely read Barnor Hesse. Outside of that, Salman Sayyid, under whom I worked in Adelaide, became someone of influence for me. It sparked a move into decolonial thinkers: Walter Mignolo, Ramon Grosfoguel and the like. All of these became influential in shaping my thinking.

I began to deal a lot with critical race theories. I loved reading bell hooks; it just connected with me. And I also dealt with a lot of what they typically call postmodern theorists early on in my political theorizing – Jacques Derrida, Michel Foucault – and my thesis critiqued liberalism. So I was unfortunate enough to read a lot of dead white male scholars from Hobbes all the way to Rawls. Most of my academic journey has been around political theorists dealing with theorizing of the state, the nation, the people and ultimately how racism works in that. But look, I don't like the term 'postmodern' because it's been politicized, weaponized and abused, but I guess I fall into that 'critical postmodern tradition' of questioning and critiquing identity.

The overlap, ultimately, was Fanon. Without Fanon, I wouldn't have got to where I am with my thinking. He shaped my political aspirations. And of course, I learned from a lot of

Indigenous scholars here in Australia. I'm indebted to them. I recall reading *Australian Indigenous Knowledge and Libraries* by Marcia Langton and Martin Nakata (2005). I came to the book because it was coedited by Martin Nakata, the father of a colleague, Sana Nakata. Sana and I worked under the same supervisor at Melbourne University where we completed our PhDs and taught alongside each other. If I remember correctly, her father's co-edited book summarized a two-day colloquium that brought together professionals, practitioners and academics to discuss future directions in maintaining Indigenous knowledge. When reading that book, I recalled Sana's conversations about disrupted histories, which made it a powerful and meaningful read. It struck me how much of a need there is to preserve and archive resistance, to archive Indigenous knowledge.

And on this point, I owe a debt of gratitude to Gary Foley for his work in documenting the struggle for Aboriginal self-determination. His works showed me an impressive past, taking from the genealogy of anti-imperial movements and Black liberation movements worldwide. But above all I read Foley as making a powerful case for why this history should not be forgotten. Similarly, I recognized the importance of the theories in Aileen Moreton-Robinson's *The White Possessive* (2015) and *Whitening Race* (2004) for my work; her insights into critical Indigenous studies really struck a chord. I found her call to disrupt the 20th-century knowledge produced by non-Indigenous scholars significant; I could sense her calling for the formation of a new discipline. Her work questioned how Indigenous studies became embedded in academic institutions and explored the epistemology of the field to uncover fresh prospects for critical inquiry and practice.

DB: Yassir, speaking to other non-Indigenous academics categorized as non-white in Australia, it is fast becoming an expectation to position and introduce themselves as 'settlers'. However, for people from refugee backgrounds, people seeking asylum or those who have undergone forced migration, for example, their situations are complex. They may struggle to view themselves in that way. Feeling forced to identify as a 'settler' seems little more than a performance. The turn to expect non-Indigenous peoples to locate themselves as settlers has been driven primarily by scholars who have been influenced by Australian anthropologist and historian Patrick Wolfe's (2006) essay, 'Settler colonialism and the elimination of the native'. While Wolfe may have sparked the surge in settler-colonial studies in Australia, as Kanaka Maoli (Native Hawaiian) scholar J. Kēhaulani Kauanui (2016) asserts, 'Wolfe insisted on making it clear time and again that he did not create the field of settler colonial studies – that Native scholars did – within the field of American Studies (as just one example), he tends to be most frequently cited as if he had'. There is a failure to recognize this, which is telling. We know that positionality matters, but what does it mean to engage: researcher reflexivity without criticality? Some people, most often white female academics, stand up and locate themselves as a 'settler' at a conference, confess their privilege and just move on. They fail to include Indigenous theorizing or question their complicity in the oppressive processes or practices of coloniality, continue to gatekeep Indigenous knowledges.

YM: In effect, they recentre whiteness and continue to gatekeep Indigenous Knowledges. Thank you for sharing that, you have brought a memory back. I participated in couple of Australian Critical Race and Whiteness Studies Association events, which I initially enjoyed. But more and more I found it fatiguing to be surrounded by this kind of performativity. It felt like most of the time that we were having these conversations, we were just checking boxes. I acknowledge that I am an extension of the settler, but it felt like the conversation was restricted to the focus on 'Are you aware that you are also a settler being a person of colour?' And yes, I am. But it often felt even among people of colour, there was a need to trace how white we all were. And I think there is value in that work but honestly, a lot of people are just comfortable just doing that – just doing the 'Are you aware of your positionality?' And it gets a little bit exhausting, not because the work is not important, but because 'And then what?'

DB: Non-performativity in race and racism work is problematic. As Sara Ahmed (2012) shows us, both performativity and non-performativity are problematic in race and racism work. David Theo Goldberg, Ray Victor and Alana Lentin, among others, make clear that not all race and racism work is critical race theory.

YM: Yeah. It felt to me like this kind of performativity was a crowding of the space. New work, new ideas, new conversations, new literacies became harder to come by. I didn't fully leave academia, but I did take a different direction.

DB: Do you find that the 'publish or perish' culture enables the reproduction of the same 'old wine in new bottles' scenario?

The writing over and over of the same with a 'new' name attached. It's like the need to be seen or to be recognized as 'the first'.

YM: Well, I bumped into a few papers before I 'left' academia that speak to the idea of a slow ontology. One of the things that academia embraces, as you said, is the publish-or-perish culture. With the speed of neoliberalism, the need to fill your CV with publications, and even when applying for a job, people are not reading your articles, but are only interested in knowing where you have been and how much you have published. And that really means that we have turned towards an industry more concerned with form than content. When you strip away all the verbose language, it is pretty much saying the same thing: racism exists, and this is how it works. But it is not exploring its evolution or the various ways anti-racism is collapsing or failing at different times. I have found it is even worse in the literature on Islamophobia. There are some incredibly intelligent people across all fields, but the standard drops a little when it comes to Islamophobia, partly because of little real questioning or critique of liberalism and democracy as instruments of the state that have racial histories. In all that, it turned out I was 'too Muslim' to be in a politics department and 'too political' to be in a Muslim department.

DB: Yassir, in your chapter in the edited collection by Asim Qureshi (2020) titled *I Refuse to Condemn: Resisting Racism in Times of National Security*, you write beautifully about '[t]he (im)possible Muslim' through a metaphor of 'being in the park'. Could you speak about what you 'lost' and 'gained' in that park in relation to your position as a Muslim scholar of Islamophobia and racism? And how do you see yourself now in relation to that park? Have things changed in how you perceive yourself now you are not officially employed within the academy?

YM: The park served as a metaphor for nature, while racism, in my view, disrupts one's core natural needs for play, belonging and pursuit of higher spiritual ground; it drags you into the mud. Fighting racism results in some type of existential crisis. I am convinced of this. It is not easy or fun. You lose a lot of friends, trust, reputation. Because you are drowning in societal constructs and false narratives and become estranged from yourself in navigating, reading, archiving and naming power, which often leads to yours and others' discontent and cynicism. In turn, society measures you based on this context and perceives you as lacking commitment or involvement in institutions and national norms. This disruption makes the childhood park a lost place of innocence, an apt metaphor. I can't return to something innocent. However, I should also say that I chose to write creatively using a particular style of creative non-fiction to express my subjectivity and challenge the rigid disciplinary knowledge produced by non-Indigenous scholars. This aligns with Moreton-Robinson's calls for different modes of critical inquiry. Although social scientists view figurative language with suspicion, I believe such language enables us to express our experiences more vividly. And you know what? It is precisely their suspicion that piqued my interest. Through this style, I want to show how racism denaturalizes individuals and a childhood park turned unfriendly represented estrangement. I guess that is part of the reason I made my decision to move out of academia. Institutions do not own the pursuit of knowledge or the accumulation of knowledge, or how I use it to educate, mobilize. But it does own its titles and status, authority. I felt that too much of my job was about securing a career. For the lack of a better phrase, it expected of me to perform in ways that uphold white supremacy; having the correct temperature of racial literacy; not too much, not too little. It is that nice middle ground that lets white folk deal with their guilt, think they are doing enough – but not enough to imply we are all still part of the problem – or demand a type of politics that moves a little quicker than it is. So, the idea of slow ontology is helping me to figure out what it means to go slow and study something thoroughly and meaningfully. It is where I think new work will arrive, the kind of work that is dying out because that kind of pace is dying out. It is no wonder that a lot of us, as well as our students, suffer from imposter syndrome because we are expected to perform in a certain way. I would like to learn more, know more, understand more. And I do not think we are imposters, but the industry is demanding that we fake it till we make it.

DB: I agree with you, Yassir. In terms of educating in the fields of Islamic studies and social inquiry, how do you deal with the racial backlash and the pushback against the position that Islamophobia is not racism?

YM: Well, I have to read the room. Sometimes, people are open to me expanding and educating and having a conversation and learning from them. At other times, people are not listening but just trying to assert their worldview. Normally, I educate by unpacking the concept of race and what constitutes

	racialization and how that works historically; that Islam is a religion of colour, first and foremost; and that there cannot be just a biological underpinning to race as there is a cultural and religious one. I also focus on the role both the body and the soul played in the historic construction of whiteness. I feel there is an important need for us to have that conversation, but honestly, most of us have two jobs at the same time and we are forced to navigate a narrow corridor.
DB:	It makes us wonder how far do we go and how far do we push? Because what I have learned being in the academy is that there is little institutional support behind us for doing work on race or racism, whether it be in research or teaching. What do you think the need is for the wider university staff or educators to help develop racial literacy?
YM:	You know what I think the problem is, Debbie. I think that will happen, but they will choose a convenient type of race literacy. In the same way they have chosen, in the public media space, the idea of the 'good Muslim', as someone who is inevitably and fundamentally, beyond their Brown or Black exterior, liberal and democratic. I am not critical of liberalism and democracy in and of itself. I have a criticism of erasing its racial histories, and how it has been used to justify wars, occupation and genocide. So, I think what will happen is that there will be a nice lukewarm form of race literacy.
DB:	Is it about morality, then?
YM:	Exactly. And since they have moralized the question, the material, economic, political, institutional ways racism functions is erased. And, in turn, continues to exploit people of colour and Indigenous folks, and their land resources, histories, labour, bodies, and so on. So, I think they will eventually find a tokenistic critical race theory. Even though the institutions have an obligation to increase racial literacy, I worry that because we do not have a critical mass here, our work will become appropriated. Because we are not the drivers or the owners of the decision-making around this, I am concerned they will select, like power always does, what is enough. Power is clever, right?
DB:	Yassir, in your book *Radical Skin, Moderate Masks* you vividly describe the covert ways othering and racism operate and manage to disguise the truth of racialized societies. In a neoliberal context that, as you have mentioned, prevents the kind of slow ontology imperative for deep interrogation and thought, what do you think is needed to get us moving towards

	a different academy – one that allows and promotes productive racial literacy?
YM:	Well, I see the solution through practising different modes of writing. As an academic writer, I believe writing should be therapeutic and meaningful for healing from politics. I think theory should be seen as therapy. It cannot just be about outlining an argument, making patterns, producing thought. There is an emotional tag to it. We have other core needs when we read works on social harms. We seek visibility, not just citations.
	The pressure to produce work solely for the sake of productivity by institutions and the field is a neoliberal calling that I refuse to succumb to. It has cost me, but maybe it also saved me. I don't know. I never did it. Producing work that causes further harm is pointless, especially when the same institutions have discredited Indigenous epistemologies. Instead, I see my academic life as a way to sort out my experiences as if I am on the therapist's couch, and escape the madness, melancholia, panic and fear inherent in the racial context. Writing becomes a form of therapy, a way to paint my arguments and turn them into spoken words that help me manage my disorder.
	Yes, I confess to suffering from some type of mood disorder instilled with paranoia by the war on terror. I am often my worst enemy, seeing threats where there are none, spies everywhere, and distrust in every corner. I wasn't always like this, but I cannot help it. … I keep it all in, act normal, wear masks. Only writing allows me to let it out.
	Writing, especially now that I am semi-retired from academia, is a way to connect with others who share similar turmoil and my own past experiences. It's kind of revenge against my shadow paranoid self. Yes, I have a pursuit for objective content and evidence. I take academic arguments seriously, I am not just writing fiction, but I hope to complement this with my quest for collegiality, a craving for company, with fellow 'mad' individuals through a style of writing that stiches our humanity back.
DB:	In your anti-racism praxis, how do you speak to and educate about both structural and interpersonal racisms and how they work together?
YM:	In class, I make a distinction between what I call a big 'R' racism and a small 'r' racism to ensure that students know the difference and can see that the smaller 'r' racism has come at the expense of fighting bigger 'R' racisms. The small 'r',

being everyday interpersonal issues, is no doubt important. But I personally could not care less if somebody sees me as a terrorist or not. I appreciate the need to combat the small 'r' racism, but I do think it often comes at the expense of uprooting big 'R' racism, which means more jobs for people of colour, Indigenous peoples, more positions of authority and power, more self-determination, more radical thinking about problems that impact us. Now I teach both, but I also teach how not to be seduced by thinking that a fight against small 'r' racism is enough. Students will be horrified more than me if somebody comes out and calls me a terrorist. The whole class will be horrified. And HR will get involved and everybody will be 'We are so sorry you had to go through that'. But I do not care about that. I will say the fact that I have been exploited and I do not have a continuing position and my work and labour are being used for advertising about diversity, but I am not seen, not read, not cited – now that is a function of racism that I care about.

DB: You mentioned that we will eventually see this kind of 'soft' racial literacy but considering that up until now there has been no formal race studies in Australia, how do you think that racial literacy is ever going to come to fruition if it is not mandated or we continue to not have race studies as a field or discipline?

YM: That's an important point. Even with the soft approach we are going to have to fight tooth and nail to ensure they are not going to give up easily. So, we continue to fight, fight and fight, and then we might arrive at some version that may be even more harmful because it conceals what we want fundamentally: self-determination, political integrity and dignity for people targeted by racism. Part of the reason I became a psychologist and worked in an Islamic school is because I want my anti-racism – my energy, my labour, my intellectual work – to be given to people who are targeted by racism. We need warriors who will carry on from the warriors before us. But we are up against a trillion-dollar media cultural industry that is miseducating people all the time about the way the world is built. And the few hours a week I have to give to my own people I want to make sure are effective. So, I know your question is about what can be done but at the university level I feel I am the wrong person to ask: I no longer have faith in that institution.

DB: Yassir, your writing is unique in how honest and personal your reflections are on your own experiences of truth-telling. Could

	you speak more about your reasons for leaving the academy? What the effects of the kind of truth-telling you engaged in were, as it is a particular style in integrating the personal, the critical, the unvarnished and the political?
YM:	I do not want to romanticize this, not suggesting you are – I appreciate your wording and it is welcomed because I can see that you see me and why I write the way I do. But, to address the other part of your question: my writing style has likely cost me in terms of mainstream academic acceptance. Despite its popularity among some people, the gains for me are minimal. In a peer-review of an article, I was once accused by reviewer two of writing a 'coming-of-age piece', and they weren't sure how it could be cited or whether it would qualify as 'proper work'. The journal editor 'enjoyed it', but unfortunately had to reject it. I wasn't writing to be cited. I was writing to say something. The dual messaging I received is everywhere in academia for me:

'I enjoy you, but …'
'We love your teaching, but …'
'You have amazing ideas, but …'
'You are important, but …'

I cannot tell you how many obscure abstracted authority figures like 'reviewer two' reside beyond the ellipses of 'yes, but …' Some unnamed figure with power always stops us from linking their love with money and job security. It's post-racial in a sense, like the way Australia's Harmony Day gets praised for celebrating culture and diversity, yet racism remains in the background as a material unnamed reality.

But my writing didn't come about unintentionally; I was aware of the risks when I decided to write in this way. My purpose in academia wasn't simply to become an academic – it was to learn how to fight systems of knowledge that prop up oppression. I wanted to create testimonies, blood and bone testimonies. … I read this quote somewhere, which skips my mind about writing embodied stories: 'The skin is faster than the word.'

You know how easy it is to write an article on Islamophobia to get cited but forget to make visible the very Muslim subject targeted by Islamophobia. All these Likert-scaled Muslim testimonies, all these reductive questionnaires of all these studies that reduced us to one-dimensional victims or terrorists. I remember reading how something like (can't remember the stat, because I don't care) '67 per cent of Muslims call Australia home'. What does that even mean? As if somehow, we all share a common definition of home, or our reasons are the same. But you and I know what it means. It means despite what racists say, Muslims belong. Why should I always respond to racists? It's too rushed a stat, it lacks slow ontology, it just wants to respond.

DB: In your current employment outside of the academy, how are you doing racial literacy work?

YM: At the Islamic school where I work, we have a 100 per cent Muslim population. I am a counsellor and I try to help identify and manage the precipitating factors that help somebody have maladaptation issues. I got that job partly because of my history of working with the community, something that does not translate into job opportunities in universities, right? There's no subject or course material saying: How do you deal with whiteness? How do you deal with power? The assumption is how to deal with Black and Brownness, written under the banner of cultural sensitivity and cultural differences. It is all about not offending someone. So, one of the things that I have seen is that a lot of mental health practitioners bring with them an unnamed whiteness, an assumption about what constitutes social and psychological maladaptation. And they do not bring in the political environment that impacts family structure, labour, all of this. And so I am doing two things. I am trying to understand through the DSM 5 [APA Diagnostic and Statistical Manual of Mental Disorders 5th edition] and all these categories of what constitutes a diagnosis, what constitutes mental health, and at the same time trying to bring my other understanding of the impacts of growing up Muslim in the West. So, part of the problem is the school itself, and society itself – it has no clue. They just want me to put the kids back on their feet so they can finish their schooling and become integrated members of society. And the assumption is, if you're a happy worker, you're mentally healthy, which is a maladaptation.

DB: Given the variety of families that you have in your school, you are working with a range of intersecting issues that people are subjected to in their lives. Not a single-issue problem.

YM: These families are quite poor in comparison to other families. And we have an array of political problems – families that have come out of detention centres, families that have lost lives to war.

DB: Do you feel that you have institutional support in doing your work?

YM: No, I have never had institutional support anywhere. The difference between university and school is that university is better at their stage performance. They will say they will support you, but when it comes down to the topic of racial literacy, I am ideological, I am a zealot, I am too involved. They will not make the connection that it is a function of racism that so many Black and Brown kids are neglected in their mental health. Or perhaps worse, the curriculum. I do not even know why they are reading Shakespeare. I do not understand; Shakespeare is not going to help you in your life. But it is the same thing I must continually navigate to survive in this environment to be able to do the work. It is about when to speak, when not to speak, when to fight, when not to fight, when to put on my mask and when to take it off. So, I have two jobs: survival and work. If they were serious about racial literacy, they would be connecting to the voices that exist in the community. Those voices are important and access to those voices is also important. But it comes down to urgency. For universities, there is no urgency to address race and racism; there is nothing at stake for them.

DB: They do not see it as core business. Do you find that there is solidarity among race scholars or people that are doing anti-racism education? How do you see us in the space?

YM: I do not like the space. It seems to me one of the hardest spaces to navigate. I think it is a function of the lateral violence of racism from the top down that spreads outwards. There is a lot of distrust. Another reason I went into psychology is addressing the lack of dealing with the trauma. It is hard enough fighting racism in and of itself without carrying the malignant grief, the ongoing witnessing of Black and Brown bodies being killed, maimed, shot at, destroyed, displaced. There is so very little institutional support, which makes the space we work in so very small. There have been very few anti-race scholars who have supported my growth. I have to give credit to the few overseas, but in the Muslim arena in Australia, they are mostly quite hostile and silent. I do not know why. On top of all of that, there is too much reward, too much money, too much career mobility upwards, for you to accept a definition of anti-racism that suits power. It is too seductive. Whether writing up a grant paper, accepting a teaching position or going on a panel, there is just way too much reward for you to accept their conditions of talking about racism within the parameters that are comfortable. If you question those parameters enough times, you will not get a re-invite. The ideologies in the background are working against you; you are a zealot, you are too radical, you are uncompromising. And so not only do we have to fight our own trauma, but we also must fight each other. We are supposed to be propping up a culture of forgiveness and growth for our own people. If, God forbid, a Muslim comes out and says something against Indigenous folk, unintended, does not understand positionality and so forth, they will rightly be called out, but sometimes they are called out in such a ferocious and repeated manner that excludes them from that space. I think there is too much of a power kick in that. Our white societies have made racism such a taboo and sensitive topic because at the heart of it, in its imagination, is white guilt, white people sensitivities, white morality. I am a beneficiary of racism, as well as a victim. And I am interested in recognizing how that works. It seems that this environment or circle that we are in has been overly infected by the highly moralizing issue where people think that if you find offence, there is some type of victory against racism. I do not know if that is the case; all I know is I do not have the time to figure it out – there's just too many of my people in need.

DB: Another race scholar of colour recently mentioned being policed in this way and feeling that they cannot speak about the racism targeting their community because they are 'expected' to only speak about racism as it impacts Indigenous Australian peoples. This type of policing can be paralysing.

YM: Racism has become too overly loaded with whether or not you are a good person or a decent human being, or whether you are a humanist and care for everybody. Now here is the problem: I am in an environment – whether it is a social, public or personal platform – where I have to make a decision. If I speak out against the different kinds of racisms, homophobia, sexism or otherwise, in a particular language with a particular urgency, well I am accused of strengthening Islamophobia. And having that conversation among my own is incredible. There are various degrees of religiosity, and the thinking is that if you are more conservative, you are considered more Muslim. So, I agree, it is incredibly difficult to speak about your own racism in your own community, or small 'r' racism. It is difficult because there is a failure of race literacy. Here we are not only fighting a problem; we are trying to preserve people's identities while fighting that problem. And that is too much work.

References

Ahmed, S. (2012) *On Being Included: Racism and Diversity in Institutional Life*, Durham, NC: Duke University Press.

Fanon, F. (1952) *Black Skin, White Masks*, New York: Grove Press.

Kēhaulani Kauanui, J. (2016) '"A structure, not an event": Settler colonialism and enduring indigeneity', *Lateral* 5(1).

Langton, M. and Nakata, M. (2005) *Australian Indigenous Knowledge and Libraries*, Sydney: UTS e-Press.

Moreton-Robinson, A. (2004) *Whitening Race: Essays in Social and Cultural Criticism*, Minneapolis: University of Minnesota Press.

Moreton-Robinson, A. (2015) *The White Possessive: Property, Power and Indigenous Sovereignty*, Minneapolis: University of Minnesota Press.

Morsi, Y. (2017) *Radical Skin/Moderate Masks*, Lanham: Rowman & Littlefield.

Morsi, Y. (2020) 'The (im)possible Muslim', in *I Refuse to Condemn*, Manchester: Manchester University Press.

Qureshi, A. (2020) *I Refuse to Condemn: Resisting Racism in Times of National Security*, Manchester: Manchester University Press.

Wolfe, P. (2006) 'Settler colonialism and the elimination of the native', *Journal of Genocide Research*, 8(4): 387–409.

20

Teaching Race, Conceptualizing Solidarity

Andrew Brooks

Introduction

How are we to teach 'race' in the context of a settler colony that is structured by the grammar of racialization and whose institutions refuse to confront these uncomfortable foundations? The question, in this instance, relates specifically to the settler colony of Australia, where the enduring national mythology is derived from an image of the happy-go-lucky convict who, through hard work and mateship, forges a new society in a hostile colonial outpost. The persistent idea of a nation defined by the promise of 'fair go' is at odds with the history of invasion and occupation that defines the project of settler colonialism. The establishment of the colony on top of the unbroken sovereignty of First Nations is an act of dispossession that relies upon the (re)production of racial regimes that mutate over time in order to legitimate and uphold the authority of the settler state. As the historian Patrick Wolfe (2016: 33) famously wrote, 'invasion is a structure, not an event'. It is a structure that produces shifting grammars of racialization, progressing from genocidal violence to forms of conditional recognition.

In the contemporary moment, the reproduction of the settler state involves the escalation of attacks on principles of anti-racism that increasingly take education as a primary battleground. A culture war is raging, and it has implications for the future of sovereign First Nations struggles, the safety and wellbeing of negatively racialized people and the perpetuation of racialized exploitation. One response to the politicization of education has been a retreat from anti-racism into the institutionalized frameworks of diversity and inclusion, which often focus on representational rather than material redress. Another has been a retreat from critically engaging with race and racism beyond the reductive notion that racism is an expression of individual prejudice or bias. This chapter reflects on Stuart Hall's (2021a) essay 'Teaching race' in order to consider the challenges of critically teaching about race from the settler-colonial context of Australia and in the midst of an escalating culture war. It begins by offering some coordinates for understanding the current attacks on anti-racism before historicizing this culture war in relation to the longue durée of settlement. Turning to the practice of pedagogy, the chapter asks what is required in order for the classroom to be a site that, on one hand, allows for a confrontation with naturalized manifestations of racism and, on the other, creates the conditions for critical reflection and transformation. I argue that anti-racist pedagogy requires a confrontation with the violence of racism, as well as a readiness to attend to the ways that this violence becomes manifest in the classroom, through discourse, received history, presumed knowledge and affect. To acknowledge this possibility complicates recent calls for the classroom to be rendered a 'safe space'. Taking seriously the possibility of an encounter with racial violence requires that the teacher approach the question of safety as an ongoing process, and it is from this position that we can locate the possibility of anti-racist solidarity.

The war on anti-racism

On 21 June 2021, Senator Pauline Hanson, leader of the marginal populist political party One Nation, stood on the floor of the Australian Senate to introduce a motion that called on the then-sitting Coalition government to reject 'critical race theory' from the national education curriculum. Hanson's motion was triggered by the release of a draft of the proposed revised national curriculum in April that year. The national curriculum is a framework designed to provide consistency across primary and high school education systems (including public, private and religious schools) that are managed by different states and territories (Department of Education, 2022). The cause for objection by conservative politicians and commentators in response to the release of the draft was a set of changes to the teaching of 'Aboriginal and Torres Strait Islander Histories and Cultures' that underpin the curriculum and reflect First Nations people's calls for truth-telling in relation to the violences of settler colonialism (ACARA, 2021). While former curricula obscured the ongoing processes of invasion and occupation, stating that 'Aboriginal and Torres Strait Islander communities maintain a special connection to and responsibility for Country/Place', the revised curriculum proposed the following change: 'The occupation and colonization of Australia by the British, under the now overturned doctrine of *terra nullius*, were experienced by First Nations Australians as an invasion that denied their occupation of, and connection to, Country/Place' (ACARA, 2021: 9). While these changes were implemented in Version 9.0 of the curriculum in 2022, the politicization of the curriculum coincided with the release of the proposed changes and an accompanying ten-week period of feedback from April to July 2021.

Before turning to the moral panic that followed these proposed changes, it must be noted that the revisions themselves contain historical and political incongruities. In the first instance, to frame this history as 'the occupation and colonization of Australia' is an impossible construction, one that situates colonization as happening 'to' Australia – which is itself a settler-colonial construction – rather than to the many First Nations that preceded the construction of the settler nation-state. Such a move prefigures the emergence of 'Australia' and has the effect of rendering it preordained rather than the product of violent dispossession given by the terms 'invasion' and 'occupation'. In the second instance, the reference to First Nations 'Australians' imposes the authority of the nation-state – an authority that can be understood as illegitimate precisely because it arises from invasion and occupation – on top of the incommensurable sovereignty of First Nations that both precede settlement and continue, unbroken, despite it. Despite best intentions, the proposed revisions contribute to the naturalization of colonization. This, however, is *not* what catalysed the objection of increasingly vocal and aggressive conservatives. It was the very suggestion that colonization was a form of dispossession that has denied First Nations people access to, and connection with, Country that whipped the angry mob into action. Conservative think-tanks and media outlets – such as the Institute for Public Affairs, Sky News and *The Australian* – came out swinging, arguing that the revised draft curriculum 'highlighted the growing influence of critical race theory' and dismissing it as 'preoccupied with the oppression, discrimination and struggles of Indigenous Australians' (Urban, 2021).

It was in this context that Hanson's motion passed the Senate with the support of members of the then-sitting Coalition government. Here it must be noted that 'critical race theory' – which cannot be reduced to a single, monolithic theory but rather describes a diverse scholarly tradition that emerges from the nexus of critical legal studies and the US civil rights movement to theorize the way social, political and legal structures (re)produce racial inequalities and preserve the status quo – is not, nor has ever been, part of the Australian National Curriculum. The journey of 'critical race theory' from US academic institutions to the Australian Senate floor can be directly linked to the former-Liberal senator and former Assistant Attorney-General Amanda Stoker, who in April of 2021 applied pressure to the Australian Human Rights Commission to pull a tender after it invoked 'anti-racism' (Remeikis, 2021). The AUD140,000 tender was intended to enhance the Commission's campaign, 'Racism. It Stops With Me', and proposed the production of educational resources designed to supplement existing school curricula. The Commission did not invoke 'critical race theory' as part of its framing of the campaign, but the resource is framed as concerned with structural and systemic racism (AHRC, 2022). A related project, 'Racism. No Way', was launched in 2000 as a co-development between State and Territory Government education systems, the National Catholic Education Commission, the National Council of Independent Schools' Associations and the Commonwealth Department of Education, Training and Youth Affairs, and continues to be updated and used in schools (NSW Department of Education, 2000). So while Hanson's claims about the teaching of a national curriculum concerned with racial literacy stretched the truth, there is some substance to the idea that organized and publicly funded resources concerned with combating racism exist.

Stoker's justification for calling for the tender to be pulled was that it was being used to promote 'critical race theory' in schools, but her fixation on the mention of anti-racism betrays her actual concern: a fear that collective anti-racist mass movements are building momentum in the struggle to dismantle white supremacy and colonial capitalist exploitation. Racism, as Ambalavaner Sivanandan (2019: 147) pointed out during the British war on anti-racism waged under Margaret Thatcher, is 'hydra-headed, and rear[s] its different heads in different ways in different times (prosperity and depression) and in differing areas (employment, housing, schools) and different places (inner city, suburbia)'. Because racism is a many-headed hydra, Sivanandan (2019: 147) tells us that anti-racism is 'a portmanteau word meant to carry all these differing ideas and ways of combating racism'. It is a programme that insists everything must change, which is what makes it threatening to established orders. It is no surprise that the renewal of attacks on race critical pedagogy come in the aftermath of the mass uprisings that swept across the world in 2020, beginning with the irruption of riots across US cities in the wake of the killing of George Floyd by a Minneapolis police officer and that sparked solidarity actions across the world. In Australia, where Blackness and Indigeneity are irreducibly intertwined, the mass protests that took place in 2020 were simultaneous expressions of solidarity with the George Floyd rebellion and articulations of resistance to ongoing racialized state violence faced by First Nations people. Calls to end Indigenous deaths in custody and abolish the police and prisons rang loudly in the streets.

Writing two years on from the motion to ban 'critical race theory', and after a change of government, this event might be dismissed as a desperate attempt by Hanson's One Nation party and the conservative Liberal-National Coalition to stoke the fear of difference that has, in the past, reliably generated votes. There is also a temptation by centrist or progressive commentators to dismiss the event as the simple importation of American cultural politics into our domestic arena, an example of hysteria imported from elsewhere. While there may be some truth to the latter position, the ease with which moral panic spreads from one context to another should not be dismissed so lightly; rather, this trend indexes shared global conditions in which fascism is openly and publicly rearing its head. The condemnation of anti-racist movements is an attempt to maintain the current terms of order: the white possessive claim that underpins the settler colony; the equation of whiteness with property; the reproduction of the capital relation that exploits racial and gendered differentials in the ongoing project of accumulation. If education is, in part, an encounter with the history of concepts that allow us to make sense of the world, then it should come as no surprise that this has become a crucial terrain over which differing political forces attempt to win popular consent for their ideological programmes. Culture war attacks on curriculum extend from primary and high school education to Australian universities, which are caricatured as elitist institutions and hotbeds of radical leftism that are out of touch with the values and beliefs of 'everyday' people. Terms such as 'cultural Marxism' and 'wokeness' revive anti-communist red scare tactics that have been a continuous feature of liberal political discourse throughout the 20th century, deployed to describe an all-encompassing idea of 'political correctness' that supposedly curtails free speech and places hard limits on open discourse, social cohesion, economic prosperity and humour. Former Deputy Prime Minister John Anderson (2022) wrote that '[w]okeness is a direct attack on what Churchill called "variety", that is, different ways of thinking and living'. We must note the irony of the conservative appropriation of this term from its roots in US Black social life as a vernacular expression to describe practices of survival and political consciousness-raising in the context of racial segregation in the late 19th and early 20th centuries. One of the earliest appearances of the phrase on record is a spoken word coda to a 1938 protest song by the inimitable Blues musician Lead Belly called 'Scottsboro Boys', which documents a legal case considered to be a miscarriage of justice in which nine Black teenagers were accused of raping two white women in Alabama, an event that led to extra-judicial white supremacist lynch mobs taking to the streets. At the conclusion of the song, Lead Belly says, 'I made this little song about down there. So I advise everybody, be a little careful when they go along through there – best stay woke, keep their eyes open' (Lead Belly, 2015 [1938]).

The conservative redefinition of 'woke' as out-of-control political correctness involves positioning dominant ideologies – such as the naturalization of settler colonialism and white supremacy, or the equation of gender with a binarized conception of biological sex and the reproduction of heteronormativity – as marginalized. Well-established social norms, and by extension the large swathes of the population that adhere to them, are cast in the role of victims under attack by 'neo-Marxist and postmodern ideology' (Anderson, 2022). This inversion of power relations should be understood as an act of censorship that attempts to protect racism, transphobia and homophobia from condemnation and critique. Statements like Anderson's diminish and marginalize those who experience racialized and gendered structures of domination, trapping discourse in questions of intention rather than effect and keeping the focus on isolated incidents. This discursive sleight-of-hand casts racism and other forms of domination as a right to expression rather than an act of violence.

Attacks on 'wokeness' are not relegated to the margins, but have penetrated mainstream discourse, entering the halls and chambers of parliament, dominating national news coverage and becoming the stuff of water-cooler conversations. The success of conservative culture war strategies can be seen in Anthony Albanese's assertion to commentator Joe Hildebrand during an interview during the 2022 federal election campaign: 'I am NOT woke' (Hildebrand, 2022). That the leader the Labor Party, the political party with historic ties to the workers' movement and progressive social platforms, would take such pains to distance himself from social movements that oppose racism, sexism, homophobia and transphobia indexes both the culmination of his party's long march into conservatism and the widespread adoption of conservative definitions of 'wokeism'. Casting himself as an 'everyman', Albanese would go on to win that election and become prime minister.

Historicizing the culture wars

The culture war in which we find ourselves requires historicization. We can trace it through the so-called history wars that were ignited by the conservative Prime Minister John Howard in the mid-1990s; he articulated a vision of nationalism grounded in a celebration of Britishness that turned away from the realities of colonial violence and dispossession. Howard's dismissal of what came to be disparagingly termed 'black armband history' sought to recentre the notion of Australia as a white possession and did so, as Aileen Moreton-Robinson (2015: 20) points out, by mobilizing within the white body politic 'both the fear of Asian "invasion" and of "dispossession" by Indigenous people'. One can follow this culture war all the way back, in fact, to the acts of invasion and occupation that led to the establishment of a British colony on sovereign Aboriginal land. The settler colony is no mere transfer of ownership from one authority to another, but describes a system of rule motivated by access to land on which settlers arrive with the explicit intention of making a new society. The historian Patrick Wolfe states:

> Territoriality, the fusion of people and land, is settler colonialism's specific, irreducible element. Settlers' seizure of Native's land is not simply a transfer of ownership. That can occur in a regular fashion within a system of ownership – by sale, inheritance, foreclosure and the like, rival claims being resolvable by appropriate arbitration. Rather

than replacing one owner with another, settlers seek to replace an entire system of ownership with another. The settler/Native confrontation, in other words, is not between claims to ownership but between frameworks for allocating ownerships. It is between sovereignties, which are primordially external to one another. (Wolfe, 2016: 34)

Moreton-Robinson (2021) extends this analysis by describing this confrontation as a clash between 'incommensurable sovereignties'. Indigenous ontologies, she writes, 'are inextricably connected to being in and of our lands. This is an inherent sovereignty not temporally constrained' (Moreton-Robinson, 2021: 259). In this assertion, we are reminded that Indigenous sovereignty both precedes the imposition of settler sovereignty *and* cannot be structurally incorporated within the jurisdictional limits of the settler state. As a result, the settler state attempts to resolve the problem of incommensurable Indigenous sovereignty through, as Patrick Wolfe (2006) famously theorized, violent logics of elimination and replacement. Working in concert with varied techniques of racial domination are a range of discursive strategies that come together to produce what Moreton-Robinson (2015: xi) terms the 'possessive logics of patriarchal white sovereignty'. The concept of possessive logics, for Moreton-Robinson, refers to

> a mode of rationalization, rather than a set of positions that produce a more or less inevitable answer, that is underpinned by an excessive desire to invest in reproducing and reaffirming the nation-state's ownership, control, and domination. As such, white possessive logics are operationalized within discourses to circulate sets of meanings about ownership of the nation, as part of commonsense knowledge, decision making, and socially produced conventions. (Moreton-Robinson, 2015: xii)

Possessive logics of patriarchal white sovereignty are reproduced in myriad ways: through law and policy; through the media and public discourse; in collective acts such as the booing of the Indigenous Australian Football League players Adam Goodes and Lance Franklin. Subjects, too, can embody possessive logics, and Moreton-Robinson (2015: xii) offers the example of the conservative commentator Andrew Bolt's breach of the Racial Discrimination Act 1975 in 2011, in which he accused ' "fair-skinned" Aboriginal people of only claiming their Aboriginal identity in order to gain access to social and economic benefits'. The current iteration of the culture wars – with its attacks on 'critical race theory' and 'wokeness' – adheres to the possessive logics of patriarchal white sovereignty, seeking to naturalize the white possessive claim that is foundational to the establishment of the settler colony. Albanese's eschewal of 'wokeness' reveals the success of conservatives to render the term a crude container for all of those things we find in arts and humanities programmes of universities, such as social theories of race and gender, and analyses of structures that shape social relations. In this picture, 'critical race theory' comes to act as a catch-all for any critical analytic work concerned with theorizing and unpacking what race *is*, and equally importantly, what race *does*. In the moral panic of the culture wars, diverse theories, debates and practices are reduced to a singular homogenizing position that misrepresents the breadth of race critical work as stoking existing social divisions and preaching hatred. Here we might more accurately understand the war waged on 'critical race theory' as an attack on the heterogeneity of race critical theories.

If critical theories understand race as a floating system of signification and a way of organizing and meaningfully classifying the world, as Stuart Hall (2021b [1997]) described it, in order that we might ultimately undo the way this system of meaning is linked to domination and exploitation, then the attacks on such a project can only be understood as a defence of current racial orderings of the world. What is really at stake in all this talk of culture war – in the shifting objects and terms that become new moral panics for constellations of conservatives, liberals and fascists to coalesce around – is the maintenance of a hegemonic ideology that is coming under attack by people made surplus to the needs of capital, whose forms of struggle insist on a world beyond racialized and gendered forms of domination. The culture wars are not merely a struggle over semantics, or a struggle disconnected from political-economic realities, but rather an expression of historic and economic conditions that in turn shapes the distribution of social and political power.

Teaching race, confronting violence

In 1980, in the midst of the large-scale economic and political restructuring of the United Kingdom that we commonly call Thatcherism, the cultural theorist Stuart Hall delivered an informal talk to the London branch of the Association of Teachers of Social Science that reflected on the challenges of teaching race: 'You have to recognize the strong emotional ideological commitments people have to positions about race—this isn't an area where people simply think they know things but it is very strongly charged emotionally and this fact has to be recognized and be brought out' (Hall, 2021a: 123–4). Hall implores the teacher who enters the classroom with their own lived commitment to anti-racism to not only recognize the uncomfortable presence of racism lurking beneath the surface of the classroom, but to draw it out, to make these naturalized and emotionally charged positions the substance of the classroom. 'I do think you have to create an atmosphere which allows people to say unpopular things', Hall tells us. 'I don't think it is at all valuable to have an atmosphere in the classroom, which is so clearly, unmistakably antiracist that the natural and "commonsense" racism which is part of the ideological air we all breathe is not allowed to come out and express itself' (Hall, 2021a: 124). What are we to make of Hall's imperative? And how is one to create an atmosphere in which people can say unpopular things without putting the wellbeing of other students or themselves at undue risk?

One way to begin is by acknowledging the seeming impossibility of these two positions: to create the conditions in which the 'ideological air we all breathe' is allowed to express itself places certain limitations on the classroom as a safe space. We cannot proceed from the presumption that the classroom will be free from certain forms of violence. To be clear, I am speaking about epistemological and ideological violence rather than physical violence – although, of course, the former underpins the latter. To recognize that ever-present threat of violence in the classroom perhaps feels like shaky ground from which to commence, dangerously close to the territory of conservatives who invoke 'free speech' or 'academic freedom' while attacking 'trigger warnings' and 'wokeism' in order to continue to espouse racism and transphobia and other forms of hate speech under the guise of scholarship and pedagogy. A simpler departure point would be loudly and boldly proclaiming that the classroom *is* a safe space that simply will not tolerate the articulation of racism and other forms of structural domination. But the ideological air we breathe unfortunately permeates such proclamations. As Christina Sharpe (2016: 104) puts it, 'the weather is the totality of our environments; the weather is the total climate; and that climate is anti-black'. Considering this statement from the settler colony of Australia involves reflecting on the irreducible relation between Blackness and Indigeneity – the total climate is shaped by the confrontation between settler and Indigenous sovereignties.

What, then, does it mean to understand that violence is present in the space of the classroom that deals with the social, cultural, economic and political relations? To accept such a proposition might entail that we rethink safety as the dominant paradigm that governs how to approach the classroom ethically. Or it might lead us to rethink what is meant by safety, understanding it not as something that can be established at the outset of a class or course, but as that which must constantly be negotiated in relation to what arises within the classroom. Safety not as an absolute but as an orientation. The task of the teacher is to mediate the classroom environment in order to collectively stage an encounter with the ideological air we breathe, analysing how the total climate within which we live relates to a series of structures, as well as how it comes to be naturalized and presented as the way things have always been. Put another way, the concept of safety as an operative method for teaching refers not to the eradication of violence from the classroom, but to an approach that allows a managed confrontation with it. The articulation of naturalized ideological positions – such as the legitimacy of settler sovereignty (the Australian nation-state) – might necessarily involve the surfacing of things that Hall (2021a: 124) notes are 'pretty horrendous to hear'. And the experience of hearing these things will be experienced differentially by students depending on their own relation to ethnicity, race and other markers of identity. The violence that haunts the classroom is unevenly distributed, yet there is simply no way of absolutely safeguarding against it even if we wished to.

Violence, then, might be understood as an unavoidable feature of pedagogy, especially those pedagogies that seek to contribute to the struggle of transforming the social toward liberatory ends. Recall Frantz Fanon (1963: 35–6), who wrote that 'decolonization is always a violent phenomenon. Decolonization, which sets out to change the order of the world, is, obviously, a programme of complete disorder. But it cannot come as a result of magical practices, nor of a natural shock, nor of a friendly understanding'. I want to be careful not to collapse Fanon's materialist analysis into the realm of metaphor and to take seriously his insistence that decolonization is a material struggle to overturn colonial rule and repatriate land. My invocation of Fanon is not an appeal to 'decolonize pedagogy' via such strategies as the diversification of reading lists (even if this has pedagogical importance), but about the role that violence might play in the transformation of social relations within the classroom. If we follow Hall's (2021a: 124) call to 'create an atmosphere in which those questions [of race] can openly and honestly be discussed', acknowledging that such an atmosphere involves the possibility of an encounter with ideologies underpinned by violence, then we might also consider what this confrontation with violence enables. The capacity to name and unpack naturalized ideological positions is crucial to the project of unsettling them. In order to unsettle what appears to be common sense, we must, as teachers, move quickly from individual manifestations of racism to their structural underpinnings – that is, we must show how individual expressions arise from specific social and historical conditions. We must move beyond reductive notions that racism describes a form of prejudice that is singularly locatable in the actions of individuals – the commonsense idea of a 'bad apple' that spoils the otherwise healthy crate. This framing of racism is reproduced even by campaigns that seek to do more and interrogate the structural underpinnings of individual behaviours. Recall the Australian Human Rights Commission's campaign 'Racism. It Stops With Me' or Australian schooling resource 'Racism. No Way' with which this chapter began, and that was the cause of so much consternation among conservative politicians. The use of the full-stop after racism in both cases betrays the fantasy that racism is self-evident and able to be clearly identified, and that it is located within individuals rather than emerging from an interplay between historical, economic and political forces. The effect is to locate the struggle against racism as an individual rather than collective project. Against this rendering, we must insist that racism describes acts of racial ascription that arise from specific economic and political conditions and that, via repetition, come to create the impression that race is a stable entity. In other words, race is produced by racism and not the other way around.

To approach the teaching of race with attention to its structural foundations requires an interdisciplinary approach to teaching that is capable of thinking across political economy, sociological, biology, media, culture and technology. But, as Hall (2021a: 126) notes, 'no matter how deep you go into structural factors, you need to show that they do generate particular interactions between groups of people, but you have to be able to show that you can get a deeper understanding of those surface relations'. Consider, for example, the statistic at the time of writing that Aboriginal and Torres Strait Islander people account for 32 per cent of all incarcerated people across Australia, despite only comprising 3.8 per cent of the total Australian population (Australian Bureau of Statistics, 2022). It is not, unfortunately, uncommon to hear people invoke this staggering statistic presented as 'evidence' of innate criminality or deviance. In the classroom, one might move from this surface position to an account of the historical structure of settler colonialism, noting that the establishment of the colony is motivated by a desire to expropriate land. In the context of the Australian colony, a ready supply of convict labour would be put to work by the British to transform the newly established colony into a successful pastoral economy. As such, from the inception of the colony, First Nations people were rendered a surplus population to be eliminated or managed through the coercive mechanisms of police and prisons. The movement from a singular expression of racism to an interrogation of its historical and structural underpinning enables a comprehension of the way race is reproduced over time. The movement from the surface to the structural does not inevitably lead to transformation, but it is one crucial way in which the perceived stability of 'the way things are' is forced to encounter the weight of its own construction.

In making space for dominant ideology to be openly articulated, we encounter the possibility of twin violences, both of which must be navigated with care and caution: on the one hand, there is the violence that negatively racialized students might experience when the classroom becomes a space for the interrogation of the racist air that we are forced to breathe as an everyday reality; on the other, there is the possibility of violence directed inward by the student who confronts, perhaps for the first time, their own ingrained and naturalized racism and is shocked by what that confrontation engenders. Teaching race must be animated by a commitment to create the conditions in which the latter might occur while doing what is possible to safeguard negatively racialized students from potential harms. Of course, it should be noted that classrooms are never unidirectional exchanges solely determined by the actions of the teacher. My own experiences of teaching race have been shaped by the generosity and rigour that students show towards each other and to me in the process of collectively confronting violence. The movement from surface manifestation to structural examination and back again is one way to confront this violence without either validating the articulation of racism or rendering the exercise a performance of anti-racism that forecloses the possibility of analysis and learning.

To approach the teaching of race in this way requires that we proceed, to repurpose another of Hall's (1986) phrases, into a politics without guarantees. For Hall, the idea of a politics without guarantees was first developed to push back against a conception of politics that was solely determined by economic conditions of production that would, as such, inevitably lead to immediate class unity. Building on the work of Antonio Gramsci, Hall argued that hegemonic power is something that has to be constructed and maintained – an open-ended process in which dominant classes develop shifting strategies to maintain their influence. By extension, resistance to hegemonic power is not a given, not merely found in shared class or race relations but in the identification of mutual interests. It is at the intersection of the twin violences that code the race-critical classroom that we might find the possibility of shared commitment to anti-racist struggle. Attention to the structural interrelations of race, class, gender, sexuality and ability can engender a recognition that the violence of racial capitalism is a violence that is killing us all, albeit in markedly different ways. In other words, it is here that we can locate the possibility of a solidarity that is grounded in incommensurable difference – attentive to both the way colonial capitalism shapes social life *and* the differential experiences of its harm.

Anti-racist solidarity beyond diversity

To frame the teaching of race in relation to the cultivation of solidarity is to imagine a pedagogy invested not only in understanding race but in the project of dismantling it. Despite the framing of universities as hotbeds of leftism, advocating for institutional support of anti-racism initiatives within the governance structures of contemporary universities offers little promise of meaningful action. The language of diversity and inclusion has come to replace the paradigm of anti-racism, shifting the fight against the reproduction of racializing grammars within institutions towards a representational politics largely concerned with the ever more granular production of metrics that account for the cultural and ethnic composition of student and staff bodies. One impact of the granularity of cultural diversity reporting has been the fragmentation of multi-ethnic, anti-racist coalitions that have historically come together around experiences of racism. 'The language of diversity, masquerading as anti-racism, has become completely unmoored from social meaning', writes Tithi Bhattacharya (2021). She goes on to argue that the horizon of diversity initiatives within large institutions such as universities has become the production of an optics of inclusion in which 'women and people of color are now hired as purveyors of violence to shield the system from criticism'. Bhattacharya repurposes Cheryl Harris's concept of predatory inclusion, which was originally used to describe the way Black families in the United States were trapped by predatory mortgages in the name of economic inclusion, to describe the elevation of culturally diverse people to positions of power within large institutions. Here institutional diversity and inclusion initiatives can be understood as expressions of what Sara Ahmed (2006) calls 'the non-performativity of antiracism'. Ahmed explains that

> documents that are authorized by institutions (such as race-equality policies, which are often signed by, say, the vice-chancellor on behalf of an institution), make claims about the institution (for instance, by describing the institution as having certain qualities, such as being diverse), or point toward future action (by committing an institution to a course of action, such as diversity or equality, which in turn might involve the commitment of resources) [function as non-performatives because] they 'work' precisely by not bringing about the effects that they name. (Ahmed, 2006: 104–5)

In this theorization, Ahmed inverts J.L. Austin's account of performative speech acts, which posited that an utterance is performative when it instantiates a material change. The famous example that Austin gives is the marriage vow: the speaking of the words 'I do' enact a material transformation in which one changes legal and social status. Judith Butler would later extend Austin's speech act theory into a larger theory of performativity that focuses on the way social constructions such as the gender binary emerge not via singular or one-off acts, but 'as the reiterative and citational practice by which discourse produces the effects that it names' (Ahmed, 2006: 105). The concept of non-performativity describes speech acts that do *not* bring about the effects they name. Such discourse conversely upholds and extends the opposite of that which it names, namely the status quo.

If institutional governance is not the answer to how we might develop anti-racist pedagogies within the university, then what is? Or how can we teach race in order to find and foster multi-ethnic, anti-racist coalitions within institutions that are at best indifferent, and at worst hostile, to the project of dismantling race as a structure of domination? The answer lies in the classroom itself, which remains relatively autonomous despite the ever-increasing layers of governance that surround the teaching and learning. Fred Moten and Stefano

Harney (2013: 126–31) teach us that when we enter the classroom, we retain the possibility of refusing to call the classroom to order, an act that constitutes a refusal to become an instrument of governance. In the minor gesture of refusing to call the classroom to order, we can find the conditions in which study can proceed unshackled from the strictures of university governance: learning outcomes, assessment criteria, non-performative diversity frameworks and so on. To refuse the call to order, however, is not to disavow the authority of the teacher, whose very presence cannot but alter the atmosphere of the learning space. Rather, it is to suggest that this small gesture might move against forms of governance that are designed to safeguard against the risk of violence in order to stage a confrontation with them. It is in the confrontation with that which is uncomfortable – or even, as Hall suggests, horrendous to hear – that we can establish the conditions for a form of collective study conducive to the production of anti-racist solidarities. The task of the teacher is to manage this encounter without their authority weighing too heavily upon proceedings. Teaching race must involve cultivating an open and honest atmosphere in which reflections on the naturalization of racism can move, with care, into interrogations of the way racial regimes are structured and constructed. This task remains vital in the context of a culture war that seeks to demonize the diverse and varied practices that are concerned with abolishing race and that can be grouped under the umbrella of anti-racism. The teaching of race must proceed as a politics without guarantees.

References

ACARA (Australian Curriculum, Assessment and Reporting Authority) (2021) *Review of the Australian Curriculum F-10: Cross-Curriculum Priorities – Aboriginal and Torres Strait Islander Histories and Cultures*, https://www.australiancurriculum.edu.au/media/7137/ccp_atsi_histories_and_cultures_consultation.pdf

Ahmed, A. (2006) 'The nonperformativity of antiracism', *Meridians*, 27(1): 104–26.

AHRC (Australian Human Rights Commission) (2022) *Racism. It Stops With Me*, https://itstopswithme.humanrights.gov.au/about-the-campaign

Anderson, J. (2022) 'Why we must fight back against the forces of woke', *The Australian*, 28 August, https://www.theaustralian.com.au/inquirer/why-we-must-fight-back-against-the-forces-of-woke/news-story/e2c28884f1508f13763308a11d319c13

Australian Bureau of Statistics (2023) *Prisoners in Australia*, Canberra: ABS, https://www.abs.gov.au/statistics/people/crime-and-justice/prisoners-australia/2022

Bhattacharya, T. (2021) 'Fuck mindfulness workshops', *Spectre Journal*, 24 March, https://spectrejournal.com/fuck-mindfulness-workshops/?fbclid=IwAR1ZLOSDbIR-8xz8_7-q2AZvmYtBFgpOLrc1uxbewGbJI-KCtSJ0vhKWc80

Department of Education (2022) *Australian Curriculum*, https://www.education.gov.au/australian-curriculum

Fanon, F. (1963) *The Wretched of the Earth*, trans Constance Farington, New York: Grove Press.

Hall, S. (1986) 'The problem of ideology: Marxism without guarantees', *Journal of Communication Inquiry*, 10(2): 28–44.

Hall, S. (2021a) 'Teaching race', in P. Gilroy and R.W. Gilmore (eds), *Selected Writings on Race and Difference*, Durham, NC: Duke University Press, pp 123–35.

Hall, S. (2021b [1997]) 'Race, the floating signifier: What more is there to say about "race"?' in P. Gilroy and R.W. Gilmore (eds), *Selected Writings on Race and Difference*, Durham, NC: Duke University Press, pp 359–73.

Hildebrand, J. (2022) 'Albo's rapid-fire answers on Captain Cook, China', *Herald-Sun*, 22 March, https://www.heraldsun.com.au/news/national/federal-election/federal-election-2022-anthony-albanese-to-change-labors-class-war-rhetoric/news-story/f276923ff8dc247f89c38472ccc4ab6e

Lead Belly (2015 [1938]) 'Scottsboro Boys', recorded 1938, on *Lead Belly: The Smithsonian Folkways Collection*, SFW40201.

Moreton-Robinson, A. (2015) *The White Possessive: Property, Power, and Indigenous Sovereignty*, Minneapolis: University of Minnesota Press.

Moreton-Robinson, A. (2021) 'Incommensurable sovereignties: Indigenous ontology matters', in B. Hokowhitu, A. Moreton-Robinson, L. Tuhiwai-Smith, C. Andersen and S. Larkin (eds), *Routledge Handbook of Critical Indigenous Studies*, New York: Routledge, pp 257–68.

Moten, F. and Harney, S. (2013) *The Undercommons: Fugitive Planning and Black Study*, Wivenhoe: Minor Compositions.

NSW Department of Education (2000) *Racism. No Way*, https://racismnoway.com.au

Remeikis, A. (2021) 'Human Rights Commission vows to continue anti-racism program after Amanda Stoker complaint', *The Guardian*, 28 April.

Sharpe, C. (2016) *In the Wake: On Blackness and Being*, Durham, NC: Duke University Press.

Sivanandan, A. (2019) 'Left, right and burnage: No such thing as anti-racist ideology', in *Communities of Resistance: Writing on Black Struggles for Socialism*, London: Verso, pp 145–52.

Urban, R. (2021) 'Curriculum pushes radical racial theory', *The Australian*, 23 May, https://www.theaustralian.com.au/nation/politics/curriculum-pushes-radical-racial-theory/news-story/2bfb3f27df48975438a1808480ee7dcb

Wolfe, P. (2006) 'Settler colonialism and the elimination of the native', *Journal of Genocide Research*, 8(4): 387–409.

Wolfe, P. (2016) *Traces of History: Elementary Structures of Race*, London: Verso.

21

In Conversation with Alana Lentin: Racial Literacy – an Act of Solidarity

Debbie Bargallie and Alana Lentin

DB: Alana Lentin, you and I got to know each other around 2019 when, as the then President of the Australian Critical Race and Whiteness Studies Association (ACRAWSA), you asked me whether I would stand for a position on the executive committee. This was after you had examined my PhD thesis the previous year.

AL: Yes, I was looking back through my emails to see when it was we first started corresponding, because we had met before at the ACRAWSA conference in 2014, very briefly, and again at a dinner in Sydney, but we never really had the opportunity to chat properly. Your email was so kind. You wrote, 'Now that I am officially Dr Debbie Bargallie, I wanted to reach out and thank you for examining my thesis. I honestly had no idea that you were marking it and I feel so honoured and proud that you examined my thesis. Your comments were so detailed, considerate and constructive and really gave me an incentive to advance my work.' I was really moved by that, because I felt honoured to have been asked to examine your thesis and it's been such a thrill to see it developed into your first book, *Unmasking the Racial Contract*. You also wrote, 'I hope that we can get to do some race work together in the future.'

DB: Yes. And we have been doing that work. After I joined the ACRAWSA committee in 2019, we started working closely together and, in 2020, during COVID-19, and after our term at ACRAWSA ended, we applied for a research grant on racial literacy. We didn't get that, which was instructive as to the kind of research that gets funded and the kind that doesn't. It seems very hard to get institutional support when you emphasize race as a technology of colonial power rather than, for example, racist discrimination that occurs within given circumstances.

AL: Yes, I have resigned myself to not getting research funding. But that is okay for me because I have the advantage of being a full professor and of not having my legitimacy as a researcher questioned by the university. It's not so simple for negatively racialized scholars, early career researchers or people who are trying to enter the academy. People don't have the same luxury of refusing to play the grant game. All of this is not dissociable from the advantages I have as a white, middle-class European woman.

DB: Yes, but it's important to say that you are also Jewish. How does that impact your understanding of race, anti-racism and racial literacy?

AL: It is foundational to my experience and understanding. But it's not simple or straightforward. Within multiculturalism, there is a reductiveness, a flattening out of how racialization emplaces people differently and how that changes across time and space. So, from the perspective of the state, it treats people as members of these different, but supposedly equal, minority groups, organized around a white core, without much thought given – until more recently perhaps – to how we are all positioned in relation to the ongoing practices of colonization and the consequent dispossession of Indigenous peoples. So, as someone who has migrated multiple times across the course of my life, being Jewish – whatever that means to me as an individual – is necessarily relational to where I am. And of course, that is also articulated with gender and class.

So, I was born in occupied Palestine, the descendant of Romanian Jews who, on my mother's side, had fled fascism. I moved to Ireland shortly after because that is where my Dad is from. His grandfather came from Lithuania as a 14-year-old boy in the late 1800s, sent alone by his family to avoid being conscripted by the Imperial Russian Army as a Jew. This was a common migration story. Growing up in Catholic Ireland in the 1970s and 1980s was a very different experience to, let's say, that of a white Jewish person in London, Paris or New York, even Sydney or Melbourne. There was a tiny number of Jews. But when I left Dublin, and lived in the United Kingdom, in various places in Europe and now Australia since 2012, my racialized positioning changed, and of course I always benefited from whiteness.

I find it is interesting how I am apprehended as an anticolonial – specifically an anti-Zionist – Jew who does not hold back on my political allegiance with the fight for Palestinian self-determination. Although it is not a majority position, I have heard it said in some quarters that I must be posturing to gain 'anti-racist brownie points'. There is something profoundly anti-Semitic about the insistence that all Jews must be Zionist, whether than comes from the right or the left. I have to say that this doubting of my true commitment has led to my place as a race scholar and anti-racist activist being questioned in Australia. But I think that, in addition to other reasons, this is also because of the lack of a solid community of race scholar-activists here, which is a structural problem.

DB: Yes, throughout this book, various contributors have discussed the problems of doing race scholarship and teaching in Australia because of the lack of infrastructure. How do you think that impacts racial literacy here?

AL: It is very hard doing this work when there is little to no community. However, I also resist the notion that there is no one doing this work. As this book and your research project show, there are actually many scholars doing critical research and teaching across the continent. The problem is joining it up because of a lack of opportunity and structure. There are no programmes, centres or departments dedicated to the study of race and people are doing their work often alone or teaching within other modules. In fact, looking back over old emails again, I came across another one from ACRAWSA in 2016, inviting me to give a talk at a symposium (which eventually didn't take place). It read: 'As you well know, whereas the UK and US can point to a strong anti-racist intellectual tradition, the same arguably cannot be said of Australia. The symposium may consider the circumstances of this absence and whether it is now timely to introduce dedicated postgraduate courses examining theories of race and ethnicity.'

So this absence is a widely acknowledged problem, one that has not yet been resolved.

Indeed, I think I am one of the only academics at an Australian university who teaches a full subject on race at both undergraduate and postgraduate levels. But the question for me is not so much whether this work is being done – it is, even without the structures – but how to build community to sustain the work and ourselves. The lack of community breeds a notion of reinventing the wheel; everyone is forging out on their own, braving a new frontier. Or others imagine themselves as having been the only ones, without giving due recognition to the work of others, whose work is perhaps less cited, or less internationally recognized, but important nonetheless. I might be so bold as to say that if those of us with more secure positions and established networks did more to create opportunities for others, then we might have the community we so desperately need. But power hoarding is a problem within neoliberal academia, a minefield that is only exacerbated under colonial conditions.

DB: So, as someone who had already published several books and international recognition as a race-critical scholar before coming to work in Sydney, what do you do to foster those opportunities?

AL: When I first came to Sydney in 2012, there was rather more institutional support for activities from within my university. Over the years, as we all know, budgets have become tighter and there is less internal funding available for initiatives that don't necessarily lead to big research grants. This is an institutional problem that affects marginalized areas of study like ours especially. But in the early days, I organized various events, such as a symposium on the fiction of post-racialism in 2013, or master classes on Islamophobia or asylum seeker detention. I instigated a public engagement series that was massively successful. We had a brilliant event on race and comedy, for example, and another on resisting Islamophobia through art. Then the funding was cut, despite the fact that we had a large turnout and our second event was broadcast on ABC Radio National. It was said that this was my 'special interest topic' and not of general relevance. I found this strange, as Western Sydney University is of course easily in the most racially 'diverse' region in Australia, so how is race a minoritarian topic? This, to me, says a lot about how the academy considers the significance of race as an area of study and public interest. I think there is embarrassment among, particularly white, academics. I think they often don't know where to look when you say the word 'race'. Interestingly, this is improving in recent years, especially due to the struggle of Indigenous Black Lives Matter and Palestinian organizers. I think, against the backdrop of the global Movement for Black Lives, that certain things became untenable and could no longer be ignored. But that, of course, also precipitates other problems, such as cooptation and the consequent watering down of activist demands.

DB: Could you maybe say a bit more about that before you go on?
AL: Things have certainly fired up since 2020, less regarding race scholarship specifically, but definitely in terms of Indigenous studies. There is a lot more institutional support for Indigenous academics and students, the bolstering of funding for research and infrastructure. This is absolutely vital. But, as you and I argued in a few articles we wrote about racial literacy, there is a problem of collapsing things together. I think, from the institutional perspective, the thinking is that if support is given to Indigenous studies, then that also deals with the question of race. On the one hand, yes, redressing the atrocious marginalization of Indigenous scholarship and representation of Indigenous activists and students is vital. However, Indigenous studies and race studies, as many Indigenous race critical scholars have pointed out, are not the same thing (cf Kauanui Kēhaulani, 2008). In other words, you don't get more racial literacy by dealing with the problem of representation alone. This is like dealing with the problem of institutional racism via a human resources (hiring) strategy. That does not deal with the problem of a systemically racist institution.

The problem with regard to the growing institutionalization of Indigenous studies is a bit different because there is a bit more room for Indigenous leadership and decision-making (although this is still far from adequate). But while people can now speak more openly about Australia's colonial 'legacies' and even about ongoing 'gaps' in Indigenous and non-Indigenous opportunities and access, or about the injustice of Indigenous incarceration and deaths in custody, this does not automatically translate into a commitment to investing in studying what, from a race critical perspective, the root of these problems is: the persistence of racial-colonialism and its embeddedness in institutions, politics, law and culture, including universities.

As we wrote, after Black Lives Matter, when race and racism were more openly on the agenda, we started to hear talk of racial literacy, but within existing frameworks, such as cultural competency, which have long been used to talk about structural racism against Indigenous people (Bargallie and Lentin, 2020). In this framing, Indigenous people are badly served by institutions such as healthcare, due to a lack of cultural understanding from settlers. However, a race-critical stance would say the problem is not a lack of understanding or appreciation for Indigenous culture – a heavily essentialist notion to begin with, which cannot be generalized across different Indigenous peoples – but rather it should be plainly named as institutional racism. You do not need to have an in-depth understanding of someone's culture to not treat them in a racist manner. The fact is that a white Australian person does not have to know the first thing about Swedish culture, for example, but a white Swedish person would not run the risk of being 'made vulnerable to premature death', as Ruth Wilson Gilmore (2006) puts it, if she comes into contact with an institution of the Australian state.

The point is that Australian universities do not deal with the problem of the lack of racial literacy that feeds structural racism merely by supporting Indigenous studies. It also remains to be seen what the longevity of this investment will be. I don't want to sound overly cynical, but we should be attuned to what has happened elsewhere – for example, in the United Kingdom and United States, where Black studies scholars, hired in the wake of Black Lives Matter in 2020, have subsequently been fired, or even whole centres shut down. This is not the same as the right-wing political attacks on critical race theory and ethnic studies in the United States. This is about the shutting down of programmes citing 'budgetary reasons', particularly in the wake of COVID-19, where money becomes the reason to axe long fought-for programmes of study seen to be serving a minority community. This is, of course, silly. As the great Trinidadian anti-colonial scholar C.L.R. James (1992 [1969]) remarked in 1969: 'Now to talk to me about black studies as if it's something that concerned black people is an utter denial. This is the history of Western Civilization. I can't see it otherwise. This is the history that black people and white people and all serious students of modern history and the history of the world have to know. To say it's some kind of ethnic problem is a lot of nonsense.'

As he said in an interview the following year (James, 1970), Black people are best equipped to do this work, but that doesn't mean it is only for Black people. I fear that, rather than investing in the serious work of scholarship, universities take a trickle-down approach centred around narratives of 'Black excellence' and the like. According to this, having what Joy James has acerbically referred to as 'Black faces in high places' (she was referring to Barack Obama and Condoleeza Rice) will have a positive knock-on effect for other, less-monied Black people (Yancy, 2021). However, history has taught us otherwise. The lack of activism within Australian campuses feeds into this problem. Who will fight for Indigenous studies if they come under attack? Again, we can learn lessons from overseas as we see critical race and ethnic studies programmes being decimated in parts of the United States. Black studies scholars such as Charisse Burden-Stelly (2016) have written about the problem of Black studies being coopted by academia, invariably leading to a watering down of the demands for what Joshua Myers (2023), Robin D.G. Kelly and others call Black study, to distinguish it from the institutional appropriation signified by 'Black studies'. What happens when there is a gulf between the people and the academy?

There are many academics, particularly Indigenous, who are grounded in community. However, there is a lot of extractive work being done too, in which people latch onto the latest thing and hoover up research money to work with, say, refugee African communities or Muslim women. Scholars from these communities have been highly critical of these tendencies, but we shouldn't shy away from the fact that, in order to secure a scholarship or a post-doc in academia, they often accept to work on such projects, often led by white academics who need their insider status to gain access to these groups. Is the problem worse in Australia than elsewhere? No. But maybe it seems more apparent because of the lack of visibility of more critical work that purposefully refuses these engagements. I wrote a few years ago about what I called the 'postracial silences' in migration studies (Lentin, 2014) and we could apply the same analysis to what I call 'racism studies' – to distinguish them from race-critical studies – more broadly. It is the failure to centre race as a mechanism that continually produces and reproduces hierarchies and divisions for the benefit of more effective white rule that feeds this vicious circle. But it is clear why this situation is perpetuated, because it does not serve individual careers. Academia is the hunger games, as you once wrote to me in an email!

DB: Alana, you cover a lot of useful ground in your analyses to link the extractive and competitive processes and practices of research funding, with the uncritical approaches to doing race in the academy. And you are correct that framing race through a cultural lens and offering greater representation will not uproot the persistence of racial-colonialism and its embeddedness in institutions, politics, law, culture and so on. Your teaching syllabus is unique in this regard, and beyond that, your generosity in sharing this knowledge, teaching materials and pedagogies online through your blog and extra-curricular initiatives are brilliant examples of innovative and effective forms of building racial literacy. Going back to the

	question of your own contribution, you were saying that your initiatives no longer get as much support as they did ten years ago.
AL:	Yes, I have to say that I still managed to get some funding through circuitous routes, for example to support the 2018 symposium we organized as ACRAWSA on race, Blackness and Indigeneity with Alexander Weheliye and Irene Watson among many other wonderful speakers. We were also able to support Patricia Hill Collins' trip to Australia in 2020, including a master class at Western Sydney University and of course her keynote at the 2020 ACRAWSA conference. During COVID-19, in 2021, we organized an online panel on critical race in Australia where you spoke alongside Aileen Moreton-Robinson, among others. We had a huge turnout for that. In 2023, together with my colleague, Quah Ee-Ling, we organized an online seminar series, 'Radical Antiracism Today', with a marvellous lineup of speakers. So, of course, these things are happening – on a shoestring budget, I might add. However, they are not the same as building community. What I do in that sphere is a lot less visible than the events I help organize. It includes creating opportunities for early career scholars, and mentoring students and colleagues, both here and overseas. At the time we are speaking, what occupies most of my time is organizing to oppose the genocide and epistemicide in Palestine. Every single university in Gaza has been destroyed! Most significant for me is my teaching, which I make accessible beyond the university by sharing open-access resources through my website. I have made a lot of use of social media in the past, but that has become less safe for me in recent times, due to attacks – including one of physical violence.
DB:	When we were leading ACRAWSA, we were creating the kind of community that you note is important.
AL:	Or at least we were trying to. I took over ACRAWSA in 2017 after a period in which not much had been happening with the association. ACRAWSA was such an important entity for that community-building with so much important work done under the aegis of its founders, Aileen Moreton-Robinson, the world-renowned Goenpul critical Indigenous and race scholar, and Fiona Nicoll, a white scholar from Queensland, whose work on Australian whiteness has been foundational. A lot of significant work was achieved in the first few years after the founding of the association in 2005. In the middle years, the association became much more focused on the study of whiteness and

was led mainly by white scholars. But it continued to produce important work through the *Critical Race and Whiteness Studies* journal and regular conferences. This was before I came to Australia. I attended the 2014 conference in Meanjin (Brisbane) where you and I first met and in 2017, I was brave enough to put my hand up to become president. A lot of things had to be built back up, from the ground up. The website, which housed the open-access journal, had been hacked, so that had to be redesigned and put back online as a matter of urgency, because no one could access the articles that had been published. We did that and we also started a blog, edited by Marilena Indelicato. We had different streams for early career and more established contributors, the early career people receiving mentoring in crafting their blog posts. There were reports on events, film reviews and open letters on a variety of issues that arose, such as the Ramsay Centre for the Study of Western Civilization or the publication of an article 'In defence of eugenics' in the *Monash Bioethics Review*.

We also organized some events, including the 2020 annual conference, just before COVID-19 hit. I think we were just starting to build up a community around the association when the conference took place. At the conference, there was an annual general meeting and a new committee was elected. Sadly, it was effectively disbanded shortly thereafter and the association has ceased to function. The website no longer exists, which means that the archive of the journal cannot be found. This is the legacy of 15 years' work, theorizing race in Australia, so it really means something that it is no longer accessible. This is where the lack of community becomes a real problem because there was an insufficient basis built for other people to step up and take responsibility. It seemed to me that, while ACRAWSA was active, people were happy to avail themselves of its offerings, but when it ceased to function, few questions were raised about what had happened. We hadn't created enough of a community around the association to make people feel responsible for it when it disappeared, to care about it enough to step up, or at the very least to ask why it wasn't there anymore. I'll be honest that I continue to feel a great sense of loss but also of responsibility, that I could have done more. However, a big problem that I have personally faced is being perceived as having a lack of legitimacy. Australia is a very insular society, and even in the area of race scholarship there are loud voices asking, 'Who are you? And what is your place here?' I understand and even have

	a certain respect for that. So, for better or worse, I am keeping my work very low-key now. I work with my students in the classroom where I feel the real work of racial literacy-building can be done, and I develop solid relationships with individuals, like you. I feel this is what I can do at the moment.
DB:	So, what do you feel should happen now?
AL:	I don't think that's really up to me to say. There are other people taking up the mantle of race critical work in Australia – younger people than me, or you – and it is up to them to decide on the future direction it takes. I am happy developing my teaching because this is the space where I feel I can be of most use. I develop resources that I know many people use, and I actively reject the gatekeeping around resources that is common in academia. One thing I like to remind people of is that there are no original ideas as such, maybe just different angles on things. What I do stand by, however – and on this I insist – is that it is vital to show how you came to know what you know. We must pay more attention to the politics of citation. And by that I don't mean paying lip service to the most well-cited people in academia, effectively bragging that you have this or that book on your shelf. In a blog post I wrote a few years ago (Lentin, 2021), I spoke about the importance of 'showing your working out' (as they tell kids in maths class). How did you come to have this particular thought and write it down in this way? Be honest when answering that question. I wrote about this because I noticed a phenomenon which I called 'power plagiarism' in the blog. This is when people refer to references that they find in other people's work, but do not acknowledge that that is where they came across them. It is referred to officially as 'second source plagiarism'.

I wanted to stress the power dimension, because this is a practice often used by people trying to stake a claim to a field and crowd others out. By doing so they fail to acknowledge that all learning is done in community, that there are always those who came before you. Being attentive to citation is also vitally about acknowledging the myriad sources of knowledge. Maybe a particular idea came up while you were having a conversation with a friend, a student, in an activist meeting, or with someone at a café. Cite that! What you are doing is modelling knowledge-making as a community practice, a lived practice, not something that just exists in books. This for me is linked to my conception of racial literacy, which I see as a solidaristic practice, an idea I take from an interview I heard with Marcus Gilroy-Ware (2021).

Contrary to the wilful misconception that racial literacy assumes that ordinary people are 'illiterate' and need educating on race from 'detached academics', I see literacy as an active process of knowledge-building and sharing. It is necessarily dialogical, grounded in the understanding that there is no way of separating theory from practice and experience. It has become all too common, as I think others have noted in this book, to mindlessly defer to those 'with lived experience'. Many people have rightly critiqued this notion because it often ends up with an essentialist notion of 'experience' that has more to do with external markers of identity than true knowledge of a given topic (Táíwò, 2022). But, more than this, it is important to remember that people are the theorizers of their own experiences. We develop theory every day to help us navigate the simplest things in life and we do this from a young age. So it is preposterous to claim 'theorists' are detached from real life. Rather, in our dialogues with others in the community, we commonly develop theories that help all of us. Racial literacy is part of this; we read the world together, building a picture of what the practices and processes of race look like. How do they change over time? How do they shapeshift? Or, to use a concept I have learned from the political theorist Robert Nichols in his work on Indigenous dispossession, how does race recur? In other words, to borrow from what Nichols (2020: 9) writes about dispossession, race 'produces what it presupposes', with each iteration building 'on or augment[ing] its original postulate'. It is similar to what Cedric Robinson (2007) refers to as the recalibration of the racial regime. This is a complex process that requires tracking. As A. Sivanandan (1990: 64) remarks, racism 'changes shape, size, contours, purpose, function – with changes in the economy, the social structure, the system and, above all, the challenges, the resistances of that system'. This is a set of processes, spanning centuries, with iterations across location, often working in different, apparently contradictory, ways at the same time. We need all hands on deck to even begin to understand this. So, for me, developing racial literacy is an act of solidarity, of community building, born of love and care for each other. I hope to contribute to this, even if only in a small way.

DB: And that is how we see this book collection: as a project of solidarity.

References

Bargallie, D. and Lentin, A. (2020) 'Improving racial literacy: What will it take?', *Croakey Health Media*, 1 October, https://www.croakey.org/improving-racial-literacy-what-will-it-take

Burden-Stelly, C. (2016) 'The modern capitalist state and the Black challenge: Culturalism and the elision of political economy', dissertation, http://digitalassets.lib.berkeley.edu/etd/ucb/text/BurdenStelly_berkeley_0028E_15992.pdf

Gilmore, R.W. (2006) *Golden Gulag: Prisons, Surplus, Crisis, and Opposition in Globalizing California*, Berkeley: University of California Press.

Gilroy-Ware, M. (2021) 'Neoliberal feelings don't care about your facts: Interview with Marcus Gilroy-Ware', The ReImagining Value Action Lab, https://soundcloud.com/reimaginevalue/gilroy-ware-facts

James, C.L.R. (1992 [1969]) 'Black studies and the contemporary student', in A. Grimshaw (ed), *The C.L.R. James Reader*, Cambridge, MA: Blackwell, pp 390–404.

Kauanui, Kēhaulani J. (2008) *Hawaiian Blood: Colonialism and the Politics of Sovereignty and Indigeneity*, Durham, NC: Duke University Press.

Lentin, A. (2014) 'Postracial silences: The othering of race in Europe', in W.D. Hund and A. Lentin (eds), *Racism and Sociology*, Berlin: Lit Verlag, pp 69–104.

Lentin, A. (2021) 'Power plagiarism', *AlanaLentin.Net*, 11 July, https://www.alanalentin.net/2021/07/11/power-plagiarism

Myers, J. (2023) *Of Black Study*, London: Pluto Press.

Nichols, R. (2020) *Theft is Property! Dispossession and Critical Theory*, Durham, NC: Duke University Press.

Robinson, C.J. (2007) *Forgeries of Memory and Meaning: Blacks and the Regimes of Race in American Theater and Film before World War II*, Chapel Hill, NC: University of North Carolina Press.

Sivanandan, A. (1990) *Communities of Resistance: Writings on Black Struggles for Socialism*, London: Verso.

Táíwò, O.O. (2022) *Elite Capture: How the Powerful Took Over Identity Politics (and Everything Else)*, Chicago: Haymarket Books.

Yancy, G. (2021) 'Reaching beyond "Black faces in high places": An interview with Joy James', *Truthout*, 1 February, https://truthout.org/articles/reaching-beyond-black-faces-in-high-places-an-interview-with-joy-james

22

Teacher/Decolonizer

Ambelin Kwaymullina

When people ask:
How long have you been an educator?
I say:
All my life
Because as an Aboriginal person
educating others
is something I was born into
an attempt
to stem the tide of ignorance
before I drown in it
before we all do

When Aboriginal people
are hired to teach
the work we're paid for
is a tiny part
of the educating we do
We are called on to educate
not only our students
but our colleagues
our bosses
passing visitors
basically anybody
associated with the university
who wants to know something
about being Aboriginal

All this ignorance
comes at a cost

but there is no space
in workload allocation models
for worry
fear
grief
pain
anger
exhaustion

No space at all
Barely any room
even to breathe
even to exist

I believe
decolonization will come
when the pathways of settler-colonialism
are replaced
by pathways grown from
and answerable to
respect
for Indigenous peoples
and our belongings to our Countries
But this cannot be done
without conversations
yarnings
with local Indigenous peoples
nations
I cannot speak
for all the many nations
but I can help these yarnings along
through building understanding
of Indigenous peoples
Indigenous worlds

I think this begins
with recognizing
challenging
the artificial context
of settler-colonialism
which comes from the founding lie
of settler-colonial states
that Indigenous peoples are 'less than'

and that only knowledge-ways
law-ways
landholding-ways
of the West
have value

This context has become normalized
naturalized
embedded into structures and behaviours
including at unconscious levels
forming a filter
which distorts knowledge about Indigenous peoples
such that even those who want to understand
struggle to truly hear our voices
or engage with our worlds

Understanding this context
requires understanding the threads of thought
that shaped it
Racism
is one of these threads
but it does not stand alone
because in a settler-colonial context
racism served dispossession
and present day manifestations of bias
against Indigenous peoples
cannot be understood
without understanding
it was always about the land

As a teacher
it is important to me
to articulate how and why
I teach as I do
to demonstrate the standards
I hold myself to
expressed below
in the form of some of the questions
I ask myself about curriculum

Have I embedded respectful behaviours
not as an aspiration
but as a skillset

including through teaching
the Indigenous cultural and intellectual property protocols
developed by Indigenous peoples?[1]

Is my curriculum strengths-based?
To be clear
not every dialogue that speaks of Indigenous disadvantage
is a deficit discourse
A deficit discourse
is one which defines Indigenous peoples
only in terms of disadvantage
and suggests (expressly or by implication)
that disadvantage is a natural condition
of being Indigenous
A strength-based approach
values the great resilience
knowledges
cultures
of Indigenous peoples
and interrogates the structures of settler-colonialism
the pathways of dispossession
that block Indigenous potential

Is my curriculum evidence-based
and does that evidence
centre the voices of Indigenous peoples
as the primary sources
of our own cultures
laws
histories
systems?

Have I measured impact
with reference to how curriculum is likely to be experienced
by Indigenous students
even if
there are no Indigenous students
in the class?
Because an inclusive classroom
will never emerge
when content is shaped
by the expectations of the unexcluded
just as a culturally safe space

cannot by created
by reference to those not in danger

Have I made sure
that different forms of communication
are accepted and valued
so Indigenous students
can interact in cultural ways
such as through silence
avoiding eye contact
or speaking/writing of vastness of connections
that surround the subject matter?
Have I created opportunities for Indigenous students
to share their insights
without fear of misappropriation
and to engage with the words
of all the Indigenous peoples
who walked the academy before them
including through the work done
on Indigenous knowledges
systems
research methodologies?

In Aboriginal cultures
the points where two worlds meet
such as the in-between light
as night changes to day
hold great possibilities
perhaps classrooms
could be places of possibility too
carrying us all
into the dawn
of decolonized futures

Note

[1] In Australia, such protocols include the Australian Institute of Aboriginal and Torres Strait Islander Studies Code of Ethics; the Australia Council Protocols for using First Nations Cultural and Intellectual Property in the Arts; the National Health and Medical Research Council Ethical Conduct in Research with Aboriginal and Torres Strait Islander Peoples and Communities: Guidelines for Researchers and Stakeholders 2018 and Keeping Research on Track 2018.

Index

References to figures appear in *italic* type; those in **bold** type refer to tables.

4K1G (radio station) 253, 254
14 Nations (Moore) 130–1

A

ABC radio 252, 253, 254, 308
Aboriginal and Torre Strait Islander children 17, 20, 44n, 102–3
 see also Stolen Generation
Aboriginal and Torre Strait Islander Commission 17
Aboriginal and Torre Strait Islander peoples 8
 Closing the Gap 233, 243n
 deaths in police custody 20, 44n, 52
 incarcerated 300
 national census 20, 249
 New South Wales 229
 voting rights 26n
 see also First Nations people; Indigenous people; Voice to Parliament Referendum 2023
Aboriginal and Torre Strait Islander perspectives 38–40
 cultural competency vs. racial literacy 40–2
Aboriginal and Torre Strait Islander students 33
Aboriginal English 252, 254–5
Aboriginal Legal Service 195, 198
Aboriginal Provisional Government 196
Aboriginal sea law 196
Aboriginal studies 16–18, 33–5
 curriculum 36–7
 definition 39–40
 teaching and research staff 35–6, 38–9
Aboriginalism 264
academic precariousness 52, 140–3
 see also publish-or-perish culture
Accomplices Not Allies (Indigenous Action Media) 43
affect-emotions 262–3
Africa 64, 65
African diaspora 170–3
Agozino, B. 140–1, 142

Agung-Igusti, R. 173
Ahmed, S. 81, 210, 213, 262–3, 302
Ahmida, A.A. 65
Albanese, A. 295, 296
Alexander, J. 84
alt-right 49
 see also far-right ideology
American law schools 191–3
AMKA 170–1
Ampe Akelyernemane Meke Mekarle report 20
Anderson, J. 294
Andrews, L. 22–3
Annihilation of the Blacks (Foley) 125–8
anti-colonial frames 80–2
anti-colonial theory 18
anti-intellectualism 13–15
 history wars 15–16, 20, 26n
 and Indigenous studies 16–18
anti-racism 240
 non-performativity of 302
 war on 291–5
anti-racism work 182–3
anti-racist community praxis *see* Community Identity Displacement Research Network; community psychology
anti-racist education 111–21
 see also teacher education
anti-racist feminist leadership 116–18, 121
anti-racist pedagogy 18–19
anti-racist solidarity 301–3
anti-woke awakening 21–3
anti-woke culture 13–14, 15
anti-wokeness 18, 24
Anzaldúa, G. 165, 206, 217
art 123, 124
 AMKA 170–1
 Annihilation of the Blacks (Foley) 125–8
 Courting Blackness (exhibition) 130–2
 Hedonistic Honky Haters (Foley) 128–9
 Incantation 205, 206–7, 210
 decolonial feminisms 211–13

INDEX

enacting decoloniality 213–20
Sisterships (Fernando) 221–2
Next in Colour 171–3
Asian Australians
  model minority myth 179, 180, 181, 182, 184, 186–7
  personal narratives 181–5
  racial literacy 179–81, 182, 184, 185–6, 187
Asian immigrants 178–9
Asmar, C. 33
austerity 52, 140–3
Austin, J.L. 302
Australian Critical Race and Whiteness Association (ACRAWSA) 1, 305, 307, 312–13
Australian Indigenous Knowledge and Libraries (Langton) 278
Australian settler pedagogies 67–73

B

Badtjala Country massacre 125, 126
Baker, A. 88, 89
Bandung 208, 222n
Banks, C. 193
Banks, M. 206
Bargallie, D. 2, 19, 38, 52, 95, 252
becoming/unbecoming 87
Behrendt, L. 196
being/non-being 166–7
Bell, D. 95
Bellear, B. 195
Bhattacharya, T. 302
Bianchini, M.L. 63
Birdsell, J. 85
Biting the Clouds (Foley) 131
'black armband' view of history 16, 26n, 36, 295
Black historical consciousness 197–8
Black Lives Matter 51–2, 310
Black News Service 250
Black psychology 167–8
Black public spheres 247–50, 255
Black studies 310–11
'Blak' 3
Bodkin-Andrews, G. 41
Bolt, A. 50, 296
Bringing Them Home report 36, 44n, 195
broadcasting *see* Indigenous community radio
Buchanan, C. 250
Bulhan, H. 167
Burden-Stelly, C. 311
Burney, L. 131
Burns, M. 155, 159
Burrows, E. 248, 250
business schools 111–16
Butler, J. 302
Byrd, J. 87

C

Calabria 63–4
Capers, B. 192
capitalism 113
Centre for Global Indigenous Futures (CGIF) 25
Chant, K. 22
Chatterjee, P. 141, 142
Chávez-Moreno, L.C. 20–1, 27n
Cherbourg Radio 253, 254
children 17, 20, 44n, 102–3
  see also Stolen Generation
Closing the Gap 233, 243n
Clough, P. 262
Coe, P. 195
Collyer, E. 216
colonial law 137, 138, 142
  see also law; Voice to Parliament Referendum 2023
colonial technologies 139–40
colonial wars 65–6
colonialism 63–5
  and the curriculum 138
  see also anti-colonial frames; anti-colonial theory; settler-colonialism
coloniality 166, 167, 211
  see also decoloniality
colonization 79
  see also decolonization
colour-blind racism 173, 183
Combahee River Collective 208
Commonwealth Aboriginal Studies Working Group 39
community art 170–3
Community Identity Displacement Research Network 165
community psychology 166–7, 173–4
  and Black psychology 167–8
  and Indigenous knowledges 168–9
  solidarity work 170–4
  and whiteness studies 169–70
community radio *see* Indigenous community radio
conspiracy theories 21–3
contact zones 165, 168, 267
Council of Australian Law Deans (CALD) 154–5, 161
counter-hegemonic racial literacy 179–80
'Courageous Conversations About Race' (Singleton and Linton) 160
Courting Blackness (exhibition) 130–2
COVID-19 pandemic 21, 51, 52, 178, 254–5
Cowlishaw, G. 37
Creamer, J. 196
creole 254–5
criminology 143–9
critical auto-ethnography 180–1
  hegemonic racial literacies 187

model minority myth 186–7
personal narratives 181–5
critical hope 24
critical Indigenous scholarship 2, 3–4
critical Indigenous studies (CIS) 18
critical race theory (CRT) 15, 18, 19, 21, 57, 73–4
  and anti-intellectualism 13, 14
  business schools 111–12, 114
  conservative dismissal of 49–50
  and culture wars 297
  in national curriculum 291, 292–3
  in racial literacy praxis 104–5, 107
  tokenistic 282
critical racial literacy 2, 4, 18–19, 23
  see also racial literacy
Crowley, L. 196
cultural competency 40–2, 182
cultural interface 100
cultural positionality see racial and cultural positionality
culture wars 14, 294, 295–7
  see also anti-racism: war on; wokeness
curriculum 137, 320
  and colonialism 138
  criminology 143–9
  law 154–6
    and racial literacy 155, 156–61
  national curriculum 57, 291–3
  and race 36–7, 79–80

D

data sovereignty 230–3, 238–9, 243
Davenport, J. 21
Day, M. 70–1
Deacon, D. 3
death 263–5, 270–2
deaths in police custody 20, 44n, 52
deciphering practice 218
decolonial feminist praxis 205–7
  Incantation 210, 211–13
    enacting decoloniality 213–20
    'Sisterships' (Fernando) 221–2
  positionality 207–11
decolonial praxis 18–19
  community psychology 166–7, 173–4
    and Black psychology 167–8
    and Indigenous knowledges 168–9
    solidarity work 170–4
    and whiteness studies 169–70
decoloniality 210, 212, 213–20, 218
decolonization 82, 299, 318
decolonization of universities 32–3, 42–3
  Aboriginal and Torre Strait Islander perspectives 38–40
  Aboriginal studies 33–5, 39–40
  and austerity 52, 140–3
  cultural competency vs. racial literacy 40–2
  curriculum 137

  and colonialism 138
  criminology 143–9
  and race 36–7, 79–80
  social theory teaching 53–9
  staff 35–6, 38–9, 40, 41–2
decolonized futures 73–4
decolonizing frames 80–2
Decolonizing Sociology (Meghji) 53
Demonic Grounds (McKittrick) 85–6
dialogic learning 54–5
diaspora see African diaspora
Dillon, G. 23
disability inclusion 236–8, 240, 243
Disorient (website) 118
displacement see Community Identity Displacement Research Network
diversity 238–40, 301–2
diversity, equality and inclusion (DEI) 112–13
Dodson, M. 195
Donnelly, KJ. 49

E

education
  anti-racist 111–21
  legal 155, 156–61, 190–1
  see also English language imperialism; national curriculum; teacher education
embodied learning 269
embodied literacies 80–1, 82–3
  becoming/unbecoming 87
  hairdressing story 85–6
  Mother's story 83–5
  Unbound Collective 87–9
emotional governance 262
emotions 81
  and race 261–3
    teacher education 266–71
    voluntourism 263–6, 267–8
engaged reflection and representation 100–4
English language imperialism 268–9
epistemic violence 126, 138, 165, 169
equality before the law 158–9
Eurocentrism 53–4, 55, 167
Everingham, P. 268
experiential learning 159–61

F

Fair Work Act (FWA) 140, 141
Fanon, F. 56, 81, 128, 132, 166–7, 277, 299
far-right ideology 21–3
  see also alt-right
feminist leadership 116–18, 121
feminists of colour 208, 209–11, 215
First Fleet, The (Australian Children's Pictorial Social Studies) 67–9
First Nations people
  in Australian law 152
  embodied literacies 80–1, 82–3
    becoming/unbecoming 87

INDEX

hairdressing story 85–6
Mother's story 83–5
Unbound Collective 87–9
in national curriculum 291–2
see also Aboriginal and Torre Strait Islander peoples; Indigenous people; Voice to Parliament Referendum 2023
Fletcher, M. 199
Flinders Island Chronicle 250
Floyd, G. 293
Foley, G. 278
formal equality 158–9
Fraser, N. 248
Fredericks, B. 38
Frontier Wars 66

G

Gainsford, A. 194
Gaztambide-Fernández, R. xix
gender 113
gender roles 70
Gilmore, R.W. 310
Great Awakening 21–3
Griffith University 124, 126–7
Grosfoguel, R. 166

H

Habermas, J. 248
hacking 271
hairdressing story 85–6
Hall, S. 291, 297–8, 299, 300, 301
Hanson, P. 14, 57, 291
Harris, C. 302
Hart, V. 127–8, 130
health outcomes 51
healthcare 182
Hedonistic Honky Haters (Foley) 128–9
hegemonic diversity 238–40
hegemonic power 301
hegemonic racial literacies 179
heterosexualism 70–1
Hickling-Hudson, A. 97
higher education *see* universities, decolonization of
history wars 15–16, 20, 26n, 295
Hobbs, H. 194
Hollinsworth, D. 42
hooks, b. 88, 116
Howard government 13, 16
Howard, J. 17, 20, 295
Huntress (yacht) 196

I

I Refuse to Condemn (Qureshi) 280
identity 57, 160, 183
see also identity, non-Indigenous; racial identity; settler-colonizer identity
Identity magazine 250

identity, non-Indigenous 95–8, 278–9
engaged reflection and representation 100–4
in relation to others 98–100
shifting from self to system 104–7
see also African diaspora; Asian Australians; 'other others'
identity politics 57
Immigration Restriction Act 1901 *see* 'White Australia' policy
Incantation 205, 206–7, 210
decolonial feminisms 211–13
enacting decoloniality 213–20
'Sisterships' (Fernando) 221–2
Indigenist research 169, 252
Indigenous children 17, 20, 44n, 102–3
see also Stolen Generation
Indigenous civil rights movement 195
Indigenous community radio 246–55
and Black public spheres 247–50
historical background 250–1
Indigenous data sovereignty 230–3, 238–40, 243
Indigenous futurism 23–5
Indigenous internship programme 25
Indigenous knowledges 168–9
Indigenous lawyers 190–1
outsider storytelling 197–9
Indigenous people 8
racist abuse towards 23
in settler pedagogies 67–9, 72
see also Aboriginal and Torre Strait Islander peoples; First Nations people; Voice to Parliament Referendum 2023
Indigenous public sphere 247, 250, 255
Indigenous queer studies 25
Indigenous Remote Communications Association 246–7
Indigenous scholarship *see* critical Indigenous scholarship
Indigenous sovereignty 19–21, 24, 72, 196, 296
Indigenous students 33
Indigenous studies 309
see also Aboriginal studies
individualism 238
institutional racism 240, 310
insurgent texts 217
interest-convergence 95
internet technology 21
see also social media
internship programme *see* Indigenous internship programme
interpersonal racism 113, 283–4
intersectionality 209–10, 236
Islamophobia 280–2, 286–8, 308
Italy 63–5
It's Fun to Read (Infants' Reading Committee) 69–72

J

James, C. 24
James, C.L.R. 310
John, C. 192
Jones, D. 1–2
Jordan, J. 219
justice *see* social justice
Justice, D.H. 25

K

Keating, P. 20, 249
Kēhaulani Kauanui, J., 279
Kelada, O. 2
King, L. 197
Ku Klux Klan 128
Kwaymullina, A. 216

L

land ownership 26n, 67, 295–6
  see also terra nullius
language 246, 252, 254–5, 281
  see also English language imperialism
lateral violence 42, 44n
law 137, 138, 142
  and race 152–3, 156–9
  see also Aboriginal sea law; Voice to Parliament Referendum 2023
Law Admissions Consultative Committee (LACC) 154, 157
law curriculum 154–6
  racial literacy 155, 156–61
law schools 191–4, 199
Lead Belly 14, 294
leadership 116–18, 121
Learning Law (Marinac et al) 158–9
Ledbetter, H.W. 14
legal education 155, 156–61, 190–1
  see also law schools
legal equality 158–9
legal profession 190–1
  outsider storytelling 197–9
Lentin, A. 305–15
Leroux, R. 22
liberation approaches, psychology 168
life stories 83–5
listening positions 215–16
literary archeology 83
Liu, H. 111–21
Living on Stolen Land (Kwaymullina) 216
Liyanage, C. 21
Lobo, M. 209
Lohmeyer, B. 269
Lorde, A. 4, 219
Lugones, M. 208, 220

M

Mabo case 190
Machado de Oliveira, A. 261
Makata, M. 100
Maldonado-Torres, N. 166
Mansell, M. 196
Marshall, T. 198
Martín-Baró, I. 168
Martin-Chew, L. 124
Martin, K. 96, 169
Master of Business Administration (MBA) students 115
Mathews, R.H. 130
Maxwell, C. 171
McAvoy, T. 196
McDermott, L. 194–5
McKittrick, K. 80, 82, 83, 85–6, 89, 90
media *see* Indigenous community radio
mental health 286–7
mestiza consciousness 165, 206
Mignolo, W. 218, 220
migrants 306
  see also Asian immigrants; postwar migrants
Mills, C.W. 2
Milner, H.R. 93, 95, 104
Miranda, D. 83
model minority myth 179, 180, 181, 182, 184, 186–7
Monture, P. 190
Moore, A. 130–1
Moore, T. 39
Moore, W.L. 192
Moreton-Robinson, A. 19, 24, 56, 72, 82, 84, 152, 166, 207, 271, 278, 281, 295, 296
Morrison, T. 83
Morsi, Y. 276–88
Moten, F. 302–3
Motta, S.C. 211
Moya, P. 207
Mullenjaiwakka 194–5
multiculturalism 306
Mussolini, B. 64
Myers, J. 311

N

Nakata, M. 18, 128–9
Nakata, S. 278
National Aboriginal Education Committee 39
national census 20, 249
national curriculum 57, 291–3
National Tertiary Education Union (NTEU) 42
Native American mythology 199
Native Title Act 1993 194
neoconservatism 270
neoliberal managerialism 173
neoliberalism 267, 270, 280, 282–3
New South Wales 229, 236
New World Order conspiracies 22
Newfong, J. 250
Next in Colour 171–3

Nichols, R. 315
Nicoll, F. 130, 131–2
non-being *see* being/non-being
non-Indigenous identity 95–8, 278–9
  engaged reflection and representation 100–4
  in relation to others 98–100
  shifting from self to system 104–7
  see also African diaspora; Asian Australians; 'other others'
non-performativity of antiracism 302
Northern Territory Emergency Response 20
NQ Messagestick 250

O

Organisation for Economic Co-operation and Development 267
Orientalism 56–7, 264
O'Shane, P. 195
'other others' 208, 216, 222n
othering 19, 167, 208, 282
outsider storytelling 197–9

P

patriarchal white sovereignty 72, 227, 228, 239, 240, 296
pedagogies, racialized 67–73
  see also anti-racist pedagogy
'people of colour' 208
performance art 170–3
  see also Incantation
performative speech acts 302
Persard, S.C. 210
personal writing *see* testimonio
Phillips, G.L. 84
Phillips, J. 103
Phillips, S. 128
poetry 219–20, 221–2, 317–21
policy document cycle *231*
politics without guarantees 301
positionality 206, 207–11
  see also racial and cultural positionality
postwar migrants 65–6
power plagiarism 314
predatory inclusion 302
primary textbooks 67–73
prison population 300
privilege 159–61
provocative art 123, 124
  Annihilation of the Blacks (Foley) 125–8
  Courting Blackness (exhibition) 130–2
  Hedonistic Honky Haters (Foley) 128–9
psychology *see* Black psychology; community psychology
public service 229, 230
public spheres 247–50, 255
publish-or-perish culture 279–80, 283
Purewal, N.K. 211

Q

QAnon 21, 27n
queer studies *see* Indigenous queer studies

R

race 51, 79, 80, 112–13, 227
  and emotions 261–3
    teacher education 266–71
    voluntourism 263–6, 267–8
  and law 152–3, 156–9
  silencing of 81
  teaching of 297–301
  and solidarity 301–3
racial and cultural positionality *94*, 95
  engaged reflection and representation 100–4
  researching self 95–8
  researching self in relation to others 98–100
  shifting from self to system 100–4
Racial Discrimination Act 1975 20, 296
racial hierarchies 63–4, 66, 192, 240
racial identity 160
racial isolation 186
racial literacy 1–3, 4, 19, 20–1, 80–1, 271, 276
  as act of solidarity 305–15
  Asian Australians 179–81, 182, 184, 185–6, 187
  business schools 111–16
  vs. cultural competency 40–2
  and legal education 155, 156–61, 192–3
  in social policy 227–43
    disability inclusion 236–8, 240, 243
    framework **241–2**
    and hegemonic diversity 238–40
    Indigenous data sovereignty 230–3, 238–40, 243
    policy document cycle *231*
    service delivery strategy 230–3, 239, 243
  soft approach to 282, 284
racial literacy praxis in and for teacher education *94*
  engaged reflection and representation 100–4
  researching self 95–8
  researching self in relation to others 98–100
  shifting from self to system 104–7
racial microaggressions 186
racial states 25, 37, 43–4n
racial stereotypes 69
racialized pedagogy 67–73
racism 3, 80, 81, 85
  against Aboriginal and Torre Strait Islander staff 42
  colour-blind 173, 183
  and COVID-19 pandemic 178
  denial of 37
  institutional 240, 310
  interpersonal 113, 283–4

in the legal profession 195
personal experiences of 66–7, 72–3, 125
and power 166
structural 114, 283–4, 309
systemic 114, 159–61
vernacular 73
see also anti-racism; Islamophobia
racism studies 311
racist abuse 23, 37
Radical Skin/Moderate Mask (Morsi) 277, 282
radio see Indigenous community radio
reading practice 218
Redeeming Leadership (Liu) 116–18
Redfern Park Speech 20, 249
referendum see Voice to Parliament Referendum 2023
reflection and representation 100–4
Reproducing Racism (Moore) 191–2
researcher positionality 95
researching the self 95–8
  in relation to others 98–100
Reyes Cruz, M. 169
Reynolds, H. 127
Richmond, M. 127
Ricœur, P., 57
Rifkin, M. 87
Rigney, L.-I. 169, 252
Roach, A. 102–3
Robinson, C. 315
Roy, A. 118
Royal Commission into Aboriginal Death in Custody 20, 36, 44n, 52, 190
Rudd, K. 20

S

Said, E. 56–7, 264
Santa Cruz Feminist of Color Collective 208, 211
Santos, B. de S. 55
Schick, C. 267
school textbooks 67–73
'Scottsboro Boys' (Lead Belly) 14, 294
second source plagiarism 314
self-determination 239
self-determined community art 170–3
service delivery strategy 230–3, 239, 243
settler-colonial wars 65–6
settler-colonialism 318–19
  see also colonialism
settler-colonizer identity 95–8, 278–9
  engaged reflection and representation 100–4
  in relation to others 98–100
  shifting from self to system 104–7
settler futurism 23–4
settler pedagogies 67–73
settler state 290
sexism 85
shadow writing 217

Sharpe, C. 298
Simon, B. 72
Singleton, G.E. 160
'Sisterships' (Fernando) 221–2
Sivanandan, A. 293, 315
slow ontology 280–1
social justice 19–21
social media 21, 23
social policy, racial literacy in 227–43
  disability inclusion 236–8, 240, 243
  framework **241–2**
  and hegemonic diversity 238–40
  Indigenous data sovereignty 230–3, 238–40, 243
  policy document cycle *231*
  service delivery strategy 230–3, 239, 243
social theory teaching 53–9
sociological imagination 54, 55
Socratic method 192
soft skills 157–8
solidarity xix, 57, 118, 207, 220, 301–3
  racial literacy as 305–15
solidarity work 170
sovereignty 84
  see also Indigenous data sovereignty; Indigenous sovereignty; patriarchal white sovereignty
space 220
spirit murder 193
Squires, C. 247, 248–50, 255
Stein, S. 271
'stickiness' 81
Stoker, A. 292, 293
Stolen Generation 20, 36, 102–3, 195
  see also *Bringing Them Home* report
stories see embodied literacies
storytelling see outsider storytelling
structural inequality 266
structural racism 114, 283–4, 309
Suffla, S. 167–8
systemic racism 114, 159–61

T

Táíwò, O.O. 57
teacher education
  interest-convergence 95
  racial literacy praxis *94*
    engaged reflection and representation 100–4
    researching self 95–8
    researching self in relation to others 98–100
    shifting from self to system 104–7
  and whiteness 266–71
teaching see Vice-Chancellor's Award for Excellence in Teaching
teaching race 297–301
  and solidarity 301–3
Tent Embassy protests 250

INDEX

terminology 8, 208
terra nullius 26n, 67, 84, 90n, 190
testimonio 165
textbooks 67–73
'Third World' women 208
Threshold Learning Outcomes (TLOs) 155–6, 157
Tindale, N. 85
trauma 287
travelling 219–20
Triple A (radio station) 247, 251, 252–3, 253–4
Trudgett, M. 41
truth-telling 284–5
Truth-Telling (Reynolds) 127
TwoSixtyProject 212

U

Uluru Statement from the Heart 36, 44n
unbecoming 87–8
Unbound Collective 87–9
United Kingdom 15, 297, 310
United Neytions, 2018 (Moore) 131
United States 14, 191–3, 310
Universities Australia Best Practice Framework 2011 40, 41
universities, decolonization of 32–3, 42–3
  Aboriginal and Torre Strait Islander perspectives 38–40
  Aboriginal studies 33–5, 39–40
  and austerity 52, 140–3
  cultural competency vs. racial literacy 40–2
  curriculum 137
    and colonialism 138
    criminology 143–9
    and race 36–7, 79–80
  social theory teaching 53–9
  staff 35–6, 38–9, 40, 41–2, 52
University of Queensland 130–1
Unmasking the Racial Contract (Bargallie) 2
Urban Aboriginal Art 125

V

Veracini, L. 64
Vergès, F. 211, 215
vernacular racism 73

Vice-Chancellor's Award for Excellence in Teaching 143–9
violence 297–301
  see also epistemic violence; lateral violence
visual arts 123, 124
  Annihilation of the Blacks (Foley) 125–8
  Courting Blackness (exhibition) 130–2
  Hedonistic Honky Haters (Foley) 128–9
Voice to Parliament Referendum 2023 20, 138, 139–40, 196
voluntourism 263–6, 267–8
von Doussa, J. 158
Vosters, H. 87–8
voting rights 26n

W

Watego, C. 83
Watson, I. 194
WEIRS 208, 222n
'White Australia' policy 66, 72, 179
White Possessive, The (Moreton-Robinson) 84, 278
white spaces, law schools as 191–4, 199
white supremacy 2, 19, 114, 186, 192, 228, 235, 238, 239
whiteness 82, 127, 261, 294
  and teacher education 266–71
  and voluntourism 263–6, 267–8
  see also patriarchal white sovereignty
whiteness studies 169–70
whiteness theory 160
Whitening Race (Moreton-Robinson) 278
Williams, P. 193
Wing, A.K. 191
'woke' 14, 115
wokeness 13, 24, 294–5, 296–7
  see also anti-woke culture; anti-wokeness
Wolfe, P. 278–9, 290, 295–6
women/feminists of colour 208, 209–11
'women of colour' 208
world travelling 219–20
writing 215, 217, 283, 285
  see also testimonio
Wynter, S. 80, 218

Z

zones of being/non-being 166–7